The Process of Financial Planning

The Process of Financial Planning
The Adviser's Guide

First edition

Chris Gilchrist and Danby Bloch

Danby Bloch, Series Editor

taxbriefs
financial publishing

Taxbriefs Limited
Centaur Media plc
St Giles House
50 Poland Street
London W1F 7AX

Telephone 020 7970 6471
Facsimile 020 7970 6485
info@taxbriefs.co.uk
www.taxbriefs.co.uk

ISBN 978-1-905482-45-0

Printed and bound in Great Britain by Intype Libra Ltd, London.

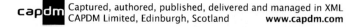 Captured, authored, published, delivered and managed in XML
CAPDM Limited, Edinburgh, Scotland   www.capdm.com

About the Authors

Chris Gilchrist

Chris is a director of a firm of IFAs specialising in investment. His 35-year career includes financial journalism and authorship as well as roles in financial services businesses. He is the author of five financial books including *Unit Trusts - what every investor should know* and *The Sunday Times Guide to Tax-Free Savings*, and a contributor to *Managing Collective Investment Funds*, the definitive guide for operators and regulators of collective funds. He edits a monthly investment newsletter, *The IRS Report*.

Danby Bloch

Danby Bloch is editorial director and co-founder of Taxbriefs Financial Publishing which produces many of the UK's Chartered Insurance Institute's examination learning texts. The company also produces customised newsletters and other publications for firms of financial planners and accountants. Taxbriefs is part of the Centaur Media Group.

Danby is chairman of City of London IFAs Helm Godfrey and has been in the financial services industry for over 30 years. In 2010 he became a director of wrap operators Nucleus Financial Group. Danby has written five books on financial planning and innumerable articles for the UK national and trade press. He is also a regular lecturer and trainer on tax and financial subjects.

Part 1: The scope of financial planning

Chapter 1
Defining the scope of financial planning and considering priorities

1 Theory and practice

Financial planning is a discipline that has evolved over about a century but has changed profoundly in the past 30 years. Only in the past 25 years has it developed as a defined methodology in the UK. The increasing complexity of tax systems in developed economies, the vast increase in the methods, strategies and funds available for capital investment, and the changes in lifestyles (see chapter 4, 'Different types of client') have all played their part in making comprehensive financial planning valuable to the client. The development can be seen in two dimensions, the content of financial planning and its practical application, which could also be seen as the theory and the practice.

- **Content.** Most of the complexity of tax systems faced by individuals in developed economies has arisen since 1945. Since many more decisions have tax consequences, often severe, financial planning has to consider the interaction of taxes to produce an optimal or 'tax-efficient' strategy. Frequent legislative changes (for example in pensions) have meant that individuals' entitlements and needs have also changed. At the same time, proliferation of products (mortgages, insurances, investments) means advisers need to have a much wider range of technical knowledge today than they did even 20 years ago. Today, this content falls within the scope of professional regulation and the adviser's knowledge is tested by increasingly demanding examinations.

- **Application.** Tax law and product features deal with facts but financial planners deal with people, which in the UK (though not the US) was done often in an informal way. In recent years, regulation of the advice process has required advisers to progressively formalise the way they run their businesses and deliver advice. Historically, financial planning tended to deal with client circumstances and needs as if they were objective facts. Today, there is a wider range of approaches, with many planners adopting methods that may require emotional engagement and commitment by both planner and client. Given the growing understanding of prevalent biases in human reasoning and decision-making (see chapter 3, 'The impact of behavioural finance'), it can be argued that the ability to facilitate understanding of complex financial issues is more important than knowledge of the law and products.

2 Style and scope

A financial plan covers the entirety of an individual (or couple's) financial affairs, from the day-to-day issues of budgeting to the long-term ones of saving and investing. Its timescale ranges from the immediate to the far distant and, indeed, to beyond the individual's death and the transfer of their assets to their heirs. Its essential feature is that it represents a carefully considered allocation of resources to a defined set of objectives, an allocation that is periodically reviewed and adjusted in the light of changing personal circumstances and financial and fiscal conditions.

Advisers can choose to provide financial planning in an almost entirely objective way. In this case, the client's choices, such as to save more for their retirement, are regarded as rationally determined and objective inputs to the planning process. At the other extreme, practitioners of life planning methods will question the client's motives and feelings not just about financial decisions but about the factors that underly them, including their relationships, ambitions and attitudes. The life planning school has been gaining ground in the UK as well as other markets such as the US and Australia where it is better established. Led by specialists such as the US financial planning/life planning author and lecturer George Kinder, the extension of financial planning into the wider sphere of life planning involves devoting significant time and resources to this approach as well as a carefully developed process and skills of questioning and probing key issues.

Kinder argues that life planning is a natural extension to what most planners already do; that it lays the foundations of much more meaningful and robust relationships that improve the quality of the financial planning process and that it can greatly increase the clients' commitment to the process and recommendations. He believes that planners can and generally should charge separately for the life planning which has a substantial value in its own right.

The adviser's decision as to what style of financial planning to adopt will therefore determine not just the methods they use but also the scope of their planning. So while the description of the content of financial planning later in this section adequately describes the factual scope of the discipline, it does not cover the effective scope of planning as experienced by the client.

To create a comprehensive financial plan requires wide ranging knowledge covering the nine topic areas outlined below. Such knowledge is embedded in the curriculum for the 'diploma' level of qualification for advisers. But in each of these areas, clients may have specific needs for advice that go beyond the financial planner's knowledge or competence, and planners will normally refer clients to specialists such as tax accountants, trust lawyers or employment lawyers. Some of these possible needs are highlighted in the relevant sections.

Most financial planners tend to develop greater specialist knowledge and qualifications in one or more of these areas, and may make this a feature of their advice proposition (see chapter 7, 'The advice proposition'). For example, accountants who become financial planners will tend to offer more detailed advice on tax issues, while those from a legal background may focus on trusts and estate planning. In financial planning practices, individuals may have different specialist qualifications so that each practitioner can draw on the relevant expertise when needed.

The boundaries of financial planning therefore vary to some extent depending on the background, skills and qualifications of the individual planner and their colleagues.

Priorities

One possible definition of financial planning is that it is about priorities. In most cases, people's resources fall short of what they need to fulfil their desires, so in making financial decisions they have to rank their needs and desires in order of importance to them. Many practitioners would assert that it is people's inability to undertake this prioritisation for themselves that is the cause of most poor decision making, and that it is therefore the core of financial planning.

The two styles of financial planning, which we could call factual and relational, approach prioritisation in different ways.

The **factual approach** is to set out the issue in numerical terms, specifying the shortfalls between resources and objectives, listing options that close the gap, and requiring the client to choose between these options. The **relational approach** involves querying the desires and encouraging the client to engage in 'what if?' scenarios in an open-ended way, initially without reference to the numerical outcomes. Often the result will be a decision that lies outside the original frame of reference.

Most financial planners use elements of both, reflecting the fact that some clients are more receptive to one or other of these approaches. 'Life planning' practitioners, though, see their role as wider than merely facilitating good financial decisions. They see themselves more as financial coaches, engaged with their clients in the same way that sports coaches are with athletes, helping them to make not just financial choices but 'life choices'.

Clearly adopting this style of financial planning requires a set of methods and techniques that are beyond the scope of this book, and also requires the practitioner to develop interpersonal and emotional skills to a greater depth than is necessary using a more conventional approach.

Holistic or partial

Some practitioners use the term 'holistic' to convey the notion that they are going beyond routine methods of financial planning. It could be argued that financial planning must be holistic or it is not financial planning at all. If a client requests advice purely on a single issue, such as a pension transfer, this is not 'financial planning' as discussed in this book. In the 'single issue' situation, the adviser takes into account only those factors the client permits them to consider, whereas if the issue is considered within a financial planning context, it is related to the whole of the client's circumstances and needs and to all their existing plans and investments.

Accordingly, while the content of financial planning can be divided into the categories discussed below, the practice of financial planning is about the totality of an individual's finances both current and prospective. This is the perspective adopted throughout this book.

3 The content of financial planning

The nine categories listed below include the core content of financial planning. They are listed here in ascending order of complexity and technical difficulty. The table (see page 16) identifies essential core areas of knowledge and skill and areas where planners may refer clients to other specialist services.

Employment and income

The degree of security of employment and income is a key issue. Financial planning involves undertaking financial commitments to savings and protection and in the case of many such commitments it is better not to enter them at all than to cancel them soon after commencement. 'Affordability' is regarded by regulators as a fundamental feature of appropriate financial advice.

Recent decades have seen a progressive reduction in the level of employment security. Short-term contracts and part-time employment have been used by employers to make their workforces and costs more flexible. For many people, therefore, flexibility in their financial plans is equally important.

Business proprietors and the self-employed will rarely have the same security of income as employees, but the longer they have been in business the less likely it is that they will suffer a catastrophic fall in income. Nevertheless security of income has implications for the appropriate level of liquid savings, as well as for the level of commitments to mortgage repayments and savings plans.

Advice to business proprietors will normally include issues such as methods of remuneration, pension contributions, business ownership within a family and other items that interact with the taxation of the business itself.

Retirement saving and protection are common employee benefits, and few people value them at their true worth. Where they constitute a significant element of a financial plan, it is important that the individual understands the importance of these benefits and includes them in any evaluation of alternative employment opportunities.

For young couples, a major issue is who will be the main breadwinner at what stages of their children's lives. Historically, it would have been the man throughout the period of dependency, but today couples may pass the baton of main earner back and forth several times before their children become independent. This makes financial planning a much more challenging task.

Following the abolition of employers' ability to set mandatory retirement ages, it is expected that many more people will continue to work into their late sixties and beyond. While some will do so from necessity – only by putting in several more years will they have enough capital in their retirement funds – others will do so because they enjoy their work, and some of them may be in danger of over-accumulating capital in pension funds.

Issues in employment

- How secure is the client's employment? Would redundancy insurance be worthwhile?

- What is the likely trend in future earnings? Is the client being over-optimistic about this?

- Are there key benefits (e.g. final salary pension) that the client would sacrifice if they changed their job?

- If the client has other forms of income such as buy-to-let properties or private company dividends, how secure are they?

- Are business proprietors' interests defined by a shareholders' agreement?

- Is remuneration from the business tax-efficient?

Budgeting

People vary enormously in the way they handle their day-do-day finances. Some are meticulous in managing bank and credit card statements and bills while others have only the vaguest idea of where their money goes.

Creating a budget that tracks all income and expenditure is a basic discipline, which was routinely practiced in households until quite recently. But today many people enter employment without having been taught it and never apply it for themselves. Often for these younger people, an encounter with an adviser will be the first time they have ever tried to create a budget.

Experienced advisers know that simply creating a monthly budget that accounts for all income and expenditure within relevant categories will often prompt major changes in behaviour. Simply acknowledging the amount they are spending on items like entertainment or holidays or gadgets can be enough to cause someone to change their spending habits. Overspending is the cause of a large proportion of financial problems, so the process of creating a budget is one of the most powerful tools in the adviser's box.

The degree of detail that is useful in a household budget depends on how much control the clients appear to have over their spending. For those with serious spending problems, an extremely detailed budget, assembled by keeping daily records of every item, will be desirable.

Analysing expenditure in appropriate categories will reveal the scope for savings. Often people fail to appreciate the way a regular small expenditure builds up, the classic example being the daily Starbucks coffee that adds up to £50 per month.

People also tend to stick to existing spending habits, so even when their income falls, they are reluctant to trim spending, especially on items like holidays or Christmas presents.

Budgeting is dealt with in depth in chapter 16, 'Immediate cashflow planning'.

Issues in budgeting

- Is cash being accumulated for items like holidays, or are they being paid for on credit cards and then paid off afterwards?

- Do clients have outstanding balances on credit cards and how do they plan to pay them off?

- Do clients clearly know their monthly outgoings on utilities, council tax and other regular bills?

- Do clients plan for seasonal variations in outgoings, for example in utility bills, holidays?

- Is the current account usually in deficit at the end of the month before the next salary payment is made?

- Are clients making regular large cash withdrawals without being able to account for where the money is going?

- Are current account surpluses regularly swept into a deposit account or savings plan?

Saving and liquidity

Common sense leads most people to decide that they need a rainy day fund of easily-accessible cash. But some people lose sight of the ease of accessibility and instead pursue higher interest rates at the expense of lengthy notice periods, which can create problems in an emergency. Determining an appropriate emergency fund and placing it with ease of access as the primary factor and interest rates as a secondary factor is an essential in financial planning and can be seen as an extension of the budgeting process.

Setting future goals such as private or university education for children, building capital to start a business or purchase a home, or providing children with funds to buy their first home, usually require prioritisation and careful allocation of limited resources. Most people have short, medium and longer term goals and need different forms of savings plan to meet them. Their prioritisation of these goals is likely to change as their circumstances alter.

Most people have limited ability to forecast changes in their circumstances more than five years ahead, so flexibility is a key issue in medium and longer term savings plans.

Saving is dealt with in chapter 18, 'Saving and investments'.

Issues in saving

- Given clients' circumstances, income and commitments, is there a sufficient sum in a rainy day fund?

- Are separate plans in place for defined short, medium and longer term goals?

- Does the content of each plan match the client's needs and timescale of the plan?

- In the case of couples, could any joint plans be divided easily in the event that they separated?

- Are plans reviewed regularly and updated to meet any change in needs and circumstances?

- Are longer-term plans making use of the annual ISA allowance?

Financial protection

A young single person in their first job, living in rented accommodation and with life insurance and health benefits as part of their employment package, has minimal needs for protective insurances other than for their possessions. But from then on throughout life, people add financial responsibilities and liabilities: more possessions (houses, cars, goods), more liabilities (mortgages, children) and more commitments (savings plans). Looked at in balance sheet terms, the individual accumulates larger and larger liabilities and while they may not be able to afford to insure all of them, there are good arguments for insuring as many as possible.

For young people, insuring against loss of income through ill health or redundancy will rank high; for couples with children, insuring the life and health of breadwinners; for couples with older children, insuring for the costs of taking their children to the point of financial independence; for older people, insuring against the costs of care in old age.

In each case, there are usually a variety of ways in which liabilities can be insured, and particularly for young couples with limited resources, creating an appropriate protection package is often a challenging task in several dimensions.

Protection is dealt with in chapter 17, 'Insurance and financial protection'.

Issues in protection

- Is insurance in place to cover living expenses in the event of loss of income through ill health?

- For couples with young children, is critical illness insurance or income protection insurance the most suitable way of covering mortgage repayments against the risk of ill health?

- Is it worth paying higher premiums to secure guaranteed insurability in future?

- Are existing life insurance policies written under trust?

- Have existing life policies been reviewed to see if they can be replaced at lower cost?

- Do clients have appropriate cover for their properties and possessions?

Mortgages and borrowing

Day-to-day borrowing to finance consumer purchases through the use of credit cards falls within the category of budgeting. But larger and longer-term loans including loans for car purchase or home extension, and mortgage borrowing for first and other homes, constitute a separate category. There are two reasons: the presence of the element of investment return to be compared with the interest rate payable, and the issue of the affordability of debt repayments.

In recent years regulators have focused sharply on the affordability issue, partly as a response to the mortgage lending excesses of the 2005-07 period. The proportion of net income used in debt repayments is the key consideration. For first-time homebuyers, a figure of about a third has often been taken as a reasonable maximum.

In the post-war era in the UK, house purchase using the largest possible mortgage has been a reliable way to build wealth, thanks to house prices rising faster than inflation and debt being devalued by inflation. But in conditions of very low inflation and house price growth, the strategy of capital accumulation through debt-financed home ownership will fail. It is safest to construct borrowing strategies on the basis of affordable cost (especially relating the costs of ownership to the costs of renting) rather than on the assumption of capital accumulation.

With the proliferation of mortgage products in recent years, borrowers face complex choices between variable and fixed rate mortgages; traditional, flexible and offset mortgages; and repayment and interest-only mortgages. While 'best buy' internet shopping for the mortgage with the best interest rate is now easy, determining the most suitable borrowing strategy is not so simple.

It is notable that people in many European countries rent throughout their working lives while accumulating capital sufficient to buy a retirement home. As the difference in running costs between old homes and new energy-efficient ones becomes better understood, the pattern of home ownership in the UK will probably continue to change.

Business proprietors today often have pension schemes that own properties used by their business, so that commercial borrowing to finance such purchases can fall within the scope of financial planning.

Borrowing is dealt with in chapter 16, 'Immediate cashflow planning'.

Issues in borrowing

- Are realistic plans in place for repayment of borrowings?

- Are shorter-term debts at high interest rates being paid off as rapidly as possible?

- How exposed are clients to a general rise in interest rates, especially on mortgage repayments?

- Is the term of debt repayments realistic, given clients' expected employment?

- Would an alternative type of mortgage (e.g. offset) be more advantageous?

- Could the client benefit from switching their current mortgage?

Retirement and pension planning

Accumulating sufficient capital to generate adequate retirement income is the single biggest financial issue facing many people in the UK. The historical pattern of lifetime employment with a final salary pension scheme generated satisfactory outcomes for millions of people, requiring little thought or effort. Today a very small minority of employees are in this position. Greater job mobility, the closure of final salary schemes, the reduction in employer contributions towards pension schemes and the erosion of the flat-rate State pension as a proportion of average earnings have all contributed to the situation that most people need to save more than they can afford in order to accumulate enough capital to support them in a much longer retirement than their parents'.

Added to this have been a series of changes to the rules governing private pension provision that have created uncertainty, and reductions in interest rates that have made the purchase of the traditional lifetime annuity with pension fund capital a deeply unappealing proposition to many retirees.

For many people, the question will be whether and how much to save in pension plans as opposed to other forms of saving. This is a highly complex issue where tax factors, life expectancy, health and investment returns all play a part in shaping the optimal solution. These same issues also arise when considering the transfer of existing pension arrangements to new plans.

On top of this, the UK's dysfunctional system of funding long-term care provision means people need to make provision for private care and seek ways of protecting their assets if they do enter care.

The historical pattern of accumulation of capital during a working life and decumulation during retirement is gradually changing. Abolition of employers' ability to set a mandatory retirement age and the progressive increase in the qualifying age for the State pension mean many people will work for longer, delaying the point when they start to decumulate. Part-time employment at 65-plus will become more prevalent, giving retirement funds longer to grow before decumulation begins.

Retirement planning is dealt with in chapter 19, 'Capital accumulation for retirement' and chapter 20, 'Retirement decumulation'.

Issues in retirement planning

- Is there a realistic estimate of the monthly saving required to accumulate a sufficient retirement fund?

- Is the client making maximum contributions to an employer-matched retirement scheme?

- Have all existing retirement saving plans been reviewed, and inefficient or poor-value plans terminated or transferred?

- Could the non-earning spouse advantageously contribute to a stakeholder pension?

- What is the appropriate balance between pension plans and other forms of retirement saving?

- Should tax-free cash from pension plans be used to accelerate mortgage repayment?

Tax planning

UK tax law now runs to several thousand legislative pages with many times that number of pages of HM Revenue & Customs (HMRC) interpretation and guidance. The system is widely acknowledged to be over-complex and the system of tax credits, reliefs and allowances in urgent need of radical simplification. The present system offers many opportunities for legitimate avoidance of taxes, which can be useful even for those on modest incomes. An example is the potential benefit from salary sacrifice, which can prevent the loss of benefits worth more than the net salary foregone.

For higher earners, tax reliefs (pensions, Venture Capital Trusts (VCTs) and Enterprise Investment Schemes (EIS)) enable the avoidance of tax on substantial incomes. Business Assets Relief can be used to avoid inheritance tax. Capital gains tax liabilities can be deferred through EIS investments. Even for those on lower incomes, use of the annual ISA allowance can permit the accumulation of a tax-exempt fund in excess of £300,000 over a 25-year term.

While artificial tax avoidance schemes have come under increasingly heavy fire from the legislature and HMRC in recent years, simple tax avoidance using entirely straightforward and legitimate opportunities usually offers people far more scope than they realise to lower their tax bills. For example, independent taxation of husband and wife means there are potential tax savings from a transfer of assets wherever one pays tax at a higher rate.

Tax avoidance is a field with ill-defined edges. While use of VCTs and EIS schemes is sanctioned by legislation, the use of business investment schemes utilising capital allowances, or sophisticated schemes for other forms of business finance, can fall into a grey area where they are neither subject to the HMRC pre-notification rules that govern avoidance schemes nor constitute straightforward investment propositions. Advisers can choose whether to offer advice in this area or to refer clients to specialists.

Tax planning for very wealthy individuals may involve issues such as residence and domicile and registration of businesses, and is the field of firms usually employing highly qualified tax specialists. Such issues are beyond the scope of this book and advisers will usually refer clients needing such services to one of these specialists.

Tax planning is covered in chapters 16, 'Immediate cashflow planning' to 21, 'Estate planning'.

Issues in tax planning

- Is the client's current tax code correct?
- Does the client have outstanding tax liabilities or repayments due?
- Is the client's income tax status (basic or higher/additional rate taxpayer) likely to remain the same or to change?
- Could the client benefit from a salary sacrifice arrangement?
- Are clients using the relevant allowances and exemptions such as the annual gains tax allowance and gifts exempt from inheritance tax?

- Are couples' investments registered in the most tax-efficient ways in terms of ownership?
- Are clients making best use of their annual ISA allowances?
- Has the client failed to comply with UK tax law?

Investment

For most individuals, investment involves allocation of capital to investment funds ranging from the safety of near-cash to the speculative specialisms of funds investing in China or biotechnology. For the extremely wealthy, bespoke investment strategies using purpose-built vehicles may be appropriate, but for the vast majority of investors, relatively conventional fund portfolios can be designed to match their needs and risk tolerance.

An increasing number of investors create DIY fund portfolios using platforms such as Vantage, Alliance Trust or FundsNetwork, or use execution-only stockbrokers to create share portfolios. But once the sums at stake become sufficiently large and the risk becomes more obvious, investors generally prefer to entrust the task of creating a suitable portfolio to an adviser.

Individuals may have specific needs in mind when investing, such as the marriage of a daughter, purchase of a second home or repayment of a mortgage. But the majority of people investing capital are doing so with the long-term aim of generating cash to support them during retirement. Conventionally, this has been described as retirement income, but in practice most people who live for 30 years after retiring draw upon their capital as well, so the term 'decumulation' is now generally used.

Until the 1990s, advisers tended to allocate lump sum investments to generalist funds such as with-profit funds and managed funds. Then the use of portfolios of unit trusts and OEICs became prevalent, a trend encouraged by the development of platforms and wraps on which these assets could conveniently be held. But the severe losses suffered by many investors in 2008-10 have since led to a trend away from advisers' use of advisory portfolios to the use of discretionary portfolio management services.

Historically, financial planners have tended to offer investment advisory services using UK-authorised collective investment funds. But advisers can also choose to manage portfolios with discretionary mandates, or to outsource the management of investments to a third party, usually a discretionary fund manager. They may also do both, for example offering their own advisory services for core portfolios and using specialist discretionary services for investment in alternative asset classes or in VCT and EIS schemes. The adviser's level of professional qualifications will increasingly determine the scope and style of the investment service they offer.

Behavioural finance (see chapter 3, 'The impact of behavioural finance') has shown that for most people, losses are far more painful than profits are pleasurable, so that loss aversion tends to dominate their attitudes and responses.

The investment process is covered in chapter 6, 'Investment planning' and and investment planning in chapters 18 'Saving and investments', chapter 19, 'Capital accumulation for retirement' to chapter 20, 'Retirement decumulation'.

Issues in investment

- What experience has the client had of investment and what has been their response to it?

- Are the client's attitudes, especially to the risk of loss, so fixed and inflexible that it would be dangerous to recommend any form of investment where capital is at risk?

- Is the client's income tax status (basic or higher rate taxpayer) likely to remain the same or to change?

- Have timescales and purposes for investment been thoroughly investigated and agreed, to minimise the chance of early withdrawal of capital?

- Does the client clearly understand the risk-return trade-off (see chapter 6, 'Investment planning')?

- If spouses do not share the same attitude to risk, would they be happier having separate portfolios?

- Do the client's investment needs require specialist solutions?

Estate planning

Only a small minority of the population have estates liable to inheritance tax, but almost all those with assets face choices about the disposition of their assets after their death. Gaining clarity about their desires and implementing their intentions through a will is both a legal and a financial planning issue.

It is rare for people to have thought through all the consequences of their intentions, and often the adviser will need to establish what the real purpose is. Bequests may, for instance, be made to avoid the risk of capital falling into the hands of an in-law and not reaching the grandchildren. Only after fully discussing such issues can an adviser propose the most efficient measures, some of which may be better achieved by lifetime dispositions.

Since most people dislike making wills, they tend not to review them, making this an important part of the financial planning process.

For elderly people, advising on establishing suitable powers of attorney is also important. Especially when an elderly person has gone into care and becomes unable to make decisions, having a power of attorney (POA) already established can avoid problems for their children and heirs.

For people with potential liabilities to inheritance tax, a well-framed will is one aspect of the tax mitigation process. But planning measures such as purchase of business assets, altering property ownership to a 'tenancy in common' basis, or making lifetime transfers, are likely to be the key to reducing tax liability. Though recent changes in the law have reduced the financial advantages of trusts, there are still many situations in which transfer of assets into a trust is the most effective way of achieving a client's objectives.

Since ownership of business assets is the only way of escaping tax on very large estates, this is likely to involve highly complex issues of ownership, transfer of ownership and management, which may require specialist and legal advice.

Estate planning is covered in chapter 21, 'Estate planning'.

Issues in estate planning

- Are the children and heirs fully apprised of the client's intentions?

- Are there conflicts of interest between beneficiaries that need to be resolved before the client's death?

- Does the adviser have a good working relationship with the lawyer responsible for the will?

- Is spouses' ownership of assets efficient in terms of estate planning and inheritance tax?

- Are clients aware of the cost and tax drawbacks of trusts as well as their advantages?

- Have existing trusts been reviewed and updated?

- Is use being made of annual exemptions to minimise inheritance tax liabilities?

- Are business assets owned and managed in the most effective way for tax purposes?

In each of these areas, establishing the facts, identifying needs and agreeing priorities are the key steps in the financial planning process and are all covered in Part 2 of this book.

The scope of financial planning

Field	Core	Optional	Beyond the scope of financial planning
Employment	Tax status and coding; qualifying State pension national insurance contributions; use of tax allowances and reliefs	Life planning; tax-efficient employee benefits; non-UK employment	Divorce; employment disputes
Budgeting	Monthly household budget; short-term debt repayment	Budgeting software	Debt counselling
Liquidity	Emergency fund; short-term capital and income needs	Cash management service	Provision of credit or banking facilities
Protection	Life, health and income insurances	General insurances	
Borrowing	Personal loans, mortgages	Mortgage broking	Disputes with lenders
Retirement	Pension and other savings plans	Business tax planning	Business management issues
Tax planning	Tax efficient ownership and use of tax concessions	Tax avoidance	Tax evasion
Investment	Risk profiling, targets for returns, allocation of capital to tax wrappers	Own advisory service, own discretionary service, referral to discretionary fund manager	Advice on shares, business ventures
Estate	Wills, POAs, inheritance tax mitigation	Tax avoidance; foreign domiciles	Business ownership and management

4 Determining priorities

In each of the nine categories set out above, people may have conflicting aims. A young couple may, for example, want to protect both their incomes in the event of ill health and also insure their lives for their children's benefit, but be unable to afford the cost of complete cover. They would then face the question of whether to have some (but less than adequate cover) in all these areas or whether — for the time being at least — not to purchase one of these insurances.

And there will also be conflicts between needs in different categories. Our young couple, for instance, may have started a long-term savings plan. Should they reduce their monthly saving in order to buy more insurance cover?

Deciding on questions like these requires careful analysis of needs. While clients will see issues in terms of what they want, often with a bias to the short-term, the adviser's job is to work out what they need.

Clarifying needs is the necessary precursor to prioritisation – see chapter 10, 'Client aims and objectives' and chapter 13, 'Summarising and analysing needs and priorities'.

Wants and needs

Many clients enter discussions with advisers having simply a set of wants that they have not translated into monetary terms.

Example 1.1

A couple wish to send their two young children to private schools from the age of 11. The adviser works out that on the assumption that fees rise in line with inflation at 2%, the annual fees when both are at school in ten years time will be about £12,000. The couple may be able to pay £7,000 a year out of income. They therefore need to accumulate a capital sum of some £45,000 in the next ten years. They also need to purchase additional life insurance to ensure that sufficient funds are available to pay the fees if one of them dies.

In the context of financial planning, a need is the expression of an objective in monetary terms.

Clients may think they know what they need but unless they have really articulated their wants and desires their formulation of needs is likely to be inadequate or inaccurate. For this reason skilful advisers encourage clients to 'dream a little' in expressing their wants. If the round-the-world cruise, the visit to the relatives in Australia, the vintage car, the photography course or the mobile home is what the client really wants, this should form part of their plan. Often the client will have wants that they subsume in the general aim of 'having enough money', but it is part of the adviser's job to find out what they really want so that it can be realistically costed and planned for.

Formulating objectives

When questioned on their objectives, people tend to make general statements of their aims such as "I want to have enough to live on when I retire". In order to convert this into an input for a financial plan, an aim has to be converted into one or more specific objectives. A need has to be specific (for example in terms of retirement age), measurable (the retirement income should be the equivalent of £2,000 per month in today's terms), action-related (capable of being affected by action taken now), realistic (an extra contribution of £200 per month is affordable) and time related (the retirement fund should be £300,000 in six years' time).

Qualitative statements (like the quotation in the preceding paragraph) help the adviser understand how the client thinks and feels, so they are a good starting point. If the client makes quantitative statements ("I want to retire on the equivalent of three-quarters of my pre-retirement earnings") it is advisable to encourage them to make qualitative statements as well.

Identifying and formulating aims and objectives is covered in chapter 10, 'Client aims and objectives'.

Prioritising objectives

People usually want many things and understand that they probably cannot have them all. Translating wants into aims and objectives enables people to identify what is essential. These most important needs will form the core of their financial plan and will usually be 'must have' (retirement income, protection) as opposed to 'nice to have' (new car, bigger house).

The table lists the most important objectives typical of each life stage, and these are likely to have the highest priority. This does not mean that they necessarily absorb the largest share of resources. For a couple with young children, arranging adequate protection is a high priority because of the potential consequences if one of them dies or becomes seriously ill without having suitable insurances in place. But the overall monthly cost of this protection may be less than they contribute to medium-term savings plans.

Common objectives related to life stages

Life stage	Objective
Young, single	Purchase first home
	Build capital fund
Young, married with children	Create security for the family
	Private education for children
	Create retirement fund
Middle aged with older children	Help children to financial independence
	Pay off mortgage as soon as possible
	Build financial assets to support retirement
Retired	Finance new leisure activities
Older	Help grandchildren
	Pass on wealth to heirs

When the adviser works out the cost of meeting the client's objectives, there will usually be a gap between the resources available and what would be required to fully meet the objectives. The gap can be reduced by adjusting goals (for example, retiring five years later) so that they require less resources, or by increasing the resources (through reducing current spending) that can be devoted to these goals.

People normally focus on their immediate aims and may not think much about longer-term issues such as retirement planning or long-term care provision. Usually, creating a realistic plan will involve shifting more emphasis to the longer term and may well involve sacrificing some shorter-term goals (replacing the car, having a kitchen makeover) to improve the chances of achieving longer-term aims (paying off the mortgage early, being able to afford to retire at 65).

5 Formulating recommendations

The discipline of financial planning involves treating recommendations as the outcome of the process. This is what differentiates it from selling financial products, where the analysis of needs is undertaken solely with an end in mind, or 'single issue' planning, where other issues and considerations are set aside.

In the financial planning process, recommendations should be clearly linked to the aims and objectives by analysis.

Usually, financial planners create a formal plan, which states a set of objectives, and may include a wide variety of recommendations. The planner will usually update this plan at regular intervals and make fresh recommendations in response to changing circumstances.

Analysis

Most people make decisions in a largely intuitive way, using 'rules of thumb' which often operate unconsciously. As shown in chapter 3, 'The impact of behavioural finance', the perceptual and behavioural biases that are a normal feature of human psychology make this a poor way of reaching financial decisions.

In contrast to this, the financial planner assembles all the data relevant to an issue and analyses it. In some cases specialist tools are needed, for example in analysis of pension transfers. Much of the time simply understanding and using compound interest is all that is required. Advisers increasingly use cashflow projections and analysis (again, primarily based on compound interest) to assess the achievability of a client's objectives.

Because the scope of financial planning is so wide, it is essential to adopt a disciplined process for each of its stages, and this process is explained in Part 2 of this book.

Chapter 2
Financial planning — the benefits for clients

Financial planning is a relatively new profession, especially in the UK, and many people are unclear what financial planners can do for them and the benefits that they would derive from using the services of one. How financial planners describe themselves is a helpful starting point to understanding their function. Some advisers describe themselves as financial problem-solvers, referring to activities such as calculating the amount of inheritance tax that might be payable on an estate and recommending an appropriate mitigation strategy. Equally it might mean helping a client choose the right financial product to meet a specific need, for example the provision of enough income in retirement. Such a description accurately describes what financial planners do, but it seems rather limited. It may describe what they do for most clients, but financial planners would probably prefer to think of their function as more encompassing and in some sense more creative.

Product providers and even regulators have adopted the expression 'distributors' to describe the financial advisory sector. Clearly providers see advisers as the people who sell their products to the retail public. That is not how most financial planners regard themselves, although they would almost certainly concede that they are likely to recommend financial products to clients to help them meet their aims.

A growing number of advisers would describe themselves as holistic planners, life planners or even 'financial architects'. The reality is that while most clients are initially prompted to consult a financial planner on a specific issue, they then find that their actions have repercussions in other areas; estate planning often leads to retirement planning and raising a mortgage for house purchase is typically followed by a conversation about life and health insurance needs. No financial problem is an island.

One of the distinctive features of financial planning is that it follows a process that is broadly common to all practitioners. A key difference between the way in which a client might try to solve their own financial problems and a financial planner's approach should be the use of a planning process. This process ought to be logical, ordered and lead to an effective plan that brings a number of valuable benefits to their clients.

1 What clients want – helping them to define their aims

Inevitably the process of trying to solve a specific problem will start with the planner's need to understand the client's general short and long-term aims and objectives as well as the financial circumstances of the client. This is likely to involve the client in one of the most in-depth conversations about their wishes and aspirations that they might have ever experienced. Few other professionals ask for this degree of intimate understanding of the client that financial planners require – with the possible exception of psychotherapists.

Most people live in the present and seldom contemplate the future other than in the very short-term or possibly in a very general way. Few think with any coherence or clarity about their long-term future or the financial implications of their ambitions. Likewise and perhaps even more understandably, it is rare to encounter a client who has thought about the potential consequences of their death or serious illness. One of the great values of the financial planning process is that clients are forced to consider their future lives and what this might mean for their financial arrangements. Until they undertake the process of thinking about their future plans and finances, most clients seem able to displace hard questions about these issues with vague hopes and intentions. As human beings we have a strong propensity to focus on the here and now and defer thinking about the future, especially if the problems are hard to grapple with or might require altering one's current behaviour by, for example, saving more and spending less – see chapter 3, 'The impact of behavioural finance'.

Financial planners have differing views on how much they should concentrate on general life planning for clients as opposed to pure financial planning. In many instances the former approach can lead to stimulating clients to examine their life's ambitions for their lives in a deeper and more considered way than they may have done before. Moving into this wider sphere – although without ever extending into the territory of the therapist – is something that some financial planners resist. Some regard this as an area in which they are already active to some degree, although in considerably less depth. Others have concerns about moving so far out of the financial sphere.

Many financial planners are still reluctant to move away from the strict bounds of financial planning into this wider focus of activity, despite the claims that the relationship and the understanding of a client's wants and needs are so much stronger.

Whether financial planners accept the whole-hearted life planning approach or opt for a much purer financial focus to their questioning, it is clear that clients will be invited to think of issues they have seldom considered before. Even if they have worked with a financial planner in the past, they will almost certainly find that they need to reappraise their expectations and wishes in the light of their changed circumstances. The death of a relative, the birth of a child, a marriage, separation or divorce, a house purchase, promotion or period of unemployment may all stimulate a client's attitude to their future and the financial planning that will be required.

So a key benefit of the process of financial planning is that clients will be induced to consider whether their plans, wishes and aspirations for the future developed continue to be realistic and appropriate. But in many instances, clients will be contemplating these matters for the first time.

Example 2.1

John had a new born son. John assumed that he could afford to send his son to the same expensive boarding school as he had attended some 20 years earlier. He also had dreams of retiring to the country at age 55 or a little later. Even without the benefit of a full life planning exercise, several things became clear and meant that John needed to rethink his aims. His wife did not necessarily share his ambition to send the child to this particular school – at least probably not as a boarder. What was more, it looked as if they could not afford to buy the house they wanted and also afford the substantial school fees without a significant uplift in their income. The other possibility was that the grandparents would contribute very substantial sums, which did not seem very realistic. Finally, it turned out that John was less keen to retire at 55 when he thought more carefully about what he would do in retirement.

The process of discovering a person's aims, objectives, wishes and aspirations – let alone their approach to risk in all its forms – can be time-consuming even without the use of fully-fledged life planning techniques. This element of the planning process lays the foundations for the rest of the planner/client relationship and may therefore take several hours and more than one meeting. This process has a value that cannot be directly linked to the level of investment and the investment returns that might be achieved. A person of relatively modest means may need to have as much time (or more) spent on this aspect of planning as someone with substantial assets. Some argue that clients can do this for themselves and that it does not require much technical expertise. In some cases, this might well be true, as some clients have very well developed ideas of their aims and objectives. But even in these instances, clients may well benefit from the questioning of a skilled practitioner who can draw on the experience of conducting many such interviews to stimulate more in-depth thinking.

The planner should always compare a client's stated aims and objectives to the main financial problem areas, such as adequacy of retirement funds or lack of realism about investment returns or understanding of risk. The financial planner has important advantages over the do-it-yourself method of financial planning: the financial planner should be familiar with most of the main issues and can provide an objective view of the situation. Many clients will find the conversations about future plans and aims illuminating and helpful and unlike any other dialogues they may have had with friends or other professionals.

Helping a client to understand the nature of financial risk is often time consuming. Some clients will have a reasonably good understanding of themselves – both what they can afford to lose and what they feel they can afford to lose. But in most cases, clients misunderstand their own position and the actual risks involved in investment – and the risks that should be covered by insurance.

The value of summarising and analysing the position

Greater clarity of purpose and understanding of aims should be accompanied by a very much clearer understanding of the financial position by both client and planner and the financial realities that they need to grapple with. It is often surprising how little grasp many clients have of their finances. Most people know what their homes are worth and the amount of their monthly mortgage payments, but other details can be vague. Typical areas where clients would benefit from a clear presentation of the facts are:

- Gross and net income
- Expenditure
- Borrowings and their associated costs
- Trusts
- Investments
- Life assurance and other protection policies
- Pensions
- Wills and estate issues and potential inheritance tax liability

In some cases, the simple and systematic listing of the financial facts is very valuable to clients. But the financial planner should aim to go further by summarising the facts in an illuminating way. The main approach to presenting this type of information meaningfully is to point out the relationships between the figures. So for example, income should be related to expenditure, expenditure examined under different headings to identify possible savings areas, borrowings should be related to their costs, related assets and income flows.

One of the key steps is the synthesis and analysis when the financial planner examines whether the client is meeting their aims and objectives now and in the future. It is the essential reality check.

Then it makes sense to look for the gaps. The client has — or possibly should have — a set of aims and objectives. The gap analysis should identify where there is a difference between those aims and the reality of the client's life. For example, the client should have enough life and health protection to provide a capital sum of £X and an income of £Y; but the actual provision is half that amount; net income is £Z and expenditure is 105% of £Z; so perhaps expenditure needs to change. The target savings for retirement is £A, but the client is only on track to provide 30% of £A. The client has a risk profile that is not compatible with the risk rating of their investment portfolio.

A powerful set of techniques in the analytical stage is to consider the individual client and their family rather like a business. Clearly, this has some limitations — businesses tend to be focused on profitability and growth and do not have the range of considerations and aims that an individual might have. But looking at the purely financial can be very illuminating, producing businesslike statements such as:

- Income and expenditure account broken down by main income and cost centres.

- Cashflow — many people have high and low cash points in the year and identifying these can be very helpful.

- Balance sheet — assets and liabilities with liabilities broken down by type, term and costs.

- Future cashflow projection to identify when the client might run out of money in retirement.

- Risk analysis — an analysis of the main hazards that the client faces and analysing these in terms of impact, likelihood and how they have (or have not) been dealt with.

- Contingent cashflow — what would be the consequence of one of the key hazards — e.g. death, ill health, unemployment, drop in the value of investments.

- SWOT analysis — a statement of strengths, weaknesses, opportunities and threats.

The benefits of this stage for the client are: a clear statement setting out their financial position and an analysis of the gaps between their aims and the reality of their position.

Clear recommendations

Identifying solutions to the issues raised in the analysis stage is a critical function of the financial planner; likewise making recommendations. Most clients would find it hard to carry out these tasks, especially where the planner brings together the knowledge and skills needed to become a qualified adviser – encompassing tax, legislation, pensions, protection, investment and comprehensive planning. The nexus of tax and investment planning can be especially complicated and in particular the need to choose the appropriate combination of tax wrappers. It is difficult to keep up-to-date with the issues.

The plan itself is likely to be enormously valuable to the client, as it will contain:

- A summary of the key facts about the client.

- A schedule of detailed information about existing investments and other financial products.

- A statement of the client's aims and objectives and an appraisal of their priorities and capability of being realised.

- An analysis of the main gaps in the existing provision and planning.

- A programme for immediate and long-term action.

- Detailed recommendations.

A client working alone to carry out their financial planning is unlikely to provide themselves with this essential road map to their financial future. As a result, without the benefit of professional help, clients are likely to display many kinds of weaknesses in the preparation and execution of their planning. With insufficient time and knowledge, their analysis and recommendations are likely to be incomplete. With little or no written statement of the key aspects of the plan, they may well lose the thread of their strategy and follow inconsistent approaches, especially if there are changes in the financial environment such as an investment downturn.

Choosing the appropriate products for clients still requires considerable skill. There are websites that help investors to select products, but understanding the technical issues, knowing the providers, reading the detailed terms and conditions and understanding the implications of the statements requires a degree of expertise and sheer time commitment that most clients do not have.

But it is perhaps in identifying – and helping the client to choose – the main priorities for action where planners can come into their own. Typically it is not possible to achieve all the objectives immediately. There may be a limited budget, or it may not be possible to achieve both the required return on investment as well as the risk rating that the client wants. The planner can help tease out the key issues and come up with a suitable compromise or order of implementation.

The weaknesses of do-it-yourself financial planning

Financial planning for a client requires a number of attributes that make it difficult to carry out for oneself. As a result even financial planners do not always plan for themselves very successfully:

- **Time** – most people do not have the time to gain the technical knowledge to make good decisions about their finances. Many clients are financially rich but time poor, although this may change for some when they retire.

- **Commitment** – even where they do have the time to study the technicalities – and some clients do not have especially complex affairs especially once difficult one-off pensions complications have been sorted out – they often lack the commitment to devote time to a subject that many people do not find very interesting.

- **Self-discipline** – sometimes financial planning requires difficult decisions – buying one investment in difficult circumstances (say after a market fall), selling investments that have underperformed and seem likely to continue to do so, and buying insurances when other areas of expenditure seem much more immediately inviting.

- **Knowledge** – most clients have insufficient knowledge of both the key financial planning issues and the products that are available, together with their costs, benefits and potential drawbacks and risks. In other words, financial planners help their clients to make better decisions about both strategy and detailed solutions.

The costs and value of advice

There is a temptation for some commentators and regulators to relate the costs of advice simply to the investment returns that clients earn as a result of the advice they are given. There is some merit in this approach; it can help to keep costs in proportion to the outcomes. In most situations it would clearly be absurd for a client to incur costs of £5,000 in relation to an investment portfolio of less than £20,000 and very little prospect of it being added to in the future. Rich clients can afford to pay relatively more for a financial planner's services. But it is also a very limited view of the function of financial planning which may well be concerned with far more than the purchase of investments.

In some respects financial planning resembles the prosaic function of completing a tax return. The accountant's charges may turn out to be less than the tax saving they can achieve, but they may turn out to be more. Complex clients with substantial resources are more likely to need tax advisers to complete their tax return and provide advice than someone with a simple situation. But both may feel they need to have an expert to carry out a function, giving the satisfaction of knowing that they will not have to undertake a tedious chore and they will enjoy the peace of mind of knowing that an essential task has been carried out on a timely basis. So it is with financial planning. Much of the value may lie outside the selection and management of investment products.

Knowing the boundaries of competence

It is important that financial planners appreciate their limitations. The skills sets of financial planners vary greatly. The ratcheting up of standards in the course of the implementation of the retail distribution review has meant that levels of knowledge for financial planners are more uniform, so that a basic understanding of key concepts is more widely shared. But like medical general and specialist practitioners, it is essential for financial advisers to understand when they should advise clients to call on the services of other types of adviser.

Financial advisers who undertake life planning, for example, must be keenly aware of the limitations of their activities. Assuming that they are not psychologists, they should not venture into psychological treatments and advice. It is potentially dangerous and is certainly inappropriate. Equally, where a client needs legal services, they should be recommended to consult an appropriately qualified person.

The aim of many financial planners is to become the trusted adviser who is at the centre of their clients' financial affairs, coordinating and liaising with other advisers, but always able to bring the strategy together. In reality other professionals may well undertake this role, most often the lawyer or the accountant.

Comparison with other professions

Other professions provide both a pattern and a contrast to the work of the financial adviser.

Accountants share many of the functions and characteristics of financial planners and some financial planners are also accountants by training. Accountants are sometimes and perhaps unfairly accused of being overly focused on looking backwards to previous years' accounts or tax returns in contrast to the financial planning function of looking forwards and preparing for the future. Many of the accountant's basic tools of scheduling accurately, balance sheets, profit and loss accounts and cashflows statements are central to the financial planner's work.

Management consultants share many of the attributes of financial planners. They are often concerned with holistic multi-faceted aspects of their clients' problems and solutions. Many of the issues are financial and relate to their clients' ability to withstand changes in circumstances and be prepared for the

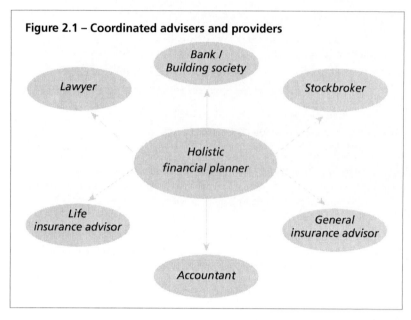

Figure 2.1 – Coordinated advisers and providers

future. In some respects an individual can resemble a business organisation with its need to balance income and expenditure, build reserves for the future and adjust to change. Indeed some clients own businesses and their financial futures are intimately bound up with the future of their businesses. So it is perhaps not surprising that financial planners can draw on many of the techniques of management consultants such as SWOT analysis (strengths, weaknesses, opportunities, threats).

Psychologists and counsellors both share characteristics with financial planners both in the way that they work and their aims. They know that it is important to understand what drives the client and generally have well developed methods of questioning and analysing their behaviour and intentions. They know that people are motivated by both rational and irrational beliefs and understand that clients often have to change their behaviour and in particular their spending patterns if they are to meet their goals.

Lawyers have to help their clients meet personal objectives within the constraints of the legal system. Much of the work of financial planners also involves the discipline of solving legal and tax based problems.

The financial planner could come from most of these original core disciplines. Many financial planners are by training accountants, lawyers or other types of professionals before they focused on financial planning. The distinguishing feature is the process of planning.

Chapter 3
The impact of behavioural finance

1 Introduction – rational and irrational thinking

Financial planners often expect their clients to be able to assess risks realistically, be prepared to spend money on insurance where it is needed and save for the future. Accordingly, the financial planner finds out their clients' goals, summarises and analyses their circumstances and recommends the best way to achieve what they want. But the reality of how their clients will behave can be very different.

Any financial planner with practical experience of advising clients will be well aware that people do not always behave in this cold logical way when it comes to money. Clients may be clear about what they want to achieve, but they often seem curiously unwilling to engage with the necessary means to those ends. For example, every financial planner has encountered clients who know that they are overspending on luxuries and are getting into serious and avoidable debt but seem to be incapable of changing their habits. It is very common to come across a client who agrees that they want to retire in reasonable comfort and seem to accept that it will be necessary to save a certain amount each month to achieve that, but is then curiously incapable of committing to the required level of saving.

The behavioural finance experts applied the insights of psychology to the ways that people actually make decisions. People commonly, systematically and often unhelpfully make mistakes and snap judgements about their financial lives. Financial planners need to understand these insights.

Financial planners can take many of the ideas and lessons from the field of behavioural finance and make the best use of it in their work with clients in a number of ways. Financial planners should be able to:

- Identify when their clients' behaviour undermines their long-term financial well-being and take steps to help clients to change or avoid that behaviour.

- Use some of the insights and techniques developed by behavioural finance experts to mould their clients' behaviour in a positive direction e.g. to save more for their retirement.

- Explain to clients such investment phenomena as crazes, crashes and panics and how the investment markets operate.

- Exploit other investors' behavioural mistakes to gain additional rewards in the investment market place, although this is aspect is not the focus of this chapter.

This chapter focuses on the first three of these aims. The ways in which the ideas of behavioural finance can be used to second-guess investment market movements are beyond the scope of this book. Some commentators have serious doubts as to whether it is often possible to use behavioural finance in this way. However, it is helpful to understand that markets can be irrational because they are governed by the emotions of human beings. When faced with an investor who had bought an investment because it was currently 'wrongly' priced, the economist John Maynard Keynes is said to have uttered the words: "The market can remain irrational longer than you can remain solvent". Financial planners need to be aware that fund managers like all professional investors are by no means immune from biases and mistakes.

In selecting funds and management teams, an important part of the process should be to check the systems and controls that provide disciplines to prevent fund managers from making many of the systematic mistakes that behavioural finance has identified and that can lead to underperformance.

Behavioural finance has become very widely discussed in financial and government circles with many of the key concepts covered in the press on a daily basis. The high priests of behavioural finance, such as Daniel Kahnemann, Richard Thaler, Dan Ariely, have become advisers to governments, banks and regulators around the world. In the UK for example, the government's decision to introduce auto-enrolment into pensions legislation was directly prompted by the work of such behavioural finance specialists as Richard Thaler and Shlomo Benartzi.

2 Background to behavioural finance issues

Many experts trace the birth of behavioural finance to the discussion of prospect theory in a paper (Prospect Theory: An analysis of decision under risk, 1979) written by Amos Tversky and Daniel Kahnemann. Kahnemann (who was awarded the Nobel prize for economics in 2002) and Tversky came to the crucial conclusion that investors are much more unhappy with a loss of £1,000 than they are pleased with a gain of the same amount. This asymmetry of attitudes to profits and losses often leads to skewed and illogical behaviour in the choice of investments. Mostly, investors choose investments that are excessively cautious, but in extreme circumstances fear of realising a loss can drive some people to taking very high risks and gambling amounts that they may not even have in order to regain their losses, particularly after a heavy losing streak.

Tversky and Kahnemann and the many other authors and academics who have followed in their footsteps have identified a range of irrational behavioural patterns that are predictable because they seem to be hard wired into the human brain. They describe how people actually make their financial decisions, rather than how they logically *should* make decisions to maximise their needs and wants and meet their expressed goals. Even if people know and understand what they should be doing to achieve their goals, they may well still make bad decisions. This might be because of their lack of self-control or because they have various ingrained habits of thought and response.

There is not space here to do justice to the reasons why psychologists, anthropologists and even neurologists believe that irrational thinking often prevails over rational approaches to life. The human brain seems to be well adapted to the many millennia that humans have spent as hunter gatherers on the savannah and has not yet evolved to suit the relatively brief period of life in large and economically complex communities. The basic emotions of fear and greed are much more quickly triggered than the rational thought processes of calm calculation and logical appraisal and they are also much more powerful. We have developed short cuts and habits of thought and feeling that allow us to make rapid decisions. These are hard-wired into us and are systematic and predictable. One of the aims of behavioural finance has been to identify these short cuts that people persistently use and which influence their behaviour and cause them to make systematic mistakes.

These short cuts have important implications for financial planning. Financial planners aim to make their clients think and behave rationally about their financial affairs. This is likely to involve balancing income and expenditure, saving for the future, investing in a sensible way and buying insurance where needed. Yet behavioural finance experts warn that this kind of rational behaviour often runs counter to many of people's most basic instincts and thought patterns.

3 The key behavioural finance concepts

Financial planners increasingly find it helpful to be aware of the main strands of thought in behavioural finance. In particular it is worth having an understanding of the main terms used so that they can identify, categorise and analyse clients' mistakes. The following is a quick guide to much of the key vocabulary or behavioural finance.

Adaptive attitudes

Most people tend to develop the same attitudes as the people they associate with. This applies to money issues just as much as other matters. Adaptive attitudes lie behind such crowd behaviour as financial market panics and bubbles. They also help to explain the tendency for people to make roughly the same level of pension contributions as their colleagues, rather than making a choice that is based on their own individual needs and wants. Adaptive attitudes are often very apparent in people's choice of investments and funds. When they are told what their friends and colleagues have chosen, there is a strong tendency for people to follow suit. Keynes was an early student of behavioural finance in some respects and he said, "Investors may be quite willing to take the risk of being wrong in the company of others, while being much more reluctant to take the risk of being right alone".

Attachment bias

Attachment bias is the tendency to hold investments and other assets for emotional reasons, e.g. because they are inherited or the shares are local or they are in the company that employed the client. See also 'Endowment bias' and 'Status quo bias' effect.

Anchoring

People naturally tend to attach to one particular value or reference point. For example, suggesting a particular number to a person can lead them to focus on that number and become emotionally attached to it. Anchoring can be important in many situations. Advertisers often use numbers because they know that investors will focus on them, so they may emphasise the target 9% returns on income or growth bonds, rather than the complex conditions that have to be met to achieve this attractive return. Investors also have a tendency to anchor on a particular price as the appropriate value for an investment and below which they would not be prepared to sell whatever the merits of the investments and its suitability for them.

Typically this would be the price that the investor paid for the share or fund or it might possibly be the value that it achieved at the peak of its performance. Investors are very reluctant to sell investments at a price they consider to be a 'loss' – i.e. below the value on which they have anchored – because they would regard it as realising a loss about which they would have feelings of regret, see 'Prospect theory'.

Attribution bias

There is a tendency for people to attribute successes to their own skill and judgement and poor outcomes to bad luck or to events outside their control. Investors (like car drivers) are often prepared to take more risks when they feel they are in control, even if the feeling is illusory, see also 'Over confidence'.

Availability bias

The most vivid or salient events that can be most easily imagined have the greatest impact on people's memories and their predictions. Colourful and vivid anecdotal experience and stories often carry more weight than cold statistical evidence, see 'Representativeness bias'.

Clients are more prepared to buy life assurance after the death of a family member or friend, rather than simply when they need it. Most investors feel that a sudden loss is more painful than a slow decline in value.

Behavioural finance or behavioural economics

Behavioural finance is the application of psychology to financial and economic behaviour. It is the study of how people actually make financial decisions rather than how they should, if they were being coolly rational, make them. There is a particular emphasis on the ways in which people make predictable mistakes.

Clustering illusion

Clustering illusion is the ability to discern patterns, or clusters, where they do not exist. Closely associated with hindsight bias and extrapolation bias (see below), clustering illusion is often observable in the interpretation of investment statistics. Cynics suggest that chartist investment is almost entirely based on clustering illusion.

Cognitive dissonance

When trying to reconcile conflicting opinions, information or attitudes, there is a temptation to blank out the unpleasant or that which does not conform to the individual's preconceived ideas (see 'Confirmation bias'). Examples include investors who believe that they are successful stock pickers, remembering the stocks that were profitable but not those that lost them money. Similar traits can be observed in gamblers. Cognitive dissonance also extends to recalling the positive aspects of a situation (e.g. the prospect of retiring on an adequate pension) but ignoring or forgetting the negative aspect (e.g. having to spend less now in order to save enough for retirement).

Confirmation bias

The habit common to most people of accepting or remembering information that confirms their preconceived opinion is called confirmation bias. For example, "I am a successful investor and the proof is that most of the investments I have chosen have been profitable". They tend to ignore or forget any evidence to the contrary, see also 'Cognitive dissonance'.

Endowment bias

Many investors are impelled to hold onto investments that they have been given or inherited. Psychologists' experiments have established that people who inherit a portfolio of investments are much less likely to change its individual investment composition than people who simply inherit cash deposits. Endowment bias is a subset of attachment bias, which is a more general desire to hold onto assets for emotional reasons, see also 'Status quo bias'.

Extrapolation bias

This is linked to availability bias and describes the general tendency to believe that very recent trends will continue into the future. So people will more naturally feel that share or property values will continue rising if they have been rising in the recent past or that they will keep falling, if they have been declining recently. Extrapolation effect explains why investors seldom come into the market when prices are cheap and feel comforted by the notion that prices have already risen a long way; they buy at the top and sell at the bottom.

Familiarity bias

People have a prejudice in favour of the familiar, partly because it seems safe. Investors may be over-optimistic about local investments, shares in their employer or residential property, all because they are familiar. This can lead to such mistakes as excessive risk taking and lack of diversification.

Fear of regret or loss aversion

People may prefer to do nothing rather than act in such a way that they may have cause to regret their actions by, for example, realising a loss on an investment. Part of the worry is that if they sell a loss-making investment too soon, the price might later rise and they would regret the sale and feel even worse. The effect may be to induce people to hold onto unsuitable loss making investments for too long. Some clients, when faced with a portfolio in which some investments have declined while others have increased, will focus on the losses rather than the performance of the portfolio as a whole, see 'Framing'.

Framing

Decisions can be framed or presented in different ways. The context in which something is presented can greatly influence decision making. For example, at its simplest, people are more likely to accept a proposal that is presented as having a 50% success rate rather than exactly the same proposal that is presented as having a 50% failure rate. An investor who bought a share for £1 might regard the current price of £2 as providing an opportunity to realise a profit. Alternatively, they might frame the situation by anchoring on the peak price of £6 that the investment reached last year and regard any disposal at less than £6 as a loss — and therefore a cause for regret. See also 'Mental accounting' and 'Prospect theory'.

Hindsight bias

Hindsight bias is closely associated with the curse of knowledge: that once a person knows something, they find it hard to imagine that they could have ever thought otherwise. Hindsight bias can lead people to think that they could have forecast a past event — e.g. in some sense, they feel that they would have known that the credit crunch was coming (even though they did not actually predict it). The bias leads to unrealistic expectations of investment managers as well as over confidence in their own abilities or possibly even those of new advisers.

Hyperbolic discounting

People greatly overvalue money they receive now in comparison to money that they will receive in the future. One of the results is that the pain of saving a pound now is much greater than the pleasure of receiving a pound in the future. Immediate gratification is much more powerful than deferred gratification. Saving is painful and the expectation of future benefits does not seem to be adequate compensation.

Hyperbolic discounting also leads people to undervalue future pain or discomfort. It is much easier to persuade someone to agree to make a speech in six months time than in six hours or six days time. So the unpleasantness of a future impoverished retirement is discounted in comparison with the desirability of the additional net spendable income of not having to save now. Interestingly hyperbolic discounting can be used to induce people to commit to starting a savings programme in at a future date.

Magical thinking

Even the most rational of people may accept magical thinking at some level. Superstition or irrational belief that one event causes another, even where there is no logical association between them. For example, an investor buys a share and it immediately falls in value; this sort of experience can lead some people to believe that they are 'unlucky with shares'. A run of the same number on dice throwing is strongly suggestive of a trend, although everyone knows logically that dice have no memory.

Mental accounting

Mental accounting is a form of 'Framing' (see above). Instead of regarding their investments as a whole, people often divide them up into imaginary boxes or separate accounts which they think of as being very different from each other. People tend to consume some types of wealth and not others. For instance, they may be prepared to spend money in their current account but not draw on any special retirement accounts. Mental accounting can help nurture self-discipline, especially for saving (a 'pot' for school fees, a 'pot' for holidays and a 'pot' for retirement). But it can also be unhelpful if each of the separate mental accounts turn out to be excessively risky or cautious when considered as a single portfolio because of duplications of holdings leading to excessive concentrations. Mental accounting can also lead to serious mistakes in borrowing, such as running up expensive credit card debt at the same time as holding risky or low yielding investments.

Over confidence

Excessive confidence has been described by Kahnemann as one of the most 'robust findings' of behavioural finance. People are often very sure of the rightness of their decisions, especially when they have relatively little evidence on which to base this certainty. The strength of people's emotional attachment to short cuts and biases makes them hard to change and tends to override cooler and more rational behaviour. People are often overconfident about such things as their future earnings, the returns that their investments will make, and often their skill in making investment decisions. Where people feel they are in control, they are even more likely to be excessively optimistic about the outcomes — this is sometimes referred to as self-attribution bias. It is feelings like this that can lead investors to become day-traders.

Prospect theory

Most investors dislike making a loss much more than they derive pleasure from making the equivalent gain. It seems that experiencing a loss has an emotional impact on an investor that is roughly two and a half times the effect of the equivalent gain. So an investor who loses £10,000 would need a gain of about £25,000 to compensate for the bad feeling caused by the loss. The ability to realise a loss is crucial in making rational investment decisions. For example, it is essential in order to be able to hold a balanced portfolio. Investors need to be prepared to take losses and sell investments that have not been successful or that are no longer suitable.

Representativeness bias

Most people are prepared to draw conclusions and make decisions on the basis of very little evidence. Information that is more salient because it is more obvious or more recent will often have a much bigger impact on opinions and decisions than information that is less dramatically presented or is older and maybe hazier in the memory.

Status quo bias

People are resistant to change — especially to changing their strategies or behaviour. Change often requires an immediate cost in order to achieve higher future returns. Loss aversion also plays a part in status quo bias. If a person keeps their existing investment, they will not have to experience the regret that might arise if any replacement investment were to perform badly. Status quo effect is also evident in the very strong tendency for people to follow the path of least resistance and take the default route that is presented to them. This might be in the form of the default route of joining a pension scheme under automatic enrolment or choosing the default fund offered by a pension scheme.

4 The validity of the behavioural finance approach

Perhaps people are so irrational that they cannot overcome their intrinsic psychological attributes and improve their financial decision making. A team from the London School of Economics (LSE) produced a pessimistic report in July 2008, FSA Consumer Research 69 Financial Capability: A Behavioural Economics Perspective. "Behavioural economics has been directed more to explaining choices than changing them . . . A relatively small amount of literature has looked at remedies for cognitive biases. Little of this specifically applied to personal finance." The report held out little hope for the effectiveness of consumer education and in the best academic tradition called for more research.

But the extreme position of some behavioural economists may be too pessimistic. Even though people make mistakes and are often irrational about their finances, they might not be irretrievably illogical and never able to make good decisions based on their long-term economic self-interest. Clearly, many people save regularly, invest with some success, buy insurance and generally behave in an apparently rational way with their finances much of the time. Writers like Tim Harford – the *Financial Times*' Undercover Economist – believe that behavioural economists exaggerate the extent to which people are irrational and believe that in very many aspects of their lives people react logically to economic incentives.

The LSE group felt that the FSA's general financial capability initiatives would have a modest impact on the public's ability to make good financial decisions. They thought that face-to-face counselling could be effective and cited some evidence to support this contention. This, they said, works where "the individual knows they are in trouble and gets specific advice what to do and perhaps help with filling in forms . . . Counselling is rather likely to deliver immediate benefits, but it is not clear that there are long-term effects in helping people avoid getting into such situations." Such counselling would be the kind provided by the citizens' advice bureaux to people in trouble with debt or similar advice provided on television shows.

If academic evidence is sparse, considerable amounts of anecdotal evidence will have to suffice. It is clear that on an individual basis, considerable changes can be made to behaviour and habits, although there may still be powerful tendencies to behave irrationally from time to time. The LSE team were hopeful about individual counselling and would perhaps be equally optimistic about the impact of a skilled financial planner's advice and help on an individual basis.

5 What financial planners can do about clients' irrational behaviour – the general approach

A highly effective way to help people to understand their behaviour and possibly change it is to provide them with a vocabulary to label and characterise behaviour. If clients can identify that their reluctance to sell an investment is attachment effect overlaid by both endowment and status quo biases, it may be easier for them to see their irrational behaviour for what it is and contemplate the possibility of making the right decision. But financial planners should not underestimate the challenge of overcoming mental short cuts even when one is aware of them. Warren Buffet's long-term business partner at Berkshire Hathaway, Charlie Munger, has long said that removing perceptual biases is the single most difficult task facing investors but also one of the most important because these biases are the cause of so many disastrous mistakes.

Curt Weil, the US fee-only financial planner of Weil Capital (Investment Advisor July 2005) points out that the predictable mistakes that people make are due to human evolution, not individual stupidity. "I started to recognise that (behavioural finance) would be a good thing to use with clients who had made, shall we say, embarrassing errors. If I can explain to them that they made a mistake not because they are a bad person or they're stupid, but because we're just wired in this fashion, it lets them off the hook." Until clients are aware of these mistakes, they are most unlikely to avoid them. Even then, it can be hard to override ingrained instincts. US financial planners report some successes in educating their clients away from acting on their more basic and illogical instincts about financial decision making.

Optimists would argue that humans may often be irrational, but there is no necessity for them to be so. In many aspects of our lives we succeed in curbing our most primitive instincts because we think through the consequences of our actions and amend our behaviour accordingly. This may or may not be a valid view of the prospects for society as a whole, but there is no reason why financial advisers should give up helping their clients become rational with money on an individual basis. An effective way to help someone see where they have made a mistake is to label it and describe the feelings that it evokes and the probable underlying causes. Simply putting a name to a type of behaviour can help clients come to terms with it by recognising their feelings and making a conscious effort to behave in a more rational manner.

People can and frequently do change their habits, both of thought and behaviour, although it can be difficult. Those who habitually overspend can learn to live within a budget and after a time it can become more or less automatic by a process that some psychologists would describe as conditioning. Often the initial step change can only be achieved with the assistance of a ploy that uses the insights of behavioural finance. For example, over-spenders would be forced to hesitate before making a purchase if they have cut up their credit cards and would have to draw out cash for the purpose.

It is clear that professional investors make the same kinds of mistakes and short-cuts to which ordinary investors are prone. Indeed in some cases they are even more prey to feelings of overconfidence, mental accounting and the all rest. This can be a considerable comfort to clients, as well as a lesson that it is necessary to select professional fund managers with care. We are all hard-wired in the same way.

So the general approach to helping clients overcome their irrational biases is to:

1. Find out what the client wants to achieve and make sure that their objectives are clear and agreed.

2. Explain the rationale for a particular recommendation or strategy and make sure that the client accepts it as right and in line with their aims and objectives. As far as possible the aim should be made as clear and simple as possible so that clients remember it and become motivated by it – e.g. "Your retirement fund should be a minimum of £1m".

3. Explore the underlying bias that is stopping them from committing to the action that both the adviser and client have agreed is appropriate and rational. This is likely to involve identifying the bias or behaviour in behavioural finance terms and considering the feelings that lie behind it.

4. Reinforce the client's understanding of the tension between the intellectual acceptance of the rational behaviour or actions and the emotional pull of the biased emotion.

5. Use the insights of behavioural finance to help make the change in the client's behaviour – e.g. to stop over-spending or to start saving.

6. Try to turn the new behaviour into a habit.

The following are some common problems and possible ways of dealing with them.

6 Procrastination

Many clients are reluctant to take action to deal with important financial matters even though they know that they should. They procrastinate – literally put off until tomorrow what they should do today. This universal behaviour is at the heart of many financial problems that people face and look to financial planners to help them solve.

For example many taxpayers defer completing their tax returns, but then regret leaving the job until the last minute and in a rush. The HMRC flat rate fine of £100 for late submission is intended to provide an incentive to get the return in. Yet thousands still leave the process until the very last minute and many of them miss the deadline. Given that they have to do the job eventually, its illogical that so many people choose to do the task after the deadline and incur penalties. It may be illogical but we can all relate to the feeling of putting off an unpleasant experience until later.

Back in the 1980s Access credit cards employed the powerful advertising slogan, "Take the waiting out of wanting". It appealed to atavistic instincts to accelerate pleasure and defer pain, to seize the day and live for the present. Many people build up substantial credit card debts despite the very high interest charges. Saving rates in the US and UK are surprisingly low. The tendency to spend at excessive rates is at the heart of many people's financial difficulties. Most people know that they should save a proportion of their income to meet such medium-term wants and needs as the costs of Christmas and holidays, as well as long-term requirements such as weddings, school fees or retirement. There are several explanations why instant gratification tends to win.

Decision making about spending and saving involves two very different parts of the brain. The emotional or limbic system is designed to ensure basic survival and is stronger, more immediate and more short-term than the thinking analytical parts of the brain. The limbic system produces feelings of fear, greed and excitement that prompt rapid decisions such as fight or flight that would have helped ensure survival in a more challenging environment than modern urban society. The analytical system tends to kick-in later to consider issues in a more reasoned and logical way. These cognitive parts in the cortex can override the limbic system and allow deferred gratification. But the basic emotions are initially stronger and more urgent. Conditioning can change these habits of thinking and feeling and inhibit spending impulses.

Example 3.1

A client has difficulty completing relatively simple administrative tasks such as filling out tax forms. The problem here might be the client's reluctance to regret the time spent in completing the forms rather than doing something more amusing. The intellectual argument for completing the tax return is clear; there would be no fine or interest charge for late submission, they would make fewer mistakes, they might suffer less anxiety, and completing the job would take no more time regardless of when it is undertaken. The spur to complete such tasks might be to help the client envisage the feeling of achievement when the task is done. Agreeing a deadline might help so that the regret of not meeting the deadline might counteract the original reluctance. Several years of completing a tax return on time might turn the behaviour into a habit.

Procrastination can be a serious problem in many contexts in financial planning. The feeling in each case is likely to be different and suggest different solutions. In all cases, it is essential to make the rational case for taking the appropriate and logical action, whatever that might be. But that is unlikely to be enough in many cases. It is then necessary to explain what the client is thinking and feeling in the hope that they will recognise its universality and then suggest specific solutions to change the pattern of thinking.

Example 3.2

The client is reluctant to sell or buy an investment. The main fear is that the decision may turn out to be wrong; in particular the investment that is sold might turn out to do better than its replacement. Part of the client's unspoken and unthinking assumption is that making the sale or purchase is a decision, whereas doing nothing is neutral. It is important to remind the client that doing nothing – not making the sale or purchase – is just as much a decision as taking the action – even though it does not feel like that. The more clients become used to buying and selling investments, the easier the decisions may become.

Example 3.3

The client is reluctant to reduce expenditure to start a savings programme or reduce debt. This action would involve the possibility of experiencing regret as a result of not spending the money on more pleasurable things. The financial planner needs to employ both positive and negative approaches: it is important to help the client to see as clearly and with as much impact as possible the speed at which high interest rates charged by credit cards can build up. Vivid pictures and graphics work with some people; the spectre of insolvency and bankruptcy may be more effective with others.

Spending a lot is a habit, keeping to a budget is also a habit and cultivating the feeling of regret when a budget is exceeded can also work. The potential for disapproval and encouragement of a group or an individual can also be very supportive in much the same way as people who have joined Gamblers Anonymous have discovered.

7 Not saving enough

Most people find it very difficult to save enough for their retirement or indeed for shorter term goals.

Part of the reason is that they do not know or remember how much they need to save. The first step therefore is to make sure that clients understand and agree their need for a substantial amount to meet their stated goal. The financial planner will have to produce evidence which is clear and comprehensible, so that the client really understands the case, believes it and very importantly remembers it. So the financial planner must produce salient and memorable information and goals.

A very good way to illustrate the gap that most clients have in their retirement provision is to use a lifetime cashflow model that graphically shows when the money will run out. Longevity in the UK and the rest of Western Europe seems to be increasing at an average rate of two years average extra life every decade. The need for a surprisingly large amount of capital in retirement can be remembered by the rule of thumb: for every pound of income, you need £20 to £25 of capital.

Once the client understands and buys into the real problem and what needs to be done about it, the financial planner needs to deal with the irrational issues. There are likely to be several of these.

The most important reason for saving insufficient amounts for retirement is probably the tendency to hyperbolic discounting – to value future income and capital much less than current income and capital. Most people prefer £100 today to £110 tomorrow but also prefer £110 in 31 days to £100 in just 30 days. So they have high discount rates for the very short-term, but their discount rate is much lower and arguably more accurate for longer term periods. Of course, at the end of the 30 day period, the much steeper discount rate will apply and reverse the original longer term preference. Linked to hyperbolic discounting is the fear of feeling regret for forgoing immediate rewards.

Clients tend to underestimate the level of resources needed to fund the cost of retiring. Partly this can be explained by the effort that is needed to learn a good deal of tedious information about finance and longevity. Partly anyone embarking on such a programme of self-education would be aware from an early stage that the end result is likely to be a greater awareness of the unpalatable truth about the need to save more. The general ability to estimate such amounts as future capital requirements is as poor as other quantitative guesswork required of people. The guesses are based on notoriously poor short-cuts, where the salient data is far more important than the logical or 'common sense' information.

Overconfidence is another factor. This might take the form of the unconsidered expectation that everything will work out well in the end. The optimism may be about the likely performance of investments or the financial security offered by the capital value of the home. In some cases, it takes the form of a significant underestimate of the individual's probable life expectancy: "The chances are that I will be dead within a few years of retirement". Such views tend to be more confidently held by the relatively young client.

Cognitive dissonance or reluctance to accept evidence that conflicts with their beliefs or assumptions can also play a part in the unwillingness of the young to contemplate making serious preparation for old age. "I am young now; I do not wish to contemplate the possibility now that I will grow old and feel differently about the need for having savings."

Social norms and peer pressure – or the lack of these – can make a difference to the willingness of people to save. Online, supermarket and workplace based Christmas clubs have helped low income families to save during the year to pay for their Christmas presents and festivities, albeit often at expensive prices and within insecure savings plans (as highlighted by the collapse of Farepak in 2006). Some behavioural finance experts like Benartzi studying workplace saving for retirement have noted a strong peer pressure to save at a particular norm. There are limited circumstances in which a financial planner can suggest social norms as a means of helping clients to take an appropriate action. The workplace is one; financial planners working in the employee benefits area may be able to help establish norms for retirement saving or taking out insurance cover that are widely accepted among groups within a workforce and that can help reinforce these habits among those who might otherwise reduce their commitment.

Some behavioural economists like Thaler and Benartzi have suggested using hyperbolic discounting as a tool to induce people to commit to future saving. Employees are persuaded to commit to starting a saving programme in a few months time. Because they discount the cost at that future time, employees are much more prepared to make that commitment now than they would be to start the savings programme the next day. Fear of loss of pride should help them to keep the commitment at the due date. If it can be arranged for the start of the savings programme to coincide with a salary increase, this should reduce the pain and feelings of loss that would occur if the individual had to sustain a clear and salient reduction in net spendable income. A similar approach could be taken to arranging to start insurance policies.

It is unlikely to be a one-off process, instead the process of persuasion will need to be revisited and repeated. Regular reviews of a client's financial position are essential, as their circumstances will in all probability change. This will mean adjusting their goals, and the means of achieving them. The financial planner must remake the intellectual case, present it in a simple and memorable way and then revisit the irrational issues that place the usually unspoken barriers to action.

8 Taking excessive investment risk

A very common mistake among clients is taking too much investment risk. Mostly this happens because they concentrate their investments within just one or two asset classes. Excessive concentration of investments could occur in several ways and the most common are:

- Holding too much in cash deposits.
- Over concentration in residential property.
- Ownership of a block of shares in a single company.

None of these is necessarily wrong in certain circumstances, but it is important that clients are aware of the very serious dangers that are involved if they take the decision to persist with this undiversified strategy in a considered and logical way. For example, exclusively holding cash deposits may be the appropriate strategy for some investors who cannot afford any short-term fluctuations in their capital.

The first step is to make the case against such undiversified investments and make sure that the client understands and remembers the rationale behind the recommendation to spread the risk. In many cases, clients will underestimate or not know the level of risk that they are running. Equally it is important for clients to understand the argument in favour of the recommended spread.

Then it is necessary for the financial adviser to consider the powerful feelings that lie behind the client's reluctance to change the investments. There could be a number of explanations, including:

In the case of cash, the relatively high interest rates that deposit accounts traditionally generate are much more salient than the potential for future returns from other investments such as equities. However, at the time of writing (November 2010), deposit yields are historically very low, but clients could be tempted to concentrate excessively on bonds or property because of their high immediate yields.

'Familiarity bias' (see page 34) is likely to underlie the excessive focus on any of these asset classes. Most clients are very accustomed to cash and residential property, with which they are comfortable and familiar. A client may hold a large proportion of their assets in a single share. They might have inherited this or it might be a shareholding they built up as a result of employment with a previous company.

Equities, bonds and commercial property are generally more alien, and clients need help to become used to dealing with them. Introducing clients to long-term savings programmes in these other asset classes, with regular feedback on performance, can help to induce feelings of familiarity. One way to help clients accept new investment ideas is to introduce them through the medium of familiar and trusted investment organisations.

'Endowment' and 'Status quo bias' (see page 33 and page 36 respectively) are both likely to play a considerable part in clients' reluctance to diversify away from unsuitable existing investments.

Example 3.4

A client might harbour a feeling that old uncle Peter who left them the shares was a very clever man who knew a thing or two about investments, and that it would be foolish to go against his judgement. The client might even be prepared to admit feeling that the long dead uncle Peter might be hurt by the sale of the asset that he had bequeathed. Such feelings might not be sustained once they are admitted and examined critically. The financial planner would need to point out that circumstances had changed and that uncle Peter would have been the first to recognise that what was appropriate for him 40 years ago might no longer be right for someone else in very different circumstances and in another set of market conditions.

Example 3.5

Mary was left some shares by her late mother in a once leading but gradually declining company. Mary was very reluctant to sell these increasingly poorly-performing shares. The reasons were various: she did not really understand what was going on at the company and was not prepared to listen; the dividend stream was kept very high for as long as possible and she focused more on the income than the underlying business (saliency); she was used to holding the shares (familiarity); she thought that her mother was good at investments (endowment); selling might turn out to be a mistake (fear of regret); her (deceased) mother and the directors of the company (whom she did not know) would disapprove and even feel a little hurt by her disloyalty (magical thinking); the shares sometimes went up in value despite their long-term decline (confirmation).

'Mental accounting' (page 35) can be at the heart of some excessive concentration on particular asset classes or even assets. It can even lead to a client effectively borrowing in order to buy an investment when that is something they would not normally wish to do. For example, clients may split up their investments into several different portfolios of investments — 'mental accounts' in the language of behavioural finance.

One consequence of this might be that there are excessive duplications of certain types of investment, such as cash or perhaps FTSE 100 shares. When the portfolio of individual shares is considered together with the pension scheme and the other collective investments, there might even turn out to be an excessive concentration of certain individual shares. Another consequence is that the client might have run up expensive short-term borrowings at the same time as holding cash and other investments. It is sometimes paying a price for liquidity, but the cost may be excessive and the cash may well be unnecessary.

Economists expect people to do what they judge is in their own interest, while behavioural finance assumes that the truth is more complicated and that people very often act illogically and in ways that defeat what they should do or in some sense might even want to do. There are often several explanations for people's behaviour. Behavioural finance has enumerated a number of individual ideas and themes, but is still very much a work in progress.

Chapter 4
Different types of client

1 Introduction – categorising clients

Financial planners encounter a number of recurring themes among their clients, both in terms of kinds of people and types of problem. So it can be very helpful for planners to become familiar with these themes and understand the broad issues and their solutions. But they should always be aware of the temptation to stereotype both clients and situations, and to analyse clients as types rather than as individuals and that this can lead them to propose stock solutions.

However, characterising clients into broad categories can be useful for several purposes, including:

- Deciding what broad types of client to target and service. It is increasingly recognised that financial planners need to specialise to some extent in order to build the appropriate expertise in terms of knowledge and skills. High net worth individuals in their 30s to 50s who have built up their fortunes from working in the City of London tend to have very different circumstances, attitudes and needs from ex-teachers in their mid-60s and older.

- Determining the categories for different types and levels of service, e.g. clients for whom a high cost/high level of service is appropriate and others who would prefer a lower cost/level of service.

- Choosing what products to promote in newsletters and mailshots to specific market sectors.

- Deciding on the training and development needs of financial planners and staff.

In the early years of a person's career, they probably need to borrow to buy a home and also to insure their health and life as protection against death or illness. As they grow older, the need to build up short and longer term savings takes on greater importance, with the need to accumulate funds for retirement reaching its highest priority in late middle age. In their 60s and 70s, most clients generally need income from their pensions and other accumulated investments and often start to show an interest in estate planning.

This is the stereotypical pattern with which most financial planners are familiar. Age is not the only variable – the others include health, family situation, occupation, income, assets, personality and aims. The variations and permutations are many and other issues like nationality and early inheritances make every client meeting a fascinating and unique encounter.

But there is a danger that excessive generalising about client types can lead to planning mistakes. People are individuals and often do not conform to neat patterns. Stereotypes usually embody useful truths, but financial planners must always work with the individual who is sitting in front of them rather than the imaginary stereotypical figure in their own head. People's lives can be complicated and seem to be becoming increasingly so.

2 Standard life stages

There are several approaches to understanding the main stages through which a person is likely to pass. A useful model is essentially financial and is based on income and expenditure and the growth in assets and liabilities. This can then link into the other model which describes events and circumstances.

Graph of life stages

The graph shows a fairly typical family pattern of income and expenditure for first a single person and then a couple.

Figure 4.1 shows a series of balance sheets giving a snap shot of main assets and liabilities at different possible life stages. The light shaded box on the assets side represents the pension fund and the dark box represents the house and other investments.

1. As a single person at the start of a career, income and expenditure are likely to be more or less in balance. But if they have been to university, the chances are that they will have built up some debt.

2. In the first few years as a couple, while they have two incomes and before having children, a couple's income probably exceeds their expenditure. They have the opportunity to build up a small amount of capital, which they probably use to pay the deposit on a home. If they buy a property, their balance sheet will show a large increase in their assets, offset by a large amount of debt in their home. But they may still be able to build up savings on a regular basis. The main financial needs at this point are likely to be for a mortgage, short-term savings and some — mainly health — insurance.

3. With the arrival of children and a larger mortgage, expenditure rises and income may fall or be static. The result could be that there may be a deficit of expenditure over income — financed and represented by a big increase in borrowing. If they buy a larger property, the overall size of the balance sheet will rise in terms of a more expensive house and a much bigger mortgage, but the net worth or difference between assets and liabilities might not increase, and might even fall if overall borrowing rises. These are the tight years of high expenses and lower incomes. The main financial needs are for mortgage and perhaps other finance, as well as substantial amounts of life and heath cover and probably some retirement planning.

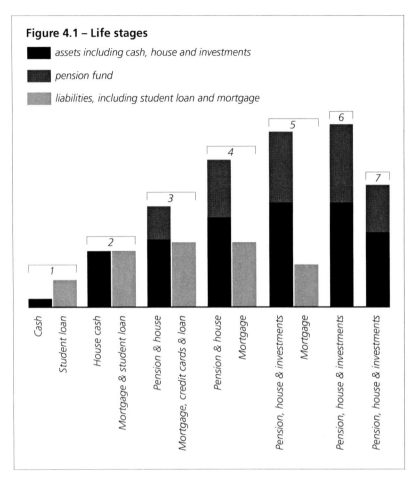

Figure 4.1 – Life stages

■ *assets including cash, house and investments*

▓ *pension fund*

░ *liabilities, including student loan and mortgage*

4. In middle age (40s to 50s), the need to make provision for retirement often competes with the costs of educating the children in terms of school fees and possibly also university education, as well as the desirability of paying off the mortgage before retirement. There may be more discretionary income that could be used for pension investment and mortgage repayments may have made some inroad into indebtedness, although capital repayments are a relatively small proportion of total monthly mortgage payments. On the assets side, the value of the house should have increased and the pension fund should have started to build up to a significant level.

5. As middle age turns into late middle age, retirement planning becomes even more urgent, while the children's financial demands on their parents may decline as they leave home and become economically more self-sufficient. The couple's investment objective is capital growth inside registered

pensions and in other investment vehicles. But for many couples, the need for mortgages and protection is still present. Around this time, it is common for people to start inheriting from parents or other relatives and the advent of these resources can make a substantial difference to their financial circumstances, allowing the earlier repayment of mortgage debt and the bolstering up of retirement funds. The value of the house is now generally substantial in relation to the mortgage, which may even have been paid off. The pension should have grown and couples should have accumulated other assets.

6. The date or period when clients are stopping work is often the time when the most financial planning is needed. They are making the radical change from working for their money to requiring their money to work for them. The process of retiring may be sudden and rapid; one moment the client is working and the next moment they are retired or it may be a gradual process lasting several years. Some people never entirely retire. Drawing funds from the pension in the form of the tax free pension commencement lump sum and income will be a high priority. Other investments will need to start producing an income. Normally the mortgage should be paid off — unless the home is virtually the only asset and equity release is the best way to raise income and/or capital. Life and health protection is probably no longer required except possibly for life assurance as part of IHT planning. At this point, the client starts using the fund built up in the pension and drawing it down in some form. Expenditure may well exceed total income and the investor may have to start to eat into non-pension capital.

7. As clients reach their 70s and 80s, income planning continues to be very important. IHT and estate planning also takes on greater significance for many people. Making sure that they have made adequate provision for long-term care may also become a priority. At this point or earlier, a client may have traded down their property or undertaken equity release.

3 Income and expenditure

Income and expenditure are closely interrelated over a person's lifetime. Expenditure tends to rise with income over a person's working life, then drops at retirement and may rise sharply in later old age with the need for long-term care. In the first part of a couple's working life, expenditure normally outstrips income. Then, income starts to exceed expenditure if the mortgage and other expenses become less of a burden and take up a smaller proportion of the family budget. The clients build up wealth in the form of equity in the home, funds in the pension scheme as well as the value of other investments and assets.

At retirement and after, clients start to run down assets, turning them directly or indirectly into spendable income.

Most people's spending is roughly correlated with their income. As a very general rule, most people spend more as their income rises, but they also find it easier to save as their income increases. This is a very broad generalisation. Like a few legendary pools and lottery winners, some people find that their expenditure rises even faster than their income; while a minority of very careful clients spend roughly the same amount regardless of how much their income grows. There may well be spikes and troughs in expenditure – and income. A large purchase such as a house, school fees, a car or investment in a business could lead to sudden changes of cashflow. Likewise, large bonuses, capital disposals or a period of unemployment or low pay could lead to spikes or troughs in income.

But this neat and conventional process of accumulating wealth and then drawing on it is far smoother than most real life family situations. It is worth considering some of the main variations on this story of life stages. Some of the key variations are:

- Client's gender
- The range of family situations
- Whether clients have children
- Age of clients
- Clients' level of earnings
- The relationship between clients' income and expenditure
- Clients' level of wealth
- Clients as business owners
- Clients with an overseas dimension
- Clients' knowledge of investment and financial issues
- Clients who are financially rich but time poor
- The personalities of clients

Gender

The lifetime financial profiles of men and women are often very different. Initially, there may be little to distinguish their career patterns and economic circumstances; they tend to earn much the same and have broadly the same needs for financial services. The big divide generally takes place when women have children. Women's earning capacity can be reduced – often permanently – following the interruption to their careers and the less intense paid work patterns in the early years of child rearing. However this is neither inevitable nor universal. There are many examples of women who maintain high earning levels through their child-bearing years and beyond; but it is a very common pattern and seems to account for much of the differential between the earnings of men and women whereby on average women still earn about two thirds of men's earnings.

With their lower and more interrupted earnings, many women build up lower savings and pension entitlements than their male counterparts. As a result for much of their lives women may find themselves financially dependent on their male partners (or former partners).

One of the gender based generalisations that still holds good is that women tend to live longer than men. In addition, women have tended to marry men slightly older than themselves the combination of these factors means that women predominate among the very old and generally die substantially more wealthy than men.

The range of family situations

The sexual revolution that mainly started in the 1960s has led to much greater complexity and variety in people's relationships. The traditional order of life events is predictable. Stereotypical family life follows a clear pattern of single life, getting married, having children, the children leaving home, children marrying, birth of grandchildren, retirement, death of the husband and finally death of the wife. Of course there have always been variations: people who have never married, people who are divorced, childless couples and many other more exotic deviations from the norm. One of the biggest changes has been the greatly increased number of people who live together without being married, and those who have children without being married both within single parent families or as unmarried couples. By the 90s and the first decade of the 21st century, the order of events and their variations on the norm had changed markedly. It is very hard to generalise about the great variety of family arrangements. But it is perfectly possible to envisage a family scenario in which two single people live together, have children and only then get married. After a few years they split up and the husband goes off to live with another partner and her children, while the wife moves in with a new partner and his children. They then decide to divorce; the ex-husband remarries his new partner but his ex-wife does not. The children go to university and take on various jobs away from home, but then return to live with mother or father during a period of unemployment. By this time father or mother has moved to another partner — whom they may or may not eventually marry. Retirement happens very early for father but late and only rather gradually for the mother.

All of these changes can have a very considerable impact on the family's financial circumstances and their financial planning needs. Complicated family finances may lead to changes in life and health protection, wills and trusts, mortgages, ownership of property and investments as well as the structure and level of pension provision. Yet many financial structures like pensions were designed for a simpler age and such products as pension annuities may turn out to be too inflexible for many family circumstances.

Whether clients have children

Children are very expensive and have an enormous impact on their parents' financial planning. Some of the extra costs are obvious, but others are less predictable – or at least they are often not foreseen. The build-up in costs tends to happen gradually, and many young parents benefit from family help which may cushion the initial shock. Childless couples are generally presented with far more straightforward financial planning decisions and have rather less difficulty in achieving their financial goals. Some of the main additional costs that children bring include:

- **Day-to-day expenditure**
  There is a rising burden of additional regular expenditure, including extra food, heat, cleaning, clothing, travel costs, larger car, toys, equipment and as they get older transport and communications.

- **Loss of income**
  Even with maternity pay, there is likely to be an initial loss of income as the mother (normally) looks after the child in the early months or years of life. The chances are that one of the parents (typically but not invariably the mother) will decide to pursue a less demanding career and experience a significant loss of potential earnings.

- **Housing**
  Accommodation that is acceptable for two adults is probably not suitable for a family with children. Extra bedrooms and other space are likely to involve moving to larger and often significantly more expensive properties, although this might be partly offset by choosing to live in a less expensive area, which in turn might lead to additional travel to work expenses.

- **Childcare**
  The corollary of both parents continuing to work after the arrival of children is the considerable additional cost of childcare. In a few cases some or all the childcare may be free if grandparents are able and willing to take on the role.

- **Education**
  Private education is notoriously expensive, especially if it involves boarding. But sending children to maintained schools can also involve some additional expenditure, especially if extra tuition turns out to be desirable. Parents may also wish to help their children with the increasing costs of university education.

- **Getting started in adult life**
  Parents often want to help their children in their early adulthood. This

could just involve adult children continuing to live at their parents' home, but it could also require subsidies while they take internships or low paid jobs. Children might also be provided with such items as cars, help with house purchase, capital for a business and eventually help with the costs of grandchildren.

- **Estate planning**
  Estate planning may turn out to simply consist of ongoing financial help rather than in-depth inheritance tax planning. Whatever the reality, most parents and grandparents feel more obligation to make gifts of income and capital to their children and grandchildren than most childless couples consider appropriate for their more distant relatives.

Age of the client

There are considerable differences between the financial planning strategies that are appropriate for people as they get older. In addition, the range of possibilities has been extended by rising life expectancy.

The financial preoccupations of the young tend to focus on budgeting, borrowing, insuring and possibly short-term saving. As people get older, their priorities change with the need to invest accumulating capital for growth. Once past retirement, income generation and estate planning generally become preoccupations. Looking after children or other dependents tends to take place at different times of life.

- **The old are mostly richer**
  Income and wealth generally rise with age and financial planning tends to become more complicated as income and capital rise and tax becomes a more significant factor (see income and wealth on page 56).

- **Age and risk**
  Age also affects people's ability to tolerate risk. The young mostly have relatively little capital or income, but they do enjoy considerable future potential and a long-term investment timescale. They can generally afford to take risks with their careers and finances and then either reap the benefits or wait to recover from any adverse consequences.

  Then as people get older, they acquire income, assets and liabilities. They then find they have more to lose and the timescale in which they can take risks and recover losses becomes shorter. They may also find that they become more cautious as they take on family responsibilities. People who are still building up their pension funds can generally afford to take greater risks than those who are actively drawing their pension income.

- **Different generations see things differently**
  Some social commentators characterise different ages and generations by

their attitudes and characteristics. The generation of people who were born immediately after the war – the so-called bulge or baby boomers – are supposed to share certain characteristics; likewise those who are categorised as say Generation X or Generation Y. These differences can be the basis for amusing parlour games; whether they have any practical use in financial planning is more doubtful.

Financial planners tend to grow older with their clients – the people with whom they feel most comfortable – although it is important to be able to communicate with, and be trusted by, people of different ages and generations.

Level of earnings

Someone on national average earnings of £20,000 to £25,000 is likely to have rather different attitudes and requirements from someone who is earning six or seven figure amounts. But the type of earnings may be even more significant than the amount in terms of the impact on their financial planning.

- **Peaks and troughs**
  A client's current earnings level may be permanent or temporary. Someone might be on a low wage because they are starting a business, are undertaking training or have simply chosen an occupation that pays modestly. Conversely some high incomes are temporary. It is important to know about a client's future prospects.

- **Long-term earnings progression**
  Some employees can expect their earnings to rise more rapidly than the average increase in incomes. As they grow older, their earnings grow with promotion, responsibility and greater expertise and recognition. This tends to be the pattern for professional and managerial employees. Other workers generally see a much flatter curve in their earnings, which in comparative terms may even reach a peak in their 30s. Manual workers typically experience a decline in their real earnings when they reach 50 and can no longer carry out heavy labour. A few people, such as sportsmen and women and entertainers, may experience very brief periods of very high earnings.

- **The source of the earnings**
  Certain careers are more secure than others. Self-employed people often regard their earnings very differently from many employees. Employees are sometimes over-confident about the security of their positions, while self-employed people may be excessively cautious. However, some employers – generally larger ones – may offer greater security to employees in certain circumstances, for example in the event of pregnancy or illness.

- **The regularity and volatility of earnings**

  Clients with fluctuating earnings should aim to be more flexible in their commitments and have more robust financial reserves than those whose income is reasonably predictable. Those with relatively low regular earnings but high commissions or bonuses have to plan the disposition of those bonuses with care if they are to accumulate savings. For them it is especially important that they have the self-discipline to save on an irregular basis.

- **Type of employers**

  The person who remains with the same large employer all their lives — such as a bank or the civil service — will probably face rather different financial challenges from the person who has a succession of jobs in a variety of firms and sectors. The pension scheme and other employee benefits from a long-term single employer will help to take care of many of the long-term financial pressures.

  However, careers are now generally less predictable than they were in the past. Changes in employment patterns mean that increasingly those who have started on the large corporate career cannot expect the stability that their parents may have experienced. The disappearance of defined benefit pensions has also reduced the differentials between large and small employer careers.

The relationship between clients' income and expenditure

A client's level of expenditure is not necessarily closely linked to the absolute amount of their income. Some high income earners overspend and some low income earners are able to save on a regular basis. But not surprisingly, the rich do generally find it easier to save. Some people run what may be described as a structural surplus; they always have a large enough income to cover their spending commitments.

There are also those clients who have a structural spending deficit and their income never seems to be enough to cover their spending commitments. A deficit might be sustainable on a temporary basis (perhaps during a short period of unemployment) but it cannot last unless the client has capital that can be run down. Financial planners frequently encounter clients who are high earners but spend all their incomes and then borrow to spend more. Cars, holidays, consumer durables, entertainment and clothing are the highest priority. They undertake no saving and carry little insurance. Any wealth they might have is in their home and may well be mortgaged to the maximum to pay for current expenditure.

The level of clients' wealth

"The rich are different from you and me", says Nick Carraway in Scott Fitzgerald's *Great Gatsby*. The absolute amount of wealth is an important factor.

A family worth many millions has a different outlook and problems from one that has very little. In the UK the distribution of wealth is very uneven, so the very rich tend to be looked after by relatively few advisers.

Who is considered rich? Most people relate the answer to their own circumstances. The multi-millionaire publisher Felix Dennis categorised total net worth as follows:

£1m – £2m	The comfortable poor
£2m – £5m	The comfortably off
£5m – £15m	The comfortably wealthy
£15m – £40m	The lesser rich
£40m – £75m	The comfortably rich
£75m – £100m	The seriously rich
£100m – £200m	The truly rich
£400m – £999m	The filthy rich
Over £999m	The super rich

Source: How to Get Rich by Felix Dennis, Ebury Press 2006

Felix Dennis was clearly not wholly serious in his categorisations at the upper end. But it is interesting to note that those whom he calls 'the comfortable poor' would be considered extraordinarily fortunate by most inhabitants of the UK, let alone the rest of the world. Rich is a relative term in terms of wealth – as it is with income. Some of the key variations and relationships are:

- **Wealth in relation to liabilities**
  Net wealth is the crucial measure. Where substantial liabilities are set against a person's substantial wealth, it is important to remember that the wealth can be quickly eroded by even relatively small falls in its value. For example, a client worth £2m with liabilities of £1.5m only has a net worth of £0.5m and this could be wiped out by a 25% fall in the value of their assets. It then becomes very important to understand the terms on which the client owes the £1.5m. If the loan is for a fixed term regardless of the changing value of the underlying assets, then they may well be able to ride through the storm of a temporary fall in the value of their assets. But plenty of loans are subject to revaluation or are at least repayable on demand – especially overdrafts and business loans. It is also important to understand how quickly rolled-up interest on loans can increase the total amount of the debt; for example at 7% a year, rolled-up interest doubles the outstanding debt in roughly ten years.

- **Wealth in relation to liquidity**
  People are said to be asset rich and cash poor if their wealth is illiquid and

especially if their assets generate little or no income. Owners of agricultural or development land are the classic asset rich and cash poor clients.

Such people are often relatively restricted in the financial planning they can undertake without disposing of assets. For example, pension planning may be restricted to making transfers of land from their personal ownership to that of a self-invested pension, thereby achieving possible tax savings — but not diversification.

They may also find themselves short of income, a classic position of elderly homeowners who have a valuable property but no income or cash resources. Selling and trading down is often the sensible approach but they may not wish to do this. In such circumstances, the normal strategy is to borrow, although this is bound to involve some downside risk as the interest would need to be rolled up and added to the principal.

- **Acquired wealth or inherited wealth**
  It is hard to make meaningful generalisations about the differences between those who made their wealth themselves and those who inherited it. Those whose wealth has been derived from working in a highly paid job, such as investment banking or from building up a successful business, may generally be older than those who have inherited it. In addition there are probably more variations in social class and attitudes to money among the 'self-made'.

  People who inherit wealth may have a stronger feeling that they are stewards of the family fortune for the next generation. But if the wealth depends on their managing a family business, they may find that drive and entrepreneurial skills are more important and may not be passed onto their children and grandchildren. An entrepreneur from a poor background may build-up the family fortunes, only for the children to lose it and the grandchildren to end up socially and financially where their grandparents first started — or "Clogs to clogs in three generations" as the expression from the north of England goes.

Clients as business owners

People who own their own businesses are different from other clients in certain respects. Much depends on the size and profitability of the business and its state of development. Particularly in their early stages, businesses can be all-consuming of time, energy and resources. At some points, they can expose clients to levels of risk that would be unknown to other clients; but at other times businesses can provide a degree of insulation from financial storms.

Business owners are often more financially aware than other clients and may be generally more decisive because they are used to making major financial decisions.

Business owners also tend to be overconfident about their financial futures. Irrational optimism is a precondition for starting most businesses. As investments, many small and medium-sized businesses are high risk, illiquid and excessively dependent on the talents of their owners and senior managers. Owners often overvalue their businesses and business assets. The business idea that was the basis for success in the early years may turn out to be outmoded and in decline by the time the business owner comes to retire. Many clients regard their businesses and business assets as substitutes for more diversified forms of long-term investment such as a pension and therefore need to understand the value of diversification, even where it involves investing in assets that might grow more slowly than their businesses.

People who inherit businesses from previous generations tend to regard their businesses differently from those who set them up. They may not share the driving passion to succeed; they may have been persuaded to join the family firm against their better judgement and they may have to work with other members of the family, possibly in an atmosphere of disagreement. Clearly there are many family firms that do successfully make the transition to second and even subsequent generations, but the challenges should not be underestimated. The implications for financial planning can be very substantial.

Clients with an overseas dimension

Many clients have overseas connections and these can play an important role in their financial planning. Where there is an overseas dimension to a client's affairs, it may be necessary to liaise with advisers who have specialist knowledge of the overseas territory in question. Issues may arise in such areas as: tax, property ownership, pension rights, exchange control, wills and estate planning. Some planners may be mistakenly tempted to take the laws and taxes of non-UK jurisdictions less seriously than those that prevail in the UK. This could rebound on both their clients and themselves.

- Clients who come from overseas to live in the UK may continue to have assets and other links with their country of origin as well as other jurisdictions. They may well be able to take advantage of the UK non-domicile tax rules. These have less long-term importance for all but the very richest clients following recent changes in UK tax law, but the IHT planning opportunities can be considerable.

- Clients who leave the UK to work overseas face a number of challenges with respect to tax, social security, pensions, insurance protection, mortgages and investment. They may be presented with an opportunity to accumulate funds in a relatively low tax environment, or they may be simply going to another broadly equivalent country in say Europe or the US with different tax and financial rules. They will need to decide what they wish to do with their UK assets while they are overseas.

- Clients who own assets abroad such as property may find that they encounter particular complications. In many continental European countries there are rules about inheritance which may necessitate clients making a will in the country concerned. Clients with property or investments outside the UK may decide not to declare these or the income from them to HMRC. Financial planners should be aware of the dangers that this could present to both their clients and themselves.

- Many UK clients think about the possibility of retiring overseas. Depending on the chosen country of residence, this can have valuable tax benefits if the client is able to establish non-UK residence (which is less easy than it was thought used to be the case). Financial planners should help clients to think through the implications.

Clients' knowledge and experience of investment and financial issues

One of the biggest differences between clients is between those who are familiar with investment and financial issues and those who know relatively little about financial matters, even though they may be able to manage their income and expenditure perfectly capably. Some financially naïve clients may turn out to be highly expert in particular areas while some sophisticated investors may well have unexpected gaps in their knowledge.

There are also specific regulatory definitions of sophisticated and professional investors that are covered in more detail in chapter 9, 'Regulatory requirements and financial planning'.

Clients who are financially rich but time poor

Many clients do not have the time to look after their finances properly and can afford to pay for someone to do it for them. These are the classically 'asset and income rich but time poor'. They need and are generally prepared to pay for administrative work to be done for them and will appreciate financial reporting that allows them to understand their financial position quickly and easily.

Those who are 'time rich' are less prepared to pay for convenience and administration especially if they enjoy looking after their own finances or at least the administration of them.

The personality of clients

The behavioural finance specialists have identified a number of traits and behaviours that seem to be hard-wired into human beings and which lead clients into making irrational but predictable mistakes (see chapter 3, 'The impact of behavioural finance'). Some clients display these and other characteristics more than others.

Certain clients seem to be naturally happy to plan their finances and look after their affairs in an orderly way. Others are chaotic, indecisive and incapable of controlling their expenditure – even to meet goals that they agree are important. Well organised people are less work for planners, but do not necessarily make better clients. The added value to bringing order out of a muddle can be very considerable and gratifying.

Financial planners need to decide how best to deal with different types of clients. In some cases, there is an important issue of even whether to take on a particular client or couple. Straightforward observation while establishing objectives and fact-finding is the key, with financial planners noting clarity of thought, understanding of issues, degree of organisation or paperwork.

Financial planners can help themselves and their colleagues decide how to deal with different clients by using personality tests like Myers-Briggs. For example, the Myers-Briggs test might help a financial planner find out which clients want carefully built-up cases for action backed by logically argued hard evidence and those who prefer a more intuitive and emotional approach to decision making.

Part 2: The financial planning process

Chapter 5
The planning process

1 Process for efficiency

The adoption of professional standards in financial planning involves the use of a model for the process. Specifying the steps in the process, their order and content, and establishing procedures for monitoring the completion of each stage, has the following advantages:

- Clarity for both client and adviser regarding intended outcomes.

- Control over procedures in each step of the process.

- Ability to delegate more routine work to administration staff.

- Greater productivity through better case management.

- Clear documentation in the event of a complaint.

Experienced advisers can often reach the outlines of a realistic plan quickly in an intuitive way, but following a set process ensures that there are no errors of oversight and that all recommendations are clearly linked to fact-finding and analysis. It can also help to ensure that the advice given by different advisers in the same firm is consistent.

2 The six-step model

In its standard ISO 22222, the International Organisation for Standardisation (ISO) set out a six-step model for financial planning. Advisers could use a different number of steps — for example, they might make risk profiling a separate stage — but the stages should link in a logical order and it should be easy to define when one stage ends and another begins.

The following outline of the financial planning process in six steps does not exactly follow the ISO but corresponds to methods in common use.

Step 1: the client and planner relationship

Many advisers begin their relationship with prospective clients informally, in general discussions where the client has the opportunity to assess the adviser and decide whether to establish a relationship with them. Such meetings may end with the adviser providing written details about their firm and their services. These should include:

- The scope of the service that can be provided by the planner.

- The planner's qualifications and experience.

- The cost of the service.

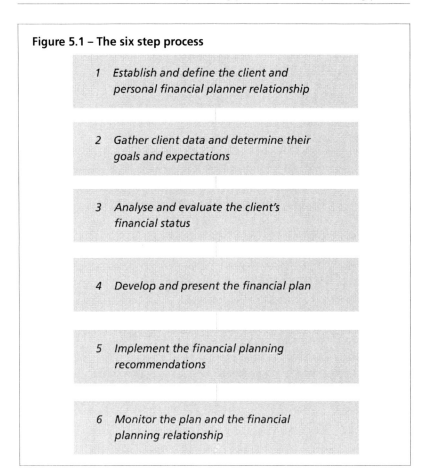

Figure 5.1 – The six step process

1   Establish and define the client and personal financial planner relationship

2   Gather client data and determine their goals and expectations

3   Analyse and evaluate the client's financial status

4   Develop and present the financial plan

5   Implement the financial planning recommendations

6   Monitor the plan and the financial planning relationship

Once the client has decided to engage the planner, they should be provided with the full terms of engagement in written form, including:

- The basis of remuneration.
- Any identified conflicts of interest.
- Details of the service to be provided including timescales (e.g. of regular reports).
- The duration of the agreement (e.g. annual).
- The frequency of contact.
- Confidentiality provisions.

These will be covered in the firm's services and cost disclosure document (SCDD) (see chapter 9, 'Regulatory requirements and financial planning') and/or client agreement (which may incorporate the SCDD). The formulation of the advice proposition including scales of fees and scope of service is covered in chapter 7, 'The advice proposition'.

Step 2: gathering client data

The planner needs to acquire a large quantity of information from the client in order to create a comprehensive plan. This will often proceed in stages:

- Essential personal information.
- More detailed data on items such as pension entitlements.
- Documentation on the client's existing plans, policies and investments.
- More detailed information obtained from product providers.

Risk profiling is often undertaken separately.

Many advisers use printed fact-find forms to gather much of this data. Some advisers use online forms that clients can complete. In some cases paraplanners or other assistants to the adviser will gather some of the information. In almost all cases they or the adviser will need to follow up the initial data gathering with supplementary questions in person or by telephone.

The methods of fact-finding are covered in chapter 10, 'Client aims and objectives'. Each method has its advocates among practitioners. The most significant distinction is between advisers who undertake their own fact-finding and advisers who use paraplanners or assistants.

Fact-finding by paraplanner/assistant

Advantages:

- Less involvement with client, so easier to follow a set process.
- Less liable to be distracted from facts by planning and analysis issues.
- Likely to be more consistent in recording data.

Disadvantages:

- May overlook information uniquely relevant to client and circumstances because it is outside the frame of reference.
- Makes the fact-finding process a routine instead of creating opportunities for open-ended discussions.
- May limit scope for exploration of attitudes to risk.

The adviser's aim is to gather all the information that may be relevant to the client's needs, goals, resources, liabilities and attitudes.

The information may be stored in the form of scanned documents, or entered into a 'back office' administration system. Files need to be maintained so that each version of a fact-find, and fresh client information added at a later date, are kept in date order. Often supplementary information is gathered in person or by phone, and this too needs to be noted on the file.

Personal information

Date of birth, employment status, marital status, dependants, state of health, residence.

Financial information

Entitlements to state benefits and pension; life and health insurances; liquid assets; savings plans; financial investments; occupational and other pension entitlements; additional properties and other assets; mortgages and other debts; other liabilities and commitments; Will.

Planning inputs

Monthly surplus/deficit of income over expenditure; expectations of future capital; short, medium and longer term goals; immediate needs; social, ethical and environmental attitudes; family relationships and children; tolerance of risk.

The last category will almost always require extensive discussions with the client, to help them formulate their goals and to prioritise them, and to clearly identify their attitude to and tolerance of risk. The result is usually a score or a 'risk profile' (see chapters 6, 'Investment planning' and 11, 'Risk profiling'), and before using this as an input in the planning process the adviser needs to obtain the client's confirmation that they accept it as a basis for their plan. Likewise, it is best to secure the client's verification of specific analyses such as monthly budget analysis, cashflow analysis or pension entitlement analysis before using them as a basis for recommendations.

Step 3: analysis and initial conclusions

Depending on the complexity of the situation, the adviser will employ a variety of analytical tools, such as cashflow analysis, balance sheet analysis, and pension transfer analysis.

This analysis will typically identify goals which the client is unlikely to achieve given the resources available. For example, the client may plan to retire at age 63, and may have a specific target income – but this may not be achievable given the amounts currently being contributed into their retirement funds.

The initial analysis may reveal a very wide gap between the client's goals and what is realistically achievable. The adviser will need to discuss this gap with the client, and the usual consequence is that the client will adjust their priorities and timescales. There may be several iterations before the situation is reached in which a realistic plan encompassing all the client's goals can be produced.

This process frequently results in adjustment of the client's goals, timescales and even tolerance of risk, and this needs to be documented. Some advisers will produce a revised statement of goals, timescales and risk profile for the client to 'sign-off' before producing the final plan.

The analysis stage is usually the most valuable to the client, since it brings together their goals and priorities and in a way they often find hard to achieve on their own. It is therefore important that the adviser engages the client in the process so that they understand the reasons for the adjustments. A financial plan that does not secure the commitment of the client is one that is unlikely to be successful.

The analysis stage of the process is dealt with in chapter 12, 'Client management'. Creating suitable investment recommendations forms a major part of the process for many clients. It also benefits from a disciplined approach, and defining an investment process (which falls within this stage of the overall planning process) has similar advantages. This is covered in chapter 6, 'Investment planning'.

Step 4: presenting the financial plan

The plan should be provided in written form. The client's goals/timescales, resources, intentions and tolerance of risk should be restated in the form they have taken following the revisions that may have occurred in the previous stage. In the case of a change in risk profile, the reasons for any change should be carefully documented.

The adviser's main conclusions and recommendations should be clearly stated, preferably under relevant headings such as emergency fund and short-term cash requirements, protection, and estate planning, followed by more detailed explanations as necessary, with any technical details confined to appendices.

In the case of long and complex plans, advisers may present the overall plan in one document including only summary recommendations, and produce detailed recommendations, for example for an investment portfolio, as a separate document.

Where action is required by the client, this should be clearly specified.

Chapter 15, 'Communicating recommendations' covers the whole area of explaining proposals to clients.

Step 5: implementing the financial plan

From the client's point of view, the adviser's generic recommendations (such as amounts to be contributed to retirement plans, type of protection policies and sums assured) are far more important than the detail of the specific plans and policies. The plan should not provide excessive technical detail. However, the adviser needs to have a robust process for product selection in all areas within their advice proposition. The product selection process is covered in chapter 14, 'Selecting appropriate products and services'. The ideal is for this process to be sufficiently well planned and documented that standard wording can be used to explain the selection of each product recommended.

The implementation of a plan may involve the cancellation or alteration of existing plans or policies, the establishment of new plans, asset transfers, will revisions and other items.

The adviser and/or their administrators should set-up an implementation plan for each client with checklists for each step required. The adviser or delegated administrator should monitor each action required by the client as well as the adviser's own actions in progressing implementation. Often this will depend on the actions of third parties, such as life insurance companies in effecting pension transfers, and chasing by administrators is almost always necessary. Best practice is to advise the client of likely timescales for each of these steps and update them as each item is completed.

If the client declines to follow any of the adviser's specific recommendations, this should be confirmed by the adviser in writing.

Step 6: reviewing the financial plan

The adviser's agreement with the client should specify the frequency of review of their financial plan (see chapter 7, 'The advice proposition'). The adviser should establish a review process whereby the client is asked about any changes in circumstances, tax status, relationships and so on that might require changes to their plan. This should be done far enough in advance of the review date to permit the adviser to assess whether fresh recommendations need to be made.

The adviser should take the time to record and review any such changes. This could require adjustment of goals and priorities, amounts saved, needs for protection, income requirements from investments, or changes to the risk profile and hence substantial changes to the portfolios of investments. If the adviser recommends changes to the plan, they should refer back to the original so that the client is clear about what has changed and why.

The review should also cover any legislative changes relevant to the client and their use of any annual tax allowances or reliefs. The nature and content of investment reviews is covered in chapter 6, 'Investment planning'.

3 Managing the advice process

The process as outlined above is a blueprint advisers can use to design their own systems. Within each step of the process an adviser firm should have the following:

- Procedures for advisers
- Checklists for administrators
- Filing procedures
- Case checking

Procedures for advisers and administrators

A checklist will usually be helpful for most of the individual steps below, provided both administrators and advisers can refer to it and that it is updated daily until the initial plan has been fully implemented. It should contain 'stops' for critical steps (e.g. no action can be taken for a client until money laundering checks are complete; no investments can be purchased until evidence of client authority is provided).

Procedures for advisers and administrators

	Procedures for advisers	**Procedures for administrators**
Step 1: Establish the relationship	Deliver the advice proposition. Issue SCDD, client agreement.	Complete money laundering requirements.
Step 2: Fact-finding	Complete fact-finding document. Obtain supplementary client data. Risk profile and client attitudes/preferences.	Establish client files. Obtain data from product providers.
Step 3: Analysis	Budgeting/cashflow analysis. Balance sheet analysis. Pension analysis. Affordability analysis. Prioritise goals. Investment plan. Product selection.	File completed analyses Obtain quotations and illustrations.

Step 4: Presentation	Summary of objectives, generic recommendations. Detailed recommendations and suitability explanations. Technical details.	Obtain key features and product documentation.
Step 5: Implementation	Check applications, fund transfers, policy and issue documents to the client.	Submit applications. Issue documents to client.
Step 6: Review	Gather fresh client data. Review goals, priorities, timescale, risk tolerance, portfolio. Make recommendations.	Update client files.

Filing procedures

Financial planning is a complex process – significantly more so than most routine tasks undertaken by accountants or solicitors. An adviser firm will only be able to monitor and control the quality and consistency of advice if all of their client files are maintained using the same methods.

For some practitioners, the ideal financial planning filing system is one where all relevant client information is entered into a purpose-designed system that enables advisers to extract and manipulate any of the data for planning purposes. A variety of such systems are available from financial software firms. In this case, all fresh data gathered from the client is immediately entered into the system, and a large part of the output for financial plans (such as cashflow projections) is generated from within the system.

Entry of all this data is a lengthy process and even if it is undertaken by administrators, it often requires checking by advisers. Hence some advisers prefer only to record a small amount of client data in a more limited administration system and use separate software tools for activities such as pension transfer analysis, cashflow modelling and risk profiling. In this case, the results of such analyses need to be attached to client files in the administration system.

While responsibility for the client relationship rests with the adviser, responsibility for the client files is usually divided between adviser and administrator. It is therefore advisable for an adviser firm to have a procedures manual to which they both adhere.

Case checking

Adviser firms need to monitor the quality and consistency of advice. This can be partially achieved by discussion of cases by advisers during the planning process. However, an adviser firm should establish case checking procedures as part of its own process.

Case checking has two objectives:

- To ensure that administration and filing procedures have been correctly followed at every step.

- To ensure that appropriate advice has been given and that all the documentation necessary to justify that advice has been delivered to the client and/or appropriately filed.

The two are interrelated in that it is often impossible to show that appropriate advice has been given if key documents are missing from the file. In particular:

- Fresh client data gathered informally in person or by telephone should be added to the file as soon as possible and where necessary confirmed to the client in writing.

- Any change in circumstances requiring a significant review is likely to affect attitude to risk, so it will almost always be appropriate to review the client's risk profile.

- Analysis forms the link between information and advice, so the results of analyses undertaken by the adviser during the planning process should always be added to the client files.

- A random sample of every adviser's client files should be checked periodically and the results of each review discussed with adviser and administrators. These reviews may be carried out by a director of the firm (who should be authorised to do so by the director having responsibility for compliance with the FSA/Consumer Protection and Markets Authority (CPMA)) or by independent consultants employed for this purpose.

Chapter 6
Investment planning

1 The importance of process

When successful investors are interviewed or write books, a striking common feature is the emphasis they place on following a process. And almost all confess that their biggest losses came from breaking their own rules.

The kinds of rules used by investors in securities may differ in their details from those used by advisers, but the principle is the same. Successful investment is based on having a set of rules and a process that you have confidence in, and sticking to them.

Historically, few advisers have tended to treat investment as a process, but the reasons for doing so are the same as those that apply to the financial planning process as a whole. Having a clearly defined investment process can enable the adviser to:

- Ensure consistency of advice for clients with similar circumstances and needs.

- Monitor the quality of advice and its implementation.

- Provide full documentary evidence of all stages of the process.

- Justify the recommendation of investments in relation to the client's tolerance of risk.

- Accurately assess the resource requirements and profitability of ongoing services.

The process of formulating and delivering investment advice, like the financial planning process, can be broken into different steps or stages. Here we adopt an 8-step model that applies to the common advisory mandate, and this is followed by a discussion of variations where advisers use third party discretionary fund management services.

2 The 8-step investment planning model

This model includes strategic asset allocation and fund selection, which are both features of a common advisory mandate. Both elements may be outsourced as part of an agreement with a discretionary fund manager (DFM), and this alternative model is discussed below.

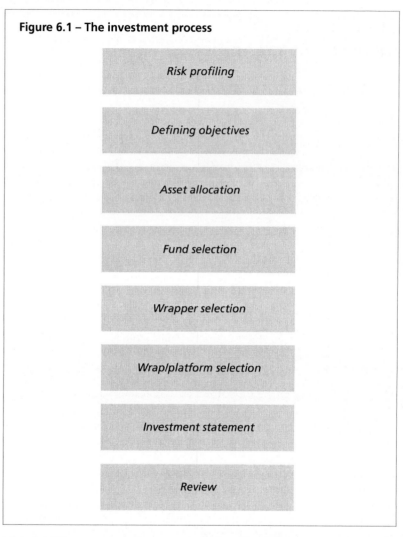

Figure 6.1 – The investment process

Risk profiling

Defining objectives

Asset allocation

Fund selection

Wrapper selection

Wrap/platform selection

Investment statement

Review

Risk profiling

Under the UK's regulatory system, very few people have ever been awarded compensation based on the poor performance of their investments. The vast majority of awards have been based on the non-disclosure of factors affecting risk, or the recommendation of investments that did not match the risk tolerance of the client.

The consequence has been that most advisers now undertake a more detailed and rigorous assessment of the client's risk tolerance, often using questionnaires to provide numerical ratings linked to 'risk profiles'. These may simply be ranked in numerical order, say from one (lowest risk tolerance) to ten (highest risk tolerance). Or they may be given names such as 'cautious', 'cautious balanced', 'balanced growth', etc. Each such profile corresponds to a strategic asset allocation with defined percentages of capital in each of a set of asset classes.

Risk issues

Online tools or printed questionnaires about attitudes are relatively easy to apply. But they may cause advisers to overlook the multi-dimensional nature of risk and appropriate ways of assessing it. In order to arrive at an appropriate risk profile, the adviser needs to investigate three dimensions of risk:

- **Risk capacity** – an objective measure based principally on the client's circumstances.

- **Risk perception** – the individual's current, subjective view based on their own experience to date.

- **Risk tolerance** – the individual's general attitude to risk as shaped by social factors.

Risk capacity

During the fact-finding process the adviser will form a clear picture of the individual's circumstances. The principal factor to consider here is not the probability or scale of loss but the consequence of loss.

Example 6.1

Mr Jones has asked for advice on investing a lump sum of £100,000. He is 57 and wants to retire at 65. His pension entitlements are likely to provide a net income of about £15,000 a year and he is looking for additional income from the investments of about £6,000 a year. He has no other assets apart from his home, where he wishes to stay when he retires. The consequence of a loss of capital or significant income shortfall to Mr Jones would be a severe reduction in his standard of living. His capacity for risk is low.

Clients with large secure sources of income or capital may have a much greater capacity for risk, in that losses would not have a major effect on their standard of living.

Significant elements of the fact-find regarding risk capacity are:

- Health, since ill health may reduce employment income or increase the need for income in retirement.

- Marital status, since separation or divorce may reduce pension entitlements.

- Expectations, since certainty regarding future possession of more capital can increase current risk capacity.

Risk perception

An individual's perception of risk is usually easy to ascertain, since it will emerge in discussing their situation. For example, it is common for clients to fail to recognise the danger that inflation poses to capital held on deposit. Their benchmark for assessing risk is nominal rather than inflation-adjusted returns. Commonly, once people understand the potential scale of capital erosion through inflation, they adjust their perception of the risk involved in other financial investments. This shows how perception of risk can change as people acquire greater knowledge. Likewise, experience of the actual day-to-day variations in the value of investments will, after some time, alter the way people with no former experience of investing think and feel about it.

As behavioural finance has shown (see chapter 3, 'The impact of behavioural finance'), current perception is heavily influenced by availability. If recent stock market performance has been turbulent and negative, people's perception of risk will be more acute than it will be after a long period of gently rising prices. Familiarity may also colour perception of risk — often people feel comfortable having a high proportion of their capital in one investment if it is shares in the business that employs them. Yet these same people would often baulk at the idea of placing that amount of capital in any other single investment. Even relatively sophisticated investors can also suffer from the endowment effect, and hold on to (or even buy more of) an investment they inherited. These perceptual biases distort perception of risk, and people can usually recognise this provided it is skilfully brought to their attention.

Risk tolerance

Risk tolerance, or attitude to risk, is what has been formed by the individual over their lifetime, with strong family influences and often subject to peer group pressures. It is less likely to change in response to changes in the environment than their perception of risk.

People's feelings about risk are often conditional and contextual, and since at the point when they ask for advice many lack the context to assess investment risk, their answers to hypothetical questions about loss may be unreliable. Their responses to actual events that have happened to themselves or to their family and friends are likely to be more reliable.

An important aspect of fact-finding as regards investment is attempting to ascertain how the client feels about risk not just financially but in other areas of their life. Advisers can, for example, enquire about friends or acquaintances who have been successful or unsuccessful with their careers, businesses or money to see how the client feels. Other behaviour can also provide useful evidence — hobbies such as paragliding, porcelain collecting or travelling independently in third world countries can provide insights into their attitudes.

Risk questionnaires

Many advisers use printed or online questionnaires as part of their risk profiling. It is advisable to use a combination of objective and subjective questions. The way questions are posed is also important. Behavioural finance has identified the 'framing effect', which may lead people to try and appear to be what seems to be normal; to do so they may skew their answers so that they come out at about the mid-point of a range of risk profiles. Avoiding obvious links between answers and risk profiles can help to avoid this.

Example 6.2

Objective risk questions

What savings and investment products have you purchased in the last ten years?

Have you taken advice before when making investments?

Which of the following three statements best describes your experience and knowledge of investing?

A. I have very limited knowledge of investments and have made little or no investments in the past.

B. I have a reasonable knowledge of investments, have made several investments in the past and take an interest in their performance.

C. I have strong interest in and knowledge of investment, and have made a wide range of investments and follow their progress regularly.

Subjective risk questions

Which is more important for you with regard to investments: the risk or the potential gain?

With five possible answers ranging from Strongly Agree to Strongly Disagree:

I would prefer lower returns with safety to higher returns with some risk of loss.

I would expect my investments to return more than my cash deposits every year.

Psychometric profiling appears to offer a more scientific assessment of risk tolerance, but bigger questionnaires are not necessarily better questionnaires.

Many risk profiling tools offered on provider websites link to the creation of portfolios supposedly corresponding to the individual's risk tolerance. Since these tools can produce significantly different asset allocations, they clearly use different methods and assumptions, and effectively replace the adviser's own decisions about asset allocations to match risk profiles with those of the provider or its agents. Independent software tools that match risk profile to asset allocation avoid this bias, but require the adviser to fully understand their construction and methods. Notably (see 'Asset allocation' on page 80), these models often use probabilistic risk modelling to generate the asset allocation.

Risk profiles

Taking risk capacity, risk perception and risk tolerance into account, the adviser allocates the client to one of a set of risk profiles. The number of these in common use varies from three to ten. Clearly, it is difficult from people's experience and questionnaire responses to identify ten different character types or profiles in relation to risk. In reality, such models are usually reverse engineered: the adviser creates a set of ten asset allocations — a typical set is shown in the table — and then these are given labels (cautious, adventurous, etc). The decision as to which of these labels fits the client is, in the end, often at least partly subjective, to the extent that many clients could justifiably be placed in the category either immediately higher or immediately lower than the one to which they are actually assigned.

Sample set of ten asset allocations to match risk profiles

Profile	Percentage of capital allocated to				
	Cash	Fixed income	Commercial property	Equities	Alternative/ absolute
1	20	35	10	15	20
2	17.5	32.5	10	20	20
3	15	30	10	25	20
4	10	27.5	10	32.5	20
5	7.5	25	5	40	22.5
6	5	20	5	47.5	22.5
7	2.5	17.5	5	55	20
8	0	15	5	62.5	17.5
9	0	10	0	75	15
10	0	10	0	80	10

Defining objectives

Most clients do not need 'income' or 'growth', or rather the fact-find should have established that the client has specific needs for cash at certain points in the future. Cashflow modelling may be used to help the client become clear about what they need when. In the investment advice process, all the client ever needs is cash.

The more precise the adviser and client can be about how much cash is required when, the easier it will be to create an appropriate asset allocation and portfolio. The worst case scenario can arise when a lazy adviser is faced with an uncommunicative client. The adviser settles for a 'growth' label, creates an asset allocation with a high equity content, and then a year later – just after the market has seen a sudden fall – the client unexpectedly asks for a chunk of capital towards a need they forgot to mention. The discussion between them will fall into a familiar pattern:

Adviser: *"But you never told me you would need the cash now."*

Client: *"But you never asked me."*

The adviser needs to flesh out all the needs and objectives identified in the fact-finding stage, ensuring that the scale of priority attached to them is realistic. Often this will involve further discussions with the client about the timing and scale of likely capital and income requirements. Frequently clients are vague about the future and the adviser may need to prompt them – for example:

- "Do you think you will want to pay for both your daughters' weddings?"
- "Are you likely to want to consider contributing to the cost of private education for your grandchildren?"
- "Should we make allowance for a third of the cost of a holiday home, assuming you will get mortgage finance for the rest?"
- "Are there any special things you may want to do or buy immediately after you retire?"

In order to create a suitable portfolio, the adviser needs to work with objectives framed along these lines:

- To create a capital fund of £150,000 at the end of six years, capable of generating annual cash for income of £7,000, assuming that up to £10,000 will be withdrawn at some point between the fourth and sixth years.
- To generate an immediate income of £4,500 from the capital of £90,000, with the aim of income and capital rising in line with inflation.
- To increase the pension fund capital from its current £250,000 to £500,000 over a ten-year period assuming no withdrawals of capital or income.

People often use 'mental accounting' (see page 35) to handle multiple goals. In financial terms, this often takes the form of setting up plans with specific objectives (to pay for the school fees, to top up the retirement income, etc). This can result in having quite different objectives for different pots of money. For example, many people are happy to set less demanding return targets for their pension funds than for other assets, provided they are confident that the risk of loss will also be lower.

Portfolio theory would suggest that having separate portfolios is inefficient and that a single portfolio would deliver a better trade-off between risk and return. In practice, married couples or civil partners may prefer to have two portfolios, one with lower and the other with higher risk/return objectives rather than having one portfolio with an intermediate rating. Individuals may prefer to have, say, a low-risk pension portfolio and a high-risk ISA portfolio. Regardless of the theory or the actual returns, the fact that this gives clients confidence and enables them to keep track of things makes it a sensible solution, provided that any cost penalties involved in running multiple portfolios are fully understood.

Asset allocation

Today the division of capital between asset classes is usually taken as the starting point for portfolio construction. Portfolio theory asserts that it is the division of capital between asset classes that is the primary driver of portfolio returns. This claim has to be seen in the context of voluminous academic research showing that attempts to 'time the market' by switching between (say) cash and equities fail most of the time, and portfolio theory's axiom that investors do not get paid for taking-on risk they could avoid by diversifying. The first makes strategic asset allocation the most important investment decision, and the second defines the scope and merit of diversification strategies.

Strategic asset allocation takes a set of asset classes and uses data for returns, correlation and volatility to create portfolios with expected returns and volatilities. The role of correlation is crucial, since a portfolio's risk and return will not be the weighted average of its constituents unless they are all perfectly correlated. The degree of non-correlation will reduce the risk, giving rise to the familiar 'efficient frontier' curve.

Historical data for returns, volatility and correlation are often used as inputs for portfolio modelling. However, there has been a wide range of variation in these factors over five-year periods in the past century, so using recent data (say for the last decade) or long-term averages can both be criticised. Some tools allow the adviser to substitute their judgment for history, and use their own expectations of return, correlation or volatility. Where such judgments apply 'reversion to the mean' to any recent trend in the historical data, they have history on their side, since such reversion is amply demonstrated over the long-term in almost all financial data series. But it must also be noted that such reversion may itself take as long as a decade to complete.

Portfolio modelling tools generally use standard deviation as the measure of risk. However, it is only a valid measure when applied to 'normal' or Gaussian distributions, and it is well established that investment returns do not form a normal distribution. For this reason it is inappropriate to make statements (which used to be common in investment literature) such as 'Returns will fall within one standard deviation of the mean two-thirds of the time'. Experiences such as those of 2008-10 falsify such claims. Making those claims conditional ('except in crisis conditions') invalidates their use as a means of guiding clients towards realistic expectations.

Volatility measures based on standard deviation (such as the Sharpe and information ratios) can be useful in assessing the performance of individual investments, but their use in portfolio modelling can lead to asset allocations that in practice embody risk greater than is appropriate. A further danger is that where such tools use recent data, they will allocate more capital to the asset class that has most recently shown the best returns. Advisers need to avoid falling into the error identified by Berkshire Hathaway's Warren Buffett: "Pension fund managers continue to make decisions with their eyes firmly fixed in the rear-view mirror."

The actual range of returns from asset classes during the past century over periods ranging from one to 15 years is a better guide to the likely range of returns and volatility. This data is updated annually in the Barclays Capital Equity-Gilt Study and the Credit Suisse Global Investment Returns yearbook. Recent returns or volatility well above or below the long-term historic average have generally been a reliable signal that 'reversion to the mean' is likely to occur in the next few years.

While fund managers generally prefer to talk about returns, the key point about asset allocation is that it is fundamentally a defensive strategy, as pointed out by Warren Buffett, "Diversification may protect wealth, but concentration builds wealth". Often, those who invest capital have accumulated it by concentration in their own business and now wish to 'take risk off the table', while the classic 'little old lady' has never wanted to take any investment risk she could possibly avoid. It is important for advisers to ensure that their strategic asset allocation decisions focus on this primary aim of protecting wealth.

Asset classes

An asset class consists of a set of assets that can be expected, on the basis of economic theory, to share certain characteristics, including the pattern of returns and volatility. Today, many practitioners define asset classes purely with reference to the historical data: if this shows sufficient divergence, especially in terms of correlation, this justifies defining an asset class.

In practice, terminology is often loose and what practitioners mean by an asset class is in fact a sub-class. For example, UK large-cap, mid-cap and small-cap stocks are all sub-classes of UK equities. While sub-classes may have delivered quite different patterns of return, it is clear that they must share a common set of risks and that in crisis conditions they are almost certain to behave in the same way. Sub-classes therefore offer limited diversification benefits: in the conditions when risk reduction is most valuable to the client, they will not deliver it.

Until recently, four major asset classes were in common use but the advent of 'absolute return' investing and the wider use of hedge funds have resulted in the use of a fifth asset class, often termed absolute/alternative. Care must be taken if this class is used to include within it only genuinely alternative items. For example, equity funds investing in infrastructure, water or private equity are not 'alternatives' in this sense: they are simply sub-classes of equity investment.

Characteristics of the main asset classes

	Cash deposits	Fixed income	Commercial property	Equity	Absolute/ alternative
Principal characteristic	Fixed nominal capital, variable interest	Fixed income, variable nominal capital	Relatively secure income, real asset	Variable income and capital, both with growth potential	Limitation of risk to income and capital
Benefits when	Low inflation	No or low inflation	Moderate inflation	Low or moderate inflation	Any conditions
Suffers when	Moderate or high inflation	Moderate or high inflation	High inflation	Erratic inflation	
Liquidity Max*** Min*	***	**	*	**	**
Volatility	Minimal	Low	Moderate	High	Low to moderate
Expected returns	Low	Low to moderate	Moderate	High	Moderate to high

Asset sub-classes

The main sub asset classes in common use are listed in the table. For such a category to be valid in terms of portfolio modelling, it must be possible to obtain historical data showing its return, volatility and correlation with other classes. From the adviser's point of view, it must also be possible to easily access funds that invest exclusively in this class of assets.

Asset classes and their subdivisions

Primary asset class	Common sub-classes	Categories in sub-class
Fixed income	Developed nation government bonds	Long-term, medium-term, short-term
		Sterling, US dollar, Euro
	Emerging nation government bonds	
	Index-linked bonds	Government, other
	Corporate bonds	Investment grade
		High yield
		Short, medium and long
		Convertibles
	Asset-backed securities	Residential mortgage backed securities
Commercial property	Real property	National, regional, global
	Real Estate Investment Trusts	National, regional, specialist
Equity	Developed markets	National markets
		Sectors (e.g. financials)
		Large, mid and small cap
	Emerging markets	National, regional, global
		Large, mid and small cap
Absolute/alternative	Absolute return	Equity long/short, Credit, Macro
	Hedge funds	Global macro, Credit, Market neutral
	Tangibles	Gold and precious metals, gemstones, fine art, antiques, stamps, wine

Using asset allocation methods

The key point about asset allocation methodology is that the investor thinks about the risk and return at the portfolio level, not just at the level of the individual holding. If a 'risky' asset (such as gold bullion) shows low correlation with other risky assets, then its inclusion in a portfolio containing those other risky assets will reduce the overall volatility of the portfolio.

This does not correspond to the normal 'intuitive' way of thinking about risk, which is commonly represented as a pyramid (see Figure 6.2). Here the investor adds or subtracts risk by changing the size of the layers in the pyramid (increasing or reducing capital invested in more or less risky assets). In contrast, asset allocation methodology requires the more sophisticated mathematics of algebra to assess the effect on both risk and return of adding any new investment to an existing portfolio.

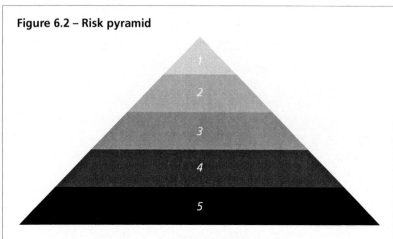

Figure 6.2 – Risk pyramid

1 *Very high risk (gold, resources, technology).*
2 *Higher risk (small cap equity, emerging market equity).*
3 *Moderate risk (large cap developed market equity, absolute return).*
4 *Low risk (fixed income).*
5 *Minimal risk (cash).*

While clients do not need to understand this process, it is vital that they do understand that the adviser's aim is to construct a portfolio having the desired risk-return characteristics, and that it may well contain individual investments that do not display those 'average' characteristics.

At present there is a disconnect between the regulator's view, which requires advisers to demonstrate their ability to use portfolio theory in designing portfolios, and the Financial Ombudsman Service, which has tended to judge individual investments as appropriate or inappropriate in relation to the client's risk profile. Making it clear that risk is assessed at the portfolio level and explaining the reasons for inclusion of individual investments having volatility greater than that of the portfolio are therefore desirable in the communication of recommendations.

Fund selection

Clients' capital will almost all be allocated to investment funds or structured products (SPs). There are four ways an adviser can research funds:

- Research and select actively managed funds in the relevant asset classes.
- Research and select passively managed funds in the relevant asset classes.

- Research and select multi-manager funds.
- Research and select discretionary fund managers.

The first three require the same type of research and selection process. Under the Financial Services Authority's (FSA) 'whole of market' rules to comply with the Retail Distribution Review (RDR), an adviser must research those categories of investment that could be appropriate for the client. The categories of fund that may be relevant to UK clients will include:

- UK authorised unit trusts and open ended investment companies (OEICs).
- Investment trusts and investment companies.
- UK life and pension funds.
- Offshore funds including hedge funds.
- Exchange traded funds.
- Unregulated collective investment schemes (UCIS).

As wraps and platforms (see below) widen their fund offerings, it will usually be desirable to take the entire universe of UK authorised unit trusts and OEICs falling within the relevant asset classes as the source for selection. Advisers using risk profiles are unlikely to use multi-asset class funds, managed funds or risk-profiled funds and could therefore exclude these and other fund categories from their research process. Likewise, advisers may take the view that for reasons of risk and the difficulty of the due diligence process they will not recommend any offshore hedge funds and will therefore not research them. They might limit their research on exchange traded funds into those listed on the London Stock Exchange. Such limitations to the scope of research should be documented in the description of the adviser's research process.

Independent advisers may also recommend unregulated collective investment schemes (UCIS) — see chapter 9, 'Regulatory requirements and financial planning'. UCIS invest in areas such as residential property, oil and gas exploration and forestry. They require considerably more diligence in research since the managers are often unknown and custodial and management contracts may vary significantly from the UCITS standards. There may be conflicts of interest between managers and investors. Advisers may choose not to recommend any UCIS, in which case they would need to justify this with reference to the risks involved.

It is difficult to incorporate quantitative methods into the selection process for discretionary fund managers, since there is not normally sufficient data available in a form that can be compared with alternatives. Qualitative assessment will focus especially on the efficiency of the service and quality of reporting both to client and adviser.

Qualitative and quantitative assessment

The adviser's aim is to select funds likely to deliver risk-adjusted returns greater than the average for their peer group. Three factors enter the assessment:

- Historic performance.
- Quality of management.
- Style.
- Costs.

Quantitative analysis of historic performance examines cumulative and discrete period returns and volatility. Comparisons are made with the relevant sector index and also with individual funds identified as forming a peer group of above-average funds. Care is taken to make relevant comparisons — for example, the performance of UK special situations funds should be assessed relative to their peer group rather than to the IMA UK All Companies sector index. For passive or index funds, the analysis focuses on tracking error.

Volatility can be compared with the relevant index or peer group. The Sharpe ratio or information ratio can be used to compare risk-adjusted returns.

Quality of management includes aspects such as fund manager tenure and remuneration. Direct links between manager bonuses and fund performance may seem desirable but may create incentives for taking on additional risk. Equity ownership in the fund management business by managers is likely to mean longer tenures. The scale, resources and capital available to the fund management group must be judged in relation to the relevant funds. For example, a global network of offices and analysts is of little relevance to the management of UK fixed interest funds but could be highly relevant to the management of a global equity growth fund.

The style of a fund manager or management group is also a relevant factor in creating portfolios. Some fund management groups place heavy emphasis on a common process that is applied across all their funds. This process may have a bias towards macro-economic analysis, or to thematic or value investing, or to some other dominant factor. In each case, this style is likely to enhance fund performance at some stages of the economic/market cycle but to hamper it at others. Hence diversification among styles can help to lower portfolio volatility.

A few fund management groups give much greater scope to individual managers to apply their own methods subject to some general 'house rules'. In these cases, too, the individual manager's methods will usually work better in some stages of the cycle than in others.

In the case of passive funds, costs are a key factor in fund selection: the lower the total expense ratio (TER) for a given index tracking proposition, the better. For actively managed funds, TERs are one factor but will usually be important only if they are significantly above or below the average for the peer group. However, any performance fees need to be carefully evaluated to estimate their effect on net returns, especially if other similar funds do not levy such charges.

Some multi-manager funds now use risk profiles or label themselves as 'cautious', 'balanced', etc. In this case the adviser needs to understand the manager's asset allocation process and ensure it corresponds to their own definitions. Moreover, they need to ascertain the extent to which the multi-manager will vary the asset allocation, since this could cause the fund to become riskier than is appropriate for the intended group of clients. Multi-manager funds are also likely to apply a style whose success varies through the market cycle.

Model portfolios

Investment advisers often create model portfolios where the risk profiles are converted into fund portfolios with percentages of capital allocated to each fund. This is done using a set of funds identified through the research process.

The use of funds of different types and styles within the relevant asset classes can substantially alter the risk-return characteristics of the portfolio. An example is shown in the table, in which a 'Balanced' asset allocation is converted into a portfolio with risk-return characteristics respectively lower or higher than would be achieved with an 'asset class' portfolio using passive funds.

Asset class	Balanced Index	Lower Risk Balanced	Higher Risk Balanced
Fixed Income	FTSE All-Stocks Gilt tracker	Gilt fund	Strategic Bond fund, High-Yield Bond fund
Property	FTSE EPRA/NAREIT UK property tracker	UK real property fund	Fund of global REITs
Equity			
UK	FTSE 100 Index tracker	UK equity income fund	UK special situations fund
Overseas	FTSE Developed World Ex-UK tracker	Global growth fund	Natural resources, technology funds

To accommodate the construction of portfolios with different characteristics, advisers need to populate their fund lists with funds of different types.

The number of holdings in a fund portfolio could be as few as five or as many as 35. While diversification in the asset classes can be achieved with five funds, diversification within the asset classes can be achieved only by using larger numbers of funds or by using multi-manager funds.

Expanding the number of funds within an asset class will affect both returns and volatility. In crisis conditions, however, correlation will almost certainly increase, so the primary benefit of such diversification is enhancement of returns. There is good evidence that 'value' and 'small-cap' strategies do reliably generate long-term returns superior to the market index, but at the cost of higher volatility (in the case of small-cap) or periods of sub-market returns when value strategies fall out of fashion. Inclusion of both strategies together with a more conventional (or possibly passive) large-cap fund could therefore be seen as creating a better risk-return trade-off than simply holding an index tracker.

Even for those with substantial capital, a portfolio of 30-40 funds (a typical number for a multi-manager fund) should be sufficient to incorporate as many sub-asset classes as are needed. These could include gold, natural resources, agriculture, infrastructure, forestry/timber, private equity, renewable energy and biotechnology as well as regional small-cap, property funds and specialist fixed interest funds.

Core and satellite

Portfolios can combine actively managed and passive funds in 'core and satellite' structures. The intention is to assemble a core of funds investing in the major asset classes that are held for the long-term, while 'satellite' portfolios contain more specialist funds that may be held for shorter periods.

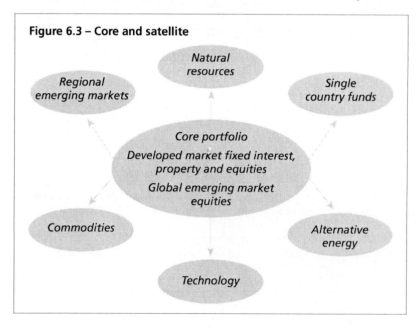

Figure 6.3 – Core and satellite

Natural resources

Regional emerging markets

Single country funds

Core portfolio

Developed market fixed interest, property and equities

Global emerging market equities

Commodities

Alternative energy

Technology

Promoters of passive funds argue that passive funds should form the core since evidence shows it is hard to find actively managed funds that consistently beat their benchmarks. It may also be possible for managers to add more value in less well researched and liquid markets.

However, it can also be argued that if the adviser has complete confidence in the long-term abilities of a manager, then having their fund as a core holding is also a viable strategy, and that passive funds can more easily be used for 'in-and-out' trading.

If the core and satellite structure is used, it should be documented and the policy with regard to core and satellite holdings clearly articulated.

Structured products

Advisers may recommend structured products (SPs) for all or part of an investment portfolio. These are fixed-term products that offer some element of capital protection or mitigation of risk as compared with direct investment in equities. They are relatively complex products that use derivatives and require careful evaluation.

Structured products may take the form of structured deposits, in which case they are technically and legally deposits covered by the banking compensation regime, or structured products, in which case they are covered by FSA/CPMA rules and investor protection.

SPs offer 'hard' or 'soft' protection.

Hard protection: the investor is assured a return of their original capital regardless of what happens.

Soft protection: if a reference index falls below a certain level during the term, the investor may suffer a loss of capital.

Products where an investor's capital is at risk are termed structured capital at risk products (SCARPS). Sometimes referred to as 'precipice bonds', these were the focus of a misselling scandal in 2003-04.

Whether products offer hard or soft protection, the investor is exposed to counterparty risk since a bank underwrites the returns. The degree of counterparty risk depends on the bank's financial status, which as the bankruptcy of Lehman Brothers in 2008 showed is not always accurately measured by credit ratings. To some extent counterparty risk can be mitigated through collateralisation, where the counterparty pledges to the product provider assets or cash sufficient to match the guaranteed element of the return.

The typical form of a 'plain vanilla' SP is as follows:

- Fixed term 5.5 years.
- Return of original capital guaranteed at maturity.
- If the FTSE100 index is higher than its initial level at maturity, the investor receives a return of orginal capital plus 70% of the gain in the index.

Small print variations in conditions can substantially alter the actual return. In this case, the final value of the index may be defined as its average over the final six or 12 months of the contract rather than its final value. The initial value may also be taken as an average over a period instead of the level on the contract commencement date. In all cases, the relevant index is the capital-only version, so the investor does not benefit from dividends, which account for the bulk of the long-term return of equities above the risk-free rate.

In the case of soft protection products, the conditions in which the investors may suffer loss need careful evaluation. Any such potential loss of capital must be very clearly explained to the client.

'Kickout' plans, where a product has a life of, say, six years but terminates on any anniversary and pays a fixed return where the index is above its starting level, are a recent development.

SPs can only be assessed using probabilistic analysis which few advisers will be capable of doing. Several websites offer their own analyses and ratings of SPs for advisers.

SPs appear to offer a lower-risk way of investing in risky assets, especially equities. Against this, counterparty risk has proved to be a potential source of loss for investors.

With many SPs, investors give up the potentially unlimited upside of equities in exchange for capital protection. For those with genuinely long-term horizons, this has historically been a poor trade. Nevertheless, for extremely risk-averse investors, or as part of a portfolio with medium-term objectives, SPs can play a part in portfolio construction.

Wrapper selection

The risk profile and model portfolio are selected based on the analysis of the client's objectives, needs and risk tolerance. The selection of tax wrappers within which to hold those assets then focuses on the most tax efficient method of holding those assets. The tax wrapper analysis can be taken to include the appropriate division of asset ownership between spouses holding one common portfolio.

Tax factors in selection

The taxation of the individual and the taxation of the vehicle through which investments are held both have to be considered to determine optimal tax efficiency.

The principal tax factors are summarised in the table.

Taxation of returns within wrappers

	Direct	ISA	Pension	Onshore Bond	Offshore Bond
Deposit interest	0%, 10%, 20%, 40% or 50%	NIL	NIL	20%[1]	0%[2]
Fixed interest income	0%, 10%, 20%, 40% or 50%	NIL	NIL	20%[1]	0%[2]
Property income	0%, 20%, 40% or 50%	NIL	NIL	20%[1]	0%[2]
Property gains	18% or 28%[3]	NIL	NIL	20%[1,4]	0%[2]
UK Equity income	10%[5], 32.5% or 42.5%	10%[5]	10%[5]	10%[1]	10%[2,5]
Equity gains	18% or 28%[3]	NIL	NIL	20%[1,4]	0%[2]

1) *Possible extra income tax on encashment for higher rate taxpayers at 20% or 30%*

2) *Possible income tax on encashment at 10%, 20%, 40% or 50%*

3) *After annual allowance; realised gain added to income to determine relevant tax rate*

4) *After allowance for indexation of purchase cost*

5) *Deducted at source*

In the UK, two forms of equity investment qualify for tax reliefs: venture capital trusts (VCTs) and enterprise investment schemes (EIS). Though some advisers include these in the 'alternative' asset class, it is clear that both VCTs and EIS involve investment in equities, often in new businesses, and therefore involve higher risks than are involved in investing in established businesses. Where appropriate, they can form part of an investment portfolio, and should normally be included in the proportion allocated to equities.

Principles of wrapper selection

The general principles of wrapper selection are:

- The ISA is the simplest and most flexible tax shelter. It is also permanent (unless there is a change in legislation) and should therefore be used for long-term investments.

- Pension plans deliver worthwhile tax relief benefits to those who contribute when higher rate taxpayers and withdraw benefits when their tax rate is lower. For those whose tax rate remains the same these benefits are marginal. The inaccessibility until age 55 can be a drawback or an advantage. Tax-free roll-up is valuable to higher rate taxpayers.

- Onshore bonds can enable higher rate taxpayers to defer some tax especially on investment income.

- Offshore bonds permit deferment of a larger amount of tax on income and gains.

- Investments generating high rates of income such as fixed interest are best held in ISAs or pension funds where tax is not deferred but eliminated.

- Investments expected to generate gains such as equities can advantageously be held direct until gains exceed the annual capital gains tax allowance.

- Offshore bonds have particular attractions to higher rate taxpayers who expect to encash them when their tax rate is lower.

- Spouses' assets should wherever possible be divided to minimise tax liabilities.

Selecting wraps and platforms

Advisers will generally recommend the use of a wrap or administration platform to hold clients' investments. The regulatory issues relating to this are dealt with in chapter 7, 'The advice proposition'.

Wrap costs and benefits

The costs of third party administration systems such as wraps are paid directly or indirectly by the client. The costs are therefore an important factor and should be assessed in relation to the capital sum involved. Generally, some platforms are better value within certain bands of capital.

The cost issue is complex since the adviser can use in-house administration systems that provide most of the functionality of wraps. The costs for such a system may in this case be lower than those of external platforms, but the adviser must incur the additional costs of staff training, security, updating and so forth. Such administration costs would form part of the cost base recovered through fees charged to clients.

If the adviser aims to provide a service where portfolios are regularly rebalanced, the ability to rebalance portfolios at very low cost is an important benefit of wraps. Ease of client access to current valuations is another valuable benefit.

Wrap choice

The regulator's views on wrap and platform selection are that the adviser needs to show that the wrap selected is appropriate for the client. Given the different charging structures of wraps, advisers are therefore likely to end up using at least two wraps for different segments of their client base. Advisers need to establish clear procedures for this assessment and for wrap recommendations, so that clients of specific types or with capital falling within certain bands receive recommendations for the same wrap.

Investment policy statement

Normal practice has been for advisers to set out the client's objectives, risk profile, asset allocation and proposed portfolio in a report.

In addition, it is beneficial to create an investment policy statement for the client, since this can be included in each subsequent report and reminds both adviser and client of the agreed terms of the investment mandate. The key issues to be covered in the investment policy statement include:

- Client's objectives
- Risk profile
- Basis of service (advisory or discretionary)
- Methodology (e.g. asset allocation)
- Permitted investments (e.g. OEICs, unit trusts, investment trusts)
- Limits on investments (e.g. maximum percentage of capital in any one fund)
- Exclusions (if any, as agreed with client)
- Ethical/environmental constraints (if any, as agreed with client)
- Nature and frequency of reporting
- Procedure for changes and reviews

The statement, if included in each client report, serves as a reminder to both client and adviser to review and if necessary alter it.

Reviews

Most advisers now provide ongoing investment advisory services and will be obliged to do so after 2013, if agreed with the client. For the majority of clients, investment reviews and reports are provided either annually or half-yearly.

For advisers using asset allocation methods, the following topics should be covered in reviews:

- Performance of the investments in nominal terms, as a percentage change and compared with a suitable benchmark.

- Comment on the portfolio with reference to any holdings that have significantly contributed, positively or negatively, to performance during the period.

- Comment on the general market and economic conditions and their effects on the performance of, and implications for, the portfolio.

- Explanation for any recommendations for changes to the portfolio's asset allocation.

- Justification for any switches, sales or new purchases recommended.

Valuation statements should show current price and valuation, historic cost and percentage of portfolio value, and include an asset allocation analysis. Income statements should show the sources of income with amounts payable net or exempt from tax and any paid gross clearly identified.

Transaction statements should show the proceeds of any sales and the cost of any purchases.

3 Outsourcing investment management

Advisers may choose a business model in which they outsource investment management to one or more discretionary fund managers (DFMs). In this case, the adviser firm positions itself as financial planners with overall oversight of the client's affairs. Outsourcing can be seen as advantageous in that it distances the adviser from investment performance. In the worst case scenario of persistent poor performance, the adviser can suggest that the client replaces the DFM. On the other hand, if investment advice/management is seen by the client as the key part of the service, this may weaken the client-adviser relationship.

Adviser relationships with DFMs

Advisers who outsource investment management may introduce clients to a DFM independent of the adviser. The terms of the introducer agreement will make the DFM responsible for advising the client in relation to all aspects of investment, including risk profiling, asset allocation and investment selection. The adviser's responsibility is in principle confined to due diligence in selecting the DFM. The adviser's client agreement with the client should define the adviser's responsibilities (if any) in relation to oversight of the investments or exclude them. The DFM will normally report independently to the client subject to their own client agreement, but will copy all reports, statements and valuations to the adviser.

The traditional 'arms-length' relationship between advisers and DFMs is undergoing change thanks to wrap technology. The adviser may establish a wrap to hold a whole set of client assets and introduce the client to a DFM for part of their portfolio, or one of several portfolios, which are maintained through the wrap. In this case, the adviser retains substantial investment responsibility (especially if charges are levied by the adviser on the assets under management in the DFM portfolio) and the DFM becomes more like the manager of an individual fund within a portfolio. The client is likely to see the adviser as having prime responsibility and if the adviser's actions – in reporting on DFM investments themselves, for example – contradict an apparent delegation of responsibility, it is likely that regulators will view the adviser as having a greater liability than applies in the case of the arms-length 'introducer' relationship.

Risk profiles

A DFM will have its own methods of creating portfolios based on risk profiles. If the adviser uses their own risk profiling methods there may be a conflict between the two. The adviser can ensure this does not happen by using the risk profiling process designed by the DFM or changing their own method so that it is aligned with that of the DFM. This may not be a realistic solution if the adviser is introducing only some clients to a DFM or is introducing clients to more than one DFM.

Alternatively, the adviser can create a system that matches their risk profiles to those used by DFMs. The adviser's focus should be on ensuring that clients do not end up taking on a greater degree of risk than they were assessed for by the adviser.

A third possibility is for the adviser to undertake only a limited risk profiling exercise in relation to non-investment matters and to make it clear to clients that this profile does not apply to lump sum investments which are outside the scope of the adviser's client agreement.

Investment process

DFMs' investment management systems may permit significant variations in the asset allocation of portfolios. In this case, the level of risk may become higher than the adviser has assigned to the client. This problem may also arise with multi-manager funds if manager mandates are insufficiently precise. The adviser therefore needs to carefully consider all aspects of the DFM's investment management process and systems.

Though advisers cannot be held responsible for the investment returns or performance of an arms-length DFM, they could be liable if the client incurred losses as a result of the DFM taking more risk than the adviser had agreed was appropriate, and the adviser may still have overall responsibility in relation to risk profiling for a wrap including DFM assets.

Tax issues

The revised system of capital gains tax effective from June 2010 has created new problems for investment advisers and DFMs. The reason is that once gains exceed the annual allowance, any additional gain is added to taxable income for the year to determine whether a tax rate of 18% or 28% applies to the gain. A significant gain can cause all or part of a basic rate taxpayer's gain to become taxable at the higher rate of 28%. The tax position on directly-held assets has therefore become more complicated.

Under the old system, the rate of tax on a gain could be determined simply by knowing the client's income tax status and their use of the annual capital gains tax allowance. Under the new system, in order to know the tax consequences of incurring a gain on realisation of an investment, advisers will need to know the taxable income for the year (net of reliefs, which themselves may vary from year to year) and any gains and losses the client has incurred in their own right (for example on a share portfolio managed independently by the client, or in a DFM portfolio) in order to estimate the tax rate that will apply.

While wraps and other systems can monitor the gains potentially liable to tax, estimating the capital gains tax rate is only possible using client-specific information. Advisers wishing to ensure maximum tax-efficiency will need to devise systems for obtaining the necessary information from clients so that they can take this into account in making their recommendations.

DFMs will often exclude gains tax considerations from their investment decisions, and if all or part of the client's assets are managed by a DFM, the adviser will normally have no control over the realisation of gains. For many clients who are basic rate taxpayers, the danger is that a substantial gain in any one tax year can trigger a tax liability at the higher rate of 28% whereas smaller realisations over two or more years would incur a rate of 18%.

Chapter 7
The advice proposition

Financial planners need to have a clear advice and service proposition to put before clients. This is simply a statement of the services the financial planner will provide and the amount the client is expected to pay for them.

There has always been a need for the client proposition and indeed all advisers and planners have provided them to a greater or lesser extent, although they have often been vague and at least partly designed by product providers (who paid commission on the sale of products rather than by financial planners for the advice they provided). Financial planners are now being driven to take the initiative and formalise their proposition themselves to a much greater extent than they have done in the past.

Financial planners have been driven to define their proposition to clients more effectively by regulatory, commercial and to some extent legal pressures.

1 The regulatory and other drivers

The main regulatory drivers have been the Financial Services Authority's (FSA's) 'Treating customers fairly' (TCF) initiative and the more recent 'Retail Distribution Review' (RDR). Several of the FSA's TCF outcomes have a direct impact on financial planning firms' advice and service propositions to clients. The detail of these is set out in chapter 9, 'Regulatory requirements and financial planning'.

The treating customers fairly initiative

The TCF initiative has driven many firms of financial planners to focus on their advice proposition. The FSA is clear that the marketing of products and services must be designed to meet the needs of identified consumer groups and be targeted accordingly. Clients have to be given clear information and be kept appropriately informed before, during and after sales. Any advice to clients must be suitable and take account of their circumstances. The FSA has provided various examples of bad practice and these include:

- Taking a fund-based fee or commission with no explanation of the services to justify this to the client;
- Placing all clients on a wrap platform at the same time without conducting a review to establish the wrap's suitability for each individual;
- Not keeping clients informed of information such as changes in investment values, product charges or investment allocation rates.

They have also provided examples of good practice that they have seen and these include:

- Conducting regular due diligence on all discretionary fund managers used;
- Making market comparisons to ensure that clients are not disadvantaged by staying with a particular company;
- Keeping each client informed of product performance and of opportunities to act when circumstances change;
- Having a system to ensure service is delivered in line with the agreement with the client;
- Keeping customers informed about the performance of a product and any opportunities to act when circumstances change, e.g. if the client invests in an equity product and there is a downturn in the market.

In the TCF initiative, the FSA has encouraged firms to consider the issue of consistency of treatment between different services as well as across planners in the same firm. Clients should be able to expect consistent (although not necessarily identical) terms from different planners working within the same practice.

The retail distribution review (RDR)

The RDR has augmented the drive to reforming and clarifying service and advice propositions by requiring greater clarity from financial planners about products and services as well as a more transparent approach to charging. Financial planners and their firms would be well advised to start the process of charging on the basis of the RDR rules before they become compulsory. It is assumed that they will aim to make this transition as soon as possible in order to iron out the main wrinkles for both planners and clients before 1 January 2013. The main provisions are set out in chapter 9, 'Regulatory requirements and financial planning', and include the following:

- Before providing any advice, financial planners must make it clear to clients whether they are offering independent or restricted advice. Non-advised 'execution-only' services will also be available.
- All firms that give investment advice must set their own charges upfront and with their clients' agreement. Product providers will not be able to offer commission to adviser firms, who in turn will be banned from receiving it, although clients will be able to ask for their adviser's charges to be paid out of their investments.
- An advisory charge will not vary according to which particular product provider or investment is recommended.

- For business written from the start of 2013, advisers will only be able to charge an ongoing amount in return for an ongoing service, except where a client is buying a regular contribution product.

- Potential clients will have to be given a price list or tariff of the advisers' charging structure before receiving advice.

Many financial planning firms are moving towards adviser charging well in advance of the RDR deadline of 1 January 2013. A number have already largely adapted. There are good reasons to try and make the changes as early as possible in preparation for the time when adherence to the adviser charging rules becomes compulsory. Individual financial planners generally take time to become used to presenting such a radical new approach to old and new clients. Firms have to adapt their systems and controls. It makes sense to try different methods of adviser charging to discover which ones best suit the practice and its clients.

The commercial drivers

The market for financial services is expanding in the UK as in most western economies, but the market is becoming more demanding in a number of respects.

- There is a greater emphasis on the need for transparency and clarity.

- Clients expect a higher level of service with their expectations raised by a range of technological advances that allow clients to see online how their investments are performing.

- Financial planning firms will experience greater pressure on their margins through higher compliance and other costs and reducing income per pound invested. To some extent, commission levels have already come down as a result of both market and regulatory pressure.

- Financial planners will need to segment their clients so that they can charge them on different bases according to the types and levels of service the clients want and are prepared to pay for.

- Financial planners will need to make efficiency savings by focusing on particular markets and types of clients. Specialising in this way encourages economies of scale in marketing because firms can build reputations among particular market sectors, with word-of-mouth and networking providing the most effective route to market. Personal reputation is the most effective way of selling financial planning and wealth management services.

- Specialising also encourages efficiency in the provision of advice and economies of operations. Financial planners and staff should be able to hold down costs by dealing with familiar problems in which they have built up both soft skills and technical expertise. Training can be focused on the key areas that apply to clients. Likewise product research can be more specialised and effectual.

- Tailoring the service and expertise to fit closely with the needs of a target market will help improve the quality of the service and the perception of specialisation. Clients do not react well to financial planners learning about an area at their expense. Although this may sometimes be inevitable, generally clients expect to benefit from their financial planners' existing expertise.

Legal drivers

There are also legal issues. Financial planners may need to define their areas of expertise and the services that they provide with some care if they are to avoid litigation. It is important that clients' expectations of the services that a firm provides are matched by actual performance and the expertise to back it up. If clients believe that the service for which they have contracted with a firm entitles them to certain services such as ongoing oversight and care of their investments, they may take legal action if they are disappointed and lose money as a result of perceived negligence.

2 Designing the service proposition

Financial planning firms should consciously design different advice and service propositions for their different types of clients or market segments. They may also decide that there are specific market segments that they want to focus on — and some that they no longer wish to serve.

The proposition for a group of young middle managers in a large firm who are in their 30s is bound to be different from the appropriate service proposition for retiring entrepreneurs in their 60s. The level of expertise brought to the older and richer clients is much greater and this should be reflected in such areas as the way the firm looks after their investments, the depth of planning for clients, the detail and frequency of the reviews, the choice of wrap platform and the arrangements for working with other advisers. The following are outline service propositions that might be appropriate for each segment. The method and level of charging should reflect the services being provided in terms of both their costs and value.

Younger client profile

Summary

A straightforward advice service typically centred around immediate advice issues relevant to managerial employees in their 30s and 40s with a need for further reviews and planning in the future. Their current needs are likely to be for protection, mortgages, short-term saving and long-term pension accumulation.

Proposition

An uncomplicated advice service for clients who understand the need for expert advice and are expected to have increasingly complex financial affairs in the future.

Client benefits

Peace of mind, access to expertise, minimal paperwork, satisfaction that their affairs are being well looked after.

Client contact and support

Mix of face to face meetings and remote contact (mainly email) with a named financial planner and support team. Meetings at the firm's office.

Core services

- Financial analysis and plan, including risk profiling;
- Annual valuation;
- Face-to-face meetings usually every two to three years, but annually for some clients;
- Letter by email and phone call at valuation time each year;
- Periodic review of risk profile;
- Maintenance of records;
- Provision of named financial planner.

Charges

- Initial financial review and plan – flat fee of £n or n% of funds under advice (FUA), with minimum of £n;
- Ongoing review service £n or n% of FUA with a minimum charge of £n;
- Minimum investment typically £n.

Marketing and service communications

Annual valuation, letter, phone call and the firm's newsletter.

Older client profile

Overview

A comprehensive specialist service that includes investment and pension planning, financial, estate and tax planning, typically delivered in partnership with other advisers.

Proposition

A bespoke financial planning service for private clients with complex affairs that need continuous management often in conjunction with other specialist advisers.

Client benefits

- Peace of mind;
- A successful investment experience;
- Delegation to experts;
- Access to expertise and information;
- Clarity out of complexity.

Client contact and support

- Mainly face-to-face meetings and phone calls with the financial planner and other advisers at a convenient location for the client and also contact by letter and email;
- Additional contact with the financial planner's technical specialist team and support staff as required (by meeting, phone and email);
- Support for investment by the ABC Discretionary Portfolio Management Group.

Core services

- Financial analysis and plan, including risk profiling;
- Review of capital and income requirements including lifetime cashflow projections;
- Quarterly valuations;
- Access to valuations via online wrap account access;
- Face-to-face meetings typically twice a year and more if required;
- Phone and email contact as needed – access at any time in working hours to financial planner and technical team and other support;

- Annual review to update all elements of the initial analysis and plan and recommendations for rebalancing the portfolio;
- Proactive contact linked to relevant tax and legislative changes;
- Named adviser, technical support and administrators;
- Maintenance of records.

Charges

- Initial financial review and plan – flat fee of £n or n% of funds under advice (FUA), with minimum of £n;
- Ongoing review service £n or n% of FUA with a minimum charge of £n;
- Minimum investment typically £n.

Marketing and service communications

Invitations to hospitality events and seminars.

3 Planning the pricing policy

Pricing its products and services is one of the most difficult issues that any business faces. Many financial planners have escaped the problem in the past because their pricing policy has effectively been set by product providers' commission scales. But recent trends in the market as well as the TCF initiative and the RDR have changed the commercial landscape, and financial advisory firms now need to have a pricing policy. There are several factors in setting prices in any context or charging structure.

Costs Charges should broadly reflect the costs of providing services to clients. Costs should be the starting point for pricing decisions because it is obviously not sustainable for costs to exceed income for long. Costs have to be determined according to the appropriate time interval; the annual costs are easily extracted from the annual accounts and then broken down by quarter, month, week, day or hour. Costs can also be allocated by department, type of activity, the total number of financial planners or the total number of advisers. So it would be possible to calculate the weekly cost of the whole company, or a department or a single adviser. The firm could conclude that a specific adviser needs to earn an income of, say, £2,000 a day to cover their costs. Another approach would be to calculate the average cost per client per year, to decide what needs to be the average charge per client, although the average might cover a very wide variation in individual client cost. Even if the firm does not intend to charge fees on an hourly basis, it is good financial discipline to be able to benchmark income against the hourly fees that would be charged to see which activities and clients are profitable and which are not. The pricing policy should not slavishly follow a cost plus approach. Some services are of greater value to clients and can carry higher charges.

Remuneration structures The way in which financial planners and others within the practice are remunerated will affect the pricing structure. If personnel are paid mainly on the basis of fixed salaries, the charging structure needs to reflect this pattern of largely unvarying costs. Fluctuating incomes can be tolerated more easily if some or all remuneration varies with the level of income and profits.

Costs The business needs to do more than just cover its costs; it ought to make a profit. Without an ongoing profit in addition to the normal income that the owners should expect to earn in their capacity as financial planners themselves, it is very unlikely that the business will have much capital value. It certainly will not be in position to build up reserves for safety and the future.

Consistency Pricing should be consistent within a firm as between activities, departments, different financial planners and clients. The logic behind charging should be defensible to the regulator and even more importantly it should be justifiable to clients and their professional advisers if and when they ask. In any case, the regulator demands that a scale of fees should be presented to clients and adhered to. Consistent does not mean identical. Pricing and fee levels can vary according to the type of work undertaken and the person who does it. A more senior and experienced individual can justify a higher charge than a lower paid individual.

Clients' perception must be that the charges are fair, reasonable and represent good value for money.

Competition There will also be competitive and market pressures on the way a firm prices its services. Clients will benchmark charges against other financial planning firms and other types of professional advisers such as lawyers and accountants.

Individual financial planners' views The financial planners themselves will have to present the charges to clients as part of the process of selling the service. They need to believe that the pricing structure is reasonable both when they first meet a new client and then each year when they must be able to justify the ongoing charges to clients.

Initial or ongoing charges

Many firms are already moving away from relatively high upfront charges and commissions towards regular ongoing charges or 'trail' fees. There are several commercial pressures that lie behind this powerful trend.

- The costs of servicing a client each year are relatively heavy and frequently cannot be covered by selling new products that the client genuinely needs.

- Taking on a new client typically involves more time commitment than ongoing servicing, but the annual costs have become greater as client expectations have grown.

- Clients generally want to pay charges on the basis of the value they receive rather than the amount and value of the product they have been sold. Spreading the charges more equally over the lifetime of the professional relationship generally achieves a greater alignment of cost for the financial planner with value for the client.

- Businesses that look after a relatively stable client bank are typically regarded as more professional by employees than those that depend for survival on prospecting and winning new business for a high proportion of their income. Individuals who are skilled at financial planning are not necessarily talented at attracting very large amounts of new business each year. The financial planning practice resembles most other professional firms when it is based more on a farming model than a hunting model.

- Businesses that buy financial planning practices place a much higher valuation on businesses that have a high level of recurring income than those that follow the more old fashioned business model of generating large amounts of initial commission or fees based on bringing in new business rather than looking after existing clients.

The main drawback to switching to a recurring income stream is the potential strain that is placed on the firm's cashflow. In the longer term, the firm should build up a very resilient regular income stream. But in the few years when initial earnings drop down and the ongoing income is still building, the firm may well experience serious financial pressures. Furthermore, the new style of working involves increasing the cost base because of the need to change systems, invest in IT, spend time and money on training and perhaps even take on more staff.

There is also the risk that some of the existing clients may find the new charging structure unacceptable and decide to move on. Equally, some of the client base may not be suitable for the new charging structure. Such a firm might therefore be compelled to engage in additional marketing activity and expenditure.

Some clients resist being charged ongoing fees from their portfolio if they relate the level of charges to the portfolios income yield. At current yields and taking into account tax, even quite modest annual charges can seem very high in relation to the income that is generated from most portfolios.

4 Charging levels and structures

With the introduction of adviser charging under the retail distribution review, every financial planning firm should be considering how to charge for their services under the new regime. Before the end of 2012 firms have some time to prepare the ground and try out the most appropriate methods for them and their clients.

The main options that could be used independently or in combination are currently as follows:

- Traditional commission from providers in the traditional way — with or without commission rebating — although this option is due to disappear on 1 January 2013;
- Adviser charging based on transaction and/or investment value;
- Adviser charging based on hourly rates;
- Adviser charging based on a fixed basis e.g. for specific jobs, activities, projects and responsibilities.

Traditional commission from providers

It could be tempting to continue taking commission from providers while it is still available. One reason for delaying the switch from traditional commission is that it postpones the disruption from what is widely regarded as the easy option for advisory firms.

With products such as life assurance products, the amount of commission that can be paid to advisers is often greater than the increase in allocation that providers will give where no commission is paid. So if an adviser gives up 3% commission on an investment bond, the provider may give less than 3% credit to the policy. The reason for this is that the life office benefits from tax relief on the commission payments.

In some circumstances it may also be easier to avoid charging VAT on charges for the provision of services to clients. This could arise where the life assurance or pension commission is enough to cross subsidise other advice and services. Many firms will continue to take commission on this basis until the last possible moment, while still changing over to the spirit and to some extent to the letter of the new regime with respect to the majority of charging.

Adviser charging based on transaction and/or investment value

A typical value-based fee structure is based on a sliding scale of value. The higher initial fee should reflect the amount of work that the financial planner does at the start of the client relationship. The following is typical, but it might be adjusted to charging a lower initial fee and higher annual fee if the balance of work is likely to be different.

Clients' assets under advice £	Initial fee %	Annual fee %
0-99,999	3	1
100,000 – 249,999	2	0.8
250,000 – 499,999	1.75	0.75
500,000 – 999,999	1.25	0.5
1,000,000 and over	0.5	0.375

Where adviser charging is based on transaction or investment values or both these bases, there is a considerable degree of continuity with traditional commissions. The main differences after the implementation of RDR will be that:

- It will be financial planning firms who will be setting the adviser charges – not product providers. Nevertheless, those product providers that continue to pay the fees from the product will maintain a considerable amount of continuity for advisers.

- Advisory firms will not be able to avoid products just because the provider does not have arrangements to pay charges to advisers. Wrap platforms will provide the main method of charging clients fees in these circumstances, for example for ETFs and investment trusts. Where the investments are not held in a wrap, clients will have to pay fees direct. This might be relatively straightforward for the initial transaction when the client is paying cash for an investment, but it could meet more resistance from clients for annual charges.

- The charges will be more visible because they will be shown in addition to and separately from the cost of products. Financial planners will need to be able to justify ongoing fees because they will be subject to both commercial and regulatory pressures from clients, who will not only be looking for value but will almost certainly be encouraged to do so by the personal financial press.

- There will be a much greater emphasis on annual charges as we have already seen above.

The advantages of value based fees are:

- Value based charging is a much smaller step from the existing commission system and many financial planners will find it easier to make the switch.

- Many clients like the idea of results based remuneration and value based charging can be portrayed in that light, at least to some extent.

- The level of fees should rise over time as a client's portfolio becomes more valuable.

- The structure is simple, clear and transparent.

- The tiered structure makes it reasonably fair. The larger the size of the portfolio, the greater the responsibility and in general, the greater will be the complexity of the client's financial affairs. But a £1m portfolio does not take ten times more time to run than a £100,000 portfolio, and the tiered method of pricing can therefore look reasonable to a client.

- It is easy to arrange for payments to be made through products, funds or a wrap platform.

There are some drawbacks to this kind of adviser charging:

- It may be tempting to overcharge in relation to the value that is provided to the client. Some firms may decide to set their scales in line with the current level of commissions. In a few cases that may be possible or desirable, but it might be hard to justify to the clients and to the regulator.

- The value of the income stream to the firm will vary with the level of the stock market. In 2008 and 2009, many adviser firms that depended on value based trail fees found that their income had reduced by a third or more, but that their cost base was more or less unaltered.

- Some clients are very resistant to substantial annual fees being charged on cash deposits as well as other investments. Charges can eat into returns and turn them negative at current rates of interest, and clients do not always see the value of holding cash in terms of the expertise needed to recommend it.

Adviser charging based on hourly rates

Hourly rates should be based on the target remuneration plus associated costs of each individual divided by the number of chargeable hours in the year. So, for example, suppose there are 1800 working hours in the year — based on 45 weeks and eight hours a working day — and 60% of these are spent on client work. If the financial planner needed a target income of £200,000 a year to cover their remuneration plus associated overheads and other costs, then the hourly rate would need to be £185.

Other staff may need to be charged out on an hourly basis and it would be necessary to work out what target income they would need to cover their salary and other costs on the same principles.

The advantages of charging on the basis of hourly rates are:

- It is clear and transparent for both advisers and clients.

- Other professions charge on this basis and clients and professional introducers will relate to the system.

- Back office systems generally have time recording and billing systems so it should be relatively easy to introduce and control.

- Time cost charging introduces a valuable element of discipline into the business, making people conscious of how they use their time and encouraging them to make sure that they use it profitably.

- All work should end up being paid for by clients and there should be little or no unconscious cross subsidy.

There are disadvantages to hourly charging:

- Some clients dislike hourly charging because it seems almost entirely unrelated to performance. They resent the time spent on apparent irrelevancies and may feel that meetings and phone calls are set up to generate fees rather than to achieve anything valuable for them.

- The charges on an hourly basis may not adequately reflect the value of the financial planner's advice as much as value related charging.

- There is an administrative cost in tracking charges, issuing invoices and chasing payment.

- There may be resistance from financial planners who find the process of record keeping irksome, especially when the system is introduced.

Nevertheless, there are some jobs where time based charging or something similar is the most appropriate method to use. Undertaking the exercise of calculating the hourly charges for each individual in a firm is a very salutary discipline and worth undertaking each year even if is not much used in practice as a basis for fee charging.

Fixed price charging

Some advisory firms use fixed price charging for specific work rather than value based charging or hourly rates. A few use this approach for virtually all their client work, although most use it for particular types of tasks.

The tasks most usually subject to fixed charging are those that are easily identified and defined, such as carrying out an initial fact-find, undertaking a lifetime cashflow calculation, drawing up a budget of expenditure, producing a planning report, providing valuations or carrying out a specific project for a client such as arranging an annuity purchase.

Another relatively common approach is to ask the client for a retainer fee to cover all the basic costs of running the account in terms of record keeping, valuations, access to the wrap account, briefing newsletters and other information. It might even include a given number of contacts or meetings.

Fixed prices tend to be based on the approximate estimated hourly cost of providing the service, taking into account the other associated costs. However, the fixed price method of charging allows the firm to make larger adjustments for the perceived value of service. In some cases, the perceived value may be higher than the costs of providing the service; this might be the case where lower paid staff can perform a relatively highly automated process that is highly valued such as preparing valuations. But it might also mean that some services, such as sorting out administrative problems with product providers are likely to be valued less, and the full costs cannot always be passed on.

The firm needs to review their fixed price tariff at least once a year and possibly more frequently in the light of changes in costs and patterns of activity. Where it is felt that the charges that clients would accept are less than the full costs of recovery, the managers should consider other solutions to the problems.

The advantages of fixed price charging are:

- The firm's income is cushioned against the impact of falling stock markets – unlike value based charging.

- Clients perceive that costs are related to output rather than directly related to time spent. They do not feel that they need to watch the clock when consulting their financial planner or other staff.

- Clients and the firm have a greater degree of certainty and predictability about the charges.

- Charges can be linked to the costs of providing a service, but it is also possible to adjust for such other issues as value, importance, difficulty, urgency and responsibility.

The drawbacks of fixed price charging are:

- Pricing may seem more arbitrary to clients.

- New charges have to be considered and renegotiated every year.

- It is sometimes tempting to charge too little.

- Making decisions about the menu of fixed charges and the charges for individual clients may be time consuming.

- It is essential to keep rigorous records of time spent on clients, which some financial planners and staff might resent and/or do badly.

The balanced approach

Many firms decide to use a combination of two or all three of the main methods.

- Value charging is appropriate for portfolios of investments, because it provides a simple long-term method of charging that clients will understand. It is loosely related to results and should provide a broadly sustainable and rising income for the firm. It may also be a reasonable basis for charging for arranging some insurances. A minimum level of charges may be required for individual clients or jobs.

- Time cost/hourly rates may be the most appropriate method of charging for work where it is hard to predict how long the job will take and time cost is the only fair and transparent approach. This is likely to be the case with one off projects and investigations.

- Fixed charges are likely to be the most appropriate method of charging for work that is predictable, valuable and perhaps even routine. It may make sense as a basis for charging for protection policies or annuities – with probably an adjustment for value.

Chapter 8
Managing processes and teams

1 Introduction

Good processes are essential for any successful business and they are especially important in the complex set of actions required in financial planning. Processes do not just happen by themselves, they need devising and managing. Management is required in every kind of practice. In a single person business, the financial planner needs to be skilled and disciplined in self-management, but increasingly financial planning is undertaken by teams of people each specialising in particular aspects of the processes. Managing processes within teams requires very particular skills that are not always found in financial planners including:

- Defining the main steps, documentation and resources needed for each step of the process;

- Designing the systems;

- Determining the roles for each member of staff with their job description within the team structure;

- Agreeing the management information required to assess individual effectiveness, team performance and business trends;

- Devising appropriate reward structures and incentives.

2 Principles of managing a financial planning practice

The client service proposition as the basis for the system

The client proposition forms the basis for systematising processes. Process should follow function. A firm that specialises in wealth management and undertakes in-house discretionary portfolio management is likely to have different detailed systems and controls from one that undertakes the strategic asset allocation in-house but outsources the day-to-day investment management decision making to one or more outside organisations.

Specialisation of functions

Financial planners should focus as much as possible on seeing clients and advising them. This means that they must increasingly become used to working in teams with other people carrying out specialist functions. Qualified financial planners should not spend their time on administration that could usually be carried out by someone with appropriate skills who is probably less expensive to employ. Even if they cost the same or more, the firm would gain from their concentrating on their specialism.

In principle, decisions and work should be carried out by the lowest level team member who is capable and qualified to do them. However, no lower level employee should be asked to make decisions for which they do not have the knowledge, skills, experience, qualifications and confidence to ensure that there will be good outcomes.

But specialisation should not be excessive. Members of the team need to understand each other's functions, so that they can provide mutual support and also be able to stand in for one another when a team member is absent. Collaboration should be central to all functions.

The use of technology in a successful financial planning practice

Financial planners should welcome and embrace the use of information technology and any other systematisation or automation that allows them to reduce costs, improve service, enhance the client experience and increase value. Competitive and regulatory pressures are helping to drive down costs and margins and the way to do this is generally: use technology more effectively. It is very hard to see how the financial planning company of the future will survive without highly computerised back office systems, client relationship management systems, modelling and financial planning tools, wrap platforms, accounting packages and communications systems.

The use of the internet is crucial. It is also important for most planners to be able to work from anywhere, be it the office, home, the client's premises and so on. Systems and processes must therefore be available remotely. They should also be integrated, so that they are consistent and work together.

Every member of a team needs to be conversant with the use of all the systems used within the business, and at least one person needs to have an enthusiasm for technological innovation. The rate of innovation and change is accelerating. The developments of the last decade will almost certainly be exceeded by the rate of change during the next ten years.

The need for shared team aims and values

Each member of the team needs to understand the aims of the company, as well as its ethos and values. This is important for developing and maintaining service standards to clients and a culture of compliance. No operation manual or system can forecast every problem or eventuality and team members should understand the general operating principles and apply them to situations they have not previously encountered. They should share an enthusiasm for innovation and continuous improvement in what they do and how they do it. Very often the best ideas for changing practices will come from the most junior members of staff; but they are unlikely to make suggestions to improve service and process if they feel that they work in a conservative environment that does not welcome new ideas.

Collecting and using information within the firm

Financial planning firms have not traditionally been good at capturing and learning from management information. Yet knowing, for example, how long it takes to see a client and enter the data could lead to improvements in the process that would help both the client and the firm. Useful information can be gathered routinely through systems or informally in meetings and discussion. Both are valuable; but only if management review the information regularly and with the intention of understanding whether there could be improvements to processes and systems.

3 Defining the main steps, documentation and resources

The aims

From the service proposition, it should be relatively straightforward to discern the main stages of work for a client and then map the subsidiary steps. The process should then be documented and automated from beginning to end. The main aims should be that:

- The financial planner is able to access the documentation and resources from the computer system at every step to carry out the process quickly and efficiently; for example there should be a fact-find form for the data gathering stage and access to appropriate research at the recommendations stage.

- All the steps are clear and consistent and no step is left out. In principle, all financial planners in the firm should use the same documentation and tools for all of their clients. It may be possible to deviate from the set process and to innovate some aspects. But this would depend on the firm's view and it would involve additional work for the financial planner. It might be necessary, however, where a client or situation did not fit into the established pattern. New developments could then be incorporated into the system.

- All processes and documents relating to clients are stored centrally, so that they form an audit trail for compliance checks or for other purposes. File checking should be much easier with electronic files than paper files; they are generally more complete, easier to read and quicker to locate. It is simplest for these purposes if all documentation is stored electronically. That will mean scanning all documents that are otherwise only in paper form. This has the added advantage of obviating the need for most filing cabinets.

- Using technology reduces the costs of providing financial planning advice, implementing recommendations and communicating with clients. This is vital if financial planning is to remain affordable while standards are also improved.

- Management information is much easier and cheaper to collect and aggregate, in order to understand trends in performance by teams and individuals as well as client behaviour.

Defining the end to end process

The main stages of financial planning should follow six steps, although there will be a range of different minor steps that could vary according to the processes developed by the practice and the type of client. The central resources should include agendas, checklists, questionnaires, explanatory documents and paragraphs for common processes, services or products and research material. The main steps and associated processes and resources include the following:

1. **Establish and define the client and personal financial planner relationship**

   The key documentation and resources at the first stage should be a draft agenda (an agenda is desirable for all business meetings with clients), business card, disclosure document and some means of describing the firm's services and approach. This last could be a website and/or a printed brochure. Some firms use a very brief PowerPoint presentation. An appropriate disclosure document is a regulatory requirement and can also act as a powerful marketing tool. Anti-money laundering procedures will need to be carried out at this stage and will require a process for identity verification.

2. **Gather client data and determine their goals and expectations**

   The system should make available a range of fact-finding tools and other resources. Some financial planners can enter data straight onto the computer; most prefer to take notes on paper and have the information keyed in later. Firms normally have a standard general fact-find and there may also be specialist questionnaires for specific circumstances, such as a business fact-find. It is often helpful to have a letter to send clients before the fact-finding session. This should give advance notice of what the financial planner is trying to achieve and ask them to put together relevant information and documentation. The risk profiling exercise can be carried out in several ways. It might involve the use of a set process and questionnaire with a discussion of risk and the clients' aims and objectives for their investments or there might be a less prescriptive approach. Some financial planners use various tools to illustrate the possible outcomes of different types of portfolios with the aim of helping their clients understand investment risk and return more effectively. Whatever the approach, the conversation needs to be carefully recorded.

The financial planner should take care to explore clients' other aims and objectives, values and interests. This might need a prompt checklist of possible concerns. Where the client has expressed an interest in ethical investment, there is likely to be a need for an ethical and socially responsible questionnaire and further information on the subject.

The fact-finding stage is almost always a mix of questioning and discussion. Financial planners may need to have access to a diverse range of information resources on past investment returns from different asset classes, trends in interest rates and inflation, mortgage repayment tables, guides to life assurance rates, tax tables, school fees and university costs.

3. **Analyse and evaluate the client's financial status**

    Firms should provide advisers with a range of tools for the client to help with summarising and analysing stages in the planning process. These might include templates for personal balance sheets, income and expenditure statements, budgets, tax calculations for income, capital gains and estates. Firms might also provide tools such as: lifetime cashflow analysis spreadsheets, life and health protection needs analysis tools, research on the past performance of funds showing yields, growth and volatility, analysis of different with profit funds and pension transfer analysis.

4. **Develop and present the financial plan**

    The firm should provide resources to help advisers with both the formulation of the recommendations and also their presentation. Software should generate specific quotations and illustrations for every kind of solution: borrowing, protection, investment, retirement, tax and estate planning.

    There should be basic templates and standard paragraphs for client reports including suitability reports. It is important that these are carefully and specifically personalised to the needs and circumstances of the client. They are an invaluable method of ensuring that reports are clear, consistent, accurate, concise and compliant. They can save a great deal of otherwise very expensive time.

5. **Implement the financial planning recommendations**

    The use of wraps and electronic data transfer should help to reduce the costs and increase the speed and efficiency of implementing recommendations.

6. **Monitor the financial plan and the financial planning relationship**

Advisers and clients should both be able to have access to investment portfolio valuations, insurance schedules and other data. This should facilitate monitoring of financial plans. Reviews should involve revisiting all the first five steps of the financial planning process, although in many cases, the earlier work can often make the task shorter and simpler.

4 Key elements to the systems and information technology

As technology changes and adapts in the future, the key types of systems will develop – probably out of all recognition. Technology should be aimed at enhancing the service for clients and reducing its cost.

The main types of software for financial advisory firms should be integrated as a single system as far as possible. In principle, no data should ever need to be keyed in more than once and the system should be accessible from locations both inside and outside the firm's office and so should be linked to landlines and mobile phone systems.

Systems should be simple to use, user friendly, intuitive, logical and (within limits) flexible. They should be secure in every sense and provide an easy to follow audit trail. The process and clients' needs should drive the system – not the other way around. The main components are:

Communications with clients This is likely to be a customer relationship management system which should hold clients' details and allow easy mass or individual communications with clients by post, email or phone.

Client record keeping Client transactions and records should be held in the back office system. This system should be able to provide information about clients, fact-finds, their products, progress with work and transactions. The back office system should link to the document handling process, all wraps and the accounting system.

Document handling Practices should aim to keep all documents in electronic form. Some advisers like to work from paper and this can be accommodated in addition to electronic record keeping. Paper documents need to be scanned and all letters and documents need to be maintained in a form that cannot be altered once they have been finalised.

Word processing and document production A key purpose of these programmes is to maintain standard documents for advisers and clients so they can produce tailored reports and other papers for clients quickly, accurately and inexpensively.

A wrap platform The functions of a wrap platform partially overlap with those of the back office system in terms of providing clients with information and portfolio valuations. Wraps are also a means of trading and holding investments and provide valuable benefits to both clients and advisers. Wraps allow clients to see their investment valuations and other details online and also to buy and sell them typically in return for relatively low charges. For advisers, they enhance the service to clients while providing a means to charge clients for their services.

Planning tools Planning tools help advisers give better advice to their clients. They can assist with the process of clients deciding their approach to investment, calculate protection needs and project future cashflows for clients based on a range of income and expenditure assumptions.

5 Determining staff roles and team structure

Over the last decade many financial planners have moved away from personally carrying out all the various functions associated with creating and implementing a financial plan and providing specialised financial services. Financial planners are increasingly working in teams where each member has their own particular responsibilities and specialisms. The membership of the teams generally varies according to the chosen service proposition, speciality of the team and the size of the practice.

Types of team

The type of team will partly depend on the focus of the firm's services — e.g. whether the aim is primarily wealth management — and partly which services will be provided from within the team and which will be drawn from outside the team or even the firm.

If the financial planner is a generalist, the chances are that the portfolio management services will be undertaken outside the team. Even many wealth management planners are likely to be the liaison point between the clients and an in-house or out of house investment team.

Teams may take several forms. For example, they may comprise a whole firm or be a component part of a firm. A team may be headed up by just a single financial planner or there may be several, with perhaps one acting as the team leader. The financial planner whose time is mainly spent in seeing clients may be the prime technical expert; some financial advisers' skills are principally dealing with clients and the lead technician may be a para-planner or another fully fledged financial planner.

Roles within teams

The following is a common pattern for a team, but it is not intended to describe an ideal structure. The main distinction between different members of the team is the extent to which they interact with clients, giving advice and helping them make decisions. The main roles are financial planner, para-planner and administrator inside the team and senior management and other service providers outside the financial planning team such as an accountant, human resources, IT, marketing etc.

Financial planners are competent to give financial advice as a result of their qualifications, knowledge, skills and experience. In general, financial planners are likely to be more highly qualified than other team members, but it is also common for para-planners to be the most qualified people in a team and to be responsible for compiling the financial plans.

Para-planners carry out most or all the planning functions apart from advising clients. Meeting clients may well be desirable in many cases, even though they would be stepping outside their para-planning role if they were to give advice. Some para-planners have the requisite permissions to give advice but mainly carry out non-advisory functions. They may however be required to give clients information from time to time when the financial planner is not available or it is deemed appropriate for them to carry out this task. A para-planner may be involved in the more purely data-collecting aspects of the fact-finding function in some firms.

Para-planners who do not directly give advice do not strictly speaking need to be qualified, but they do need a high level of expertise if they are to carry out the para-planning job properly. On this basis, there is a very strong case for ensuring that para-planners at least have the minimum adviser qualifications and may well need to be more highly trained especially if they have a specialist function.

Administrators have a lower degree of contact with clients apart from such administrative roles as arranging meetings and taking messages. Administrative staff may be working towards taking on a para-planning role and so may have some technical expertise. But the skills and knowledge they employ would be primarily concerned with such tasks as producing valuations, collating the information for reports, sending reports and other documentation to clients, accounting and the production of management information, arranging meetings and preparing routine documentation for them. Their skills are likely to be secretarial, administrative and IT.

Senior management and the board of directors There are other types of staff who may not be advisers but nevertheless have a strategic role in the firm. These could be the finance director, the operations and IT systems manager or director, the compliance manager or director, and the sales and marketing director. In some cases there may also be a non-advising managing director or chief executive, although this tends to be confined to the largest firms. In many cases these functions are carried out by people who are also financial advisers. These people have overall responsibility for the direction and management of the firm and hold control functions under the Financial Services Authority (FSA) regulatory regime.

Other functions There are many other functions that might be taken on by members of the financial planning team or elsewhere if the organisation is relatively large. These are services that are important to the efficient functioning of the financial planning role, but are not directly part of it. They include: accounting, IT, human resources, office management, premises management, marketing and public relations.

Job descriptions

It is important that each member of staff should have a job description:

- Each individual and the people who work with them should be aware of their responsibilities and the boundaries of the areas of activity for which they are accountable.

- Job descriptions are essential for designing a coherent structure where all the needs are covered by appropriate levels of skills and competence without leaving any significant gaps.

- The absence of a job description for a particular employee would make assessing their performance and determining an appropriate reward structure very difficult.

- Job descriptions are essential when recruiting new staff or deciding whether to promote a person to a higher level within the team.

6 The role of management information

Management information (MI) is essential to assess individual effectiveness, team performance and important trends that affect the business. The process system should be set up to provide relevant MI to the senior management within the firm and the financial planners to which the information applies.

MI principles

MI is essential for a firm to be able to know how the business is progressing and make decisions about change. The FSA places considerable emphasis on the quality of MI. In general MI should be:

Relevant The MI provided by the system should be relevant to the firm and the individual financial planners. It can be all too easy to generate masses of data that is confusing and not focused on the key issues.

Accurate To make the right decisions, it is important to have the right information.

Timely The MI should be available at the right time and covering the right periods. Information that is out of date is useless.

Acted upon The way the MI is presented should identify the key triggers for action which then needs to be taken.

Recorded Both the information and the subsequent action should be recorded to prove how they have been successful in making improvements and delivering the right outcomes for clients.

FSA's examples of good MI practice

Firm A ensured that the compliance report produced by its consultant was discussed by the firm's board of directors and that any remedial actions were prioritised and followed up at subsequent board meetings. The office manager monitored the action points and made regular reports back to the board on how issues were being dealt with. Where the advisers had to take any specific corrective action, the administrators logged the required remedial action on the firm's back office system and monitored the advisers' progress. The firm's compliance officer would then sign off the advisers' completed remedial action and use that information in determining each adviser's level of future monitoring.

Firm B produced and used detailed key performance indicators (KPIs) as part of its monitoring. This included the spread of products and providers, number of complaints, and the proportion of lapsed, cancelled and replacement business, which helped in focusing on particular areas and/or advisers that needed closer monitoring. The firm also circulated regular bulletins and compliance updates. Specific remedial actions were sent to advisers, who would have monthly meetings with the compliance officer to discuss their progress against the KPIs and agree any specific remedial action and training needs.

Firm C operated a tailored monitoring process in line with its training and competence scheme and used appropriate MI to ensure that its monitoring remained tailored. The junior consultant at the firm was subject to much closer monitoring than the senior consultant. The firm determined the level of monitoring required by risk-rating the advisers according to the types of business they had written and the results of the regular reviews of their customer files. If an adviser did not write a particular line of business in one year, their authorisation to advise on such business would be withdrawn.

FSA's examples of poor practice

Firm D undertook regular reviews of customer files to assess the quality of advice; it also identified and recorded the problems on its file monitoring review sheets. However, the firm did not consider what remedial action would be necessary. The firm did not feed its findings from the review of client files into its MI. As a result, the firm could not identify any trends and prevent the issues from recurring in the future. Furthermore, the firm did not consider widening its review to ensure that the various problems that it had identified were not common across the business.

Firm E produced KPIs but did not analyse them or seek to identify the root causes where a KPI was not being met. The firm could not demonstrate how that information was being used as part of its monitoring or that its monitoring was effective.

Firm F conducted reviews of customer files but these focused more on completeness checks, rather than the quality and suitability of the advice that had been given. The firm was unable to ensure that their advisers had recommended the most appropriate products and providers to clients. Furthermore, the firm had no way of identifying any learning and development needs for its advisers to ensure they remained competent in the areas of business on which they advised.

7 Appropriate KPIs

The firm may wish to set a number of KPIs for advisers and adviser teams. These could be compared to previous periods, agreed budgets or target levels and the achievements of other advisers and teams where this is relevant. These might by grouped in different areas and assuming that adviser charging has been introduced, including:

Income

- Level of monthly income and profit for each team/adviser;
- Average income and profit per client;
- Split of different types of income according to initial fee and ongoing fees/charges, funds under advice charges;
- Fees by type of business (e.g. financial planning, investment, pension, protection);
- Other income associated with providers – by provider;
- Funds under advice: total and increase or reduction;
- Debtors: money due via providers and direct from clients.

Expenditure

- Adviser income: broken down as appropriate by regular income/salary and variable income/bonus;
- Other team salaries;
- Other overheads;
- Other variable costs e.g. special marketing initiatives.

Service standards

- Active clients by category;
- New clients by category;
- Clients lost by category;
- Clients reviewed;
- New insurance policies arranged;
- Interval between client meeting and production of financial plan;
- Interval between agreement of plan and implementation by main type of product.

Compliance and advice standards

- Number of complaints;
- File review assessments including quality of advice and suitability, quality of research and documentation;
- Development and CPD achieved by adviser and team.

8 Other aspects of team working

There are many aspects of working in teams that firms need to consider with care. Briefly these include:

Leadership Financial advisers may not have developed leadership and management qualities. In some cases, they may not be the most suitable team leaders and firms should consider whether another member of a team should take on this role in some circumstances. Whoever takes on the team leader function will need training and support.

Job descriptions It is essential to review and revise job descriptions as functions change over time. Products and services evolve and need different skills, procedures and practices. Members of the team will develop and take on new responsibilities, especially as work is passed down and is undertaken by the most junior person in the team who is competent to take it on (see principles above). Job descriptions are essential for helping team members know their responsibilities and in assessing how well they are doing their jobs.

Regular assessments Each member of the team needs to be assessed regularly to provide feedback on how well they are carrying out their duties and where they need further development. These need to be formally organised and documented. Training needs should be identified and plans made.

Career development Most people like to see the possibility for future development in their role and function. Administrators may have ambitions to become para-planners, who may in turn wish to become advisers. Advisers may wish to take on managerial responsibilities instead of (or in addition to) their financial planning role. But in small firms this type of advancement may not be possible and many employees may well be happy to continue in the existing role as long as they are able to develop within it — perhaps by becoming better qualified and generally more competent or more specialised.

Recruitment Taking on new team members may be necessary to replace leavers or to permit expansion and specialisation. The job description for the post should be the core document from which the person specification should be derived — setting out the qualities, skills and qualifications that it is either essential (or merely desirable) for an individual to have to fulfil the role.

9 Agreeing reward structures and incentives

Teams and team members should be rewarded on the basis of the key criteria that the firm uses to judge their performance individually and as a team. Financial planning practices are businesses and commercial criteria are important and reflect the company's sustainability and capital value. Income and profitability will be the main criterion for judging performance by financial planners and their teams. Nevertheless, it is essential that team members should not be rewarded in such a way that they are incentivised to treat clients unfairly, or to be biased towards selling particular types of products or the products of a particular provider or to be non-compliant with the conduct of business rules.

In some practices, teams are essentially small businesses and the only basis for reward is the level of income earned after taking into account costs. Other firms reward financial planners and their teams on a wider variety of performance indicators. Typically team members are paid a basic salary, which is topped up on a regular basis depending on profits and adherence to various other KPIs.

The other KPIs may include: an amount reflecting their particular contribution (e.g. bringing in more business), compliance standards achieved, services standards met, the profitability of the company as a whole.

Chapter 9
Regulatory requirements and financial planning

Regulated firms and financial planners must understand the Financial Services Authority's (FSA's) requirements and views about financial advice issues. The following is a brief guide to some of the main areas where regulatory requirements have a significant impact on firms and the advice of financial planners and the ways in which they operate in relation to clients. The sources for the information about regulatory requirements are to be found on the FSA's website (www.fsa.gov.uk) and include: the FSA's Conduct of Business Sourcebook (COBS), FSA Fact Sheets, FSA One Minute Guides and other FSA documents.

1 The FSA's statutory aims

The FSA's regulation of firms and individuals is intended to fulfil the four statutory aims that are set out in the Financial Services and Markets Act (FSMA). These are:

1. **Market confidence** maintaining confidence in the financial system.

2. **Public awareness** promoting public understanding of the financial system.

3. **Consumer protection** securing the appropriate degree of protection for consumers.

4. **Reduction of financial crime** reducing the extent to which it is possible for a business to be used for a purpose connected with financial crime.

2 The FSA principles for firms

The principles for regulation set out the high level standards firms should apply. Parallel and similar principles apply to Approved Persons such as financial advisers and senior managers of authorised firms.

1. **Integrity** A firm must conduct its business with integrity.

2. **Skill, care and diligence** A firm must conduct its business with due skill, care and diligence.

3. **Management and control** A firm must take reasonable care to organise and control its affairs responsibly and effectively with adequate risk management systems.

4. **Financial prudence** A firm must maintain adequate financial resources.

5. **Market conduct** A firm must observe proper standards of market conduct.

6. **Customers' interests** A firm must pay due regard to the interests of its customers and treat them fairly.

7. **Communications with clients** A firm must pay due regard to the information needs of its clients, and communicate information to them in a way which is clear, fair and not misleading.

8. **Conflicts of interest** A firm must manage conflicts of interest fairly, both between itself and its customers and between a customer and another client.

9. **Customers – relationships of trust** A firm must take reasonable care to ensure the suitability of its advice and decisions for any customer who is entitled to rely upon its judgment.

10. **Clients' assets** A firm must arrange adequate protection for clients' assets when it is responsible for them.

11. **Relations with regulators** A firm must deal with its regulators in an open and cooperative way, and must disclose to the FSA appropriately anything relating to the firm of which the FSA would reasonably expect notice.

3 Current main types of advisers

A financial planner who advises on specific financial products can be one of several basic types, and retail clients must be informed on a timely basis which type of advice they are being offered. The main categories are:

Single-tied agent

A single-tied agent of one product provider can only advise on the products of the provider to which they are tied. If a tied agent does not have a product that meets a client's needs, they may introduce the client to an independent financial adviser.

Multi-tied agent

A multi-tied agent of a limited range of product providers can only advise on the products of the range of providers to which they are tied.

Whole of market adviser

Whole of market advisers have access to the whole market (or a whole segment of it). They must analyse the market on a regular basis to ensure that they are continuing to offer suitable advice. Whole of market advisers must hold professional indemnity insurance. Whole of market sole traders must arrange for a locum in the form of another regulated firm or individual to deal with clients while they are away from their business.

Independent financial adviser (IFAs)

An IFA is a whole of market adviser who qualifies as 'independent' by offering their clients the option to pay by fee rather than commission.

There is an important legal distinction between a representative of a product provider and an IFA.

- The representative is the agent of the provider who is responsible for their acts and omissions.

- An IFA is the agent of the client and the IFA firm (or the network that authorises the firm) is responsible for its acts and omissions.

4 Threshold Conditions

Regulated firms must satisfy certain conditions at all times. These threshold conditions for operating and being regulated in the UK by the FSA can be summarised as follows:

Legal status

A regulated firm can be a sole trader, company, partnership or unincorporated association.

Location of offices

Depending on the entity and type of business, the registered office or head office of a regulated firm must be in the UK.

Close links

If the firm has any close links with other firms or individuals, these must not prevent the FSA from being able to supervise it effectively.

Adequate resources

The FSA must be satisfied that a firm's resources with respect to its finance, management, staff, systems and controls are adequate in terms of both their quality and quantity.

Suitability

The FSA must be satisfied that the firm is 'fit and proper' to be authorised, taking into account the management's competence and ability, and also their commitment to carrying on business with integrity and in compliance with the regulator.

5 Services and cost disclosure documents (SCDD)

Firms are required to provide information to their clients about their status, the nature of their advice and how they are paid in services and cost disclosure documents (SCDD). There is a set of rules covering these issues that applies until 31 December 2012, although it will need amending after the implementation of the Retail Distribution Review (see below).

Firms can develop their own documents by following the FSA's rule book or they can use the template documents. Whatever approach they use, they must communicate with their clients in a way that is clear, fair and not misleading. In its notes on firms' disclosure documentation, the FSA provides a number of examples of possible wordings that firms can use.

The SCDD must be given to clients on a timely basis, must be in writing and must cover a number of main areas about the services of the firm and their costs including:

Whose products the firm offers to the client

The firm might be tied, multi-tied or whole of market.

Which service the firm will provide

The main types of service a firm can provide to clients are as follows:

- The firm could provide advice and recommendations after assessing the client's needs; or

- The firm could ask the client questions to narrow down the selection of products on which it will provide details and leave the choice of how to proceed to the client; or

- The firm could offer basic advice on a range of stakeholder products (which are relatively simple and subject to maximum levels of charges and commission payments).

What the client will have to pay for the services

Firms need to set out all the payment options for clients and explain them clearly in the SCDD. The main payment options are fee, commission or a combination of fee and commission.

Fees: Independent firms must offer clients a fee alternative to commission or just charge fees. There are no prescribed wordings for descriptions of fee charging for SCDDs but firms should use clear and plain language. If the client will be required to pay a fee, the firm should explain when the fees are payable, the circumstances in which they are payable and the arrangements for any commission paid in addition to fees.

Firms should set out the basis for the fees and the amount or rates of its fees in numerical terms. For example, they could be hourly rates for different members of staff or they could be linked to the value of the client's investments. The firm should explain whether or not the fees charged are contingent on the sale of a product.

Firms should provide this information to clients and gain their agreement before undertaking chargeable work. There should be an offer to tell the client that the firm will not exceed a given amount of chargeable fees without first checking with the client. Firms should undertake to tell clients if the fees include VAT.

Commission: The text for describing a firm's commission payments in the SCDD is not prescribed, but it should also be in clear and plain language. The firm should explain that although the client does not pay any charge up front when the firm is paid a commission that does not mean that the firm's services are free, because the client still pays for the adviser indirectly through the product charges. The client should also be told that the product charges may be lower if they buy direct from the provider.

The firm must provide details in the SCDD of the typical commission that it might receive and give examples that reflect its pattern of business. Later a firm will additionally have to disclose the actual amount of commission on a product sale before the completion of the sale, and the disclosure document should state this. Firms should also state whether the commission includes payment for ongoing services such as reviews.

Combination of fees and commission: The basis needs to be set out by the firm in addition to the information on fees and commission above.

Non-monetary benefits: Firms can include in the SCDD a brief statement of these benefits from providers if they apply and offer to provide details on request.

Who regulates the firm

This section of the SCDD should normally provide details of the firm's name and address and the fact that it is regulated by the FSA, together with its FSA regulated number. If the firm is an appointed representative, it should provide details. It should state briefly and in plain language the business for which it has regulatory permission.

Loans and ownership

Where this section of the SCDD applies, it should set out a short description of any holding of more than 10% in the capital or voting power of the firm that is held by a product provider or packaged product operator. It should also disclose any credit that has been extended to the firm by such a provider.

Complaints

The document should give the contact details of the person to whom client should make any complaints and the fact that the client can refer to the Financial Ombudsman Service any complaint that cannot be settled.

The Financial Services Compensation Scheme

The SCDD should state that it is covered by the FSCS if the firm cannot meet its obligations. This depends on the type of business and the circumstances of the claim.

6 Types of clients

There are different types of clients who are accorded different levels of regulatory protection. Firms must take reasonable steps to establish whether a client is:

- A retail client;
- A professional client;
- An eligible counterparty.

The firm's disclosure and the protection requirements are much higher for retail clients than for professional clients or eligible counterparties.

Retail clients

A retail client is anyone who is not a professional client or an eligible counterparty.

Professional clients

Some professional clients are automatically classified as professional clients. These include local or public authorities, companies or other undertakings of sufficient size (based on such criteria as number of staff and level of turnover), national governments, central banks, various other state or supranational bodies and other authorised firms.

Some clients can be treated a professional clients if they wish. They must choose to be treated in this way and to understand the implications of making this choice (see also 'Unregulated collective investment schemes' (UCIS) page 144). The firm also needs to assess the client:

- The firm must conduct a qualitative assessment of the client's expertise, experience and knowledge to ensure that they are capable of making their own investment decisions and of understanding the risks involved.
- If the firm is subject to 'Markets in Financial Instruments Directive (MIFID)' (page 139), it may also need to undertake a quantitative analysis of the

client, assessing their previous investment transaction history, previous employment history and the value of their investment assets.

Eligible counterparties

Some eligible counterparties automatically include governments of countries, central banks of countries, various other state or supranational bodies, FSA authorised firms and other financial institutions authorised by an European Economic Area (EEA) state. Financial advisers are unlikely to classify any clients as eligible counterparties because the services they provide are unlikely to include eligible counterparty business.

7 Know your customer rules

The FSA's conduct of business sourcebook (COBS) requires advisers to find out and record in writing enough relevant information about a private client before giving a personal recommendation about a designated investment. In addition to basic information about the client, the FSA recommends that the key areas for advisers to consider should include:

- A detailed breakdown of the client's income and expenditure as well as assets and liabilities.

- Information about the client's existing savings, investments, pensions and life assurance arrangements.

- The terms of any wills and details of expected inheritances.

- Details of the client's occupation status and future prospects.

- Details of the client's health.

Clients' wishes and goals

Advisers should take care to find out their clients' goals and aspirations and make sure that their recommendations are clearly derived from this information. Advisers should aim to discover:

- The client's previous investment experience and knowledge, particularly the purpose and expectations that they had for their investments.

- Their planning objectives; these could include important future dates such as their retirement date, child's wedding, their silver wedding anniversary and the people whom they would like to benefit from their investments

- The client's priorities where they have several goals or needs.

- The amount of cash that the client likes to hold at all times.

- The extent to which an investment may fluctuate in value before the client begins to feel uncomfortable.

It is also important for the adviser to discover any beliefs, circumstances or fears and barriers to planning that might affect their clients. This should help establish their priorities and ensure that they are being treated fairly.

8 Suitability rule and suitability reports

Firms must not make personal recommendations to retail clients or carry out discretionary transactions for them, unless they are suitable on the basis of the needs and circumstances established in the fact-find with the client.

When a suitability report is needed

A retail client must be provided with a suitability report if the client is being recommended to:

- Buy, sell, surrender, convert, cancel or suspend premiums or contributions with respect to a life policy or pension contract;
- Make income withdrawals from a pension contract;
- Buy or sell a holding in a regulated collective investment scheme, an investment trust savings scheme or shares in an investment trust ISA;
- Undertake a pension transfer or opt-out from an occupational pension scheme.

Suitability reports are not required for increases to regular premium contracts or for single premium top-ups of single premium contracts.

Contents of the suitability report

The suitability report must at least:

- Specify the client's demands and needs;
- Explain why the recommended transaction is suitable for the client on the basis of the information provided by the client;
- Explain any possible disadvantages of the transaction for the client;
- Summarise the main consequences of the transaction and give the client appropriate details depending on its complexity;
- Explain why a recommended personal pension or free-standing additional voluntary contribution (FSAVC) is considered to be at least as suitable as a stakeholder pension;
- Explain why a recommended FSAVC (or personal/stakeholder pension) is at least as suitable as an AVC;
- In the case of income withdrawals and short-term annuities, the relevant risk facts should be included.

Suitability reports should be clear, fair and not misleading. They should avoid using technical terms that the client might not understand unless they are fully explained in the report.

Timing of the provision of the suitability report

The suitability report must be provided to the client:

- In the case of a life policy, before the contract is concluded, unless the adviser provides the necessary information orally or the client requires immediate cover;

- In the case of a personal pension scheme or stakeholder pension scheme (where the FSA's rules on cancellation require notification of the right to cancel), no later than the 14th day after the contract is concluded;

- In any other case, when the transaction is effected or as soon after it as possible. If the firm produces the suitability report before the transaction, it will have to be changed and reissued if there is any difference between the recommendations and the actual transactions.

9 Treating Customers Fairly (TCF)

Firms must be able to demonstrate that they consistently deliver fair outcomes to their clients and that their senior management takes responsibility for establishing and maintaining an appropriate culture. The FSA states that the TCF initiative should produce a number of outcomes from financial planning firms and others in the retail financial services sector:

Outcome 1: Consumers can be confident that they are dealing with firms where the fair treatment of customers is central to the corporate culture.

Outcome 2: Products and services marketed and sold in the retail market are designed to meet the needs of identified consumer groups and are targeted accordingly.

Outcome 3: Consumers are provided with clear information and are kept appropriately informed before, during and after the point of sale.

Outcome 4: Where consumers receive advice, the advice is suitable and takes account of their circumstances.

Outcome 5: Consumers are provided with products that perform as firms have led them to expect, and the associated service is of an acceptable standard and as they have been led to expect.

Outcome 6: Consumers do not face unreasonable post-sale barriers imposed by firms to change product, switch provider, submit a claim or make a complaint.

10 Complaints and complaints handling

The FSA defines a complaint as any oral or written expression of dissatisfaction — whether it is justified or not — about any financial services activity provided by a firm (or withheld by it), where the complainant has suffered financial loss (or may do in the future), material distress or material inconvenience.

The regulator expects firms to deal properly with any complaint made by a consumer, whatever the subject of the complaint. Firms need effective and transparent written procedures for dealing with complaints reasonably and promptly. When a consumer makes a complaint, the firm must:

First investigate the complaint.

Then assess fairly and promptly what the complaint is about; whether it should be upheld; and what action/redress should be taken.

Then fairly and promptly provide a clear assessment of the complaint and an offer of redress or remedial action, if that is appropriate. Any offer that is made should be settled promptly.

When a firm receives a complaint, the complainant must be sent a prompt written acknowledgement that they have received the complaint and are dealing with it. After that, the firm must keep the complainant up-to-date with progress in resolving their complaint.

The firm must send a final response to a complainant within eight weeks of receiving the complaint. If it is not possible to provide a final response at this stage, the firm must write to the complainant explaining why and when it will be possible to provide a response. The firm must also tell the complainant of their right to refer the complaint to the financial ombudsman service and provide details of this service.

Proposed changes to the complaint handling rules

The FSA proposes to change the complaint handling rules in several ways including:

- Abolishing the two-stage complaints handling process, so that a consumer will be able to go to the ombudsman service after receiving the firm's first response, rather than having to go back to them later if they remain dissatisfied;

- Requiring firms to nominate a senior individual responsible for complaints handling;

- Underlining the requirement for firms to carry out root cause analysis, by identifying and remedying any recurrent or systemic problems with complaints, and to take action where appropriate;

- Providing additional guidance about taking account of the ombudsman service's decisions and previous customer complaints, and learning from the outcomes;

- Increasing the limit on the amount the FOS can award consumers from £100,000 to £150,000.

11 The Retail Distribution Review (RDR)

The stated purpose of the RDR proposals is to give consumers confidence and trust in the retail investment market. Under the proposals, the FSA requires financial planners and their firms to introduce 'adviser charging' as well as to hold a new higher minimum level of qualifications. The FSA announced the review in June 2006 and has published a series of consultative documents and proposals since then. The main aims of the RDR are to:

- Improve the clarity with which firms describe their services to consumers;

- Reduce the potential for adviser remuneration to distort consumer outcomes;

- Increase the professional standards of investment advisers.

The main types of advice and services post-RDR

Within the RDR the FSA also aims to redefine the various types of advice and services provided to clients. Firms will have to make clear to their clients which of these services they are offering before providing any advice. Firms' services and cost disclosure documents (SCDD) should be clear on the type of advice that they are giving. Restricted advisers will also be required to disclose orally the fact that they provide restricted advice and the nature of that restriction.

Independent advice This includes a new definition of independence, where firms provide recommendations that consider all products and providers that could meet a client's needs.

The new definition is that independent advice must be unbiased and unrestricted, and based on a comprehensive and fair analysis of the relevant market. Genuinely independent advisory firms should be free from any restrictions that could impact on their ability to recommend whatever is best for their clients. IFAs will need to include in their review of the market, not just life products and collective investment schemes (CISs), but also products such as exchange-traded funds (ETFs), structured investment products and investment trusts.

Independent financial advisers will need to demonstrate how they have reviewed the market and selected products in line with the client's risk profile and suitability. The FSA has said that they do not expect advisers to review the market for products that do not meet a client's needs and objectives. IFAs will still be able to use panels to help review the market.

Restricted advice Restricted advisers will include most banks' in-house advisers, advisers who use a limited number of providers and those who advise on a limited product range. This includes 'simplified advice' and 'basic advice' (see below). Any advice that is not independent will have to be labelled as 'restricted'.

'Execution-only' services Non-advised product sales may also be provided and the definition will not change from the current position.

Simplified advice (sometimes referred to as 'guided sales') will be provided through streamlined advice processes, giving clients suitable personal recommendations based on an assessment of their needs, as in the FSA's existing rules. This is likely to be a shorter process than full advice, may involve a decision-tree, and may be limited to a more simple set of products. In contrast, full advice covers the full range of a client's needs on an in-depth basis and a suitable personal recommendation.

Basic advice is essentially simplified advice that is confined to the sale of stakeholder products. It will continue to be possible to sell these products through basic advice on a commission basis. The FSA's view is that the potential for commissions to influence advice is much more limited with basic advice because stakeholder products are sold within the constraints of a price cap.

Adviser charging

The FSA has called the new methods of paying firms for advice 'adviser charging' and they will be introduced with effect from 1 January 2013. Firms need to develop appropriate charging structures that meet the RDR requirements. The FSA is strongly recommending that firms should start focusing on their level of service and the outcome for the client rather than the type of products they sell.

- The FSA will not prescribe the type of adviser charging a firm could use; it could include hourly rates, a percentage of the client's investment and it could be taken as a deduction from investments or paid directly by the client.

- Firms must disclose their charging structure to clients upfront and in writing, so that clients have the information before the start of the advice and planning process. Firms also have to agree the total charges the client will incur which they will need to disclose as soon as they know what they are.

- From 1 January 2013, firms will only be able to receive an ongoing charge where they are providing an ongoing service, for example, regularly reviewing the performance of a client's investments. Where there is an ongoing charge for an ongoing service, the firm must confirm the details of the service, its associated charges and how the client can cancel it.

- An exception to this rule is where a client is buying a regular contribution product. In these circumstances, the firm may choose to offer a charging arrangement where the client can pay over time, without having to provide an ongoing service. This approach should help to retain access to advice for customers who may not have the funds to pay for advice upfront. However, the cost of that advice and how it is to be paid will need to be agreed at the outset between the firm and the investor.

- From the same date, product providers will no longer be able to offer commission on their products, and advisory firms will no longer be able to receive commission set by product providers.

- Clients will still be able to have their adviser charges deducted from their investments if they wish, but these charges will no longer be determined by the product providers. This will just be a mechanism for making a payment rather than setting the amount.

- Factoring (or the payment of indemnity commission) will not be allowed after 2012 under the new rules. Product providers will be able to pay adviser charges from a customer's investments to an adviser firm to settle adviser charges, but this will be on a matched basis. Product providers will therefore not be able to advance payments to the adviser firm before they deduct them from the client's investment. Clients should be able to see and understand the flow of money.

After compulsory adviser charging is introduced in January 2013, the FSA will check that firms have adapted to meet the RDR requirements. This will include supervising how firms set and operate their charges; checking for key risks, for example, whether the adviser charges set by a firm are fair and not excessive; whether there is evidence of product and provider bias and whether they can discern any trends in product churning.

The transition to adviser charging

The new RDR rules will not be applied retrospectively. For business written before the end of 2012, adviser firms will be able to continue to receive the ongoing remuneration associated with the product or with any increase in contributions that a client may subsequently choose to make.

- Where there is a change to the product after the end of 2012 a firm's approach should be based on assessing whether the product is essentially unchanged. If the product has just been amended or extended under options that have been available to the client from inception, the commission can continue to be paid.

- However, if the change is such that the product becomes a different one or needs a new contract with the client, the new adviser charging rules will apply.

- There are also special rules that apply where a new adviser takes over the contract for the product.

- Firms should not generally renegotiate commissions payable on products or try to impose an adviser charge for services that have already been paid for through commission.

- Firms can move towards introducing adviser charging in the period before the full implementation of the new rules; the FSA has not made any specific transitional rules. However, adviser charging should only be applied to new business, and not to existing business for which the firm receives commission or has already received it.

The FSA's inducements rules already restrict provider firms from offering monetary or other incentives that can cause conflicts with their duties to clients. Under adviser charging, any payments and benefits paid between firms must be designed to enhance the quality of the service to the client. Any significant non-monetary benefits that product providers offer to adviser firms (such as access to training programmes) should be widely available across adviser firms if they are to be provided at all. They should not be used to reward particular firms.

12 Wraps and platforms

Platforms are online services that are used by financial planners and sometimes investors directly. Their purpose is to be able to view and administer the investor's portfolios online. Platforms provide facilities for buying and selling investments and are typically used to aggregate and arrange custody for clients' assets.

There are several kinds of platforms. Generally, those described as 'fund supermarkets' offer access to a wide variety of unit trusts and open ended investment companies (OEICS). Platforms described as 'wraps' generally offer access to a greater variety of products and usually support advisers who want to agree their own remuneration with clients instead of receiving commission.

In the FSA's view, using a platform can improve a firm's administration. However, firms need ensure that any increases in complexity or cost resulting from adopting a wrap are justified by sufficiently valuable services. The platform a firm uses may not be suitable for all its customers. This differentiation may lead to the segmentation of customers, but it may be necessary to ensure all groups are monitored properly.

Using a single platform may affect a firm's independence, according to the FSA. A firm may, for example, decide to use more than one platform to ensure it reflects the range of choices available in the market as a whole.

13 Markets in Financial Instruments Directive (MIFID)

The European Commission's directive MiFID came into force on 1 November 2007, replacing the Investment Services Directive (ISD). MiFID widens the range of core investment services and activities that firms can passport so that they can advise clients throughout Europe. It is part of a plan to create a single market in financial services across the European Union by:

- Setting common standards of business practice by making cross-border business easier;
- Drawing a clearer line between the responsibilities of home and host states;
- Clarifying who has jurisdiction over conduct of business.

Most firms that fall within the scope of MiFID also have to comply with the Capital Requirements Directive (CRD) which sets requirements for the regulatory capital a firm must hold. MiFID covers investment banks, portfolio managers; stockbrokers and broker dealers, corporate finance firms, many futures and options firms, some commodities firms.

MIFID also affects those small financial advisory firms that hold client assets, although other firms may be affected if they wish to conduct business in other parts of Europe. The directive affects the way a firm's permissions, passporting and approved persons are recorded in the FSA's Register. MIFID affects:

- Client categorisation;
- Communications and financial promotions;
- Client agreements;
- Initial disclosure document and menu;
- Suitability;
- Preparing and providing product information;
- Training and competence;
- Complaints.

MiFID and adviser passporting

Under MiFID investment advice must be regulated in all European Economic Area (EEA) States. The UK secured an 'opt-out' from MiFID for financial advisers under which UK financial advisers are not automatically subject to MiFID obligations.

However, where a UK financial firm is advising clients located in another EEA state, the firm must ensure it satisfies that state's legal requirements. The MiFID rules are relevant even for firms that do not have an office in another EEA State. For example, if a UK client moves to another European country, permanently or temporarily, and the UK firm continues to advise them while they live there.

The firm can satisfy the local state's legal requirements by opting into MiFID and obtaining a passport for their services. This will prevent the firm needing authorisation in other EEA member states for those matters covered by the passport. Firms are responsible for determining the regulatory requirements applicable to their business and ensuring they comply with them. A UK firm that wishes to exercise passporting rights must notify the FSA.

Different passports may be needed to give advice on different products, even if the same client is being advised on a range of products or if only a small number of clients are being advised. One or more of the following passports may be required:

- The Markets in Financial Instruments Directive (MiFID) passport to be able to give advice on investments to clients based in another EEA state. MiFID does not include all investment products. Those that come under MiFID include shares and collective investment schemes, but life policies fall under the scope of the Insurance Mediation Directive (IMD).

- The IMD passport — to be able to give advice on insurance-based products to clients based in another EEA state. The IMD covers introducing, proposing or carrying out other work preparatory to the conclusion of contracts of insurance; concluding contracts of insurance; and assisting in the administration and performance of contracts of insurance, especially if there is a claim.

- A domestic authorisation in the EEA state in question for business that falls outside the remit of any passport.

Whether or not a passport is required to advise clients in other EEA States is primarily a matter of the law in the relevant EEA state.

Impact of MiFID on the resources needed by firms

If a firm opts into MiFID in order to give investment advice to clients in another EEA State, it will almost certainly become an 'exempt CAD firm', assuming in particular that it does not hold client money or client assets in relation to its MiFID business. There are special prudential requirements for a personal investment firm that is an exempt CAD firm (exempt from the Capital Adequacy Directive).

- An exempt CAD firm that is not subject to the IMD must have initial capital of €50,000 or professional indemnity insurance (PII) with a minimum level of indemnity of at least €1m for any claim and €1.5m in aggregate. A firm can opt for an initial capital/PII trade off if the combination gives a coverage equivalent to either of the requirements separately.

- If an exempt CAD firm is subject to the IMD, broadly it must meet at least the IMD's PII requirement and have additional resources of initial capital of €25,000 and PII of €500,000 for any one claim and €750,000 in aggregate; or it must have a combination of initial capital and PII resulting in an equivalent level of coverage to these options.

- Under all these options, a firm must have initial capital of at least £10,000 and must also meet an ongoing own funds requirement which is equal to the requirement for initial capital. The level of PII may also need to be higher, depending upon the firm's relevant income.

MiFID and conduct of business rules

There are some differences in the conduct of business rules for business that falls within MiFID. For example:

- The MiFID 'appropriateness' regime requires the financial adviser to evaluate the client's knowledge and experience for many non-advised sales.

- The inducements regime requires more disclosure under MiFID. Any inducements (such as free training) should be designed to enhance the provision of the service to the client.

- There are differences in how the exemptions from various requirements operate under the regime for communications with clients e.g. UCISs (see page 144).

- MiFID firms have to keep their records for five years, while non-MiFID firms only have to keep most records for a minimum of three years.

- When dealing with professional clients, there are wider requirements for suitability, prior information and reporting requirements. The thresholds for classifying a client as professional are generally higher.

The geographical scope of MiFID

Apart from the UK, there are 29 EEA States with passporting rights: Austria, Belgium, Bulgaria, Republic of Cyprus (South Cyprus only), Czech Republic,

Denmark, Estonia, Finland, France, Germany, Greece, Hungary, Iceland, Ireland, Italy, Latvia, Liechtenstein, Lithuania, Luxembourg, Malta, Netherlands, Norway, Poland, Portugal, Romania, Slovakia, Slovenia, Spain and Sweden.

Gibraltar and the UK have agreed special arrangements and the IMD and MiFID apply to them in full.

Channel Islands & Isle of Man The IMD and MiFID do not apply in these islands. Firms based in these territories are treated in the same way as firms based in a non-EEA State and do not have passporting rights. Equally, UK firms do not have passporting rights for the Channel Islands and the Isle of Man. UK firms that wish to conduct business there have to apply for permission direct to the relevant financial regulators in each territory.

14 Pensions switching

Where a person is advised to move from one pension scheme to another, this is known as 'pension switching'. In contrast, 'pension transfers' refer to moving deferred benefits (see section 15). The FSA has been concerned about a number of areas of unsuitable advice and require firms to consider their practices and where necessary review individual files and provide redress. In the view of the FSA, advice may not be suitable where:

- The switch involves extra product costs without good reason;

- The fund recommendations do not suit the client's attitude to risk;

- The need for necessary ongoing reviews is not explained and the reviews are not set up;

- The switch involves a loss of benefits from the ceding scheme without good reason;

- Firms operate tied advice models that prevent their advisers considering a client's existing pension arrangements when giving pension switching advice,

- Portfolio advice services are recommended with insufficient justification that the additional costs will genuinely add value for clients.

15 Pension transfers

Pension transfers are defined by the FSA as essentially moves of an individual retail client's deferred benefits between pension schemes. In this context, a person's pension benefits no longer continue to accrue and the client is not yet taking the benefits — even if they could do so.

The FSA has established a number of specific requirements covering advice on pension transfers and has stated that it is "difficult to envisage consumers seeking to undertake transfers on an execution only basis". These requirements include the following:

- Firms that wish to provide advice on pension transfers (and opt-outs) must obtain specific permission to carry out this regulated activity;

- Individuals who give advice on pension transfers must either have a specific permission themselves – controlled function 30 – or any transaction on which they advise must be checked by an adviser who has this permission.

- An individual must have passed one of the specified appropriate examinations in order to be treated as competent to advise on pension transfers or to check other advisers' transactions. The list of these exams is available from the Financial Services Skills Council (FSSC).

- Where a pension transfer is from a defined benefits (DB) scheme, the benefits likely to be paid under this scheme must be compared with the benefits from the personal pension or stakeholder pension before making any recommendation to a customer to transfer out. The comparison must be carried out in accordance with special rules set out in the FSA's COBS.

Pension sharing

Under a pension sharing order in a divorce settlement, the receiving spouse 'transfers' the shared benefits, and this transaction may come under the pension transfer definition in some circumstances.

- Where the rules of the pension scheme from which the benefits are coming do not allow the receiving spouse to be a member of the scheme, there is no choice and this transaction would therefore not count as a pension transfer for the purposes of the FSA rules.

- But where the receiving spouse can continue as a member of the pension scheme, then any transfer out will count as a pension transfer.

When pension transfer permission is required

The appropriate permissions are required for transfers from occupational pension schemes (OPS) to a personal pension, stakeholder pension, self invested personal pension (SIPP) or retirement annuity. OPS may be DB or DC (including individual executive pensions). They are also required for transfers from s32 buy-out bonds to a personal pension, stakeholder pension, SIPP or retirement annuity.

S32 buy-out bonds

A transfer from an occupational pension scheme to an 's32 buy-out bond' usually constitutes a pension transfer and would be subject to the FSA's rule requirements. Most s32 buy-out bonds reflect the fixed and guaranteed benefits arising from the transferring occupational scheme. If the member subsequently transfers from the s32 buy-out bond to a personal pension or stakeholder pension, the second transfer is also usually subject to the 'pension transfer' rules.

16 Unregulated collective investment schemes

Many advisers recommend unregulated collective investment schemes (UCISs) to their clients. The FSA has been concerned that UCISs have been promoted inappropriately and have also been the subject of unsuitable sales. It is important for firms to understand:

- What is an UCIS and how it is affected by regulation;
- The people to whom they can promote UCISs;
- The suitability and risk issues.

Firms that advise on and sell UCISs should review their systems and controls especially in relation to financial promotions and client risk profiles.

What is a UCIS?

A UCIS is a collective investment scheme (CIS) that the FSA neither authorise nor recognise. The FSA 'authorise' UK CISs that can be marketed to the public and 'recognise' non-UK CISs that meet their specified criteria. The FSA website lists those CISs that are either authorised or recognised. CISs that are not regulated are not subject to the same restrictions as regulated schemes, for example with respect to their investment powers or how they are run.

UCISs cover a very wide range of investments that do not fit into the FSA's criteria for regulated CIS. They may include such investments as oil and gas scheme partnerships, many types of property funds, life assurance viatical settlements, hedge funds and private equity funds.

Even though they are described as 'unregulated', the label can be misleading to some extent. In many respects UCISs are as regulated as ordinary CISs.

- The people who carry on regulated activities in the UK in relation to UCISs are subject to FSA regulation; such people include those who provide personal recommendations, arrange deals, or establish, operate and manage a UCIS.
- The FSA Handbook applies, including the COBS rules, particularly in relation to suitability for clients. In some ways, UCISs could be regarded as even more regulated than other CISs because of the restrictions on promoting them.

Promoting UCISs

UCISs cannot be promoted to the general public and there are restrictions on promotions.

It is important to understand the meaning of the word 'promotion' in this context. Promoting a UCIS involves communicating in the course of business an invitation or inducement to engage in investment activity in relation to a UCIS. 'Promoting' in this context is a broad concept and does not just mean communicating through a written financial promotion, such as marketing literature. It also includes face-to-face discussion, phone calls, emails, advertisements, websites and presentations.

Broadly speaking a UCIS can only be promoted where an exemption applies. The FSA's COBS lists eight categories of investor to whom UCIS promotions are permitted. These include people for whom the firm has:

- Taken reasonable steps to ensure that the UCIS is suitable and are established or newly accepted clients of the firm.

- Assessed their expertise and knowledge and has concluded that they can make their own decisions and understand the risks involved (see above 'Types of clients').

- Warned in writing that the firm will promote UCISs to them and who has stated in writing, and separately from the contract to invest, that the firm may make these promotions.

- Categorised the individual as a 'professional client' under the MIFID rules. The criteria for this include a minimum defined frequency of financial transactions, or a minimum size of financial holdings of €0.5m, or a minimum professional knowledge and experience in the relevant business area.

Firms that intend to promote and recommend UCISs to investors need to be very clear about the detail of these exemptions (described here very broadly). The detailed rules are contained in an order made by HM Treasury known as the PCIS Order – FSMA (Promotion of Collective Investment Schemes (Exemptions) Order 2001 (SI 2001/1060) (as amended). The FSA rules exempting the promotion of UCIS under certain circumstances are contained in COBS 4.12.

It is important to document the exemption that applies in each case and the reasons why it applies, together with appropriate evidence.

Suitability of UCIS

Before recommending a UCIS, a financial planner needs to gather information about the client to establish whether the UCIS is suitable. When making a personal recommendation or providing discretionary portfolio management services on a UCIS, the planner must establish that the UCIS is suitable for the client. This includes obtaining the necessary information about the client's knowledge and experience in relation to the UCIS, the client's financial situation and their investment objectives. In the case of non-advised business (e.g. execution only) by MiFID, firms, this can include meeting the 'appropriateness' requirements.

Risks and UCISs

A client who invests in a UCIS could lose some or all of their money, in the same way as with most other investments. However, the risk is likely to be greater with UCISs. They are therefore generally considered to be high risk and firms should always ensure that their clients understand the risks before they invest in UCISs. The risks include the following:

- A UCIS typically invests in assets that are not available to a regulated CIS. This may be because the assets are riskier or less liquid, or it may be structured in ways that are different from a regulated CIS.

- UCISs are not subject to the investment and borrowing restrictions that apply to regulated CISs and which are intended to ensure a prudent spread of risk.

In addition, investors may not be covered by the Financial Ombudsman Service (FOS), if they have a complaint about the fund. They may also not be covered by the Financial Services Compensation Scheme (FSCS), if they need to seek compensation. This should be made clear to clients. The documents from the UCIS provider should help confirm whether investors have access to FOS or FSCS.

Part 3: Identifying and analysing needs and wants

Chapter 10
Client aims and objectives

1 Getting the full picture

Even when made aware of the biases covered in chapter 3, 'The impact of behavioural finance', people will still use short-cuts or rules of thumb. Financial planners are no exception, and the danger planners must avoid is leaping to 'solutions' based on a small set of facts that confirm a limited view of the client. This intuitive leap misses out the key stage in the planning process, namely analysis, which can only be based on accumulating and then considering all the relevant facts.

But as chapter 4, 'Different types of client', has shown, clients live complicated lives, so what are the relevant facts? The planner may not know until they have asked a lot of questions. Each area of planning (protection, investment and estate) has its own set of issues that determine what facts may be relevant. Many of the specific issues are covered in part four.

This chapter focuses on the more general issues involved in obtaining relevant facts, and ascertaining the client's aims and objectives. The planner's aim should, as a minimum, be to formulate these aims and objectives in such a way that the client agrees with them. Ideally, the formulation should be such that the client commits to them and in doing so makes them the core of their financial plan.

Many advisers undertake risk profiling along with fact-finding and this topic is dealt with separately in chapter 13, 'Summarising and analysing needs and priorities'.

The use of printed fact-find documents can mislead advisers and clients into regarding the process as a simple sequence, when in practice this is rarely the case. In particular, clients can often only formulate what they want when they have some understanding of what is available or realistic. For example, a client may express the aspiration to educate children privately without having much idea about the likely total cost. Once they understand the financial commitment involved they may abandon this aim.

Planners will also encounter couples whose views on important topics differ significantly; a situation which may require several discussions before they arrive at an agreed aim. This and other issues involved in dealing with clients are covered in chapter 14, 'Selecting appropriate products and services'.

2 Aims and objectives

Aims are best defined as long-term aspirations or ambitions with often indefinite timescales, while objectives are more specific with definite timescales.

In the financial plan, aims are linked to objectives, which in turn partially define needs.

Some advisers categorise information relating to aims and objectives as 'soft facts' as opposed to the 'hard facts' covered in the section on fact-finding page 152.

Some advisers gather the hard facts before engaging in a discussion with the client about their aims and objectives. Others gather both types of information at the same time. Some advisers start the discussion with aims and objectives and leave the printed fact-find form for the client to complete afterwards.

Logically, aims and objectives come first since they are the reason for the financial planning process (if the client had none there would be no need to plan). Moreover, they to some extent determine what factual data is essential for the planning process.

Formulating aims

Discovering and formulating the client's aims can be easy in the case of clients who have thought hard about what they want to achieve. In some ways such clients are ideal since there is no ambiguity and there are often imperatives in terms of specific needs.

Example 10.1

"I plan to leave my teaching job and become a photographer after completing a professional photography course and then aim to earn a living as a freelancer."

"I aim to accumulate enough capital to buyout my brothers' shares in the family farm when my parents die and then live there as a part-time farmer."

"In five years' time I aim to take a one-year sabbatical and obtain a specialist qualification which will enable me to re-enter my profession as a more highly-paid consultant."

In most cases however, people find formulating aims difficult because they do not think much about the long-term and instead focus on day-to-day issues in their lives. In fact, engagement with a financial planner may be the first time many people have thought seriously about a range of long-term issues.

If the client has difficulty in thinking about the future, it is easy for the planner to fall into the trap of identifying aims with needs. But the client's needs (see chapter 15, 'Communicating recommendations') arise mainly out of the facts of their circumstances, which will continue to change. Their aims should be wider ranging and more general in scope and should relate to their aspirations and desires rather than to their immediate situation. An aim that is purely financial will usually be either a substitute for an aim the client could not articulate or an acceptance of the status quo, which could change in the future.

It is important to appreciate that even if a client does not have a clear aim now, they could develop one at some point in the future. So the adviser needs to have open-ended discussions that enable them to assess the likelihood of a change of direction.

While fact-finding focuses on the detailed and specific, investigation of aims and objectives is best pursued with open questions:

- "How do you feel about your job?"
- "How would you describe your ideal job?"
- "What would you say is most important for you to achieve in the next ten years?"
- "How would you describe your aspirations for your children?"
- "Can you envisage circumstances in which it was not you/your partner but instead your partner/you who was the main breadwinner?"
- "What factors do you think would prompt you to move home?"
- "What does financial independence mean to you?"
- "How much support would you expect from your children if you need care when you are older?"

Such discussions may encompass delicate issues such as marital relationships and relationships with children. For example, a couple may say they wish to undertake financial planning as a joint activity but it may become clear to the adviser that the long-term future of the relationship is doubtful. Elderly people may be in the throes of a dispute with a son- or daughter-in-law and their aims in relation to inheritance are likely to change when this is resolved.

Emotional issues of this kind should not be seen as obstacles to financial planning. Rather, emotional issues — which also underlie clear statements of aim — are the reason for financial planning. Insecurity and the desire for financial security are powerful drivers, and in the absence of a clear life aim they may form the core of a financial plan. But it is the security rather than the finance that is the client's aim. The aim of the financial planner — to improve the client's financial position — is a secondary aim for the client.

In some cases, the adviser can nudge the client towards a more realistic attitude by producing a draft formulation of their aims and asking for their comments.

Defining objectives

Where a client has a clear life aim, a set of objectives will usually arise naturally from it. Take one of the earlier examples: "I plan to leave my teaching job and become a photographer after completing a professional photography course and then aim to earn a living as a freelancer."

In this case, one objective will be to accumulate as much as possible in pension entitlements over the period until the client leaves their job. Another will be to set up suitable funds to finance the photography business, which will translate into needs for a capital fund to purchase equipment and for a living expenses fund to supplement initial earnings. A third will be to safeguard the family, which will translate into the need for suitable protection policies.

In the absence of such a clear life aim, objectives will often be defined in terms of improving the current financial position. It may help some clients to be presented with a list of relevant objectives and asked to choose those they consider most important.

Example of objectives

Increase my net spendable income

Reduce the amount of tax I pay

Safeguard my family if I die or become ill

Be confident that I am in control of my finances

Get a better return on my investments

Improve my likely retirement income

Get more income from my investments

Reduce my monthly outgoings

Increase my monthly contributions to savings plans

Understand my pension and retirement position

Advisers need to be aware of the framing and adaptive effects described in chapter 3, 'The impact of behavioural finance', as these may influence clients' responses.

In describing their objectives, clients more often make qualitative than quantitative statements.

Qualitative statement: "I would like to be comfortably off when I retire."

Quantitative statement: "I would like to have a retirement income of at least two-thirds of my pre-retirement earnings."

Normally, the adviser will need to question clients in order to convert a qualitative statement into a quantitative one so that its achievability can be assessed.

More generally, for objectives to be integrated into a financial plan, they should be:

- **Specific**: 'we want to accumulate £200,000 by age 60'
- **Measurable**: 'we want our investments to produce enough income to pay for care home fees'
- **Action related**: 'capable of being affected by action now'
- **Realistic**: 'we can afford to save £250 per month'
- **Time related**: 'our retirement fund should reach the £400,000 target by the end of the seventh year'.

In expressing their objectives clients often fail to distinguish between longer-term and immediate objectives. For example:

Immediate objective paying off credit card balances at high interest rates.

Longer-term objective accumulating enough capital to provide retirement income.

In many cases, clients over-emphasise immediate or short-term objectives at the expense of longer-term ones. As discussed in chapter 3, 'The impact of behavioural finance', this is the result of a normal set of perceptual and behavioural biases and it may assist the client to discuss these.

The adviser's aim is to identify all the client's main objectives and then classify them as immediate and longer term.

Short-term objectives would include building up an appropriate fund for emergencies and short-term commitments and paying off high-interest debts.

Longer-term objectives would include having an adequate retirement income, being able to educate children privately, and paying off the mortgage early.

Prioritisation of objectives and needs is covered in chapter 15, 'Communicating recommendations'.

3 Formal fact-finding

The purpose of the fact-finding process is to gather all the information that is required to produce appropriate recommendations for the client. While there is a core of data that is usually sought from every client, advisers need to identify areas where supplementary information is required for them to complete their analysis.

Most advisers use a printed or online form to gather information about the client. A common method is to have a relatively short basic form of six to eight pages which includes general questions about the main issues, with separate more detailed forms for topics that are only relevant to a minority of clients, such as information about share option schemes or business assets.

If the general form does not contain 'prompts' for these more detailed forms, the adviser needs to have their own prompt sheet to ensure they do not fail to gather vital information.

Some advisers gather information before meeting the client to discuss their aims. Others incorporate a discussion of aims into the fact-finding process in face-to-face meetings, while yet others delegate fact-finding to paraplanners or assistants.

Fact-finding issues

The following sections relate to commonly used divisions of the fact-find document. They cover significant points and do not cover all the data that is routinely collected.

Personal information

Where family relationships are complex or extended, it can be useful not just to gather the data but also to create a family tree.

State of health, family health history and dangerous sport participation all play an increasingly important role in determining the cost of protection policies.

Dependants or potential dependants may include not just minor children and children by former partners but parents and other close relatives who may need support in old age, or adult children in the aftermath of illness or bereavement.

People who are divorced or separated may have many unresolved or partially resolved financial issues including home ownership, liabilities for debts, death benefits under life assurance policies, and potential splitting of pension rights.

Most clients will be domiciled and resident in the UK, but where this is not the case, or where a partner is not UK resident or domiciled, the tax position can be complex and precise details about place of birth, dates of marriages and periods of residency may be needed.

Regulators' interpretations of requirements for establishing a client's identity (the money laundering rules) have been subject to change and advisers need to clearly understand the current requirements.

Prompts for the adviser

- If there is a possibility of parents or other relatives becoming dependent on the client, how likely is this?
- If a child has special needs, is funding or financial assistance available from the state or a charity?
- Is a difficult relationship with a former partner likely to cause problems in the responsibility/care/education of children?
- Have significant future dates been noted — retirement, weddings, major anniversaries?

Children's education

Some parents have firm intentions and plans regarding their children's education but they are probably in a minority. Many have not made up their minds about the possible choices and may not even have considered some of them, such as moving house to an area where the state schools are good, attending the local church to help a child into a church school, spending on extra private tuition, applying for scholarships and bursaries, or mixing maintained and private schooling at different times. The suitability of many of these options is likely to be outside the scope and competence of a financial planner, but the planner needs to be aware of them and may need to suggest that parents should seek specialist educational advice.

If others are involved or will be involved in funding children's education, apart from the parents, the planner needs to know the extent of their intended support and the sources from which they will contribute. They may need to find out how definite such commitments are and how vulnerable they would be to changes in the other parties' circumstances.

To cost educational needs correctly, the adviser will need information on the type of school and the intended period of attendance. The planner will need to be able to construct a spreadsheet or its equivalent of the time when school fees will need to be paid and at what level (depending on various assumptions about the types of school the children might attend).

A firm commitment to private education without at least one very highly paid job should prompt questions about how it will be paid for. Will sending the child to a private school require both parents to take-on paid employments? What are the realistic rates of net earnings that they can expect, especially taking into account the additional costs of child care etc? Will they have enough money to pay for the school fees or will they be able to ask any other family members for help — and if so how much?

What buffer of cash do they want to build up to pay for school fees if they encounter any financial difficulties — such as the illness or unemployment of one of the parents?

Intentions regarding University education need to be probed, and the extent of intended parental support discussed.

If the child does go to university, what are the parents' feelings about the relative merits of the child taking on the costs of their higher education versus the parents helping them by paying some or all of the costs to avoid them building up substantial debt? There may or may not be a choice about this.

In much the same way as there are financial implications of going to different schools, there are implications of going to different universities. There may be variations in the level of fees that universities will charge. But there are very considerable contrasts in the other costs — notably accommodation. Staying at home and going to the local university is probably the cheapest option; if the student is intent on going away to enjoy the full experience of higher education, they will discover that many locations are relatively cheap compared to southern cities and especially London.

Some parents are able and willing to buy accommodation – usually a house – for their student child to live in and let to fellow students. Is this feasible or desirable? There are advantages and drawbacks to this strategy that the adviser will want to consider with the parents and possibly the student. Much depends on the student's character and longer-term plans, the location of the property and the state of the property market, as well as the financial status of the parents in terms of how much they can invest and borrow.

The precise terms of any trusts that exist for the children's benefit should be obtained.

Prompts for the adviser

- Have grandparents or other relatives been canvassed for financial support?

- Is there a 'Plan B' if the parents' current intentions for private education are not achievable?

- Would the parents move home in order to obtain the education they want for their children?

Income and employment

Gross income from all sources should differentiate between secure employment income and bonuses, short-term contracts or self-employment. The security or otherwise of employment is a critical issue as regards longer-term commitments.

Employee benefits can be extensive and valuable. Entitlements under share option schemes, the terms and likely vesting dates, are essential data for tax planning.

Several years of financial data (balance sheet and profit and loss account) should be obtained for a private business that accounts for a large proportion of income.

Couples may have partnerships in which case the terms of the partnership and several years' accounts will be needed.

Future plans for employment or other form of career are central to much financial planning. Some people might intend to have a high-flying career with a rapidly rising income. This might be with one or two employers or it might be with a succession. Some may have an income that could be expected to stay more or less level in real terms. Some high flyers find themselves on an earnings plateau.

It is also helpful to have an understanding of the risks involved in different careers. Some occupations seem to be inherently higher risk than others, although an individual's actual situation may not match these preconceived views of different types of employment. It is important to listen to clients' own views on these issues and how they perceive the risks facing them in their employment. The main risk for most clients in employment is of prolonged periods of unemployment. Their fear of this will be rooted in their general confidence about themselves and the world as well as their perception of the demand for their skills.

People who run their own businesses (or aim to) generally face different issues from those who expect to be employed. They may feel that they are very secure or that their business is fragile. Business fact-finding is beyond the scope of this book.

Prompts for the adviser

- Has the client checked their tax coding?

- Are there pension rights from former employments or paid-up personal pension plans?

- Have clients utilised all the tax allowances and reliefs to which they are entitled?

Expenditure

A detailed expenditure analysis may not be essential if clients are clearly well disciplined and run a monthly surplus. Where clients are in monthly deficit or savings need to be made to finance longer-term commitments such an analysis will be essential. A study of the client's bank and credit card statements may be necessary.

Many advisers include a pro-forma monthly budget in their fact-find, with headings such as utilities, council tax, insurance, car and holidays. Some clients will find this a useful aid to summarising their expenditure and it can be a useful tool in analysing their situation.

The level of discretionary expenditure will be relevant in calculating how much clients can afford to save to meet their financial goals, for example how much they could pay for insurance cover or pension planning. This requires the adviser to ask questions about what expenditure clients could reduce or cut out entirely if they really wanted to achieve their aims. This would also help to determine how much income they would need if they hit a difficult financial patch as a result of illness, unemployment or the death of a partner.

In thinking ahead towards retirement, the planner can ask about expenditures that would not be required in retirement, for example mortgage repayments and work-related travel costs, as well as any increased costs that they might incur once they retire.

Prompts for the adviser

- If the client's expenditure exceeds their income, how long has this been happening?
- If the client's over-spending is linked to problems with addiction, have they sought medical advice or help?
- If there are large fluctuations in monthly income or outgoings, can the client explain these?

Assets

For couples, the basis of ownership (sole or joint) for all assets is essential data as is the basis of ownership of the home (joint tenants or tenants in common).

For business assets, intentions regarding long-term ownership or disposal can have important tax implications.

For assets subject to capital gains tax, their cost is essential data for tax planning.

For investments, any income and its tax status; any restrictions on encashment or withdrawal; any special terms (such as penalty-free dates for with-profit bond encashment); and reasons for the purchase of non-conventional investments, are required.

For life insurance bonds, the owners and lives assured may differ; current and cumulative withdrawals are required to compute the tax position.

The purpose of investments or clients' reasons for their purchase can help to clarify their attitudes. Why or how did the client acquire them and what is the ultimate plan for them (in the case of property in particular)? Some people have valuable art and antiques, which may be earmarked for various members of the family.

Ownership of inherited assets or private company shares may signal problems ahead with the endowment effect (see chapter 3, 'The impact of behavioural finance').

Foreign property can lead to complications. It is worth checking whether it has been properly set up in terms of the legality – some Britons have used companies to purchase foreign property, which can prove troublesome. In many cases, there is a need for a foreign will, and there may be both capital gains tax and inheritance tax charges in the relevant jurisdiction independent of the UK tax treatment.

It is always worth questioning clients on their feeling about the appropriate amount of cash to hold. Most financial planners suggest three months' or six months expenditure as an emergency fund, but clients may well feel they want to hold more than this — and the reasons are worth exploring.

Prompts for the adviser

- What is the nature of the relationship with business partners?
- If the client has a strong commitment to one investment or one type of investment, what are the reasons for this?
- Are a couple managing investments jointly or individually?

Liabilities

The redemption date of loans, in particular mortgages, is important, especially whether they continue past the client's intended retirement date, and the terms of loans (such as penalties applying to early repayments) can be significant. Mortgages may be offset, with implications for short-term savings, and any loan may have special terms and conditions.

The interest rate currently payable and any recent or imminent change in the interest rate should be noted.

Credit status: has the client recently checked their status with a credit rating agency? This is often a useful exercise and enables any errors on the record to be corrected.

Not all liabilities are obvious or visible. For example, there could be potential or contingent liabilities such as guarantees for children's mortgages, business loans or overdrafts, or guarantees to landlords under leases.

It is a good idea to ask about the client's views about using extra cash on a regular or one-off basis to pay off a mortgage early rather than investing in other assets — notably pension plans. Many clients have interest only mortgages; it is worth discussing what they want to do about capital repayment. They may be planning to use the lump sum from their pension or some other asset to pay off this liability at retirement. This might be a high-risk approach or there may be an element of double counting in the possible uses of the lump sum.

If there are tax liabilities, are there liquid funds available to pay them?

Prompts for the adviser

- What is the client's general attitude to debt?
- Has the client taken active steps to manage debt or are they in need of help with this?
- Did the client choose their own mortgage or did they use a mortgage broker?

Protection policies

Policies may be in trust or written on the life of another, or assigned to a lender. Details of trust terms are essential.

Policy conditions and options, e.g. increasability/renewability, index linking of premiums, can be significant. For critical illness policies, the scope of cover with older policies may be more limited than is available today.

The cover provided by income protection policies, especially those sold by banks alongside loans, may be very limited.

If the client is a non-smoker, policies may have been taken out when they were a smoker.

Clients may be unclear what they actually have in terms of protection, and may benefit from a simple explanation of the different types of cover.

It is an integral part of the fact-finding process to discover what clients' protection needs might be in the event of death or serious illness, taking each partner/spouse in turn. This involves helping the clients to envisage the financial circumstances they would encounter if one or both died or fell seriously ill. For example, if either parent were to fall seriously ill, the couple should consider how they would pay for help with the children and with other expenditure.

These questions should lead to the financial planner having enough information to be able to calculate how much cover will be needed, how long for and the basis on which it should be provided.

Prompts for the adviser

- Do policies taken out to cover the mortgage in fact match the term and outstanding debt?

- Has the client considered the full range of protection polices at any time?

- Is the client covered by any life policies owned by a former partner?

Pensions

Defined benefits: a copy of the scheme's member booklet and the client's latest benefit statement will be required to check pension and death benefit entitlements.

Defined contribution schemes: are the funds or funds in which contributions are invested default choices or were they active choices by the client?

Lump sum death benefits: who has been nominated by the client to receive them?

Prompts for the adviser

- Are there pension rights from former employments or paid up personal pension plans?
- What is the status of any defined benefit scheme where the client is a member or has preserved benefits?
- Has the client made additional voluntary contributions to any occupational scheme?

Retirement

Intentions about retirement are a key element in the financial planner's analysis and projections. In many cases, clients hope to retire earlier than is likely to be possible. The financial planner needs to make an assessment of the client's future estimated resources at retirement and question whether or not their aim is realistic. This might be obvious at the first fact-finding session or it might require a second or subsequent discussion.

Some clients expect to be able to carry on working indefinitely regardless of the possibility of changes in their health and capacity or demand for their services on the job market. On the other hand, clients may not be aware of the possibility of maintaining some source of income from work after they have retired from their principal occupation. Clients may need to think about this and the implications for where they live, how much additional income they will require and the need to be flexible.

A major issue is bound to be the level of income and capital that clients will need in retirement. To some extent this should be apparent from their current lifestyle and level of expenditure. But retirement brings considerable changes in expenditure. Some costs (leisure expenditure) will rise; while others (travel to work) will fall. Clients need to think about this in order to help the financial planner produce a realistic estimate of needs.

Among the relevant topics are:

- What do clients intend to do in retirement? Where do they want to live? Some people just want to stay where they are; others have a yen to be near their families or to retire to the seaside or go and live abroad. Financial planners need to probe these stated ambitions to see whether they really stand up to scrutiny in both practical and financial terms.
- If clients plan to move, will they find it easy to make a new life in the area to which they are planning to move? What are the transport connections like in the area and will they be able to get about when driving becomes problematical? Is the area really suitable geographically and in other ways? There are many people who have retired to hilly Dorset or Devon towns by the sea that seem idyllic when they go there with children or grandchildren

on summer holidays but turn out to be dead in winter and very hard to walk around once infirmity sets in.

- For those who plan to move abroad, have they thought through the problems of living overseas – language, culture, tax, healthcare, the danger of currency movements devaluing their pension and investment income?

These are hard questions to get people to think about and often it requires the financial planner to help them to imagine their future lives by encouraging them to paint a picture of how they will spend their time in retirement.

Wills and trusts

The date at which the latest will was made should be noted. Regardless of whether the provisions of the will still conform to the client's wishes, there may have been legislative changes requiring amendment. But the adviser should also question if the provisions of the will are still the client's wishes. If clients have minor children, the will should provide for guardianship in the case of the death of both parents.

Where a trust exists, a copy of the trust deed or a summary of its provisions is essential.

If any Powers of Attorney exist, the circumstances in which they are activated should be noted as well as the names of the attorneys.

Gifts made in recent years using the annual exemptions for inheritance tax should be noted, together with any larger amounts.

Clients may have very different attitudes to inheritance planning. Partly this will be a function of age and partly attitudes to inherited wealth generally. Inheritance tax (IHT) planning unsurprisingly seems to become more important with age; the urge to save tax needs to be offset against the need to provide for the donor's long-term standard of living and security. Some clients are more keen to help their children immediately – for example to help them buy a property or pay for school fees – and place less emphasis on longer term planning that may have more impact after their deaths. Other clients may want to defer benefiting their children or other family members until after they have died, either because they feel that is more appropriate or because they believe that they cannot afford to make substantial lifetime gifts. Clients' views about these matters will often gradually emerge, as they find out what is and is not possible to achieve in term of balancing IHT planning and their immediate income and capital needs.

Prompts for the adviser

- Is the client aware of being a beneficiary under anyone else's will?
- Is a nil rate inheritance tax band available from a predeceased spouse?
- Does the client have an ongoing relationship with a legal adviser?

Preferences

Some clients have strong religious or ethical views that they wish to apply to their finances. In particular this can affect investments. But clients may also have quite specific preferences such as wishing not to do business with particular companies.

Other sources of data

Advisers may need to obtain data from other sources and will need to obtain letters of authority from the client:

- **Accountant**: details of latest financial statements; current year income and tax status; details and tax status of business assets.
- **Lawyer**: provisions of trusts or wills.
- **Product providers**: details of pension policies, investments, life insurance policies.

Questioning

Even when the client completes a printed fact-find on their own, the adviser will normally need to follow this up with personal questioning. This will usually combine an exploration of needs with a gathering of additional information.

In this process the adviser needs to be aware of the biases described in chapter 3, 'The impact of behavioural finance', especially framing, adaptive attitudes, anchoring, status quo bias and mental accounting.

- **Framing**: the adviser should try to avoid formulating questions in such a way that the client can assume a particular answer is 'normal'.
- **Adaptive attitudes**: these often influence levels of saving or the types of investment held, so it is useful to explore to what extent the client has been influenced by their peer group or other social groups.
- **Anchoring**: the adviser should avoid using figures that the client may anchor on, since this may prevent an open-ended exploration of issues and these figures may become unrealistic targets.
- **Status quo bias**: since most people are resistant to change, it is best to frame questions that do not imply or assume that change is necessary.
- **Mental accounting**: many clients adopt a 'one pot for this and another for that' method of keeping track of their finances. It is best not to question this during the fact-finding process since it is in the analysis of needs that it will become clear whether or not it is an impediment to effective planning.

When seeking additional information, questions should be precise, but when exploring objectives or needs, open-ended questions are preferable.

Closed: "Are you a member of a pension scheme?"

Open: "What, if any, plans have you made to provide yourself with a retirement income?"

If the client is unaware of important needs, "what if?" questions may help.

"What would be the effects on your household income if one of you was unable to work for a long period?"

Updating

Most financial planning clients will subscribe to a service where they receive reviews either annually or semi-annually. The adviser's planning process needs to include methods for gathering fresh information that may require changes to the plan and recommendations to change existing arrangements.

There are three main ways advisers do this:

- Send a copy of the most recent fact-find document, or a printout of the data held in the client management system, to the client and ask them to note any significant changes on it and return it.

- Send a 'Review' form to the client with broad questions prompting them to provide information that would require changes to their plan or arrangements.

- Meet the client or telephone them to find out if there have been any significant changes in their circumstances or needs.

A method that is not yet in common use but may become more popular is to hold client data on a web-linked administration system part of which is open to the client so that they can change personal data themselves. The system should deliver prompts to the adviser when such changes are made.

In many cases, the fresh information will not in fact require any changes to the plan. However, if there have been significant changes to the client's circumstances, the adviser should undertake a reassessment of their risk profile.

Advisers should note that the updating of client data before fresh advice is given or new investments or plans recommended or implemented is a regulatory requirement. It is advisable to construct administration processes that check that client information has been updated before new recommendations are made.

Chapter 11
Risk profiling

1 The need for risk

Most clients do not want to take risks, but they need to in order to achieve their objectives. The purpose of risk profiling is to establish as clearly as possible the client's capacity for and attitude to risk, since this will largely determine the nature of any recommendations for investments and savings plans.

Often a client's objectives cannot be achieved unless the client takes on more risk than they want to. So the discussion of risk will almost always take place in the context of the client's objectives. And clients who are ambitious for returns or for specific objectives may alter their stated risk tolerance during the course of such discussions.

Ideally the client's aims and objectives should be explored before undertaking risk profiling. It will often be necessary for the adviser to translate these objectives into monetary terms in order to assess, at least approximately, the rates of return that would be required to achieve them. A lifetime cashflow analysis (see Figure 15.3) is one way of doing this. The client is then better placed to understand the connection between these cashflows and the risks involved in achieving them.

In exploring the client's attitudes to risk, the adviser needs to assess the client's major concerns. These could concern having a shortfall in their retirement income, or abrupt falls in the value of their investments, or even their ability to live with the fluctuations they expect from a portfolio.

While the use of formal quantitative methods of assessing risk tolerance has become more widespread, it is important to note that these are aids to the personal evaluation of the adviser, which is more qualitative in nature. Quantitative techniques are not substitutes for the in-depth discussions that in most cases are the key factor in assigning a risk profile to a client.

Risk profiling was briefly covered in chapter 6, 'Investment planning', as part of the investment planning process. This chapter covers the issue in more detail.

2 Components of the risk profile

A risk profile, more accurately a risk-return profile, is a summary of the average levels of return and risk the client expects from their investments and savings.

Because, as behavioural finance has shown (see chapter 3, 'The impact of behavioural finance'), people are more averse to risk than they are keen for gains, the emphasis in risk profiling is in defining the client's ability to tolerate losses or shortfalls in the rate of return required to meet their objectives.

The risk profile has three components:

- Capacity for risk
- Perception of risk
- Tolerance of risk

Capacity for risk

Unlike the other two factors, the client's capacity for risk is an objective measure based on their resources, circumstances and the timescales of their objectives.

The resources available often constrain the client's capacity for risk. For example, a widowed client with a small amount of capital depends on this capital to generate income to top up her state pension. Any capital loss would have a very damaging effect on her standard of living. Her capacity for risk is low, whereas that of a young single man without any commitments who has just inherited £500,000 from a relative is high.

Circumstances partially define the client's obligations, which may also constrain risk capacity. If a client faces the threat of redundancy, for example, they may have to allocate more of their resources to meeting their current obligations.

Given the very wide range of returns possible from 'risk' assets such as equities over the short-term, a short timescale may also reduce risk capacity. However, this need not be purely a consequence of the client's age. In theory, a man aged 85 has a realistic investment timescale of five years, but if he is prepared to pass investment risk on to his heirs, this fact alone would not necessarily constrain his capacity for risk.

Perception of risk

The client's perception of risk is subjective, immediate and is usually known by the client and clearly expressed, often in terms of 'not wanting to lose money'. Many will perceive cash deposits as having no risk and stock market investments as being very risky.

It is important to realise that perception of risk is heavily influenced by availability and salience. A recent stock market crash, especially if it has featured in the news, makes people perceive greater risk in equities, whereas a run of good years for shares will result in far less negative views.

Negative experiences of close friends or family, even if these are quite untypical or caused by their own rash behaviour, will also influence perceptions. One reason for 'bubbles' is that people no longer perceive the risk, bringing another behavioural finance phenomenon, adaptive behaviour or herding, into operation.

Tolerance of risk

People's perception may or may not coincide with the attitude to risk culturally and socially formed over their lifetime. Clients are not necessarily able to articulate it, which is why psychometric questionnaires can be useful since they can bring out such deeper feelings, which often have their roots in childhood experience, as summed up by journalist Katharine Whitehorn's pithy "The easiest way for your children to learn about money is for you not to have any".

However, aspects of these deeper attitudes often emerge during discussion since the individual's lifetime experiences and their responses to them will demonstrate their underlying attitudes. People who pick themselves up after personal disasters, who bounce back from business failures or successfully make career changes are likely to have a higher tolerance of risk. People who have stayed with the same employer or in the same home for many years, or have turned down business opportunities, have displayed aversion to risk. Hobbies and activities can also be suggestive.

Changing profiles

Advisers know that their clients' perceptions of and attitudes to risk will often change as they gain more experience of investment. However, there are other factors that can influence attitudes to risk:

- Discussion of common psychological factors in investment, such as the endowment effect and the familiarity effect, can help people to alter their views.

- Major changes in circumstances such as a bereavement or inheriting wealth often prompt attitudinal changes.

- Learning more about investments reduces the level of anxiety many people experience and makes it easier to accept fluctuations.

Research has shown that people's perceptions of risk are unstable, but the causative factors for changes in perceptions and attitudes have not been established. It is good practice to review attitudes to risk and risk profiles periodically.

Applying profiles

In the financial planning process, the adviser attempts to allocate a risk profile to the client. But in planning for specific objectives, advisers may then agree higher or lower risk-return profiles for different sets of assets. For example, many clients will prefer to manage their pension investments with a lower risk profile than that which applies to their other investments.

For clients with substantial assets, a 'core and satellite' (see Figure 6.3) approach may lead to the construction of a core portfolio with a moderate risk profile and satellite portfolios with higher risk profiles.

Spouses may prefer to have separate portfolios with different risk profiles rather than one portfolio with a common profile.

3 Exploring risk and return

Most advisers now use questionnaires to explore client's attitudes to risk – see page 169. However, recent behavioural finance research has revealed that people's responses to such questionnaires are neither internally consistent nor consistent through time. For this reason alone, the adviser should not rely solely on questionnaires to establish risk profiles. It is also important to note that questionnaires are not very helpful in assessing risk capacity, which requires the adviser's analysis.

Risk cannot be explored as a topic in its own right independent of return. Risk and return are two sides of the same coin. If clients do not already realise this, it is a key message they need to understand before it will be possible to go further.

A useful starting point is often the client's perception of cash deposits as being risk-free. This of course ignores the effects of inflation, which even at modest rates erodes real capital values. When clients see this – in the form of a chart or table showing the decline over a period of years of the real value of capital – they often effectively change the benchmark against which they assess risk from an unrealistic absolute to a realistic 'relative to inflation' perspective.

Usually, it will require discussion of this and the typical risk-return characteristics of the different types of investment to enable the client to understand the risk-return trade-off well enough to articulate a definite view.

Table 11.1 – Long-term returns from different types of investment

Type of investment	Annual real return over		
	10 years	**20 years**	**30 years**
Deposits	1.8%	3.1%	1.9%
Gilts	2.6%	5.4%	2.3%
Property	3.7%	NA	NA
Equity	-1.2%	4.6%	5.2%

Figures shown are annual average real returns before tax including reinvested income. Data to end-December 2009.

Sources: Barclays Capital Equity-Gilt Study 2010; IPD Databank

Useful aids to this process are figures in tabular or chart form showing the typical range of variations in returns over different time periods (as per the

Barclays Capital Equity-Gilt Study and the Credit Suisse Global Returns Yearbook). There are three key facts clients need to grasp:

1. Equities consistently deliver higher long-term returns

2. Over short periods, the volatility of equities is very high

3. Shares are more likely to beat cash over longer periods

Probability of shares producing higher returns than cash deposits if they are held for

2 years	3 years	4 years	5 years	10 years	18 years
66%	69%	73%	75%	91%	99%

Source: Barclays Capital Equity-Gilt Study 2010

Based on the client's objectives, the adviser can estimate the critical yield – the annual return necessary to achieve that objective. This can then be compared with the long-run historic average returns from the major asset classes. The client can then see what the implications are for the degree of risk they need to take to achieve their aims.

It is important not to use short-term returns, especially if they have been above the historic averages, since clients are often over-optimistic and the adviser needs to avoid reinforcing such tendencies. Faced with high target returns and therefore high risks, clients may scale back their ambitions, following JK Morley's, "In investing money, the amount of interest you want should depend on whether you want to eat well or sleep well".

Volatility measures

While risk may be expressed in many different ways, it is usually measured in terms of volatility. This statistically expresses the probability of returns falling within given parameters, usually expressed in terms such as "Returns will typically fall between 6% and 12% a year about two-thirds of the time".

However, simple explanations of volatility are difficult, because in fact volatility is normally measured on a monthly basis and its variations are expressed in terms of standard deviation, a mathematical concept few people can easily grasp. Nor is it necessarily helpful to try to do so.

For example, Table 11.2 shows the expected distribution of monthly returns for an investment with an average return of 1% a month with a standard deviation (= volatility) of 3.

The conventional description of the first line in the table would be that about two-thirds of the time investment returns would fall between +4% and -2% per month.

In practice, it is well known that investment returns do not form a normal distribution, yet it is only in a normal distribution that the column on the

Table 11.2 – Standard deviation

	Range of returns %	Range of returns %	% of returns within range
1 standard deviation	1 +/-3	-2 to +4	68.3%
2 standard deviations	1 +/-6	-5 to +7	95.5%
3 standard deviations	1 +/-9	-8 to +10	99.7%

right hand side of the table can be validly derived from the data. Allowances can be made for 'kurtosis' and 'fat tails' but the techniques for doing so are not readily available to advisers. For this reason alone advisers should be careful in their use of risk measures based on standard deviation. The fact that during 2008-2010 returns from all major asset classes showed volatility equivalent to six or more standard deviations – theoretically unlikely to happen during the lifetime of the earth – conclusively demonstrated the limitations of conventional risk assessment measures.

Many practitioners – and the theorists who created modern portfolio theory on which these techniques are based – continue to assert that these statistical methods work 'in normal conditions' and users have to expect that from time to time (in crisis conditions) they will not. Users of these methods therefore need to have robust methods for explaining to clients when they can expect their investments to conform to these expectations and when they cannot.

It is possible to explain the key concepts of risk and return without using standard deviation and its associated measures. The precision of standard deviation can be misleading. Investment returns and risks can never be measured with the precision shown in simplistic presentations of these methods. For example, calculating time-weighted rates of return using these methods will usually substantially change the reported returns from a portfolio.

An alternative measure of risk that is easier for clients to understand is drawdown, the maximum historical peak-to-trough loss in an asset class. Unfortunately the 2008-2010 period generated new records for short-term peak-to-trough losses in several asset classes, so that the use of this measure may result in encouraging clients' risk aversion. But if peak-to-trough losses are considered over longer periods of five or more years, which is appropriate if the client has committed funds for such a period, then this can illustrate how the riskiness of equities declines as the holding period lengthens.

4 Risk questionnaires

In recent years the use of questionnaires to help define the client's attitude to risk has become widespread. Initially, clients were simply given a range of perhaps five categories such as 'no risk', 'low risk', 'moderate risk' and asked to choose one. But on their own these descriptions are quite meaningless and could be interpreted in widely different ways.

Today, most advisers use either online risk profiling tools (see page 171) or more sophisticated questionnaires.

Questionnaires with only attitudinal questions may be useful provided the adviser uses them in the context of other information about the client. But questionnaires incorporating factual as well as attitudinal questions permit easy and rapid cross-checking of one against the other, so that any discrepancy prompts further investigation.

Typical factual questions include:

Have you owned any of these types of investments in the past five years?
(1) Shares
(2) Unit trusts
(3) Investment trusts
(4) With-profit bonds

In the past what level of involvement have you had with investment?
(1) No involvement
(2) Some involvement
(3) Active involvement

Compared with people you know, do you consider yourself to be:
(1) Not knowledgeable about investment
(2) Averagely knowledgeable about investment
(3) Well informed about investment

Questions about expectations can be useful, such as:

I would expect the total annual return from my investments (income plus capital growth) to exceed the return from a typical building society account by an average of:
(1) Up to 1% a year (2) 1% to 2% a year (3) 2% to 3% a year
(4) 3% to 5% a year (5) Over 5% a year

Attitudinal questions are of the type:

I personally believe that when investing, protecting what you have is most important:
(1) Strongly agree (2) Somewhat agree (3) Neither agree or disagree
(4) Somewhat disagree (5) Strongly disagree

I worry less about investment decisions than most people I know:
(1) Strongly disagree (2) Somewhat disagree (3) Neither agree or disagree
(4) Somewhat agree (5) Strongly agree

I am willing to accept that my investments will fluctuate and could fall below their original value:
(1) Strongly disagree (2) Disagree (3) Unhappy, but agree
(4) Agree (5) Strongly agree

If the answers to the factual questions indicate a low level of knowledge or investment activity in the past, then answers to attitudinal questions suggesting a high tolerance of risk are suspect. Likewise, active involvement in investment in the past combined with apparently low tolerance of risk is inconsistent.

In most cases, the adviser's personal questioning and interaction with the client will enable them to provisionally allocate the client to one of a number of risk profiles. A questionnaire is then a cross-check. If the risk profiling process starts with the completion of a questionnaire, advisers should develop their own methods of using it as a basis for discussion to ensure that the results are valid.

Typically a questionnaire will use numerical scores for each answer to create a total score that corresponds to a risk profile. A set of three, five, seven or even ten profiles may be used (see chapter 6, 'Investment planning', for a set of ten profiles). In reality, it is very difficult to differentiate between attitudes sufficiently clearly to be able to allocate to one of a set of ten risk profiles on the basis of a questionnaire alone. Even following detailed questioning by an adviser, consistently differentiating clients into more than seven categories is problematic. Unless the adviser can show that the outcomes of such categorisation are consistent, there is little point in using so many categories.

Furthermore, as discussed in chapter 6, 'Investment planning', the choice of investments within asset classes can have a large effect on the risk-return characteristics of a portfolio, so that assuming that risk profiles with different asset allocations automatically translate into consistently different risk-return bands is overly simplistic.

5 Risk profiling tools

In recent years risk profiling tools have become available to advisers. Some have been created by independent specialists while others have been created by product providers.

Two major issues arise concerning the use of such tools:

- If the tool is provided by a product provider, does it contain biases towards certain outcomes in terms of asset allocation or fund selection?

- Does the adviser understand the basis on which clients are allocated to specific categories?

Personal questioning by the adviser may appear subjective, but if advisers are consistent in their approach and line of questioning, there is no reason why their categorisations should not also be consistent. The consistency of risk profiling tools, on the other hand, derives from rule sets applied mainly to attitudinal questions. All such questionnaires suffer from a problem identified by behavioural researchers, namely that in situations of uncertainty, people often seek to appear 'normal' (see chapter 3, 'The impact of behavioural finance'). They will often interpret the wording of questions and answers to give what they consider to be the 'normal' response. While it is relatively easy for an adviser to spot this in a face-to-face discussion, it is not so easy to see it in the results of a questionnaire that has been completed by the client on their own.

It is possible to construct questionnaires that minimise this bias. The technique normally used by psychologists is to ask what is essentially the same question in subtly different ways. Discrepancies arising from adaptive behaviour and other biases can then be identified and scores adjusted for this. But to do this effectively a questionnaire may need to run to 50 plus questions.

Organisations that have a large database of responses to their questionnaires can use this to adjust for biases and can also alter the link between scores and profiles, techniques that to some extent deal with these issues.

However, a remaining issue is the weight given to risk capacity in allocating risk profiles. If a client has no risk capacity constraints, then basing a risk profile only on attitudinal questions will produce a satisfactory outcome, but if there are serious issues of capacity, then it is possible that the risk profile derived from a questionnaire will be higher than an adviser would allocate based on a comprehensive view of the client's circumstances as well as attitudes.

Advisers can explain why risk capacity factors justify a reduction in the level of risk they consider appropriate compared with that derived from the client's answers to a questionnaire. Such discussions should be documented.

6 Designing and describing risk profiles

Advisers may use a set of as few as three or as many as ten risk profiles. In each case the adviser needs to:

- Describe each profile in simple terms that can be readily understood, avoiding the use of jargon;

- Create an asset allocation matrix for the set of risk profiles showing the percentage of capital allocated to each major asset class;

- Ensure that this allocation produces no greater volatility or drawdown than is suggested in the profile descriptions;

- Review the asset allocations for each profile at regular intervals.

Descriptions

While clients would often prefer to sign up to a risk profile that said "I am not prepared to lose more than 20% of my capital in any circumstances", advisers cannot offer such assurances and their profile descriptions have to be less definite, as shown in the following examples.

Cautious

You have a low tolerance of investment risk. This implies you would accept a small amount of investment risk but only if this can be achieved without large variations in the value of your investments. This means that diversification is important – holding different types of asset is one way of damping down fluctuations in the value of your portfolio. Your answers indicate a relatively low expectation of returns, somewhat above those from deposit accounts.

Balanced

You indicate a general acceptance that returns cannot be achieved without some degree of investment risk. However, your responses indicate that you are unwilling to take much risk within your overall portfolio. The benefits of diversification will be important since this is designed to offset the unavoidable risks involved in those investments that generate higher returns. Your expectation of returns higher than those you could receive from deposits should be achievable with a diversified range of assets generating some income as well as capital growth.

Asset allocation matrix

Asset allocation matrices are often idealised and based on long-run asset class returns, volatility and correlation. At any point in time, however, valuations of entire asset classes can be well above or well below their historic averages, as commercial property was in 2007, for example. In this case an adviser would adjust the allocations across all their profiles. So while the allocations shown in the table below are probably typical, a more realistic representation of how allocations work over time would be for each allocation to be defined as a percentage range rather than a single number. In this case the percentage of capital allocated to equities in the Growth portfolio could be 60%–80% rather than the 75% shown.

Table 11.3 – Percentage of capital allocated to asset classes

Profile/ portfolio	Cash	Bonds	Absolute/ Hedge	Commercial property	Equities
Cautious	5.0%	40.0%	20.0%	5.0%	30.0%
Conservative	5.0%	30.0%	20.0%	5.0%	40.0%
Balanced	2.5%	20.0%	20.0%	5.0%	52.5%
Growth	2.5%	10.0%	10.0%	2.5%	75.0%
Adventurous	0	7.5%	7.5%	0	85.0%

As discussed in chapter 6, 'Investment planning', the allocation of capital to asset classes is only one factor in determining the risk-return characteristics of the portfolio, which can be substantially changed by the selection of investments within each asset class.

Consistency

The set of profiles and portfolios shown above is consistent. Riskier assets account for a progressively larger share of capital as the tolerance of risk increases. And over the long-term, the volatility of such portfolios would also consistently increase in the same way.

However, as advisers discovered in 2008-2010, in extreme conditions "All correlations go to 1". Prices of corporate bonds and commercial properties fell at the same time as equities and by similar percentages. The short-term volatility and drawdown of cautious portfolios in this period far exceeded predictions based on historical data, whether these predictions were generated by portfolio modelling tools or otherwise.

While there is a natural tendency to want to regard these events as aberrations, they cannot be dismissed from the record. Nor can advisers say with confidence that such conditions could not return. So in the case of all profiles and portfolios, advisers need to add the warning to their descriptions of risk and return that in extreme conditions, volatility may far exceed the norms on which their profiles and portfolios are based.

Review

The world's financial markets are subject not just to cyclical up-and-down moves in the familiar bull-bear pattern. There are also long-term secular trends that persist through market cycles. For example, since 1960 the degree of correlation between world equity markets has steadily increased, to the extent that little diversification benefit is now gained by adding large-cap US or European equities to a holding of UK large-cap shares.

Another such trend is the growing economic strength of China, India and Brazil. This has been reflected in progressively rising allocations of capital to emerging markets in most allocation models over the past decade.

A third such trend is the rise of absolute return investing, now defined as a separate asset class in most models and accounting for a progressively rising percentage of capital in many advisers' cautious portfolios.

These examples show that the asset allocations linked to each risk profile need to be regularly reviewed and adjusted not only in response to market circumstances but in the light of long-term economic and financial trends.

7 Stochastic modelling

Many portfolio planning tools now use risk tolerance or a risk profile as the basis for constructing asset allocation models or fund portfolios.

As noted above, advisers need to take into account capacity for risk as well as attitude to risk, so simply using a questionnaire-based risk profile as an input to a portfolio modelling tool can be dangerous.

Advisers using such methods need to understand the concepts underlying the technology and especially the sensitivity of outputs to changes in the assumptions used. This is one of the most complex fields in financial planning and has a substantial explanatory literature which advisers should consult.

Modelling methods

In essence, these models draw on historic databases of returns, volatility and correlation for the major asset classes. They also use a set of variables such as inflation, short-term interest rates, bond yields, dividend yields and dividend growth rates. Specific numbers or ranges for these variables are set in the model; some or all such variables can be altered by the user.

The model then performs a large number of simulations, using different combinations of variables and historic data. The original term used by mathematicians to describe the process used was 'Monte Carlo simulations', because the combinations are chosen at random ('stochastic' means random). Only a small set (at most tens of thousands) of all the possible permutations of the data (millions or tens of millions) is considered. The model then computes the numbers of simulations producing similar outcomes and generates probability estimates for each outcome. Crucially, these probabilities are based on the assumptions used, and small variations in the assumptions can usually produce much larger variations in the probability ranges for an outcome.

A typical use of this kind of analysis can be found in the Bank of England's quarterly Inflation Report, which contains stochastically modelled estimates of the future course of inflation.

Such models can take any combination of the assets for which historic data is held (a portfolio) and estimate its likely future value over time. The typical stochastic fan chart will show the most likely outcome as the darkest central band, with progressively fainter outlying bands showing outcomes with lower probabilities of occurrence. The data can be presented in monetary terms as a range of values with probabilities for each, or as percentage probabilities of reaching certain monetary values.

Possibly the most significant question an adviser should ask about such models is how long a history it uses for each asset class. Study of the historical data (in the Barclays Capital Equity-Gilt Study or the Credit Suisse Global Investment Returns Yearbook) shows that there have been several periods of up to ten years over the past century over which returns have deviated upwards or downwards from the long-term average. A run of data of less than 20 years is unlikely to capture the full range of possible variations and projections could therefore be biased upwards or downwards.

Merits and drawbacks

Advisers and clients need to be wary of the apparent precision of the projections. A moment's thought will make it clear that a projection of future returns to an accuracy of two decimal places is extremely unlikely to be accurate. Yet the presentation of precise numbers encourages both adviser and client to anchor on these numbers.

Clients may fail to make the distinction between a projection and a forecast. Even when they are clearly told that it is a projection, they may still anchor on the numbers and attach a greater certainty to outcomes than is realistic.

On the other hand, by presenting the client with a graphical range of outcomes, the models make it easier for the client to engage in the risk-reward discussion and to accept, where necessary, a higher degree of risk than they were originally comfortable with in order to stand a better chance of attaining their objectives.

For the adviser, an important benefit of using such a modelling tool is that their portfolio recommendations will be consistent. Achieving the same consistency without the modelling tool requires the creation of the disciplined investment process described in chapter 6, 'Investment planning'.

Fund selection

Some portfolio modelling tools permit the adviser to select the funds that will be used to populate the asset classes in portfolios. Others use quantitative measures based on historic performance to select funds. Tools on provider websites on the other hand often use the provider's funds for a significant part of a portfolio. Advisers need to be aware of any such bias in provider tools.

Where stochastic modelling is applied to asset classes, the model will use conventional indices for historical data. If a fund portfolio is then created using the given asset class combination, the risk-return characteristics of the portfolio can deviate substantially from a portfolio consisting of the indices. Individual funds may have returns and volatilities that differ widely from those of their asset class index.

However, it may not be possible to model such fund portfolios accurately, since many funds will lack sufficient historic data.

Modelling of the outcomes from index-based asset class portfolios is considerably more reliable than modelling outcomes from portfolios of funds.

Whether or not a modelling tool is used, advisers in practice add or subtract risk relative to the index for the asset class through their fund selection.

8 Reviewing risk profiles

On each occasion when fresh recommendations are made to a client, the adviser should ensure that any new information regarding the client's circumstances is taken into account, as discussed in chapter 10. Such new information may on its own require the adviser to re-evaluate the client's risk profile. The attainment of key objectives or milestones is almost certain to require adjustments.

Changes in circumstances

Among the major changes in circumstances that would necessitate a review of the client's risk profile are:

Bereavement: the client may have greater or lesser resources to meet their objectives, and their objectives are also likely to alter.

Inheritance: possession of more free capital will usually increase risk capacity.

Retirement: it usually requires a period in retirement for the client's lifestyle to adjust, and when it does, their requirements from their investments may change.

Children: birth of children, their progress through the educational system and their attainment of independence may all prompt changes in the client's risk profile.

Age: people tend to become more conservative in most respects as they grow older. This does not always apply to attitudes to risk, but advisers should expect some change in attitude between the ages of 55 and 70 for example.

In some cases, only the client's capacity for risk may change while the adviser may be confident that their tolerance of risk remains unchanged. However, it is good practice to check this by asking the client to complete a fresh risk questionnaire.

Additionally, most advisers recognise a change in clients' attitudes to risk as they grow more familiar with the behaviour of their investments. In general, most note an increasing acceptance of risk as compared with the situation where they had no experience of investment. Accordingly, it is good practice for advisers to test new clients' attitudes to risk through a risk questionnaire after a few years even if their circumstances remain unchanged.

Chapter 12
Client management

1 The business and its clients

Financial advisers need to deal with many issues arising from the personal relationship between client and adviser. Some of these can be dealt with by establishing processes. But many will be 'one-off' issues relating to specific circumstances that require careful and sensitive handling. As far as possible firms should establish procedures for dealing with these issues.

Financial advice is a service business and firms should seek client feedback about client's perceptions of the level of service they have received.

2 The initial meeting

The initial meeting with a client should establish the foundations for the whole relationship. It is possible to recover from a poor first meeting with a client but there is only one chance to make a first impression and it will stay in the client's memory.

The purpose of the initial meeting should be to:

- Discover whether the individual fits the criteria established for the target client profile for the business.

- Explain the adviser service proposition to the potential client in a compelling way, mapping out what the firm can achieve for the client, the process and the charging basis.

Most advisers do not make a charge for the initial meeting. A good way to establish that no meeting is free is to describe the first meeting 'as being at the firm's expense' – rather than saying that it is 'free'.

Some advisers prefer the initial meeting to be genuinely open-ended and simply respond to the client's questions and interests. Others use a structured process, and given the uncertainties most people have about what financial planning is and how it works, including a formal explanation of the adviser's proposition (see chapter 7, 'The advice proposition') is helpful. The firm's brochure may contain the proposition in detail, but the client will often merely scan this and the initial meeting is a good opportunity to ensure the client really understands what the adviser is offering and at what cost.

The client will often appreciate a clear explanation of the firm's client agreement/Services and Cost Disclosure Document (SCDD) covering the scope of the service and the costs.

As in any service business, though, 'people buy people', and advisers need to avoid too much emphasis on procedure at the expense of the 'what's in it for me?' question that will always be in the prospective client's mind.

For the client, a key feature of professional financial planning services is the continuity of the relationship with the adviser. People value this highly, but the clearer they are about this aspect of the financial planning service, the more concerned they are likely to be that they really do trust and get on with the adviser. The adviser needs to recognise this concern and respond to any opportunities to foster the trust that will form the foundation of the relationship.

One way of making the prospective client feel easier about embarking on the relationship is to demonstrate that the adviser already has clients like them. Where people have been referred by a client or professional connection, this will usually have been established already. If this is not the case, it is worth researching in advance the client's business and social connections since the adviser may have existing clients who have a connection.

3 Selecting clients

Historically, many advisers simply accepted the vast majority of people who approached them for advice as clients. When a transactional remuneration and service model is used, this can be a valid approach. But when advisers have developed an ongoing service proposition on a fee basis, then an open door policy is not good practice.

Each firm should establish the criteria for the types of people they want to have as clients (see chapters 4, 'Different types of client', and 7, 'The advice proposition') in line with their service proposition. The key indicators are likely to be such characteristics as age, level of wealth, occupation, type of problem (e.g. estate planning) or some other distinguishing features that allow the firm to build a degree of expertise and common process in dealing with clients. This is increasingly recognised as a preferable strategy for a practice than simply taking on any clients who come through the door on a 'taxi-cab rank' basis.

But there are a number of client characteristics that all financial planners should be wary of, and clients they should generally aim to avoid. Some clients can be educated out of some of these attributes, but advisers should not be excessively optimistic about their probable success rate in this regard.

The client with unrealistic expectations Some clients expect to beat the investment market in all circumstance; others hope to be able to pay no tax. Clients need to be told about the limitations of the service; otherwise there will be fall-out later on when they discover reality and feel let down.

The client with complaints Excessive and unreasonable complaints about the client's previous advisers, or very frequent moves between advisers in the past, can be warning signs.

The client who does not appreciate the value of the service The client who starts off by complaining about the costs when they are explained will almost certainly be difficult when it comes to paying the adviser's fee bills.

The client with values that clash badly with those of the adviser Some advisers specialise in sophisticated tax avoidance schemes; they should be able to look after clients who do not want that type of advice, but may have difficulty in keeping to the straightforward approach to planning. Equally, some clients want their adviser to help them with avoidance schemes; it should be possible to delegate that to a specialist adviser, but some advisers have moral scruples about such planning, in which case they would do better not to have such clients. At the extreme are people who are not truthful with the adviser, in which case they may well be untruthful with others such as HM Revenue & Customs. Advisers should be very careful about dealing with such people. The extra care and documentation required in dealing with them mean that even if they do not cause legal or regulatory problems they will certainly be less profitable for the adviser than normal clients.

4 Couples and families

Where the adviser is engaged by an individual, the relationship is simple. But when an adviser is engaged by a couple as their joint adviser, it can be much more complex.

Many older couples today still conform to a 'together for life' model in which it is assumed that all major decisions will be made jointly. But the younger the clients, the less likely this is the model for relationship or financial arrangements. As noted in chapter 4, 'Different types of client', many clients live complicated lives, and this can present advisers with some challenging issues.

Joint or individual

With couples, the key issue may be whether planning is undertaken as a joint exercise. Some may prefer to have entirely separate relationships with an adviser and entirely personalised financial plans, and in the extreme may even want to have different advisers. In the case of married couples, or those in civil partnerships, this does create difficulties since some decisions have to be made jointly. Clients need to understand that this way of working is more cumbersome, can be less efficient and will certainly be more costly than having the same adviser.

A more common situation is that couples are happy to use the same adviser and plan their affairs jointly, but have such different attitudes to risk that they prefer to have two separate investment portfolios with different risk profiles rather than one joint portfolio. If the amounts of assets and tax status of both partners are the same, this should have no negative implications, but if only one is a higher rate taxpayer and the assets are sufficiently large that they will incur capital gains tax at the higher rate while their partner may incur no capital gains tax, then individual ownership of separate portfolios could result in higher tax bills. This in turn might necessitate a different use of tax wrappers – for example, using an offshore bond as the wrapper for the higher rate taxpayer's portfolio – which would otherwise not be required. Clients may need to understand in some detail the consequences of running two separate portfolios in order to make an informed decision. Some may say that they are prepared to incur extra tax, but this 'in principle' attitude may change if the adviser presents them with scenarios showing the actual tax bills they might face.

Family issues

An adviser may over time take on several related clients. This can create interpersonal problems, for example where the younger generation want to know about provisions of the older generation's wills, or wish to restrict the possible expenditure of parental capital on nursing home care. Both parties may wish to place the adviser in the role of mediator. In this case the adviser must ensure that they obtain clients' agreements for any release of confidential information, and that all parties are aware that the adviser's actions must always be governed by their duty of care to each individual client, a responsibility which can only be set aside by the courts of law.

In extreme circumstances, in the case of bitter family disputes, the adviser may need to refuse a mediation role in order to be able to fulfil their responsibilities to one or more clients. Clarity of communication is vital in such cases.

In recommending and arranging Powers of Attorney, advisers need to be aware of any conflicts within the family. Where these are profound, it will be preferable for someone who is not a family member to be nominated as Attorney.

Advisers may find themselves in a difficult position where they have assisted in the establishment of a trust, and later act for a member of the family who is a beneficiary and wishes to alter the terms of the trust or the size or nature of its disbursements. It may be impossible for the adviser to act both for the trustees and for the beneficiary.

In the more normal situation of relatively harmonious family relationships, it is good practice to make the younger generation aware of inheritance planning measures, and advisers should encourage their older clients to engage their children in issues of inheritance and long-term care at an early stage.

An increasingly frequent issue is inheritance provisions where a married couple both have children by former partners as well as together. Both spouses will normally wish to make provision for the children of an earlier marriage as well as for the children of their later marriage. This can become contentious. It may be the lawyer arranging the wills who deals with these issues but the financial adviser can also become involved. It may be helpful to encourage an element of conditionality in the provisions to appeal to principles of fairness and to recommend periodic review of the provisions, which both spouses are likely to wish to change if the circumstances, and especially the financial well being, of their children change significantly.

5 Dealing with inconsistencies

The nature of financial planning is that people want to achieve many things but cannot achieve them all. Sometimes they do not want to accept the limitations imposed by circumstances and resources and try to fudge the issue by being inconsistent. This is not just damaging for them, since it means they are probably allowing themselves to have unrealistic expectations, but also dangerous for the adviser, who is likely to be blamed if something goes wrong. It is therefore important for the adviser to confront such inconsistencies and resolve them before they present the client with the final version of their plan.

Assumptions and intentions

In creating a financial plan, the adviser negotiates a set of assumptions with the client. They will often include expectations regarding future earnings, especially the rate of increase in real income they expect, as well as of the rate of inflation. As is well known (see chapter 3, 'The impact of behavioural finance'), clients tend to be over-optimistic, so they may prefer a scenario in which their earnings rise at a significantly faster rate than inflation over a long period. This scenario is inconsistent since if on average wages rise much faster than inflation for even a few years, the rate of inflation will accelerate and the real rate of increase in earnings will decline.

A key assumption in many financial plans for younger people is that the amount of money saved, and the proportion of net income saved, will increase. This is often inconsistent with the client's previous behaviour and is unlikely to happen without considerable effort. The adviser may need to build 'nudges' into their plan (for example, a commitment to save a proportion of every pay increase) to help them with this.

As discussed in chapter 3, 'The impact of behavioural finance'), we suffer from many perceptual and behavioural biases that are hard to override. A client may, for example, intellectually accept that they are affected by the familiarity bias, yet insist on continuing to add to their shareholding in their employer. Many clients may agree that the long-term outlook for house prices in the UK is not nearly as positive as it was in the last two decades, yet continue to assume that the value of the equity in their home will continue to grow at two or three times the rate of inflation.

Risk and return

A frequent area of inconsistency is risk and return. Clients agree a set of objectives, but do not want to accept the level of risk required to meet them. They may then qualify their statements about risk ("I know that the plan requires a moderate risk rating but really I am more cautious"). Or they may focus on reducing the level of risk on part of their investments, which may later be misremembered as having set a lower risk requirement for all of them.

Securing unequivocal client consent to a specified level of risk is absolutely essential for the investment or savings element of a financial plan.

Commitment

Most people who engage in financial planning do so because they believe it will improve their financial situation. But some people adopt a 'magical thinking' approach, that merely creating the plan is all that is required. Advisers therefore need to test the client's commitment to the plan and the processes of creating and implementing it, and particularly to any changes in their own behaviour that are agreed as essential components of the plan.

Advisers need to recognise signs of weakness in commitment, including a casual attitude to information, a refusal to undertake detailed budgeting, procrastination and a lack of communication between couples on key issues in the plan.

Giving such clients checklists of actions required from them, or questionnaires on their responses to 'what if?' scenarios ('How would you respond to a shortfall of £x thousand per year in your retirement income?') may help them to focus on their own part in the planning process.

However committed people are to their plan, they will need regular updates from the adviser. In the case of people whose commitment is weak, reinforcement can be achieved by focusing on the positive effects of changes in the client's behaviour on their financial progress. Graphical illustrations can be especially powerful.

6 Client feedback

Advisers wanting to improve and refine their proposition and service need to obtain feedback from clients. And from a business management point of view, firms need to assess the client satisfaction rating achieved by individual advisers.

The following benefits can be obtained if this is done well:

Track response If the survey is repeated regularly any pattern of change in the response will quickly be evident and can serve as an early warning sign of problems.

Adviser monitoring The firm can record the development of advisers and use this as an input to their training and competency activities.

Treating customers fairly Survey results can support advisers in ensuring they are meeting their regulatory obligations.

The two main ways of gathering client feedback are:

- Occasional survey
- Questionnaire for each client

Survey design

In both cases the firm will design a questionnaire. This should consist of neutral questions that do not lead the client to a particular answer.

The answers are best provided as tick boxes for at least three and preferably five responses. A five-response series using the following can work well with suitable questions:

Strongly agree, Somewhat agree, Neither agree nor disagree, Slightly disagree, Strongly disagree.

The same questions and answers need to be used over a period for comparison of results to be possible. A maximum of ten questions should be sufficient to assess a client's experience of the service provided by the firm and the individual adviser. Questions should cover the quality and scope of advice and how well the client understood it or felt it was explained, as well as the delivery and administration of the service.

Possible statements/questions include:

'The service is well defined – I know what I am getting.'

'I understand what I am being charged for service and advice.'

'Letters and reports are easy to understand.'

'I always receive a prompt reply to my queries.'

At least one open-ended question should be included along the lines of:

'Is there anything we could have done better?'

This enables those clients who wish to express personal views to do so.

It is good practice for the questionnaire to be sent by one of the principals of the business with a personal letter emphasising the confidentiality of the survey and the importance the firm places on gaining feedback from clients. If a printed form is used a reply-paid envelope should be provided. No other material should be included.

Occasional surveys

Firms must be wary of drawing conclusions from occasional surveys that account for only a small proportion of clients. But obtaining a sufficient response may be problematic.

One method is to randomly select a sample, say 10% of all clients of the business, to receive the questionnaire. Another is to send the questionnaire to all clients who have been taken on by the firm in the past year or some other period.

If clients are selected to receive the survey based on age, assets, location or other criteria the resulting data may have some use to the business but will not be meaningful in terms of assessing whether the firm is meeting its TCF obligations.

Regular surveys

The other main option with feedback is to seek it from every new client. In this case the survey is sent to clients at a defined point in the new client acquisition process, usually after the principal recommendations made by the adviser have been implemented and the relevant documentation has been sent to the client.

The advantage of this method is that the experience is fresh in the client's mind, so that responses may be more accurate. The disadvantage is that minor problems, such as a delay in the receipt of a particular document, may cause a client to lower their rating of the service, whereas if they completed the survey six months later they might have forgotten about this and no longer regard it as significant.

For the purposes of analysis, response scores can be compared on a monthly or quarterly basis.

Chapter 13
Summarising and analysing needs and priorities

1 Introduction

Some financial planners may be tempted to leave out the summarising and analysing stage in the financial planning process. They leap from fact-finding to recommendation without the necessary intervening stage of thinking rigorously about all the areas where they can help the client. The result is often that such advisers focus on just one problem and solution and miss many other important opportunities. A key skill that all financial planners need to develop is the analysis of needs.

This step in reality consists of three smaller steps of summarising, analysing and prioritising:

- Summarising is about bringing all the key facts together in such a way that they make sense and demonstrate the main issues;

- Analysing the situation should lead to the identification of problems and gaps;

- Prioritising needs is deciding which is the most urgent and important and the order in which to deal with them, and/or providing the resources to focus on them.

In most cases, financial planners present the summarising/analysing step with the recommendations. But in more complex cases of comprehensive planning, it may be preferable to review the summarising/analysing step separately to check the facts and the main conclusions before moving onto the detailed recommendations.

Part of the purpose of the summarising and analysing stage is to present the client with a clear statement of their overall financial position, so that they understand their situation much more clearly. Often, clients have a hazy view of their circumstances and find it hard to decide on a strategy for their future without understanding where they are now. The other reason for presenting the contents of the fact-find in a more summarised and analytical way is to check that the fact-finding process was accurate. It will also help identify if any additional information is needed.

Advisers may develop their own range of analytical tools and spreadsheets. Not all this data will be useful to clients. So what is actually presented to the client as the basis for their report will depend partly on the sophistication of the client and partly on the needs identified at the next stage of the process. For example, if a client has undertaken a detailed budgeting analysis on their own, there is little point in the adviser presenting a detailed analysis – a summary will be sufficient. On the other hand, if the client has not done this and is clearly unclear about their commitments, it may be worth including a more detailed analysis of expenditure in their report – although almost certainly in an appendix.

Gap analysis is a widely used expression that describes the process of defining and quantifying a client's needs and wishes and then comparing these with the current provision. If the current provision is adequate, there is no gap; but if the client's current provision is non-existent or inadequate, the process should help identify the gap and quantify it.

Example 13.1

Jack needs (and wants) an income in retirement that will maintain his current standard of living, after allowing for his likely changed spending pattern after he stops work. The financial planner identifies that Jack will need a net income, using today's values, of about £55,000 a year when he retires. His current pension savings levels and state pension entitlement seems likely to generate about £30,000 a year, so Jack has a projected gap in his retirement income needs of about £25,000 a year.

---

2 Income and expenditure analysis

The analysis of current income and expenditure is the basis for much future planning and so it needs to be undertaken with care. The picture should be built up step by step:

- First, current income, future income and contingent expenditure;

- Then current expenditure, future expenditure and contingent expenditure;

- Finally comparing income and expenditure in each situation to identify any gaps or dangers.

Lifetime cashflow modelling

Lifetime cashflow modelling is increasingly used to help financial planners, and their clients, determine whether they will have enough to live on in retirement from the assets they have already built up and are then likely to accumulate in the future. Specialist software packages are widely available that allow advisers and their clients to model future income and expenditure. Crucially, they depend on the various key assumptions the adviser makes about factors such as longevity, future earnings, tax rates, expenditure, savings levels and investment returns. If these assumptions are nonsensical, the projections will be very distorted and misleading. On the other hand, the model is just a what if projection; it is bound to be a rough guide not an accurate prediction of the future.

Example 13.2

Peter is assumed to have built up £100,000 of pensions and investments, and in the next ten years (up to his expected retirement age of 65), it is assumed that this will grow to combined pension and investment funds of £450,000 in current values. Peter and his adviser calculate his outgoings in retirement, which are based on his current expenditure after some reduction for changed circumstances (e.g. paying off the mortgage and no longer having access to a company car). They assume that Peter could live to 100 (to be on the reasonably safe side, although they may choose 105 to be even more cautious. On these assumptions, the life time cashflow projection shows that Peter is likely to run out of funds when he reaches the age of, say, 87 years. The precise date when the money runs out is not so important; different assumptions might lead to other conclusions and it might occur several years earlier or later. The point is that based on reasonable assumptions, there are not sufficient resources to provide Peter with a comfortable retirement.

The purpose of the projection is to help the client decide that there need to be changes to the financial plan either to increase the resources or lower the income expectations (or possibly both); but that is the subject for the later chapter on retirement planning recommendations.

3 Income summarised and analysed

The fact-finding process should provide the data on which current net and gross income can be summarised and analysed. It is also part of the process to consider:

- Future earnings;
- Future pension entitlements;
- Contingent income.

Contingent income is what the client would receive under various different circumstances, such as serious illness, unemployment or the death of a spouse/partner.

Current income

Each source of income should be shown with the amount, the rates and levels of tax and national insurance contributions and the net income. Stable income – from salary or pensions – should be distinguished from more volatile income, like bonuses, overtime or self-employed earnings. It makes sense to check that the tax deducted under PAYE is correct. Income should be summarised by the year but also quarterly or monthly if there are significant variations of the course of a year.

Example 13.3

John has an annual income this year of £80,000 of which £60,000 is a dependable salary and the balance of £20,000 consists of two bonuses. About £5,000 is paid in June and £15,000 is paid in December. Tax is deducted at source and his tax position for the year 2010/11 is as follows:

	£	£
Earnings		80,000
Personal allowance	6,475	
Taxable	73,525	
First £37,400 taxed at 20%	7,480	
Balance of £36,125 at 40%	14,450	
Total tax		21,930
Employee NIC at 11%	4,197.60	
Employee NIC at 1%	361.25	
Total employee NIC		4,558.85
Total tax and NIC deductions		26,488.85
Net annual income		53,511.15
Percentage of gross income		66.89%
Net June bonus	3,344	
Net December bonus	10,033	
Net income in June		6,688
Net income December		13,377
Net income in other months		3,344

Benefits in kind can form a substantial part of the remuneration of some people and any of them are taxable. Benefits commonly include a company car, season ticket loan, medical insurance, free life cover and income protection. They may have to be taken into account in analysing the costs of moving jobs, or becoming unemployed and considering the replacement income that will be needed in retirement. The company car and private medical insurance will probably be missed in retirement; the season ticket loan will almost certainly not be relevant.

Where the financial planner is working for two clients, it is essential to show their incomes separately in order to demonstrate their relative significance, for example, if one of them stopped work.

For higher rate and additional rate taxpayers, it is helpful to highlight the amount of their incomes subject to 40% and 50% tax rates. In the example above, the estimate is that the client is subject to 40% tax (32.5% in the case of dividends) on approximately £36,000 of income. This could be a useful pointer to the amount that the client might consider investing in their pension fund to achieve the highest possible tax saving for them. It might also help the client to change their investment strategy to some extent and increase their holdings in investments that should generate capital gains taxable at between nil and 28%.

Expectations of future earnings

A client's future earning potential will determine their likely savings capacity and will be reflected in their financial aims and ambitions. So the analysis of the client's income should take into account the safety of their occupation, their prospects for increasing income and promotion, their ability to keep working on a part-time basis (e.g. during and after pregnancy or in semi-retirement), the extent to which the client enjoys their occupation and would like to continue working for as long as possible.

The analysis of future income requires clients and planners to be realistic about the client's earning capacity and preparedness to work in different circumstances. For example, the kind of work that someone might be able and prepared to do in the early years of retirement might turn out to be quite different from what the individual has been used to at the height of their career, both in terms of the level of earnings and the type of work itself. They may find that their sources of work decline as they get older and their skills might be viewed as becoming out of date. Equally, they might find working less congenial.

If incomes decline in the future, the impact of taxation on net spendable income may be expected to fall. Equally, if a client expects to be a high flier, they can usually expect their tax rates to rise.

Expectations of future retirement income

One of the key objectives for most clients is having enough income in retirement. So it is important to be able to calculate the gap between the projected level of retirement income based on the current provision and the level of expected or required expenditure. Expenditure is discussed separately below.

There are four main sources of retirement income:

- State pension;
- Defined benefit (DB) pension schemes;
- Defined contribution (DC) pension schemes;
- Investment income and capital gains.

The pensions from state pensions and defined benefit schemes can be most easily estimated in current values. Details of a person's state pension entitlements can be ascertained by applying to the DWP. Benefits from DB schemes can be obtained from current employers and clients should generally have details of their benefits from previous employers. The further the client is from retirement age, the greater is the degree of uncertainty about the value of DB pensions; for example, the client could move employers or the employer could change the scheme.

DC schemes may present more difficulties. The normal approach is for the financial planner to assume that the fund will accumulate into a capital sum in the future, at which point the client will start to draw on the funds in a process of what has come to be called (rather inelegantly) 'decumulation'. Investment funds outside pension arrangements may be treated in much the same way for the purposes of determining whether the client has enough resources at retirement.

The financial planner has a choice between projecting future values in nominal terms and projecting future values in real terms. Projecting future values in nominal terms has to include the effect of inflation as well as real investment growth and might lead to projections based on annual growth rates of say 5%, 7% or even 9%. In contrast real growth rates should be represented by lower numbers, because the assumed rate of inflation is excluded; so if the assumption is the government's target rate of 2.5% annual inflation, this might lead to projected real growth rates of 2.5%, 4.5% and 6.5% a year.

In practice, it is usually best to project the values of the capital and income from these pensions and investments in real terms so they can easily be compared with the client's current level of expenditure. State pensions should be valued at the current levels; DB scheme benefits should be expressed as a proportion of current earnings and DC scheme benefits and investment income should reflect potential real growth with no inflation. It is possible to use nominal figures for both investments and pensions but it is more complicated in practice to inflate both income and expenditure and think about them realistically in inflated pounds.

Financial planners should help their clients understand about real rates of growth and how they compare to nominal rates. This means their having some view about future investment returns and inflation. Projected investment returns should also take into account the mix of the underlying investments. The average annual real rate of return on UK equities between 1959 and 2009 was just over 5%, with some very large fluctuations around the mean (plus 99% in the calendar year 1975 and minus 59% the previous year). The real return on gilts was much lower at nearly 1.5% a year, also with some surprisingly large fluctuations (plus 43% in the calendar year 1982 and minus 28.8% in the high inflation year of 1974). These historic growth rates relate to very different times from our own; they take into account no deductions for management or trading expenses and they assume that all income is reinvested – which would certainly not hold good in retirement.

Financial advisers should involve their clients in deciding what assumptions to make about investment returns and the likely future rates of inflation, but clients will need a lot of guidance and it makes no sense to ask them what rates of return and inflation they would like to use, at least not without first having an in-depth discussion. Prudence would suggest that it is normally most appropriate to use reasonably conservative assumptions about future real rates of growth. These assumptions can then be fed into the lifetime cashflow projection.

Example 13.4

Mike's financial adviser was able to project that in real terms, he had the following levels of retirement income starting at age 65 and at 2010 values:

- State retirement pensions of £9,080 which are index-linked;
- DB scheme benefits of £11,000 subject to limited price indexation;
- DC pension funds of £250,000;
- Investments worth an estimated £300,000.

Contingent earnings

There are three main areas in which the financial planner should work with the client to calculate their income in the event of certain contingencies:

- Death of one or both spouses/partners;
- Serious illness of one or both spouses/partners;
- Unemployment of one or both spouses/partners.

As with retirement income, the impact of tax on net income might often be expected to fall as incomes reduce, especially if the individual ceases to be an additional or higher rate taxpayer. But this may not occur if just one partner suffers a loss of income.

Death of one or both partners

The earnings of the partner would stop at their death. But the income from any investments would presumably continue and there might well be capital payments from life policies and pension arrangements that would generate some additional income or pay-off loans.

Serious illness of self or partner The earnings from employment or self-employment might be expected to stop at some point — possibly very soon. Where the client is employed, the financial planner should find out the terms of the employer's sick pay scheme. Very often, employees over-estimate the length of time that they will be paid by their employers. A few employers have income protection schemes or early retirement arrangements for people in ill-health and these should be factored into the calculations where they apply. State benefits may also provide some support, although this is likely to be relatively low and will be subject to future changes reducing their value still further.

Some clients also have individual income protection plans. A larger number may have critical illness policies whose proceeds could be invested to provide an income or a capital sum to pay off liabilities. Critical illness policies are a partial answer to this type of protection need because they do not cover a large swathe of illnesses.

Unemployment of self or partner Similar considerations apply to people who lose their jobs and need to make radical changes to their working ambitions in the light of new realities about their employability. Major life changes around work are likely to require a period of adjustment to lower earnings or perhaps even no earnings whatsoever. Clients need to be aware that state unemployment benefits are not generous.

4 Expenditure summarised and analysed

Evaluating a client's expenditure can take a considerable amount of detailed work. Many clients have only a very vague idea of their spending habits and can be surprised when they see them categorised by type and amount over a year.

Current expenditure

Current expenditure should be categorised by the main headings or cost centres, e.g. mortgage, other housing, household, clothing, holidays, leisure, eating out etc. Tax could be analysed under either income or expenditure (see above) but it is a very significant factor.

This form of analysis, which breaks expenditure down into major categories, is almost always useful and will be essential if reductions in expenditure will be required to fund protection or savings needs.

Example 13.5

Annual income and expenditure summary for Jenny and David

Item	Annual £	% of total expenditure
Jenny's net salary	42,000	
David's net salary	67,000	
Total income	**109,000**	**103%**
Mortgage repayments	19,000	17%
Other household spending	6,500	6%
Food	9,000	8%
Leisure/eating out	6,500	6%
Car and travel	13,000	12%
Clothing	7,500	7%
Debt repayments (ex mortgage)	4,500	4%
Holidays	7,500	7%
Other personal, e.g. gym	3,000	3%
Insurance	4,500	4%
Education – school fees	28,000	26%
Total expenditure	**106,000**	**100%**
Net cashflow	**+ 3,000**	**3%**

Discretionary expenditure

The analysis of expenditure will identify discretionary expenditure and essential expenditure. In practice there are likely to be several categories of expenditure, depending on the degree of ease with which it is possible for a client to change their spending patterns.

Some people have an excess of income over expenditure. But many clients find that they need to identify what expenditure they can reduce in order to be able to afford to meet their financial goals. These goals could be making the spending no more than their net income, taking on a higher mortgage, spending more on life and health protection premiums, or saving for retirement or some other important goal.

Affordability in this sense is a variable concept; the likely benefits of the route chosen need to outweigh the sacrifices. In some cases, the benefits (such as increased investment in a pension) may be rather uncertain and involve a degree of risk as to their outcomes; while the sacrifices are all too clear and immediate. That does not mean that clients should not make sacrifices to achieve goals; simply that they should be aware of the implications and uncertainties, so that they remain genuinely motivated to stick to the plan. They should also be realistic about their ability to maintain the savings they have decided to make or they may start a commitment that they cannot keep up and end up worse off as a result. The main categories of spending are likely to be as follows:

Easy economies Virtually everyone can make some economies in their expenditure. Reducing spending on eating out at expensive restaurants or taking less luxurious holidays could be relatively easy for a client to achieve.

More difficult economies Some cuts in spending hurt more than others. Clients who are determined to meet a particular goal (such as paying expensive school fees) may decide to cut-out all or almost all spending on holidays and leisure. Clothes and consumer durables like cars and domestic appliances are made to last long after their natural replacement date. They may decide not to move house even if their existing home is rather too small for their needs.

Disruptive and painful economies Some spending cuts will cause major disruption and changes in lifestyle and would only be made after very careful consideration. Moving home to take out a cheaper mortgage and reduce the outgoings would be more disruptive. Taking a child out of private education could also provide a substantial, if painful, economy.

Future expenditure

The further ahead the period for which the client is budgeting, the more difficult it is to be accurate. Financial planners should beware of spurious accuracy or precision in their forecasting and clients should be warned that the figures are very rough approximations. They are subject to changes in prices, technology, tastes, needs, inflation and general circumstances. On the whole, it makes sense to use round figures as far as possible in projections to avoid giving the impression of assumed accuracy.

The most common budgeting requirement is retirement. The estimate is likely to be based on current expenditure, with some adjustment for the changed lifestyle. The most common areas in which expenditure might change are:

Leisure spending This might tend to rise as people have more spare time, especially in the early and more active periods of retirement. However, holiday costs might drop to some extent because of the possibility of taking advantage of special off-season holidays and more leisurely means of travel.

Travel Some travel will probably reduce, notably travel to work. Certain travel costs decline because of the concessions that are available to older people. But other travel costs may rise with a greater appetite for tourism. The loss of the company car may be a cost that is not taken into account.

Housing Clients should aim to pay off their mortgage by the time they retire, or else convert it to a lifetime loan or other form of equity release if there is no feasible alternative. It may also be possible and even desirable to move to a smaller and less expensive property.

Healthcare Private medical insurance becomes very much more expensive as people get into their late 60s and 70s or older. Those who need to economise may choose less comprehensive policies or drop such insurance altogether and depend wholly on the NHS.

Long-term care If it turns out that a client needs long-term care, that could lead to an increase in expenditure of up to many tens of thousands of pounds a year.

Example 13.6

Jenny and David's discretionary spending

Based on the figures in the example 13.5, David and Jenny thought that if required, they could save up to about £11,000 a year without making major in-roads into their quality of life, although some cuts in expenditure would be more painful than others. They felt that cuts of about £6,000 could be made with very little difficulty.

Expenditure	Current spending £	Reduced spending £	Possible reduction £
Food	9,000	8,000	1,000
Car and travel	13,000	9,000	4,000
Clothing	7,500	4,000	3,500
Holidays	7,500	3,000	4,500
Personal e.g. gym	3,000	2,000	1,000
Total	**40,000**	**26,000**	**14,000**

They feel that if things became very difficult, it would be possible to go without holidays for a year or two, cut down on travel and most personal expenditure and make further all round reductions of £16,000, saving a total of £27,000.

The last level of spending cuts that they would most want to avoid would to move to a smaller home and cut back or even eliminate the school fees.

Contingent expenditure

It is also important to calculate the level of expenditure that would be needed in various unfortunate circumstances so that they can be compared with the available income to determine gaps.

Death of one or both partners Where at least two people are financially interdependent, there should be projections of expenditure based on the death of each of individual. The projection would need to take account of the changed expenditure pattern, after allowing for the repayment of any debt covered by life assurance, as well as the reduction in expenditure attributable to the deceased person (e.g. their clothing and travel) and any increase that would arise as a result of their death (e.g. increased childcare costs).

Example 13.7

If Jenny were to die, there would be some reduction in personal expenditure e.g. on her clothing and personal expenses, but this might not amount to much more than about £1,000 a month. However, this would be almost certainly more than offset by increased expenses on childcare and additional help around the home. The insurance policy covering the mortgage would mean that the monthly repayments would be eliminated, saving £19,000 a year.

Serious illness of self or one or both partners Serious illness in itself is unlikely to mean any reduction in a client's expenditure, other than the general economies that can be achieved on discretionary expenditure set out above.

Example 13.8

If Jenny were to become seriously ill, there would be no saving on expenditure; indeed there may even be an increase. Her salary would cease (say after six months) and would be replaced by relatively low state benefits. The total identified possible savings of £27,000 would not replace the £42,000 net earnings that Jenny currently receives and they would almost certainly be forced to move to a cheaper home and substantially reduce the school fees payments — probably meaning a change of school.

Unemployment of one or both partners Unemployment itself would also have very little impact on the level of expenditure.

5 Income and expenditure analysis

Comparing current income and expenditure

Income then needs to be compared to expenditure. For most people, the most fundamental issue will be the relationship of their income to their expenditure now and in the very immediate future. The first step is to take the income and expenditure figures from the fact-find and set them out clearly. The example above simply summarises information gathered through the fact-find or from statements provided by the client. Some analysis of this data is also useful. Key numbers in the analysis of income and expenditure are:

- What is the monthly amount of surplus or deficit?

- What is the surplus or deficit as a percentage of net disposable income?

- What is the monetary amount of contributions to long-term savings and what percentage is this of net disposable income?

- What is the monetary amount of debt repayments in total and mortgage repayments in particular and what percentage of net disposable income do these account for?

- What is the monetary total of fixed commitments other than debt repayments and what percentage is this of net disposable income?

In performing this analysis, the adviser should take an average of recent monthly figures, which will usually be drawn from the bank current account statements. But wide variations in monthly data should also prompt further investigation. Adjustments may need to be made if large one-off payments pass through this account, for example payment of an annual tax bill. The monthly analysis is useful because clients tend to manage cash on a monthly basis. For planning purposes, an annual statement is also useful. Clients who are reasonably disciplined will have considered their monthly budget and may have calculated an average monthly surplus or deficit.

Current expenditure should be compared to current net income, showing the short and long-term savings areas of outgoings separately, in order to determine whether the client has disposable income that can be used to meet their financial goals before making any adjustments to their current patterns of spending.

6 Balance sheet analysis

Assets and liabilities can be viewed in different ways. The top-level summary will show all assets and liabilities in one statement. This overview will include items such as properties and chattels. This will often show substantial net worth.

This 'balance sheet' way of looking at client data has some limitations. A company with a large surplus of assets over liabilities is normally ready to convert its assets into cash and back into other types of asset. Individuals are not usually prepared to do this, because they are often attached to their first and, in some cases, second homes which account for a substantial proportion of net worth. So a total statement of net worth, offsetting debt against all assets, which can be regarded as the top-level summary of a client's financial position, is often not the most useful in financial planning terms.

There may be issues concerning the client's commitment to financing property ownership that need addressing, but these are more likely to be seen in terms of the income and expenditure analysis. So the financial planner will usually focus on the client's financial assets.

7 Analysis of assets

Assets can be categorised in different ways; at the highest level they should be divided into used assets, investments and pensions. Investments and pensions count as financial assets. Some assets – such as holiday homes – may straddle the categories of used assets and financial assets, if the property is both used by the owner and also let out. Ownership of assets should be clearly set out. An example of how it can be easily analysed is in the example below.

Example 13.9

Jenny and David's total assets

Item	Jenny	David	Joint	Total	% of total
Main residence			£500,000*	£500,000	32%
Holiday home			£180,000	£180,000	12%
Chattels	£8,000	£17,000	£8,000	£33,000	2%
Total used assets	£8,000	£17,000	£688,000	£713,000	46%
Cash deposits	£12,000	£12,000	£35,000	£59,000	4%
Funds and investment bonds	£25,000	£40,000	£160,000	£225,000	14%
Total investments	£37,000	£52,000	£195,000	£284,000	18%
Pension funds+	£120,000	£430,000		£550,000	36%
Total financial assets	£157,000	£482,000	£195,000	£834,000	54%
Totals	**£165,000**	**£499,000**	**£883,000**	**£1,547,000**	**100%**
Less mortgage			**£200,000**	**£200,000**	**13%**
Net wealth	**£165,000**	**£499,000**	**£683,000**	**£1,347,000**	

* Held as a joint tenancy

+ DC schemes current values

For many people, this analysis will show that properties account for a high percentage of their net worth. For example, this would be typical of a retired couple who had paid off all or most of their residential mortgage. In effect, a large part of their cashflow over many years will have been devoted to accumulating capital in their property. For many retired people, this produces the familiar 'asset-rich, cash-poor' position. Substantial commitments to property and to mortgage repayments at younger ages are warning signs that the client may end up in this position.

The home, second properties and chattels are either fixed items or have little residual value for most people. So for the purposes of considering the accumulation of financial assets, a further analysis excluding these fixed items should be prepared.

Example 13.10

Jenny and David's financial assets

Item	Jenny	David	Joint	Total	% of total
Cash deposits	£12,000	£12,000	£35,000	£59,000	7%
Investments	£25,000	£40,000	£160,000	£225,000	27%
Pension funds	£120,000	£430,000	–	£550,000	66%
Totals	**£157,000**	**£482,000**	**£195,000**	**£834,000**	**100%**

Many people adopt different attitudes towards pension funds compared to free capital in other investments. However, as restrictions on pension funds are reduced, it is likely that clients will increasingly view all their investments as a single set. Depending on the client's attitudes, it may be useful to present information on the investments in one or both of the following formats. A notional capital value can be attributed to DB scheme entitlements for the purposes of a top-level summary. But because they cannot be analysed in terms of asset allocation, they should not be included in an asset allocation table.

Example 13.11

Breakdown of Jenny and David's total investments including pensions

Item	Jenny	David	Joint	Total	% of total
Cash deposits	£12,000	£12,000	£35,000	£59,000	7%
Fixed income	£27,000	£65,000	£20,000	£112,000	13.5%
Commercial property	£12,000	£42,000	–	£54,000	6.5%
UK equities	£75,000	£220,000	£100,000	£395,000	47%
Overseas equities	£31,000	£133,000	£40,000	£204,000	24.5%
Alternative/other	–	£10,000	–	£10,000	1.5%
Totals	**£157,000**	**£482,000**	**£195,000**	**£834,000**	**100%**

Breakdown of Jenny and David's investments excluding pensions

Item	Jenny	David	Joint	Total	% of total
Cash deposits	£12,000	£12,000	£35,000	£59,000	21%
Fixed Income	£11,000	—	£20,000	£31,000	11%
Commercial property	—	£12,000	—	£12,000	4%
UK equities	£8,000	£10,000	£100,000	£118,000	41.5%
Overseas equities	£6,000	£8,000	£40,000	£54,000	19%
Alternative/other	—	£10,000	—	£10,000	3.5%
Totals	**£37,000**	**£52,000**	**£195,000**	**£284,000**	**100%**

The most important aspect of the analysis is the current asset allocation of the investments, because this will be compared with Jenny and David's attitudes to risk and to their future needs.

If Jenny and David intend to manage their investments as a single portfolio (as in this case), the analysis of existing investments should be presented in this way. But where couples either already manage their investments separately or have made it clear that they intend to do so, the financial planner should undertake a separate analysis of the asset allocation for each of them.

Clients will tend to focus on the wrappers or containers in which financial assets are held and will usually want to see their holdings analysed in this way, even though the primary analysis is the nature of the underlying investments as shown in the tables above.

Example 13.12

How Jenny and David hold their financial assets

Item	ISA	
	Jenny	David
Cash deposits	—	—
Fixed income	£11,000	
Commercial property		£12,000
UK equities	£8,000	£10,000
Overseas equities	£6,000	£8,000
Alternative/ Other	—	—
Totals	£25,000	£30,000
Combined totals	£55,000	

Item	Pension	
	Jenny	**David**
Cash deposits	–	–
Fixed income	£16,000	£65,000
Commercial property	£12,000	£30,000
UK equities	£67,000	£210,000
Overseas equities	£25,000	£125,000
Alternative/ Other	–	–
Totals	£120,000	£430,000
Combined totals	£550,000	

Item	Direct/collective		
	Jenny	**David**	**Joint**
Cash deposits	£12,000	£12,000	£35,000
Fixed income	–	–	£20,000
Commercial property	–	–	
UK equities	–	–	£100,000
Overseas equities	–	–	£40,000
Alternative/ Other	–	£10,000	
Totals	£12,000	£22,000	£195,000
Combined totals	£229,000		

Where clients are dependent on the income from their investments for a significant part of their spendable income, a separate analysis should be produced to show the gross and net annual income from each asset class within the relevant tax wrappers.

During the fact-finding process, the adviser will have identified the client's objectives for the investments they hold. It is not always necessary to evaluate each investment in relation to this objective, if it turns out that the client has other objectives on the basis of which the adviser will make new recommendations. However, the adviser should provide an overview of the historic performance of the existing investments.

Example 13.13

Performance of Jenny and David's directly-held and ISA investments

Asset	Value	Annualised return over three years	Volatility	Drawdown
ISAs – UK equities	£18,000	4.5%	19	48%
ISAs – overseas equities	£14,000	6.5%	21	42%
Direct – UK equities	£100,000	5.1%	20	49%
Direct – overseas equities	£40,000	6.6%	22	39%

Where clients are contributing to savings plans the details can be summarised.

Plan	Term in years	Monthly contribution £	Current value £
Pension			
Jenny	21	£150	£7,500
David	19	£400	£65,000
ISA			
Jenny	NA	£200	£25,000
David	NA	£300	£30,000
Life assurance			
Level term joint life first death	25 years	£20 a month	Sum assured £200,000
			Cash value nil
Pension term on David's life	To age 65	Nil	Sum assured £300,000

8 Pension analysis

Clients' pension arrangements are often their most significant financial assets and for some people, their pension entitlements may even represent their largest single assets overall. It makes sense to consider DC pension funds within clients' financial assets and to some extent DB entitlements as well. But there are other aspects of clients' pension arrangements that generally may need to be analysed separately, depending on the circumstances and in particular the stage that the client has reached in the accumulation/decumulation processes. The key issues to consider include:

Relevant earnings This is the amount of income that defines the level of pension contributions that an individual can make.

Pension input periods (PIPs) A pension contribution normally benefits from tax relief in the tax year in which the pension input period for the scheme ends. In 2010 there is a special rule that contributions made after 14 October 2010 that fall into a pension input period ending after 5 April 2011 will fall under the tax rules and rates for the tax year 2011-12, not as might be expected in the tax year in which the contribution is made. The financial adviser should find out and note the PIP for each scheme of which a client is a member; in most cases, it should be possible to change PIPs so that they coincide with the tax year.

Accumulated pension funds in relation to the lifetime allowance This may provide scope to invest more into pensions or it may be a limiting factor. The analysis should identify the position. The annual allowance is to be £1.5m for 2012-13 onwards. There will be transitional arrangements for funds that exceed this level. The valuation needs to take into account accrued rights under DB schemes.

The level of pension contributions for the client in relation to the annual allowance The annual allowance is due to be £50,000 from 6 April 2011; in 2010/11, the anti-forestalling rules apply. The client's scope to make pension contributions for a particular year should be considered in the light of these annual restrictions. The new carry forward of unused relief from up to three previous years – up to £50,000 a year – should also be analysed to see if it will allow additional contributions in a particular year.

The main types of pension schemes These can be analysed in a range of ways:

- DC schemes could include SIPPs, personal pensions, stakeholder, occupational schemes such as SSASs or executive pensions or they might be s32 buy-out bonds.

- DB schemes might be the civil service or some other public sector scheme, or they could be in the private sector. DB private sector schemes might (rarely) be fully operational and open to new entrants as well as existing members. More likely they are either open to existing members only or possibly closed and with new benefits no longer accruing. There is a range of information that is needed for such schemes, because a pension transfer may be worth considering (which is outside the scope of this book).

- If the client is at the point of retirement and considering how to best deploy their pension funds, it is important to analyse the main options with respect to the available PCLS and the alternatives for drawing pension income benefits.

- A client who is in the decumulation phase may have little or no freedom of manoeuvre if, for example, the pension is in payment from an annuity or a DB scheme.

- With an annuity, it would be important to know whether it has been arranged on a joint life basis and the level of the survivor's pension, whether there is any guarantee or capital protection and if so, what it is, and whether the payments escalate and if so, at what rate.

- In the case of payments from a DB scheme, there would be similar issues about survivor's pension and escalation levels. In addition, there would be issues around the security of the scheme, its likely future and the possibility of additional discretionary payments being forthcoming.

9 Analysis of liabilities

There are many different types of liability that vary according to term, repayment method, rate of interest and terms.

Clients often fail to distinguish between 'good' debt (low rates, used to finance capital accumulation) and 'bad' debt (high rates, used to finance consumables). Presentation of the relevant data in tabular form may help them to see this more clearly.

Example 13.14

Summary of Maureen's liabilities

Type	Remaining term in years	Security and value	Capital outstanding	Amount pm	APR
Main residence mortgage	19	Home £315,000	£109,000	£706	4.4%
Holiday property mortgage	11	Apartment £76,000	£45,000	£469	6.1%
Credit card	—	—	£3,500	£150	13.9%
Car loan	2	−£9,000	£6,000	£270	7.4%

- Early redemption penalties on fixed term loans should be checked.

- If there are interest-only loans, the status and current value of any associated repayment plans should also be checked to see if the plans are on target to pay off the loan within the term.

- Total monthly commitments to debt repayments will have been included in the income and expenditure analysis.

10 Protection analysis

The client's current protection policies should be summarised according to type of policy, term, sum assured, premium and whether the benefits are in trust or assigned. Features such as renewability, increasability and whether policies are with fixed or reviewable premiums should also be noted.

Example 13.15

Jenny and David

Type	Insured	Owner	Term	Sum assured	Premium	Features	In trust
Level term	Joint first death	Jenny	25 years to 2020	£230,000	£15 pcm	None	No
Pension life cover	David	Trustees of scheme	To David's age 60	£300,000	Nil	Part of pension scheme	Nominated beneficiary Jenny

---

Analysis of Jenny and David's protection policies

The level term assurance is payable if either Jenny or David died during the course of the term of the policy. The survivor would then no longer be insured under this policy. The policy is neither in trust nor assigned to the lender. It could therefore be placed under trust

David's life cover under the pension is paid for by his employer. It is not clear whether there is a 'continuation option'. This is an option for David, should he leave his employer, to be able to take out a new policy with the relevant insurance company with no need for medical evidence; then if David were to leave the company in poor health, he would still benefit from the life assurance cover.

It would seem that Jenny and David have no other life assurance policies and no income protection or critical illness policies.

11 Estate planning and inheritance tax

The analysis of the estate planning should outline the tax and any other estate planning implications of the client dying. The main areas to consider are:

The provisions of the will or the impact of intestacy The aim should be to check that clients know what would happen to their estates after their deaths and are happy with the likely outcomes for their beneficiaries. In many cases, intestacy will lead to unwelcome results, leaving a surviving spouse or partner inadequately provided for. In the case of an unmarried couple, intestacy would probably leave the survivor with little or no provision.

Minor children In their wills, most couples leave all their assets to each other and then to their children (if they have any). Where the children are minor beneficiaries, assets would normally be held on trust for them until they are

18. Parents should consider whether the nominated trustees are personally suited for the task and whether the age of 18 is an appropriate age for them to benefit absolutely. It is also advisable to appoint a guardian to look after minor children if the parents were both to die.

Lasting power of attorney It is a good idea to check whether they have an enduring or lasting power of attorney, especially as a client approaches middle age or later.

Inheritance tax Clients should be aware of the potential impact of inheritance tax on their estates. With couples, this will depend on which individual dies first. Generally, the surviving spouse will inherit the deceased spouse's nil rate band. Thus if the first spouse to die leaves all their estate to the survivor, the survivor should currently have a total nil rate band of £650,000, above which inheritance tax (IHT) of 40% would be charged. Complications can arise if either spouse has been widowed in the past and inherited any previous unused nil rate band.

Where assets qualify for reliefs and exemptions e.g. business assets that qualify for 100% relief, this should be noted and emphasised.

The extent to which clients have used their annual exemptions should be noted if IHT mitigation is a high priority. The income and expenditure analysis can be used to calculate the potential for using the regular gifts from income exemption.

Example 13.16

Inheritance tax

Jenny and David have each made wills leaving all their estate to the survivor when the first of them dies. The survivor leaves all the assets to the children in equal shares in trust until they are 18 and then absolutely. This may not be appropriate. There is no provision for a guardian to be appointed if both David and Jenny die before the children are adults.

The inheritance tax position is as follows:

- The current gross value of the estate is £1,547,000. There is a repayment mortgage outstanding of £200,000. In addition, there is a joint life first death policy of £230,000, the proceeds of which would be payable to the survivor. After paying the mortgage, this would boost the value of the estate of the survivor to £1,577,000.

- There is a life policy on David's life, under which David has asked the trustees to pay the proceeds to Jenny in the event of his death. This would potentially add £300,000 to her estate if David were to die before

---

her and while still employed by his current employer. This nomination could be changed.

- On the first death there would be no IHT payable because of the spousal exemption. However, if Jenny were then to die, the position would be as follows:

Inheritance tax computation assuming David predeceases Jenny

	£	£
Gross estate	1,547,000	
Balance of proceeds of the first death term policy	30,000	
Proceeds of the pension life cover on David's life	300,000	
Jenny's total estate on her death		1,877,000
Nil rate band £325,000 × 2	650,000	
Amount of estate subject to IHT at 40%	1,227,000	
IHT at 40%		490,800
Net estate		1,386,200

12 Trusts

Trusts are important entities in some families. Trusts can be useful vehicles for helping families to achieve their financial goals, but they need to be kept under review. Clients and their financial and legal advisers need to keep in mind the function and purpose of trusts and monitor whether they are meeting their objectives. The financial planner should have a copy of the trust deed and should gain some understanding of the background from the main people involved. Trusts should be analysed under the following main headings:

Type of trust Trusts may be of very different kinds with very different consequences for the beneficiaries and with quite a range of possible tax consequences affecting their income tax, capital gains tax and IHT position. For example discretionary trusts are treated differently from bare trusts in respect to the rights of the beneficiaries and also in terms of all three of these taxes.

The settlor It is important to know who is the settlor or settlors and anyone who might be treated as a settlor. If the settlor was non-UK domiciled at the time of the trust's creation, this could well have important tax consequences, especially for IHT, for which purpose it might be 'excluded property' and therefore not subject to UK IHT.

The purpose of the trust and the circumstances of creating the trust
The trust may still be very relevant or it may have outlived its purpose. The circumstances in which it was set up may be important in understanding its role as well as the tax position in some situations, especially if it is a

discretionary trust. It is relevant to know the income and growth policies for the trust.

The trustees They are the people who are responsible for running the trust and may include the settlor. They will be constrained by the terms of the trust deed, but they may have considerable discretion, especially in relation to investment.

The powers of the trustees and the terms of the trust These will cover how and when the trust property is to be distributed as well as giving powers governing how to invest the trust assets. If the strategy is to use trust assets to help a particular beneficiary or group of beneficiaries, it is essential to know that the trustees have the power to act.

The assets and income of the trust A trust with very substantial assets and income can be managed quite differently from a small trust where the administration costs might be in danger of making the trust financially unviable.

The beneficiaries The ages and tax position of the beneficiaries may be important in some circumstances – notably when there is a decision to be made as to whether it is more appropriate to distribute the trust income or to accumulate it.

13 Key ratios

Rations are useful tools for reviewing the relationship between quantities. In analysing needs and setting priorities, an adviser should find the following ratios useful.

Liquidity ratios

There are two key liquidity ratios that should help determine whether the client has enough (or possibly too much) liquid cash readily available:

Emergency ratio This shows the client's easily accessible cash deposits as a percentage of their annual net income. The relevant investment period will depend on circumstances. For example, for a couple with school fee commitments the adviser will need to consider their commitment ratio over a longer period than for a retired couple with no major commitments.

Commitments ratio This shows the client's total cash and near-cash deposits as a percentage of their committed expenditure over the next one or two years. The calculation of the emergency ratio should only include instantly-accessible cash deposits. In the case of couples, both should have access to the account.

Liabilities/debt ratios

Debt is very useful as a means of acquiring things that clients would otherwise not be able to afford. It is also a good way to boost investment growth, as long as the rate of interest on the borrowing is less than the rate at which the investment increases and they can afford to pay the interest. For most people, their mortgage is a good example of both facets. A client with £100,000 cash who borrows £200,000 to buy a £300,000 house and sees it double in value over a period in which they pay a total of £30,000 in interest will see a profit of £370,000. If the client had borrowed nil and bought a £100,000 house which had doubled in value, they would have had a profit of only £100,000. The downside of borrowing is the risk of the property falling in value or of not being able to pay the interest. It is very possible to over-borrow. Useful ratios in debt analysis include:

Debt repayments/income This shows debt repayments of all kinds as a percentage of net disposable income.

Mortgage/income ratio This shows mortgage repayments as a percentage of net disposable income.

In terms of mortgage affordability, a level of about 30% has often been taken as a maximum appropriate level for the mortgage/income ratio. In some cases, it may be appropriate to borrow more, but the clients should be aware of the risks.

Life assurance and protection ratios

Useful ratios are as follows and should be calculated for each spouse/partner.

Capital liability ratio Life assurance cover as a percentage of all outstanding liabilities. Generally there should be a surplus.

Capital-income ratio This shows life cover as a multiple of current net disposable income. 10:1 has often been used as a rule of thumb, although actual estimated needs are a better measure in practice.

Life-income ratio This shows the total prospective income from life policies (from FIB policies and as income from capital sums) as a percentage of current annual household expenditure. This ratio is a rule of thumb measure of adequacy that can act as a starting point for need.

Health-income ratio This shows the percentage of current household expenditure covered by income protection policies. In most cases, it is not possible to arrange income protection greater than about 60% of current income and any cover in excess of this limit will not be paid.

14 Priorities

Prioritisation can be a very simple and straightforward process. But very often, they start off the planning process with different views about the clients' needs and priorities. Where there are two clients, they may not be entirely in agreement about the issues.

> **Example 13.17**
>
> A client may start off at the initial interview thinking what they need is simply a savings plan to build up a long-term nest-egg and they think it should be an ISA. The adviser after the first fact-find, may come to the conclusion that there are several areas that need attention, including protection, wills, rearranging the mortgage and other borrowings, and prospective retirement planning.

Part of the process of planning is to help the adviser understand what the client really wants and part is for the client to understand what they really needs and for these needs to become wants. Once client and adviser understand each other and they agree that there are several courses of action that need to be taken, prioritisation becomes a critical part of the planning process.

The limiting factor is usually the availability of resources to meet the objectives. Protection needs compete with saving needs; the pound that is spent on providing protection will not be available to build up savings. Income needs compete with accumulation needs; the client can either draw money from their funds to top up their income or they can leave the funds to accumulate. Safety competes with long-term growth; a cash deposit should not lose the client nominal value but in the long-term it does not provide the growth prospects of asset-backed investments.

Prioritisation then typically becomes an iterative process, as the adviser provides options and clients decide what is most important to them. Sometimes the answer is to deal with one priority now and postpone dealing with the others until later − perhaps when more income or other resources become available. Sometimes the answer is to deal with both now to some extent but to cut back on the provision for each from the ideal level.

For example, Simon and Ruth want to save as much as possible for retirement. They say that they have £1,000 a month that they can afford to devote to this. However, they agree that there is a grave need for life assurance on both their lives that would cost £400 a month in total. They have the following main choices (subject to minor variations):

- Invest all the £1,000 a month into the retirement savings plan; but that would mean having no protection at all.

- Invest £600 a month into the retirement savings plan and the full £400 into the protection plan; but that would mean cutting back very substantially on their main aim of retirement planning.

- Invest £1,000 a month into the pension and the full £400 a month into protection and reduce their monthly outgoings on other areas of expenditure; that would fulfil their financial objectives but it might not be sustainable in practice.

- Invest £1,000 a month into the pension and £200 a month into protection; that way they would meet their main objective, and have some protection – which would be better than none. The reduction in protection costs may reflect a reduced level of cover or it could involve some other change such as a shorter term or fewer other features. If the programme proved unaffordable, they should agree that they would reduce the pension investment down to £800 and try to make it up later.

Chapter 14
Selecting appropriate products and services

1 Suitability

The key regulatory requirement regarding advisers' product recommendations is that they should be "suitable". There are two aspects of this: knowledge of the client's circumstances, experience and requirements; and knowledge and understanding of the features, costs and risks of relevant products.

Advisers need to establish processes for both these elements of their advice. The first concerns fact-finding, qualification and categorisation of clients and the second, methods for researching and selecting products.

The FSA guidelines regarding suitability (below) also use the term 'appropriate'. Both terms point to the adviser's need to explain the link between the client's circumstances and objectives and the recommendation of specific products.

FSA guidelines on suitability:

- Have you established a process for assessing suitability? Have staff been trained in the process?

- Have you established a process for assessing appropriateness? Have staff been trained in the process?

- Do you have a mechanism in place to keep the information on which assessments are made updated regularly?

- Do you have a mechanism in place for reviewing suitability in the event of a material change in the circumstances of the client or product?

- Do you have a mechanism in place for reviewing appropriateness in the event of a material change in the relevant information?

- Do you have systems in place for recording relevant client information and any relevant correspondence with clients?

- Do you have record keeping mechanisms in place that adequately record the manner in which suitability and appropriateness have been assessed for each client?

- Have you confirmed that the suitability obligation applies to the transactions under consideration? If not, have you confirmed that the appropriateness obligation applies to the transactions under consideration?

2 Client categorisation

In order to make an assessment of suitability, a firm needs to obtain the necessary information in relation to the client in order to assess:

- **their investment objectives** – the length of time for which they wish to hold the investment, their preferences regarding risk taking, their risk profile, and the purposes of the investment;

- **their financial situation** – the source and extent of their regular income, their assets, including liquid assets, investments and real property, and their regular financial commitments;

- **their knowledge and experience** – their ability to understand the risks involved in the transaction or in the management of their portfolio.

This information will routinely be acquired in the fact-finding and risk profiling process.

Retail clients

The level of knowledge and experience that can be assumed (rather than obtained through detailed questioning) depends on the category into which the client falls. The majority of clients will be classified as retail clients, in which case no level of knowledge or experience can be assumed and only the information gathered by the adviser can be used as a basis for recommendations.

However, the adviser may take into account the level of education, profession or former profession of the client in order to help the firm to satisfy itself that the client's level of knowledge may be relevant for more complex products such as derivatives and structured products. Individuals who have a finance-related professional background or qualifications are more likely to understand the risks in complex products than individuals who do not.

On the other hand, advisers should also pay due care during the sales process to whether a client is illiterate or has some other incapacity which could impact on understanding – for example, when product documentation is not in the client's first language.

Professional clients

For clients defined as professional, knowledge and experience can be assumed for the products, services or transactions in respect of which a client has been classified as professional. For example, a chartered surveyor working in the commercial property sector as a negotiator on development projects could be classified as professional in respect of direct commercial property investments. In this case, in respect of products in that category only, a higher degree of knowledge and experience could be assumed than for a retail client without the requirement to establish this through detailed questioning.

It can also be assumed that a professional client has the ability to bear investment risks consistent with their investment objectives where the adviser is giving personal recommendations and investment advice, though this does not apply to discretionary management services. Again this does not apply to retail clients.

Designation of a client as professional needs to be documented with the area within which the designation applies described as precisely as possible. In the case above, for example, it would not be appropriate for the chartered surveyor to be classified as professional in relation to listed stock market property investments if they had no actual knowledge or experience in that field.

Advisers using the 'professional' designation for clients need to ensure that any relevant recommendations they make are separately identified. In most cases additional risk warnings will be required.

3 Essential information

Information

There is an irreducible minimum level of information without which the adviser will not be in a position to make a personal recommendation. However, as long as it is consistent with the client's interests and investment objectives, an adviser may be able to propose an alternative service or transaction tailored to the level of information the client has been willing to provide. For example a client may accept an advisory service relating to a portion of their portfolio, based on the provision of less information than would be required to provide a discretionary management service on the client's total portfolio.

Even if a more limited service is provided, any recommendation must still be suitable for the client (including being consistent with the client's investment objectives) and the scope of the service agreed and understood by the client.

Risk

Advisers should have a reasonable basis for believing that the client would be able to financially bear the risk, if the transaction recommended carries with it a financial risk, bearing in mind the proportion of the client's assets exposed to that risk. It is important to note that this requirement does not concern the client's attitude to risk, but their risk capacity, as assessed by the adviser.

Advisers should assess the impact of a reasonably foreseeable loss relating to recommended investments, and should also consider the risks of extreme market movements (even if relatively unlikely), particularly in the case of investments with uncertain outcomes such as structured products.

Variations

If an adviser concludes that a financial instrument is unsuitable for a client, the firm cannot provide investment advisory or discretionary portfolio management services in respect of that instrument. However, the firm could proceed on a non-advised, execution-only basis in relation to that instrument if the client wishes to do so and confirms this in writing, and if doing so is consistent with the firm's obligation to act in the client's best interests. The firm will need to check if there is an obligation to test appropriateness when providing the non-advised service. In some cases, there may be no such obligation for non-complex instruments.

Ad-hoc advice

This includes situations that require different levels of detail relating to the client's circumstances to be taken into account. For example, where a client instructs a firm only to give personal recommendations relating to an identified portion of their assets or in relation to the desirability of investing in a specific investment, without reviewing the client's entire portfolio, the suitability assessment could involve a narrower review, focusing on the client's objectives, financial situation and knowledge in relation to that particular portion of assets or specific investment.

Updating

The client information on which needs analysis and product recommendations are made should be reviewed at regular intervals. Fresh information, changes of circumstances, etc may require clients' existing holdings to be reviewed and replaced.

Suitability reports

Current regulations do not expressly require firms that have to assess suitability to provide the client with a suitability report as a matter of course, though they do require the provision of adequate reports on the service provided. But the rules do require a suitability report to be made to retail clients in relation to holdings in regulated collective investment schemes, and it is normal practice in adviser firms to provide suitability reports for all advised investment and savings recommendations.

4 Generic product selection

The adviser's needs analysis of client data should lead directly to broad recommendations linked to generic products.

> **Example 14.1**
>
> A client needs to save regularly to accumulate a capital sum over the next 20 years to repay their mortgage. They are currently making no use of their ISA annual allowance and have no capital they could transfer into an ISA. The Stocks & Shares ISA is therefore the generic product most appropriate for the client's needs.

In many cases the recommendation of generic products will be driven by several factors including tax, access to capital and investment options.

> **Example 14.2**
>
> John is self-employed and has no long-term savings plans. He needs to save over the next 20 years to build up a capital sum from which he can draw retirement income. The two most appropriate types of product are personal pensions and ISAs. Which of these is recommended will depend mainly on the extent to which he may need access to capital and his likelihood of paying higher rates of income tax.
>
> As in this case, the adviser's recommendations are likely to be specifically determined by the client's needs. If John is very likely to need access to much of the capital, then only a small proportion of proposed contributions can be allocated to a personal pension plan. If there is no such access requirement, and it appears probable that John will pay the higher rate of income tax for at least the next few years, then recommending that the majority of monthly contributions go into a personal pension plan will be more appropriate.

In many cases, there will be more than one suitable product category for the client. Advisers need to ensure they have considered all the relevant factors that may affect generic product selection and that their conclusions are clearly set out in client reports. Tax, risk, and access to capital are likely to be the most important factors in relation to the selection of investments and savings plans.

Whole of market

The 'whole of market' rules to be applied in the Retail Distribution Review (RDR) require IFAs to review all products that may be suitable for the client. In principle, the whole of market rules require IFAs to research several varieties of fund, not just unit trusts and open ended investment companies (OEICs) — investment trusts and exchange traded funds, for example, might also meet the client's needs. However, there may be reasons for an adviser to rule out an entire category of products from consideration.

Example 14.3

Joan is a 75 year old widow with a capital sum of £120,000 she wishes to invest to generate a steady income. She is risk averse and has no prior experience of investment. The adviser rules out investment trusts as an option for her because of their gearing and share price/NAV differential, both factors that increase their level of risk as compared with unit trusts or OEICs.

Advisers need to ensure that where they do exclude entire categories of product from consideration, their reasons for doing so are clearly documented.

5 Specific product selection

Once a generic product type has been determined as suitable, the adviser needs to select individual products within this category.

For each generic product type, there will be many products that might be suitable. Usually, only a small number of features are specifically relevant to the client's current needs and circumstances. It is these specific needs that should determine the criteria that are most heavily weighted in the selection process. A larger number of other product features can be assessed and compared and the adviser's choice of which of the many features to review should be based on the client's needs and circumstances and a straightforward value-for-money comparison.

Example 14.4

Arthur is investing £80,000 which he intends to hold for at least ten years and the adviser has assessed an investment bond as most suitable given his circumstances. In selecting products, the actual costs, charges and surrender penalties applying to an £80,000 investment over a ten-year term should be used as a selection criterion, not simply the overall level of charges.

Advisers may set high-level criteria for product selection. They may, for example, require an insurance provider to have a financial strength rating above a set minimum level. Such criteria can result in the elimination of products that might otherwise be suitable, so these criteria must be capable of justification and must be consistent with the actual recommendation. For example, if a selection criterion for a personal pension plan is access to a wide range of funds but the adviser in fact recommends the insurance company's managed fund, the recommendation may not be suitable — the criterion may have eliminated better-value products.

The normal selection process is to start by defining the features that will be used as the primary level of product selection. There are up to 50 features for most savings and investment products. Of these, between six and ten features will normally be of higher importance. In most such products, for example, costs and charges will usually be ranked as an important selection factor. Flexibility, on the other hand, is a feature that may be relevant to some clients but not to all, so it would normally be applied as a second-order criterion.

The first-order selection will usually generate a shortlist of five to ten products possessing the required features, and this will be further reduced by rating them on first- and second-order criteria. In principle advisers can create their own systems of ratings. However, in practice certain criteria are usually more important than others for particular clients, and a system that permits the variable weighting of selection factors (say on a one to five scale) enables the adviser to match products much more precisely to needs and circumstances. Designing and applying such a system consistently across a range of products is a challenging task.

Where products are selected primarily on cost, for example a non-underwritten level term assurance policy, then an initial shortlist may be based on premium for a given sum assured. But where protection products offer different covers (as with critical illness) or their terms vary (income protection policies) or where option terms vary (renewable or increasable term policies) then advisers need to ensure that they use relevant criteria to compare these features, and to obtain like-for-like quotations that correspond to the specific needs of the client.

IFAs subject to the more demanding post-RDR whole of market rules need to select the most suitable product from all those available. In principle this means researching all the available products within that type, for example onshore investment bonds or SIPPs. However, the search may be restricted if client requirements are clearly defined.

Example 14.5

Ian wants to switch several personal pension plans into one scheme where he has a wider choice of investments. The adviser determines that Ian does not require access to facilities to purchase property or indeed any investments other than collective investment funds. The adviser therefore restricts research to SIPPs that offer only these investment options.

For each product type, the adviser should use criteria that relate to the needs of the client. While such needs may be the same across all clients of a particular type or segment, advisers need to ensure that they do take particulars into account.

Example 14.6

An adviser researches investment bonds with the aim of choosing one for a client X with £100,000 to invest in a wide range of unit trusts and OEICs. The criteria used are costs and charges, range of funds, service standards and the life company's financial strength. Having selected the bond from company A, the adviser uses this research to justify the recommendation of the same bond to client Y. However, client Y has said they may need to encash all or part of the bond within five years, and company A's product levies a penalty charge, while that of companies B and C does not. Use of the research for client X to support a recommendation for client Y is inappropriate.

In principle, an ideal research process uses a set of criteria to generate a short list of say five products from a potential field of 80 or so. These five are then more closely compared in respect of a broader range of features such as costs and charges, options, flexibility and administration in order to make a final selection. Ideally each feature compared is scored and, where appropriate, the scores are weighted in relation to their importance to the client to produce a ranking table. Such a research process scores each feature compared and records the scores and overall ratings so that these can be held in the client's file.

Example 14.7

An adviser is researching group personal pension plans. The adviser believes low costs and charges are the most important factor to consider in selecting such plans, and therefore gives this factor a weighting double that for any other used in the assessment.

In practice few IFAs have the resources necessary to undertake such in-depth research across the entire range of products. They are therefore increasingly likely to subscribe to a specialist service, such as Defaqto's Engage, which enables advisers to use a wide range of criteria to select products from all those available. Advisers can weight the scores for different factors where they think appropriate and undertake research specific to client circumstances. They can also use the research output in client reports and store it on file.

By having access to a large product database, advisers can also compare the products available to them with products sold direct by supermarkets and banks. In many such cases, such products are known to be inferior, but actual comparisons of features and costs may be useful.

The factors advisers may use in assessing products fall into two categories:

Objective. Many product features are relatively easy to compare using quantitative methods, along the lines of Which? ratings. The scope of cover is also easy to quantify (for example, the number of conditions covered by a critical illness policy). Charges may not be quite so simple, in that the way charges are levied, as well as their level, can affect value for money. A product with high early encashment charges, for example, may rate poorly if assessed on a five-year holding period but well over a ten-year period. Care must therefore be taken to choose periods of assessment corresponding with clients' likely uses of the products.

Subjective or hard to determine. Life companies' financial strength has long been a controversial issue. Life insurance company accounting is extremely complex and published accounts are notoriously hard to compare. Professional stockbroker analysts' assessments of the financial strength of life company PLCs can vary significantly. The *Money Management* annual survey of life office financial strength has often been used by advisers in their assessments. Product researchers Defaqto use ratings from specialist actuarial ratings agency AKG. The other potentially subjective factor is service standards. While there have been occasions when the administration of an entire provider company has been poor, it is more often the case that local offices have given poor service to particular groups of advisers, or that service standards in particular departments of the company (life, health, pensions, investments) have been poor. Moreover, service standards in relation to new business may be poor while service to existing policyholders is good, or vice versa. The reasons for failure vary, but in many cases the issues are resolved within a few months. This explains why some advisers can believe Company B's administration is bad while others view it as good. Advisers therefore need to take care in using service standards as a factor in product selection. Defaqto among others has attempted to make service standard assessment more objective by conducting regular surveys of advisers, while trade publishers have also instituted service standards awards.

Historically many advisers simply ruled-out products offered by providers they did not wish to do business with. Often this was justified by reference to poor administration or service standards. Under the RDR whole of market rules, advisers are likely to need to demonstrate product selection processes that compare service standards as well as product features and costs.

Product selection criteria

The following are among the more important product features that advisers may wish to assess in selecting products.

Investment bonds (unit linked)

Insurance company financial strength

Initial charge

Allocation rate

Annual charge

Range of funds

Range of externally managed funds

Income withdrawal options

Minimum investment

Maximum age at entry

Capital guarantees

Income guarantees

Unit trusts/OEICs

Financial strength of fund management group

Annual charge or TER

Longevity of fund manager tenure

Longevity of fund

Size of fund

Recent cash inflows to fund

Annual turnover of fund

Number of holdings of fund

Top ten holdings as % of fund assets

Volatility of returns

Historic returns

Risk-adjusted returns

6 Suitability reports

Advisers are required by regulations to issue suitability reports for unit trusts and OEICs and in practice usually do so for all recommendations.

The aim is to clearly link the client facts and circumstances with needs analysis and with the products recommended.

The adviser's report to the client will normally function as a suitability report. To ensure that it adequately explains the recommendations advisers will usually distinguish clearly between generic and product recommendations.

Generic recommendations

The report will usually summarise the client data, set out the analysis and prioritisation of needs, and then proceed to identify the generic product requirements. In the report, the reasons for the generic recommendations may be abbreviated, with a more detailed explanation including details of the relevant tax, risk and other factors provided as an appendix. In practice, advisers often use standard wording for these longer explanations, since the reasons for recommending (for example) a Stocks & Shares ISA for long-term regular savings plans are normally the same. The benefit to the client (tax exempt growth and income) is the same for all clients, and the value of the tax exemption varies only in relation to the individual's personal tax status. These facts can be set out in generic terms.

However, use of standard wording can be dangerous since suitability reports are meant to be client-specific. In particular, care must be taken in the use of tax factors to justify recommendations. As noted in previous chapters, current tax rates and payments are certain but the client's future tax position is often much less so. Where it is extremely uncertain (say a self-employed person with very variable income), then the advantages of avoiding higher rate tax through the use of a particular investment, or of securing benefits from tax relief, should not form the main basis of a recommendation. In such a case, simply using standard wording outlining the tax benefits for a higher rate taxpayer could be misleading.

The normal format is to set out the need or objective and to list the factors that justify the choice of a generic product type. Advisers may do this for the whole set of needs and products, and then have a separate section on the actual products selected, or may include specific product selections after each generic product is discussed.

Product recommendations

As stated above the selection of the product for the client should be based on the criteria most important in relation to the client's needs and circumstances. The report can simply state why these criteria were used and why the product selected scored highly on these criteria.

Where the adviser subscribes to a product research tool such as Defaqto's Engage, sections of the research report such as product ranking tables can be included in the client report.

Product brochures and key features documents will be provided for each product and will usually contain all the information the client needs. But where several products are being recommended, the client will usually benefit from a brief summary of their important features.

7 Selection issues

Many of the 'bias' issues about product selection concerned commission rates. Post-RDR, there is no scope for commission-based adviser bias in product selection. However, specific products still present issues for advisers.

Wraps

The wrap market is evolving rapidly. In the context of the RDR proposals, regulators have expressed a wish to enforce transparency of charges and charging systems. This may affect the business models of wrap providers and hence their charging methods.

The key is not whether wraps are a 'product' but is that advisers need to put clients' interests first and their own convenience second. But this issue is more complex than simply a comparison of the different levels, types and totals of charges clients incur with different wraps. For example, wraps with more features and tools reduce the workload of advisers, who might otherwise charge higher fees.

So, as with other products, advisers need to assess wraps in terms of the relevance of the features they provide, which may or may not be of benefit to clients. Integrated capital gains accounting, for example, is a useful tool, but it is of no value to someone with a small portfolio who will never exceed their annual capital gains exemption. The ability to hold a wide range of assets through wraps may also be irrelevant to many clients but very useful to some. Wrap providers tend to differentiate their offerings with more features, but advisers need to focus on client benefits for the client.

The suitability principle suggests that clients should pay only for features and services that are likely to be of use to them. If they can get many extra features at no extra cost, well and good, but if one wrap offers the limited range of features that the client actually needs at a lower cost, the adviser needs to consider this.

This may result in advisers recommending different wraps to different groups of clients. In this case, consistency of advice in adviser firms will be a key issue, as an FSA review identified failings in the advice process for wraps among the majority of firms surveyed. If advisers do select wraps based on features and costs, then their recommendations of wraps to clients should be consistent with this analysis.

Unregulated Collective Investment Schemes (UCIS)

UCIS are often 'one-off' types of investment. There are rarely several of one kind among which detailed comparisons can be made. In researching them, it is idiosyncratic features that will often be most important. The legal structures through which assets are held, for example, can often be a key issue. Contractual agreements between several different parties are often involved and their details can be important. The status of the professional parties involved as auditors, custodians, legal and investment advisers is a useful if not wholly reliable criterion for selection.

As discussed in chapter 9, 'Regulatory requirements and financial planning', advisers need to take great care in framing their recommendations for UCIS. In selecting them, they also need to identify the key risk factors and draw these to clients' attention.

Enterprise Investment Schemes (EIS)

EIS investments of a collective type, like UCIS, are difficult to assess. Investment is in private firms, the terms of investment are negotiated individually between managers and business owners, and there is rarely a 'standard' deal. Advisers have to rely largely on the reputation, skills and resources of the managers. These should be researched as far as possible.

Chapter 15
Communicating recommendations

1 Introduction

Communications with clients should always be fair, clear and not misleading. So a suitability report should achieve its primary aim of explaining why a set of recommendations is suitable for the client in question and how and why the recommendations meet their needs and objectives. It is also important to explain the services provided by the firm and their costs.

The Financial Services Authority (FSA) take the view that advisers should ensure that their suitability reports:

- Use clear and plain language;

- Are tailored to the client's circumstances;

- Specify the client's demands and needs;

- Explain the reasons for the recommendations and how these address the client's needs and objectives;

- Provide a balanced view and explain any disadvantages of the recommendations for the client, including the risks, costs, charges and any potential penalties associated with the recommendations;

- Highlight any of the client's objectives that are not covered by the recommendations, and the implications of any 'focused advice' that is being provided.

The report should also make clear the basis of charging for the work and the commissions the firm is receiving or the fees being charged. The commissions and fees for individual products and services should be set out in the recommendations.

2 When suitability reports are required

A firm must provide a suitability report to a retail client if it makes a personal recommendation to the client who acquires a holding in a regulated collective investment scheme or sells all or part of a holding. The same requirement applies to contributions to a personal pension, as well as other pension related transactions including pension withdrawals, pension transfers or opt-outs. All recommendations in relation to life policies must be covered by a suitability report.

However, there are certain circumstances in which a suitability report is not required, including a personal recommendation either to increase a regular premium to an existing contract or to invest additional single premiums or contributions to an existing packaged product to which the client had previously paid a single premium or made a single contribution.

The suitability report should be sent when the recommendation is made or as soon as possible. If the financial planner prepares the suitability report in advance of the recommendation, they should be prepared to amend and re-issue it as necessary.

- For a life policy, the suitability report should go to the client before the contract is concluded, unless the necessary information is provided orally or immediate cover is necessary. If the adviser provides the necessary information orally or arranges immediate cover, they must provide the client with a suitability report in a durable medium immediately after the contract is concluded.

- For a personal pension or stakeholder pension scheme, the rules on cancellation require notification of the right to cancel and the firm must provide the suitability report no later than the 14th day after the contract is concluded.

In any other case, the firm must provide the suitability report when the transaction is effected or executed or as soon after as possible.

The suitability obligations are required for professional, as well as retail, clients in respect of Markets in Financial Instruments Directive (MiFID) scope business but the FSA do not insist on a suitability report for these clients.

3 Using clear and plain language

Many clients complain about the jargon that financial specialists use in their speech and writing. Jargon is convenient and precise, but it is off-putting for those who are not used to it and have not been trained in financial technicalities. Suitability reports should therefore aim to avoid jargon where possible. However, technical terms are sometimes unavoidable and using alternative expressions could be misleading. So where a suitability report uses a technical term for the first time, the expression should be explained in clear language. Including a glossary as an appendix to a suitability report can also be helpful.

In their suitability reports for clients and in any other written communications, financial planners should aim to keep sentences short and as far as possible they should be in the active mood. It is good practice to use bullet points and numbering to help with navigation and clarity. Paragraphs should not be excessively long (or too short). Reports should avoid pomposity, and employ short non-technical words and informal language to make the reports accessible.

It would be good practice to provide the client with a copy of the suitability report before the second meeting, so that they have an opportunity to go through it in advance of the meeting and raise any questions that might have occurred to them.

4 Making the structure of the report clear

Reports can often be so long that clients do not have the time or inclination to read them. Suitability reports need to be as short as possible to be effective. However, there are points that must be included and length is sometimes unavoidable. As the FSA says, "There is no right or wrong length". It is therefore important to try and help clients navigate the documentation. Some tips are:

- Always summarise the recommendations;
- Use a clear lay-out with headings;
- Avoid jumping from topic to topic;
- Provide a contents page especially for long reports;
- Keep the main report for the key ideas and put the detail of the recommendations and product features in appendices;
- Use bold text to highlight key risks and changes associated with the recommendations;
- Use diagrams where possible and appropriate.

The FSA provide an example of poor practice where a particular adviser made a series of recommendations for different products to a client, each one in a separate report. The result was that the client would not have understood the impact of the overall recommendations on their circumstances.

The report should make its recommendations clear. The FSA gives an example of one adviser's poor practice. This adviser's suitability report provided little more than a summary of matters discussed with the client during the meetings and just highlighted various areas that they 'could consider' (such as pension contributions, mortgage overpayments). The adviser did not make any specific recommendations and did not provide the client with enough information to consider which of the available options were appropriate.

The suitability report should not repeat the content of key features documents; the report can refer to these documents and invite the client to ask about any aspects that are not clear. Information can sometimes be missing or become lost in long, unnecessary or irrelevant text. For example, it is normally bad practice to provide basic rate taxpayers or non-taxpayers with information that is only relevant to higher rate taxpayers.

5 Tailoring the suitability report to the customer's circumstances

The FSA recommends setting out what the client wants to achieve, preferably using their own words from the fact-finding process. A good suitability report repeats and reflects the discussion that has taken place between the adviser and the client. Where the client already has some of the planning in place such as insurances, investments and pensions, the report should include details. A good practice could be to send a copy of the fact-find or clear summary of its contents with the report so that the client can check its accuracy.

The suitability letter/report should explain simply and clearly why the recommended transaction or product is suitable for the client, in light of the client's:

- Financial situation;
- Knowledge and experience of investment and financial matters;
- Investment objectives;
- Attitude to risk, both in general terms and with respect to the specific area of need and recommendation.

It should also contain the relevant specific risk warnings, which should not be hidden or diluted.

The report should make it clear where the client will derive the funds to make the investment, contribute to the pension or pay the insurance premium. The source of funds might, for example, be savings from income or existing capital resources. Where the client is switching funds from one investment to another (e.g. from a deposit account to an equity fund), there should be a clear statement setting out the total holdings after the transaction, so that the client has a picture of their situation both before and after. The report should also set out why the new investment is preferable to the old one for the client and the returns they might reasonably expect from it.

6 The use of standard paragraphs

Standard paragraphs can help advisers write suitability reports that are technically accurate and economic to produce, but there can be dangers in using them excessively or carelessly. As the FSA says, "In principle there is nothing wrong with standard paragraphs and clearly they can be useful in a number of ways — for example by helping you to issue suitability letters/reports promptly or to ensure that you use appropriate wording for any general risk warnings".

However, standard paragraphs may also lead to excessively long reports. The FSA gives an example of a firm that included too much standard general wording about products and markets in the main body of its suitability reports. As a result, the reports were both unnecessarily long and not sufficiently tailored to the particular circumstances of the clients. It is less likely that clients will read such lengthy general documents.

Another danger is that advisers who use standard paragraphs may try to fit the client's attitude to risk to their recommendation rather than the reverse. In the FSA's view, it is not acceptable to produce suitability reports solely consisting of standard paragraphs with no personalisation to the client.

The coherence of the suitability report will suffer where an adviser has pasted text into it from a variety of sources that have been written in different styles. The reader will becomes confused about the purpose and content of the report, and that could further reduce its effectiveness.

7 The use of charts and graphics

"A picture is worth a thousand words" may be an exaggeration, but graphs and diagrams can be very effective at explaining certain concepts quickly and accurately. People can grasp their meaning rapidly and they can help make a written report far more meaningful for clients.

Line graphs are useful for showing the past performance of investments, both in terms of their growth and volatility. They can also be used to compare the performance of different investments against each other and/or against a benchmark index.

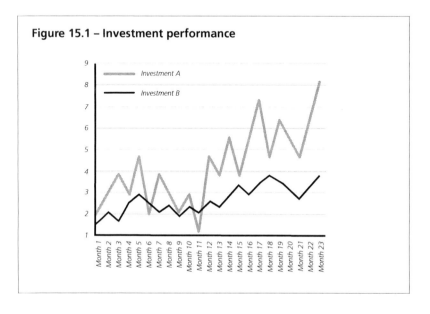

Figure 15.1 – Investment performance

Line graphs of net assets are the usual outputs of lifetime cashflow projections and are much easier to grasp than the columns of detailed figures on which the graph is based.

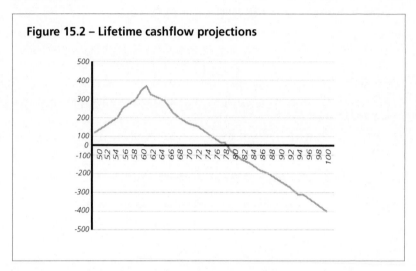

Figure 15.2 – Lifetime cashflow projections

Bar charts showing whether someone's current account is in credit or debit at the end of each month are effective for demonstrating an individual's short-term cashflow over the course of a year, e.g. highlighting the impact of the receipt of bonus payments in some months and school fees payments in other months.

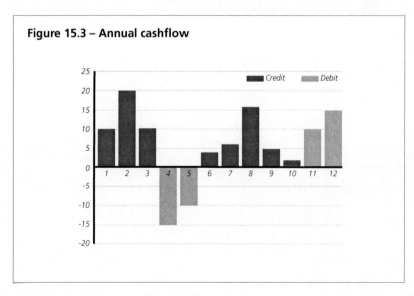

Figure 15.3 – Annual cashflow

Pie charts can be used for a variety of purposes. They are excellent for showing how a person's assets are skewed towards a particular type of asset such as domestic property. Comparative pie charts can show how a client's current investment allocation is contrasted with one that better reflects their risk profile and investment objectives generally.

Figure 15.4 – Investment allocation

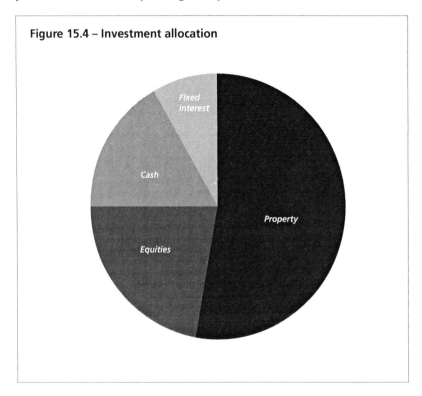

Simple bar charts can be helpful for emphasising a gap, for example between the life and health cover a client has and the cover that they need.

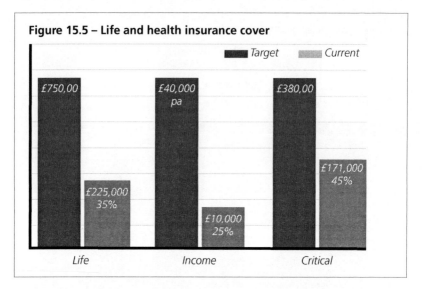

Figure 15.5 – Life and health insurance cover

8 Explaining the reasons for recommendations

Suitability reports used to be known as 'reasons-why' letters and this term describes their function well. The report must explain the reasons for the recommendations and how these address the client's needs and objectives.

Compliance consultants and managers frequently report that advisers try to explain how their recommendations meet a client's needs and wishes by describing the features of the product in detail. But the reports typically omit the reasons why the product is suitable for the client's particular circumstances. The problem may partly derive from the careless use of standard paragraphs, which are excellent for the accurate description of product features but may be less easy to personalise for a range of specific clients.

It is also advisable to set out the main alternatives to the recommendations and to explain why they are either not suitable or less suitable than those being made.

The suitability report could also include details of alternative products that the adviser has decided not to recommend, if that would help to demonstrate why the recommended product was suitable. Otherwise it is not necessary to mention them. If the adviser recommends a product which the client rejects, it could be mentioned in the suitability report.

The suitability report could include reasons for the recommendation of a particular provider. The reasons for doing so will depend on the particular circumstances of the advice and might include factors such as product features not available elsewhere, price, service levels, performance track record, underwriting criteria and reputation.

Explaining disadvantages, risks and costs of recommendations

Suitability letters/reports should be sufficiently balanced, drawing out the positives and any disadvantages inherent in the recommendations. Virtually every recommendation is bound to involve some disadvantages as well as some costs. There are almost certainly risks; with some products clients may incur penalties, for example if they withdraw from a programme prematurely.

When recommending a course of action, it is important to remember to outline the drawbacks as well as advantages. For example, by contributing to a pension the client places the funds in an arrangement that is very inaccessible until at least the age of 55 and subject to various restrictive and complex rules. In addition, there are the investment related risks. The advantages and disadvantages of recommendations are explored in more detail in Part 4, 'The main areas of financial planning in practice'.

Many investments require the client to pay initial and annual charges, and the suitability report should clearly and concisely bring them to clients' attention. A wide range of products also involve the imposition of higher or penalty charges or costs if they are accessed early. These products range from fixed term deposit accounts to many structured investment products and life assurance policies. Clients must be made aware that these penalties could affect them.

The report should set out the client's preferred risk profile and tolerance of risk. This description must be clear and should be in language that the clients will understand and reflects the discussion of their circumstances and wishes. The recommendations should explain how the products match these and meet the client's needs. For example, a suitability report might contain a simple statement to the effect that a client has a 'balanced' attitude to risk and that the recommended product has a 'balanced' profile. However, this is unlikely to provide the client with an adequate justification of the investment's suitability without explaining the meaning of the word 'balanced' that relates to the client's preferences and links it to the fund's past performance and how it might perform in the future.

The FSA provides an example of a firm that gives clients a clear written explanation of the costs and consequences of its recommendation: "There is a cost involved in this process: your money will not be invested in the period between encashment and investment. This could take several days due to the processes involved, and may result in a loss of income and/or growth, especially during periods of market volatility".

The FSA also gives an example of poor practice in explaining the costs of advice to a client. When explaining the payment options, a particular adviser referred to commission received from the product provider as an "introductory fee for introducing you to them". Later on during the meeting, the adviser stated that "we can either get paid by fee or commission", but then went on to say that most people would say "let the provider pay you". This was an inaccurate and unfair explanation of the payment options which could have influenced the customer in choosing the commission payment option.

9 Prioritisation

Many clients have to prioritise their planning, especially if they have only limited resources. The issue of prioritisation recurs throughout the planning process: first at the objectives discussion and fact-finding stages, then when the financial planner is summarising and analysing the client's position and at the recommendation stages. With some clients the priorities will be clear from the start and will not change during the planning process. Other clients will change their priorities as they understand their position better, appreciate the consequences and discover what they need to do to make changes.

There is a conventional order of priorities that most financial advisers follow in helping their clients to prioritise their needs and wishes: meeting day-to-day expenses, mortgages and borrowing, life and health protection, short-term saving, long-term savings, retirement planning and estate planning. Priorities change with age and family circumstances; older people are usually more concerned with retirement income needs and estate planning, while younger people have borrowing for house purchase and financial protection as their main priorities. But individual needs vary and this basic priority order should only be regarded as a very approximate template.

When some clients are presented with a financial report, they see their situation and what they can do about it in a single document. It is helpful to provide the client with a full report before the meeting setting out all their aims as well as the other needs that the planner has identified. At the meeting, the client can decide on the most important and urgent actions to take. The adviser can then send a second report confirming the immediate priorities agreed at the meeting.

There are two main ways to prioritise several objectives. One is simply to decide to focus on the highest priorities and postpone dealing with one or more of the others. It then makes sense to list the areas and actions that have been postponed and agree when to bring them up next, for example at the next review meeting after an interval of six months or a year when there may be more scope to take on additional commitments. The other main way to deal with priorities is to scale back the commitment to the less urgent or important issues.

For example, the client might decide that of the three main matters on the agenda for action — taking out more life cover, staring an income protection policy and increasing pension contributions by say £1,000 a month – the protection recommendations should be implemented in full, but the pension contributions should be only £400 a month. The level of pension contributions could then be revisited in six months' time.

With suitability reports that only provide advice on focused areas, advisers should draw the client's attention to the limitations of this approach in that it does not address all of the client's possible needs. Clients would then be aware that they have other needs about which they should consider seeking advice.

10 Outline structure of a suitability report

The following outline structure is purely intended as a guide to the possible contents of a suitability report; it is not an FSA recommendation or draft, although it draws on some of their suggestions and examples of good practice. This suitability report is in report format, although it could be provided as a letter. It is probably a good idea to have a very short covering letter for a report, thanking the client for seeing the adviser and perhaps suggesting the arrangements for the next meeting.

Report for A. Client

Date of the report 1 April 2011

Prepared by U.R. Adviser

Contents list of the main sections of the report with page numbers, showing the main sections and any appendices

Introduction

The purpose of the report is to provide advice and recommendations in the following areas:

This might then be followed by the main areas about which the adviser intends to provide advice, reflecting and quoting the fact-find discussion.

Example

> *Providing income and capital through insurance if either client died prematurely or became seriously ill or disabled and could not work*

> A short-term investment programme

> Building up funds for retirement

The report should state whether it is covering the full range of financial issues facing the client or if it is just focused on one or more issues that the client has raised.

The clients' financial situation

This section of the report could contain the following:

> Statement of assets and liabilities

> Summary of income and expenditure identifying surplus and agreed discretionary expenditure

Summary of the protection position and gaps

Summary of the projected pension benefits and potential shortfall

Lifetime cashflow model

Summary of the client's tax position with respect to income, capital gains and inheritance tax (IHT)

Summary of any particular issues for the client

The client's approach to financial issues

This section would normally show:

Aims and objectives

Knowledge and experience of investments

Risk profile

Recommendations

The recommendations should link to the client's objectives showing how they close any gaps or shortfalls or achieve other aims. They should explain why the product is suitable in terms of cost, risk and any other features. They should contain the risk warnings and the commissions or fees with respect to each product.

The recommendations should also set out any disadvantages of the course of action suggested.

e.g. A short-term investment programme.

I recommend that John should invest £10,200 in the XYZ global growth balanced fund. John should hold the investment within the structure of the XYZ ISA.

You said that you wanted to have long-term growth from your savings over a period of at least five years and probably more than ten years. Your risk profile for the purposes of this is medium and the fund fits this approach to investment risk. The definition of 'medium' risk is set out in paragraph xx above.

The selected XYZ global growth fund has good prospects for long-term growth in a diversified portfolio of international shares and has a high rating by Morningstar. We believe that it is prudent to spread investments over a wide range of different economies and industrial sectors, to an extent that is not possible in a fund that focuses on a single market like the UK.

Further details about the fund and its past performance are in appendix xx together with a comparison of past performance with other similar funds. The value of this investment can go down as well as up and you may not get back the amount you invested. Past performance is not a reliable guide to future performance. As the fund is substantially invested outside the UK, there is some additional risk from currency fluctuations.

I recommend that the investment should be held in the XYZ ISA. There is no additional cost to holding the investment in this form. Broadly the income from the fund and the capital gains will be free of UK tax, although it is not possible reclaim the tax credit on dividends. The tax rules governing ISAs might change in the future and there is a more detailed description of these in appendix xx.

An ISA cannot be put in trust and will therefore form part of your estate and be subject to inheritance tax. You do not think that this is a serious drawback because IHT saving is not a high priority. If the investment in the ISA makes a loss, you will not be able to offset it against any gains that are subject to capital gains tax.

Summary

The summary should list the main recommendations and describe their overall impact especially in relation to the total amount invested as a lump sum or committed on a regular basis.

e.g. The total additional monthly outlay on life and health protection policies, savings into the ISA and into your pension plan will be £xx. We discussed this level of commitment and you were comfortable that you could sustain this from your current level of regular monthly cash savings and from discretionary spending that you felt able and willing to reduce to meet your agreed financial goals.

Appendices

Summary of personal details

Brochures and key features of recommended products

Details of research on alternative products where appropriate

Part 4: The main areas of financial planning in practice

Chapter 16
Immediate cashflow planning

1 Budgeting and forecasting

Many people are in control of their day-to-day finances but cannot get to grips with longer-term planning issues. A minority have problems with the day-to-day management of their finances, and of these a small proportion has serious difficulties which if not addressed could result in financial disaster. This chapter will focus primarily on those who have minor difficulties with their short-term finances.

Usually, the fact that someone consults a financial adviser shows that they recognise they have needs or problems and are at least in principle willing to address them. In relation to budgeting, the adviser therefore initially needs to help with the organisation and interpretation of information.

Most of the problems that arise in relation to immediate cashflow planning relate to:

- Poor budgeting: failure to accurately monitor current spending.
- Poor forecasting: failure to think about needs that could be anticipated.

While many people suffer from some weakness in either or both areas, clients who have serious problems are likely to have perceptual or behavioural biases that have prevented them from getting to grips with managing their money. Advisers meeting such people need to consider whether they can in fact help them resolve their problems or whether they should suggest the individual seeks professional counselling.

Financial advisers need to try to identify not just the areas in which clients are overspending but the reasons for this.

2 Budgeting discipline

Resolving short-term cashflow issues has to start with obtaining accurate information.

Clients who are over-spending or under-saving need to prepare an accurate monthly budget. For this to be useful, spending must be accurately assigned to the relevant categories. For example, a member of a sales team meets with his colleagues every month. After the sales meeting some of them go to the pub and then have a meal together. Someone might regard this as a work-related expense, but in fact it is discretionary spending on entertainment. Clients who have spending problems will often misallocate items of expenditure in order to avoid having to acknowledge that the total for a category is too high.

Having created an appropriate set of categories such as those in the Table 16.1, the client needs to identify all the items of expense that belong in that category. This will usually require detailed consideration of bank and credit card statements. Couples may need to create separate accounts for their own personal spending as well as a joint household budget.

While most people consider their short-term finances on a monthly basis, there are many items that vary over the year and will need to be averaged over a 12-month period, such as holidays, tax and utility bills. So the minimum period for data required to create an accurate budget is usually 12 months.

If a large amount of current spending cannot be categorised – often because it is cash withdrawals from a current account – this may point to serious problems such as undisclosed spending on gambling or alcohol.

Often people are unclear about the distinction between commitments and discretionary spending. With commitments, the only way of reducing expenditure is usually to review the scale and terms of the commitment, which is often contractually defined. With discretionary spending, it is altering personal behaviour that is required.

Where the client needs to reduce current discretionary spending, the most effective ways of achieving this are:

- No cards. Credit cards are cancelled or suspended. All spending is in the form of cash withdrawn from a bank account.

- Daily accounting. Every item of personal expenditure is noted on a daily basis for a period of several weeks.

Some people are susceptible to overspending on credit cards "because it's not real money". Removing cards and turning all transactions into cash payments can help them. This is a solution people may not like but they will often recognise that it will in fact help with their problem.

Monitoring every single item of expenditure is a very tedious task that most people will strongly resist. It is often recommended by debt counsellors advising those with serious spending problems. If it is undertaken in a positive way it can be very beneficial. One way to engage clients in it is to ask them to guess the amount they spend each week/month in certain categories and then challenge them to check their daily spending to see if their guesses were correct. The records can easily be kept on most types of smartphone. Usually their predictions for at least one category will be well below their actual spending.

Recognising their actual spending patterns can alone be sufficient to help some people change their behaviour.

Some over-spenders are concealing regular spending they do not want to acknowledge. If the adviser suspects that this is the case, they need to decide whether to press the issue. Effective financial planning often requires changes in behaviour, and without a commitment to this the client is unlikely to achieve their objectives.

If clients accept that they need to exert better control over day-to-day finances, then after analysing current spending and agreeing targets for each category of spending for the following months, the adviser may need to review the budget after a few months have passed to see how well the client is keeping to it.

Since the monthly budget is the source of surplus for meeting future needs, it is vital that appropriate targets for saving as well as spending are established and achieved.

Example 16.1

Ken, aged 43, is a manager at a company that distributes parts for a wide range of commercial vending machines. His salary is £50,000 a year of which he contributes £3,500 to the firm's matched-contribution pension scheme. He receives no fringe benefits. Laura, aged 36, works part-time as an administrator at an insurance company and her net pay is £1,000 per month.

They have two children aged six and four. The younger attends a local nursery school.

Laura received an inheritance of £60,000 from her great-uncle two years ago. The couple originally agreed to use a small amount of this to cover the cost of childcare for their younger child so that Laura could return to part-time work. But in practice, they have increased their standard of living to the extent that their budget now shows an overspend of almost £500 per month, and this is eating away at their capital. Yet they are also aware that they are not putting enough into long-term savings plans since they assume that one or both children will want to go to university.

The fact-find and the discussion with Ken and Laura have not revealed any urgent short-term needs other than balancing their budget. Their employment position is stable and they have no intention of moving home. The couple have agreed they need to discuss longer-term savings needs and to review their protection policies and that they will do this once the budgeting issues and short-term savings needs are resolved.

Table 16.1 – Ken and Laura's monthly budget

Item	Monthly amount	Total
Income		
Ken's net monthly income	£4,170	
Laura's net monthly income	£1,000	
Total monthly net income		**£5,170**
Expenditure		
Utilities and fixed bills		**£156**
Council tax and water rates	£102	
Utilities (gas and electricity)	£54	
Debt		**£1,855**
Mortgage (repayment)	£1,300	
Personal loan	£305	
Credit card balance	£250	
Household		**£1,027**
Food	£650	
TV and broadband	£57	
Clothing	£320	
Travel		**£815**
Cars	£750	
Fares	£65	
Children		**£645**
Childcare	£520	
Clothing	£125	
Leisure		**£835**
Holidays	£450	
Eating out	£255	
Gym membership	£85	
Other	£45	
Insurance and savings		**£333**
Household insurance	£52	
Life insurance	£81	
ISA savings	£200	
Total expenditure		**£5,666**
Deficit		**£496**

Table 16.2 – Ken and Laura's short-term savings

Item	Ken	Laura	Joint	Total
Deposit account	-	-	£8,500	£8,500
Building society account	£1,500	£48,500	-	£50,000
Fixed term bond (2 years)	-	-	£15,000	£15,000
Totals	**£1,500**	**£48,500**	**£23,500**	**£73,500**

Once the budget has been drawn up, the potential for cost savings in each category can be investigated. As noted in chapter 13, 'Summarising and analysing needs and priorities' potential savings are of three kinds: easy economies, more difficult economies and disruptive and painful economies. In this case, Ken and Laura can achieve the required savings without the need for disruptive and painful economies (though Ken insists that his not having a car does in fact fall into this last category).

Ken and Laura are likely to focus purely on their £500 per month shortfall. They have agreed to discuss other needs but these are "in the future" and Ken and Laura are unlikely to consider the implications for their budget.

The adviser, however, has already estimated that the couple probably need to spend about £50 per month more on protection and have a savings gap of about £500 per month. The adviser will therefore urge them to aim for spending cuts of £1,000 per month. These are the major items they can consider:

Utilities

The couple signed up to a dual fuel deal three years ago and have not reviewed it since. Switching to an alternative supplier could reduce bills by about 10%.

Mortgage

The mortgage is at a fixed rate for a further two years at 4.5%, with a 3% penalty for early redemption. It has 18 years to run to redemption. There is therefore no scope at the present time for remortgaging to secure a lower interest rate.

Switching the £200,000 mortgage from a repayment basis to an interest only basis would reduce repayments from £1,300 to £750 per month. But this would simply accumulate a larger repayment liability for the future. Lenders usually permit part of the mortgage to be on a repayment and part on an interest-only basis; a 50-50 division would reduce outgoings by £275 per month, which would still defer some of the capital liability.

Personal loan

The loan, originally of £8,000, was taken out to enable Laura to purchase a car before they received the inheritance. It is at an interest rate (APR) of 11.3% and has a further year to run.

There are no penalties for early redemption of the loan, which would cost £3,300.

Credit card balance

The balance outstanding from the payment for the last major family holiday is £1,300. The couple used the card because it offered a 0% interest rate for a period of nine months, but they failed to pay off the entire balance before the concessionary rate period ended and are now paying interest at 12.9%.

Cars

Both Ken and Laura drive to work. His car, a family estate, is two years old while her hatchback is three years old. His is paid for on a lease-purchase arrangement at £475 per month. The implicit finance cost is approximately 7% APR.

Ken does not need a car for travel in his work. He could use public transport, but if this were impractical a taxi to and from work each day would cost him about £350 per month. By running one car they would save about £200 per month.

Childcare

The younger child attends a day nursery four days a week; on the other day she is cared for by her grandmother. Laura has considerable flexibility in her working hours and could work the same number of hours in a four-day week, which would cut the nursery cost by £100 per month.

Holidays

Ken and Laura are in the habit of taking a mid-price package holiday abroad for two weeks each summer with the children, a further family week at Easter and a couple of short break long weekend holidays when they leave the children with Laura's parents. They can reduce the amount they spend on holidays by about £100 per month by economising on all these items.

Leisure

Ken and Laura both use the gym. They could opt for a lower tier of membership with some restrictions on access but the saving would be only £20 per month.

If Laura worked a four-day week, she would have more time for cooking, which she enjoys, so that they could save about £100 per month on eating out.

Spending cuts

Ken and Laura agree that she will change her hours of work so she works four days a week. They aim to save £100 per month on the nursery and £100 per month on eating out.

They agree to sell Laura's car. Ken will get taxis to work and they aim to save £200 per month from this.

Laura will switch their utilities to a cheaper provider saving £15 per month. They will cut holiday spending by £100 per month.

Loan repayments

Ken and Laura will pay off the personal loan and the credit card balance with the proceeds from selling Laura's car. This will reduce outgoings by £550 per month.

They do not wish to defer capital repayments on their mortgage and will leave the loan unchanged.

Revised budget

On the basis of these actions their monthly spending will be cut by just over £1,000 and their budget will be in surplus by £500.

3 Forecasting problems

Some people end up in financial difficulties not because they do not manage day-do-day spending but because they fail to anticipate and plan for larger items of expenditure that require advance provision. These include:

- Tax bills
- Holidays
- Car replacement
- Home improvements and repairs

An essential feature of the budgeting process is to identify such commitments for the next two or three years. For each item, cash should be accumulated in a suitable savings account. Some people will prefer to have several savings accounts, one for each such future liability, and indeed this may be the only way they can actually discipline themselves to save. Earmarking savings accounts for specific purposes is one of the oldest household budget management techniques and should be used whenever insufficient money is being set aside to meet predicted spending.

Only if all such commitments are being covered by savings from monthly income can a budget be said to be in balance. This may be a new idea to some people, but they need (for example) to understand that however they finance their car, the total cost of depreciation, insurance and maintenance must be paid over their period of ownership of the car. Any amount that is not paid for now will have to be paid for later, and the cash necessary to do so needs to be saved. While lease purchasing arrangements may seem attractive, the interest paid on the often large 'residual value' or 'balloon payment' can be large and needs to be accounted for.

Cashflow projections can be useful in helping clients to understand their short-term savings requirements.

Short-term cashflow issues

Most people have financial commitments over the next few years. These may be ongoing in nature, such as school fees, or one-off, such as car replacement or home repairs.

In general, once a long-term investment portfolio has been established, it will be managed to produce the required sums of capital or income. But when a financial plan is being created, one of its components will be planning to meet such expenditures over the period (normally about five years) before longer-term investments can be drawn on.

In order to do this the adviser needs precision in respect of both the amounts required and their timing. This is relatively easy with ongoing commitments such as school fees but will inevitably be less certain (in respect of both amounts and timing) as regards one-off items. This is one reason why holding a higher quantity of cash on deposit than may appear to be desirable at first sight can in fact be appropriate for many clients.

Example 16.2

Ian and Julia have one child attending a local junior independent day school for which they are paying fees. They run one car which they wish to replace in three years' time and have minor home repairs scheduled for next year. In addition they know they will need to re-roof part of their home and paint it in five years' time.

Their projected cash needs are shown in the table.

These short-term needs can be met from cash deposits, but consideration can also be given to fixed-term deposits. Many people will prefer to keep cash for items like these separate from their 'rainy day' or emergency fund. With couples, this can also be financially advantageous, since while the emergency fund should be a joint account, other savings can be held in the name of the partner with the lower tax income tax rate.

Table 16.3 – Ian and Julia's future cash needs

End of year	Fees	Car	Home	Total
1	£2,000	–	–	£2,000
2	£2,100	–	£700	£2,800
3	£2,200	£5,000	–	£7,200
4	£2,400	–	–	£2,400
5	£2,500	–	£6,500	£9,000

In general, if capital or income is available to use the full annual ISA allowance, ISAs should be used for long-term savings because of the progressively growing value of the tax exemption. They should only be used for shorter-term cash deposits if there is no scope for using them for longer-term purposes.

Budgeting problem warning signs

Among the warning signs of over-spending are:

Personal loans. The client has regularly used personal loans for car or other consumer purchases and has not paid off the balance before commencing the next, or has used a new loan to repay the balance on the old.

Credit cards. The client has a balance outstanding on which they are paying a high rate of interest. The total balance outstanding on credit cards exceeds the amount held in short-term savings accounts. The client has regularly transferred balances from one card to another.

Transfers. Monthly deficits in the household budget are covered by transfers from savings accounts. Complicated series of transactions obscure the fact that the savings account is being run down.

Mortgage refinancing. The client has refinanced their mortgage and added to their capital balance to cover purchases of consumables.

High cash spending. Withdrawal of large sums of cash may indicate addictive behaviour.

Key issues in short-term budgeting

Borrowing

Borrowing is the source of many budgeting problems. As is widely acknowledged, we have become culturally conditioned to accept borrowing on a scale and of types that would have been unthinkable 30 or 40 years ago. Many clients fail to distinguish between borrowing that benefits them and borrowing that harms them financially.

'Good' borrowing is essentially to finance the purchase of assets whose value is expected to rise. But the interest rate must be below the expected annual rise in value.

'Bad' borrowing is to finance purchases of consumables whose value will decline rapidly. If obtainable at zero interest or very low interest rates, such borrowing is an acceptable way of financing car purchase, for example.

Since the price of much 'hardware' (gadgets, TVs, PCs, household appliances) has been falling steadily for years, people can expect to buy at lower cost in the future. So paying interest in order to buy now is an unattractive proposition. The expected decline in price of consumables should be added to the interest payable in estimating the total cost of buying on credit.

Credit cards and store cards are the worst way of financing consumable purchases since not only are the interest rates high but there are many possibilities of incurring penalties as well. The adviser should discourage clients from using these.

Table 16.4 – Beneficial and harmful borrowing

Beneficial borrowing	Harmful borrowing
Mortgage to finance home purchase with commitment of no more than 30% of net disposable income to repayments	Second mortgage or additional secured loan at high interest rate used for consumer purchases
Mortgage to finance buy-to-let property generating rental income greater than mortgage repayments	Buy-to-let mortgage where rental income does not cover repayments
Car purchase loan at 0% interest	Lease purchase and car loans at interest rates of 7% or more
	Credit and store cards at interest rates of 15% or more
	Personal loans at interest rates of 7-10%
	Mortgage in a currency other than that in which the value of the property is denominated

In theory it can make sense to pay off high-interest consumer loans by adding to a mortgage at a much lower interest rate. However, since the mortgage interest is payable for a much longer period, the total interest paid would rise if the client simply made repayments on the new balance in line with the term of their mortgage. To reduce not just the interest rate but the amount of interest paid, the client will need to increase their mortgage repayments sufficiently to pay off the extra capital more quickly — ideally within the term of the consumer loan that is being redeemed.

Currency mortgages are potentially dangerous. Would-be buyers of a foreign property may feel they are getting a better deal by extending their UK mortgage to raise the capital for a foreign property purchase. But this means that any rise in the value of sterling relative to the other currency will effectively increase the value of the loan in relation to the value of the property. Currency movements can be abrupt and sizeable and are widely acknowledged to be unpredictable. The risk involved in 'mismatching' the currency denomination of assets and liabilities is substantial.

Buy-to-let investment has grown in popularity in the past two decades. Almost always purchases are financed by borrowing. Among the issues advisers should question are the loan-to-value ratio, the cover ratio on mortgage repayments (ideally rental income should be at least 130% of mortgage repayments), the extent to which cash is being set aside for maintenance and repairs, and whether adequate and appropriate landlord's insurance cover is held. Especially important are the mortgage terms; if financing was obtained on favourable terms some time ago but refinancing may be needed, it may be that only a smaller loan or one at a higher interest rate will be available. In this case capital may need to be provided from other sources.

A different type of buy-to-let is where parents purchase a flat or house for occupation by a child while attending university. A mortgage is supported by the rent paid by other students. Often the net cost of such an arrangement can be comparable or even below the rent the parents would otherwise have paid on behalf of their child. Usually the parents have made no decision about what to do with the property after the child graduates. Recent experience in the residential property market shows owners may have to be prepared for an extended period of ownership if they want to avoid selling at a loss. Commitment to a mortgage on such a property may constrain their ability to borrow more for their own house purchase.

Joint budgeting

A household budget is necessarily a collective exercise. However, young couples often maintain their own personal bank account as well as a joint account and only defined household items are paid from the joint account. In this case, a combined household budget has to be created by identifying the relevant items from all three bank accounts as well as from personal spending on credit cards. One reason for overspending may be a lack of realism about the actual joint costs, with both partners spending too much on personal items.

Historically, the task of household budget management was often entrusted to the woman. This was indeed an almost universal practice among the working classes until the 1970s. Today, most couples tend to assume that shared responsibility is a desirable norm. In practice, however, it may be much easier if one person assumes prime responsibility for the household budget.

Changing behaviour

Once a pattern of spending behaviour has been established, it is hard to change. As discussed in chapter 3, the status quo bias and anchoring can both keep people tied to 'what is'.

It may be useful for the adviser to discuss these biases so that clients understand that they are dealing with normal effects of human psychology.

To change behaviour for good, the motivation for good budgeting and for saving needs to change from "I ought" to "I want". Among the wants the adviser can prompt are:

- Being in control
- Feeling secure
- Knowing there is money in the account at the end of the month
- Knowing there is cash to meet unexpected needs
- Not having to worry about specific items of spending
- Being confident of money management skills
- Being sure they can provide what the children need

A 'stick-only' approach to reducing spending can be difficult to sustain. If people already have negative feelings about managing their finances, failure to meet targets for cutting spending can reinforce them. So it is often best to combine stick and carrot and suggest methods of rewarding success in achieving targets.

One possibility is to allocate a fraction, say 10%, of the target savings to a 'fun' fund to be spent on treats. This trick employs mental accounting since the 'fun' fund is now a separate entity that the client will track. Or there may be some item that the clients have wanted to buy, which they agree they will buy if they achieve certain expenditure cuts within a given period (a use of anchoring).

Both these concepts will work better if they are the clients' own idea, so the adviser should start by trying to lead discussions towards these outcomes rather than making direct suggestions.

4 Budgeting solutions

Where current spending is well in excess of income urgent action may be needed to restore a balance. Table 16.5 lists some of the most obvious and easy-to-implement solutions.

Table 16.5 – Budgeting solutions – the pros and cons

Possible solution	Advantages	Disadvantages
Switch mortgage from repayment to interest only	Large reduction in monthly outgoings	Accumulates capital repayment liability for the future
Pay off loans with 0% credit card balance transfer offer	Cuts out high interest payments on other loans	Unless the entire balance is repaid within the concessionary period, even higher interest rates may then be charged
Take out loan with longer repayment period to pay off existing loans	Immediate reduction in outgoings	Involves payment of more interest
Remortgage at a lower interest rate	Substantial savings over a few years	Hassle factor
Replace one of two or more family cars with car club or taxis	Large saving in annual cost	'Invisible' costs like deprecation are not usually accounted for
Repay high-interest loans from savings accounts	Substantial saving in interest payments	Blocks caused by mental accounting
Review discretionary spending on all subscriptions and regular payments	Usually possible to save on gym, TV, etc	Focussing on this may avoid addressing bigger issues
Review life and protection insurances	Same cover may be purchasable more cheaply	Hassle factor
Abandon or reduce commitment to private education	Large reduction in outgoings	Potential damage to children; emotional attachment
Sell property and downsize	Large reduction in mortgage repayments	Loss of social status
Stop using credit cards	Avoids spontaneous spending decisions	Inconvenience

Reviews

Once a budget has been created and, where necessary, adjusted, reviews will only be needed in response to major events, such as:

- Long-term illness

- Redundancy

- Wife ceasing work to care for children

- Commencement or termination of a major commitment such as education fees

- Establishment of own business
- Transfer from employment to self-employment or vice versa
- Retirement
- Requirement for long-term care

In most cases, the cash savings and emergency fund should take the strain. Immediate cuts in some spending may be required, but it is not usually possible to create a realistic budget until several months have passed after such a change. In practice, a 'cautious' budget drawn up after a few months can be reviewed and adjusted after, say, a further six months, when the new pattern of life is clearly established. Changes to longer-term savings plans and investments should normally be deferred for several months.

Chapter 17
Insurance and financial protection

1 Introduction

Protection needs are sometimes ignored by financial planners who are mainly wealth managers, but should be central features of financial planning for many clients. The main types of financial protection to be considered are life assurance, health insurance, medical insurance and redundancy/unemployment cover. However, these hazards ought to be considered in the context of the overall risks that clients face.

Some risks are appropriate for insuring, while other risks should be dealt with in other ways. Insurance is generally the best answer for hazards that are relatively rare but would have a high impact on the individual or their family. Examples of insurable risks are the death of a parent or partner or a serious illness that leads to incapacity and loss of earnings. The chances of such a death are low but the consequences could be devastating, especially if clients have borrowed large sums in the expectation of making the capital and interest repayment from their future income.

Other risks may be less suitable for insurance, because they are low impact or happen relatively frequently — or possibly both. For these hazards, it is usually best to hold cash reserves or manage the risk in some other way. One approach is to have access to borrowing (e.g. through an overdraft facility or credit card), although this may turn out to be an expensive option and involve additional risks of their own. Dental treatment is an example of costs that are generally both relatively low and also quite frequent. Dental 'insurance arrangements' are available but for the most part they resemble savings and budgeting plans more than insurance policies.

Generally speaking those who do not have earnings and/or have access to substantial wealth have little or no need for life or health insurance, although there are some exceptions. Insurance policies are widely used for inheritance tax (IHT) planning.

2 Insuring against death — the financial consequences of a death

Life assurance is perhaps the most basic insurance need for individuals, although it is not always the most important — health insurance is a higher priority for many people. One way to consider how much life cover a person needs is to imagine the financial consequences of their dying. The following section covers the main considerations that arise when someone has died.

If someone dies the normal aim is to provide a replacement income for their lost earnings and to cover their liabilities. Where a person has no dependants, it is rare that they would need any life cover, as long as their assets cover their potential liabilities. The main issues to consider are:

Identifying who would be worse off as a result of the individual's death

The greatest financial impact of a death is likely to be on the spouse or partner and on any minor children. But there could be other people who are financially dependent on the individual, either directly or indirectly including elderly or disabled family members whom the individual supports financially or physically. An indirect liability might have arisen as a result of guaranteeing someone else's mortgage or other liability. It is also very common for business owners to guarantee a loan or overdraft or even a lease on some business premises.

The provisions of the will

Many people never make a will – or do not make a new one after their marriage or divorce. And wills are not always written so that the people who should benefit after someone has died are those who actually inherit. Dependants may miss out. In particular, unmarried partners are often left with no provision. The terms of a will might be much less tax efficient than they should be – for example in relation to income tax or IHT. At the individual's death, this might be corrected to some extent by a deed of variation, but this is generally not possible where the existing beneficiaries include minors and there are several other limitations to deeds of variation.

How jointly owned assets are held

Assets held on a joint tenancy will pass automatically to the surviving joint owner. Assets held under a tenancy in common pass through the will or intestacy.

The spouse or partner's ability to earn

In many marriages or partnerships, the surviving partner may be able to earn enough to cover their needs without any additional provision from the deceased spouse/partner. But in some circumstances, the survivor might be left in a position in which they could not work for a living or their earnings would not be adequate to maintain themselves and their family. This is more likely to be the case where a couple have dependent children and the surviving partner could not easily look after the children and earn a substantial income.

The proceeds of any pension lump sums and survivor pensions

Both defined contribution and defined benefit pension schemes typically provide substantial death benefits. These are often payable to the surviving spouse or partner. However, it may be more tax efficient for some (or all) of these benefits to be paid into a trust for the remaining family, rather than just passing them to the surviving spouse/partner. In some schemes, certain benefits under pension policies — such as a widow's pension — may not be payable to unmarried partners; it is important to check this position.

The proceeds of life assurance policies

A valuable feature of life policies is that they should provide additional financial resources at exactly the time they are required, although there can be disappointments. Policies may pay out less than assumed, for example if a policy is a decreasing term insurance and the client has forgotten this. The policy may be for a term that is too short and runs out while cover is still required. The policy may not be written in trust, in which case there is likely to be a delay before the benefits are available. Even if the policy is in trust, the terms of the trust may be unduly restrictive and inflexible. If the policy is written under a flexible trust, the deployment of the funds should be carefully considered; they may be better retained in a trust for tax efficiency and flexibility.

Trusts from which the surviving family could benefit

In a few cases, there may be family trusts that could be drawn on to supplement the survivor's income and capital provision. These need to be explored and the financial planner should pay particular attention to the provisions of the trust to see how it could be used most beneficially. Expert advice about trusts may be required.

The availability of investments or other assets that could be sold

Most clients who earn their living and have dependants need to cover their earnings with some kind of insurance. But some clients have very significant assets that could be sold or used in other ways to generate the replacement income or pay off any liabilities. In determining how much life cover is needed on a person's life, the value of their assets should be taken into account and also the ease and speed with which they could be sold. Business assets such as private company shares may take years to dispose of and could turn out to be worth very much less than expected, especially if the deceased owner was very important to the success of the business.

Tax liabilities

Inheritance tax could substantially reduce the value of the resources left to the surviving family.

- The surviving spouse may be non-UK domiciled in which case the spousal exemption would only be worth £55,000.

- If the partner is not married, there would be no exemption other than the nil rate band.

- If the main beneficiaries of the will are children (e.g. on the death of a widow), then there would only be the nil rate band(s) before the estate would be subject to 40% tax.

Business assets

Qualifying business assets are normally free of inheritance tax because of business assets relief. But if the individual was essential to the survival of the business in question, it might not produce continuing profits or be worth much after their death.

Example 17.1

Tom died leaving a wife aged 36 and two children in their early teens. Tom's widow Alicia was a manager in a large retail company but she found it very hard to continue working on a full time basis after his death. The house, which was worth £400,000, was held under a joint tenancy and passed automatically to Alicia. He had a pension fund worth £120,000 and he had nominated Alicia as the beneficiary of any death benefits. There was a mortgage on the house of £180,000 which was largely paid off by the mortgage protection policy. He had taken out a life assurance policy in a discretionary trust for Alicia and the children. With no other life assurance on Tom's life, Alicia found that the income from the £120,000 was very welcome, but nowhere near enough to cover her outgoings of £30,000 a year. She had to increase her working hours substantially to break even financially and the resulting strains in the wake of Tom's death were very considerable.

---

3 Life assurance planning

Life assurance planning should be based on the needs and the wishes of the client.

1. Identify the need for life cover in terms of who would suffer in the event of the person's death. In the case of a couple, this should be done for both

spouses/partners. It may be the surviving spouse and any children but there may be others.

2. Quantify the capital and income needed for beneficiaries. The capital would be needed for paying off liabilities, and then there would be ongoing income needs of various kinds.

3. Decide how long the cover is required.

4. Deduct any assets, pensions and life policy proceeds that could be offset against the client's life policy needs.

5. Select the right type of policies.

4 Life cover calculator

There are several ways of quantifying life cover needs; the following model of calculator is commonly used. It distinguishes capital needs from short-term and long-term income requirements. The model may need to be more complicated for some clients – for example, by providing for short-term, medium-term and long-term needs.

Figure 17.1 – Flowchart for assessing life cover

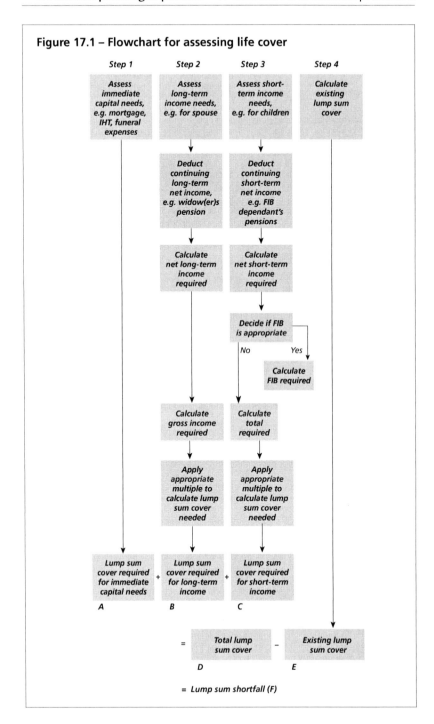

Step 1	Step 2	Step 3	Step 4
Assess immediate capital needs, e.g. mortgage, IHT, funeral expenses	Assess long-term income needs, e.g. for spouse	Assess short-term income needs, e.g. for children	Calculate existing lump sum cover

Deduct continuing long-term net income, e.g. widow(er)s pension

Deduct continuing short-term net income e.g. FIB dependant's pensions

Calculate net long-term income required

Calculate net short-term income required

Decide if FIB is appropriate

No   Yes

Calculate FIB required

Calculate gross income required

Calculate total required

Apply appropriate multiple to calculate lump sum cover needed

Apply appropriate multiple to calculate lump sum cover needed

Lump sum cover required for immediate capital needs

Lump sum cover required for long-term income

Lump sum cover required for short-term income

A   +   B   +   C

= Total lump sum cover   –   Existing lump sum cover

D   E

= Lump sum shortfall (F)

Capital needs (step 1 in Figure 17.1)

1. Funeral expenses: these vary widely, but the average cost may be about £2,500 (and could be higher).

2. Emergency funds: cash will almost certainly be needed after a person's death as their assets may be frozen during probate.

3. Specific bequests: if a person makes special bequests, they will reduce the cash available to their dependants.

4. Debts and mortgages: these will need to be repaid at death in most cases.

5. Inheritance tax: this could be payable if the surviving partner who receives the assets was not married to, or the civil partner of, the deceased. It may also be payable on assets passing to those other than the spouse/civil partner.

6. Other: there may be capital needs, e.g. to inject funds into a business to keep it going after the owner's death or buying a vehicle to replace the company car.

    A. Aggregate lines 1−6 to calculate lump sum needed.

Long-term income needs (step 2)

7. The annual personal expenses of the surviving spouse or partner (excluding children) are likely to last for the rest of their life.

    • One approach is to take into account the family's current expenses.

    • Deduct the costs associated with any children, which should be inserted below, on line 13.

    Also deduct costs that would be saved on the person's death, e.g. mortgage payments, which are covered by insurance, and direct living costs associated with the person's food, fares etc.

    • Another approach is to calculate the minimum expenditure needed − usually reaching a lower amount.

8. Additional costs: there are likely to be some extra long-term costs when a spouse or partner dies. For example there could be a need for a housekeeper or nurse. In some cases there could also be the expense of replacing a benefit in kind provided by the deceased spouse's or partner's employer, such as private medical insurance.

9. Continuing long-term net income: will the surviving spouse or partner be able to continue to work or will they have childcare responsibilities? Will some of that income continue after retirement in the form of pension benefits? The amount on this line should be continuing income after tax and pension contributions.

10. Extra long-term net income: the amount of income needed will be reduced by extra income payments that would be received following the deceased person's death, e.g. widow's pensions, proceeds of a family income benefit (FIB) plan.

11. Total long-term net income needed: this is the total income that will be required – probably for the rest of the surviving spouse or partner's lifetime. A disabled person who is a beneficiary may also need to have an income to last for their lifetime, if they earn insufficient income to support themselves.

Calculating the cover required

Long-term and short-term income needs should be distinguished because they will lead to different terms for life assurance:

A simple approach to provide for needs of up to about 25–30 years is family income benefit. Simply assess the net income required and the term and arrange the policy accordingly. Some inflation protection should ideally be included.

Alternatively, cover can be arranged on a lump sum basis. Clearly the capital required to generate an income for five or ten years is much less than the amount needed to provide for 25 years or more of expenditure.

12. Aggregate lines 7–11 to calculate the total net income needed. For lump sum cover, the appropriate factor should be chosen. Table 17.1 provides an example of factors that can be used, based on temporary annuity rates.

B. Multiply the income required by the chosen factor to arrive at the lump sum needed.

Short-term income needs (step 3)

13. Annual expenditure on children: this will include the costs of feeding, clothing and educating the children. These expenses will generally stop when they leave school or college. In most cases, this will provide the required period of cover and also the income that will need to be replaced

14. Extra short-term costs: it is a good idea to focus parents' minds on the short-term extra costs that would arise if either of them died. The obvious one is extra childcare. Clearly, if the homemaker (in many cases, the mother) died, there would be extra costs; but they might also arise if the breadwinner died.

15. Add any other short-term income needs.

16. Short-term net income: in some cases, extra net income may be generated on a person's death, e.g. many pension schemes pay dependants' benefits until children reach the age of 18 or leave full-time education/training. The

net after-tax benefit should be included. The annual payment under any FIB plan should also be included.

17. Aggregate lines 13—15 and deduct line 16 to calculate total short-term net income needed. This can be used to provide a sum assured for a FIB policy.

18. Alternatively, choose the appropriate factor from Table 17.1 to calculate a lump sum to provide for the short-term income needs.

C. Multiply the chosen factor by the income required to arrive at the lump sum needed for short-term income.

D. Add together A + B + C to arrive at the total lump sum needed.

E. Calculate any existing lump sum life cover already in existence together with the proceeds of investments that may be sold at the client's death (the income may additionally have to be taken into account if it is spent on a regular basis).

F. Deduct E from D to derive the lump sum shortfall. That should be the amount of additional lump sum life cover needed.

Income multipliers

Once the amount of net income required has been calculated, factors can be used to calculate the amount of capital needed to produce the required level. Broadly, the factors are based on temporary annuity rates and may have to be changed from time to time. The assumptions are:

- The capital will be run down over the course of the period of the cover to provide the spendable 'income'.

- The annual income will rise by about 3% a year. Additional insurance cover may be required if the income derived from it needs to increase at a higher rate.

- Tax of 20% is deducted from the taxable income element of the withdrawals. Over the longer-term periods, additional life cover may be required if the beneficiary is likely to be a higher rate taxpayer.

- The factors are rounded to the nearest 0.5.

- These figures are intended to illustrate the principles, and different figures may be appropriate depending on rates of interest applying at the time. A broad alternative indicator is to multiply the income by the number of years needed, although this overstates the amount needed for longer terms.

Figure 17.2 – Life cover calculator

Capital needs (Step 1 in Figure 5.2)

	Client £	Partner £
1 Funeral expenses		
2 Emergency funds (eg 3–6 months's expenses		
3 Specific bequests		
4 Mortgages, debts, loans		
5 Inheritance tax		
6 Other		
A Total capital needs		

Long-term income needs (Step 2)

	Client £	Partner £
7 Expenses if surviving partner etc.		
8 Plus extra long-term costs (eg housekeeper)		
9 Less continuing long-term income	( )	( )
10 Less extra long-term income (eg window(er)'s pension)	( )	( )
11 Total long-term net income needed per annum		
12 Factor to be applied for lump sum (see Figure 5.4)		
B Total lump sum needed for long-term income		

Short-term income needs (Step 3)

	Client £	Partner £
13 Annual expenses for children (etc)		
14 Plus extra short-term costs (eg extra childcare)		
15 Less extra short-term net income (eg dependant's pension)	( )	( )
16 Plus other short term needs		
17 Total short-term net income needed per annum		
18 Factor to be applied for lump sum (see Figure 5.4)		
C Total lump sum needed for short-term income		
D Total lump sum needed (A + B + C)		
E Lump sums available from existing life cover, return of pension funds and investments available for sale (Step 4)		
F Lump sum shortfall (D – E)		

Table 17.1 – Income multipliers

Period (years)	Factor
5	5
10	10
15	14.5
20	18.5
25	22.5

5 Features of life policies

In principle, it makes sense for a client to take out no more life assurance than will be needed to meet the needs of their beneficiaries. But there may be several unknowns.

- One unknown is the future rate of inflation, which can affect the amount of cover needed now to provide a future inflation proof income. It will also affect the level of cover that will be required in the future.

- It may not be easy to predict the length of time that insurance will be needed. With life assurance needs that are likely to stretch over long periods, investment issues become more important along with the need for additional flexibility.

Additional features usually involve extra costs and choices.

Inflation linked sums assured

The value of insurance cover on clients' lives should be increased on a regular basis. To some extent this may reflect increasing needs as a family grows and clients take on more liabilities. But it will also arise because of inflation causing the real value of sums assured to decline. So insurance cover of £1m should be adjusted by the rate of price inflation to keep its real value. Arguably sums assured in many cases should be increased by more than inflation to reflect rising needs. But the option to increase the amount of cover is a feature that carries a higher initial premium cost. Then as the level of cover increases over the years, the additional premiums will become proportionately more expensive with rising mortality costs.

Sufficient cover to provide inflation protected income

Most cover is used in order to provide beneficiaries with an income. If this income remains level in nominal terms, inflation will cause it to decline in real terms. Lump-sum sums assured should be large enough to generate a rising income to keep pace with inflation. Policies such as family income benefit should normally provide a rising income.

Where the income requires some inflation proofing over 10 or 20 years, the extra costs could be substantial. The amount of capital needed to provide an income of £10,000 over 20 years has to be roughly doubled to protect against inflation at 3.5% a year.

Flexibility of cover

It is not always possible to predict how long insurance cover will be needed. A reasonable assumption that the children will no longer be financially dependent on their parents after the age of 21 might turn out to be quite wrong and they might continue to be dependent for some time into their 20s or even later.

As long as the insured person remains in good health, there would probably be no difficulty in taking out a replacement policy when the original cover runs out. But some clients may find that their health has deteriorated with age, even if they are still capable of working, and a new life assurance policy may then be unaffordable or even unobtainable. The ideal solution might therefore be to have a policy that can be extended in some way, but clients would have to decide whether this flexibility was worth the extra premium costs. Depending on the age and term of the client, the extra premium for convertibility would be about 25% to 30%.

Investment linking

Some life policies have an investment element where the policyholder effectively takes on the investment risk. Others are guaranteed. In simple terms, a life policy has three main components, the mortality cost, the administration expenses and an investment reserve. The investment reserve allows the life office to charge level premiums for a policy under which the mortality cost rises each year with the insured person's age. The investment reserve builds up over the first part of the policy term and covers the extra costs of life assurance in the later years when the insured is older and is at greater risk of dying.

Insurance companies generally take the risk that the investment reserve will be enough to cover the mortality risk and other costs, so that the premium rate is guaranteed for the life of the policy.

However many whole life policies and a few term policies are not guaranteed in this way and the premiums on the policy may be reviewed periodically if the investments do not provide a set minimum rate of return. With some policies, the mortality rates may also be subject to review. In return, the premiums may initially be lower than for comparable guaranteed policies. Clients and their advisers should decide whether the risk of higher premiums in the future is worth the initial cost saving.

Term or whole life policies

Traditional life assurance salespeople have generally advocated whole life policies, mostly because of their high investment content; in contrast, financial planners have mostly argued in favour of separating saving and insurance, popularising the slogan 'Buy term assurance and invest the rest', on the grounds of flexibility, overall cost and transparency. For example, a 20 year term policy for a 40 year old man is likely to cost up to 90% less than a non-profit whole life policy with the same sum assured.

Whole life insurance should be used where there is a strong likelihood that that insurance protection will be needed for the whole of the insured person's life. However, the introduction of certain unit linked policies that are technically whole of life has muddied the waters. In some forms where the maximum cover versions are used and the investment content is low, these policies are very similar to ten year increasable convertible term.

Short-term renewable policies

One way to reduce the initial costs of insurance is to take out a short-term life policy rather than a longer term policy. If the policy is renewable, the insured can take out a new policy at the end of the initial term regardless of their state of health at the time. This can provide a short-term saving during the initial term, but the premiums in the second or third term could be much more expensive. A 20 year convertible policy may cost about 25% more each year than a ten year policy for the same sum assured. But if the same person had taken out a ten year policy and then renewed it at the end of the term, the premium would have roughly doubled with a typical company. Clients should generally be presented with the choice.

Employer's insurance cover

Many employees have life assurance as part of their employment remuneration package. The advantage is that it is free. The potential drawback is that it will stop when they leave the employment. Of course they may well have the same cover or more from their next employer or they could take out replacement cover themselves if they are sufficiently healthy at the time.

The question is therefore whether to take out more life assurance cover than they strictly need, in order to be certain that they will have some insurance should they leave the employment, or whether they should take the chance and focus on another financial priority. It is an issue that financial planners should discuss with clients.

6 Economising on life cover

There may be economies to be made after reviewing the existing life cover. This could allow the provision of higher levels of life cover, the inclusion of other essential types of insurance or the accumulation of more savings. It depends on the client's priorities after they have seen the costs of life cover. The following is a checklist of issues:

Is the existing life cover uncompetitive? Term assurance rates have been reduced in the last two or three decades and there may be scope to make savings while providing the same level and term of policy with equivalent features.

Could the term be reduced? The existing life cover may be written for a longer term than is necessary. This may be particular marked if the policy is whole life when term assurance would be adequate. However, the client should be aware of the potential dangers of reducing the term in respect of lost flexibility.

Are the additional features of convertibility or increasability still required? The considerations are very similar to the decision about reducing the term of the policy.

Is the level of life cover too high? The life assurance needs might have been calculated on an excessively generous basis. When the priorities are being looked at carefully, it might be possible to assume that the surviving spouse could get by on a lower income than the ideal level of income projected in the life cover calculator. Maybe the survivor really could move to a smaller home or have a lower standard of living or aim to earn more. Perhaps the children could be moved to a cheaper school.

For younger clients, the costs of life cover may be relatively very small and so the savings could turn out to be equally low.

7 Income protection and critical illness insurance

Virtually everyone of working age needs some kind of health insurance to provide some financial resources in the event of a serious illness or disability leading to a substantial reduction in income. Even those who are not in paid remuneration should consider having some level of health insurance cover if their disability would lead to a substantial rise in expenditure. A distinguishing feature of health insurance therefore is that it is necessary for people who have no dependants, although the need is much greater where there is a family or other dependants.

Identifying health insurance needs

The process of determining health needs is similar to that for life cover. The needs will vary considerably according to the circumstances, notably the age of the client when the illness sets in, the terms and conditions of the employment and in particular how long they will continue to be paid, the existence or otherwise of an income protection policy, the chances of recovery and re-employment, the scope for early retirement and the benefits.

In the very short-term a person who has become seriously ill will probably continue to be paid by their employer. Generally this could be up to six months at full pay, although it could be much shorter. Some employers have income protection schemes, which would start paying out at some point, although almost certainly not at the same level as the client's earnings.

Most self-employed clients would find that their earnings would dry up very rapidly. Those who own and run businesses of some size and independent existence from themselves could find that the business would be able to pay them and they might even be able to employ someone to replace them on a temporary or even permanent basis.

The serious illness or disability of a person who has been actively employed or self-employed could cause a reduction in some expenditure — notably travel costs and a few other incidental expenses. But other expenses may well increase and it may be necessary to make permanent economies rapidly. The older the client, the less likely it is that they will be able to go back to work.

In the short run, it might be necessary to cut back on some discretionary expenditure. If the illness or disability looked as if it were going to be permanent, it might be necessary to consider whether it would be worth making very substantial cuts in expenditure as quickly as possible; otherwise lesser economies might be adequate. Much will depend on the level of health insurance cover that is available and whether in fact it pays out.

Income protection or critical illness insurance

The core type of health insurance policy to provide funds for an individual who falls ill or is disabled is income protection insurance. Income protection pays out an income after the insured person has been unable to work because of illness or disability (as defined by the policy) for a set number of months, known as the 'deferral period'. This period is typically three, six or twelve months, although shorter or longer periods can be used. The policy pays out for a set term, typically to age 60 or 65. If the insured person is ill and cannot work but then recovers, the policy will pay out, then either reduce payments or stop them entirely. But if the client is ill again, the policy will also resume paying out. If the client can earn but only receives a proportion of their salary before the claim, the policy will pay a scaled-down level of benefit. Benefits can be level or they can increase in payment.

In contrast, critical illness insurance (the more popular alternative to income protection) provides a lump sum on the diagnosis of one of a number of specified illnesses, including most cancers, heart attacks and strokes. Most policies pay out the level of cover regardless of the severity of the condition, although there are now some policies where the amount paid-out is graded according to the severity of the illness or disability. The payment on a claim under the critical illness policy is not related to whether the client can work or not. The cost of £100,000 of critical illness insurance including term assurance written to age 65 for a man of 30 would be £57.10 a month and for a woman it would be £51.70 a month (Legal and General).

Example 17.3

The premium for a 30 year old man would be £20.84 a month for a benefit of £200 a week with a 13 week deferral period, index linked terms and written to age 60. For a woman of the same age, the premium would be nearly £35 a month (figures from Legal and General). Increasing the term to age 65 would cost roughly a third more. Insured people who work in a factory or other non-office based environment would have to pay substantially higher premiums. This relatively modest amount of cover could pay out a substantial amount. Assuming annual inflation of 5%, the total pay out to age 65 could amount to nearly £1.25m. The benefits are tax-free if the policy is taken out by the individual; the benefits from policies taken out by an employer are taxable.

Ideally, both policies would be used because they are complementary, but the more important and higher priority is the income protection policy because:

- The cover under the income protection policy is closely related to need. It pays out as long as the individual is unable to work – which could be relatively short or a very long time. The amount of cover may not sound very much, mainly because it is expressed in pounds per week, month or year. But the pay-out could be very substantial indeed as was evident from the example above.

- The cover under income protection is much more comprehensive than critical illness insurance. Some of the most common and serious conditions that prevent people from working are not covered by critical illness policies – notably most back conditions and mental illnesses.

However, critical illness insurance has a number of features that make it valuable in some circumstances:

- The benefits payable under income protection are limited – generally about 60% of earnings. But for high earners, the percentage and absolute limits on benefits could leave them with a substantial income shortfall. They are even more limited if the person concerned has low or nil earnings, such as a business owner with a new or temporarily unprofitable business.

- The person's financial needs may be significantly greater than the income needs.

- The critical illness policy proceeds can be used to build a retirement fund once the immediate financial needs are covered by income protection.

- The deferral period for the income protection policy may turn out to be not covered by the income from the employer or similar source. The lump sum payable on diagnosis of the condition could bridge this gap.

- The critical illness insurance policy pays out a lump sum which can be used to repay loans and settle other capital liabilities.

Example 17.4

John earned £80,000 a year before he fell ill; after tax and national insurance contributions his net income was £53,512. At this level of income his insurer imposes a limit on the benefit of 50% of earnings. So John had the maximum income protection of £40,000 a year. So with his state social security benefits his net income is less than when he worked. Critical illness insurance could be used to make up the difference, as long as the condition is covered by the policy. John's employer is no longer making pension contributions and it would also be very helpful to make some adaptations to his home to take account of his new disability. He will also need some additional help around the home. So his critical illness insurance policy for £500,000 was very useful for both his long-term and short-term needs.

Quantifying the need for health insurance

Health insurance needs should be based on the current levels of expenditure.

Generally it makes sense to have the maximum possible amount of income protection because of its wide coverage of conditions. The maximum of 60% is unlikely to be significantly more than the amount needed. For a high earner, the maximum could be much less. For a non-earner the maximum benefit may be about £15,000 a year.

Critical illness insurance should be used to make up the shortfall in income through the investment of the lump sum. Other potential uses for critical illness insurance could be the repayment of loans and the funding of pension benefits.

Choosing health insurance policies

Many of the basic principles of choosing life policies apply to choosing health insurance policies, but there are additional complications. The policy should be written to last for no longer than the cover is required to minimise premium costs, although it is very helpful to have some flexibility to extend the cover if needed. Buying cover that lasts into a person's 60s is generally significantly more costly than insurance that stops at age 60 or earlier.

Figure 17.3 – Income protection needs calculator

	Client £	Partner £
The level of current expenditure		
Plus additional expenditure incurred as a result of the illness, e.g. nursing		
Less the savings, e.g travel to work		
Net expenditure		
Gross up net expenditure for tax after allowances		
Less the state benefit		
Less any other income protection		
Less income from other sources		
Total need for income protection per year		

Figure 17.4 – Critical illness calculator

General needs in the event of serious illness – nursing, holiday etc.	£
Repayment of loans and mortgages	£
Additions and substitutes for income protection	£
Pension protection	£
Total CIC need	£

Health insurance policies may be written on a guaranteed basis or they may be renewable; the guarantees generally involve higher premium payments initially, but they avoid surprises later. It is especially important to build inflation linking into the provision of the cover and the income itself – in the case of income protection.

There are special considerations for health insurance. There are differences in the conditions that income protection and critical illness insurance companies cover. The widest cover is best in principle, although some of the conditions that have been added to certain critical illness policies are sufficiently uncommon as to make very little practical difference to the policies.

Income protection is provided by some employers; employees need to decide whether it is worth having additional cover to protect themselves if they leave the job and have to replace the employer's cover. Most clients will probably decide against this course of action because the limit on the benefit they can claim will apply to all the income protection policies in aggregate, so if the employer's scheme provides the maximum cover, the other policy will not pay any benefit.

All companies are tightening up on claims for both income protection and critical illness, but some offices have a tougher reputation than others.

8 Protection against redundancy

State unemployment benefits are very low and the mortgage interest support payments are likely to be inadequate. It therefore makes sense to have other resources to fall back on. It would be best to have an adequate cash reserve equivalent to several months' expenditure. Other strategies might include having a mortgage that is flexible enough to be able to suspend payments for a time. However, this is unlikely to be feasible in many cases, and even where it is, there may still be a case for having some kind of redundancy insurance, particularly to pay mortgage interest.

The problem with redundancy insurance is that it is very limited in its application. The policy may not pay out, particularly if the circumstances of the insured person changes, e.g. they become self-employed or they take a job that they know is insecure. People who most need redundancy cover are generally the least likely to be able to afford it or obtain cover. The insurance normally only pays out for a limited period of up to one or two years.

9 Private medical insurance

Most private medical insurance is arranged through employers. It is a taxable benefit, but the advantage to the employer is arguably at least as great as for the employee, because it allows the employee to avoid having to queue for medical treatment and can receive medical assistance at the time of their choosing.

Medical insurance is a specialist area of expertise and many financial planners pass clients who need this to specialist advisers. Personal advice on this issue may be needed for self-employed people who need to arrange cover on a cost-effective basis.

Many clients may wish to continue their medical insurance cover in retirement when the need often becomes greater in some respects but the costs tend to escalate alarmingly. Clients may need advice on which aspects of cover can be most cost effectively reduced to achieve economies of premiums.

Chapter 18
Saving and investments

1 Perceptual and behavioural biases

JM Keynes famously once responded to a criticism of his economic policies' emphasis on the short-term with the remark: "In the long run we are all dead." While this is inevitable, most people can choose to become more or less wealthy before they die. And for most people without substantial inherited wealth, the key to this will be capital accumulation from income. Investment of capital for income generation is covered in the following chapter.

It has long been recognised that people tend to save too little towards their long-term goals. Recently, behavioural finance and psychology have confirmed the existence of perceptual and cognitive biases that mean people find it hard to visualise the distant future, and because they do not do this the future is not 'available' (see chapter 3, 'The impact of behavioural finance') or vivid (salient) and hence it lacks motivational power. This is clearly one major factor behind people's tendency to under-save. This means that a key issue in fostering emphasis on the long-term and hence on beneficial savings behaviour is enabling clients to envisage their future more clearly, emphasising those elements in it that clients value most, so that they are more strongly motivated to save.

This problem is much less acute with short-term needs, since clients can usually clearly understand their need for capital sums to pay a tax bill, replace a car or pay the school fees. Few people, though, can envisage their future more than about five years ahead.

One way to deal with this issue is to create intermediate stages in a long-term plan. Instead of thinking of a 25-year savings term (appropriate for someone in their mid 30s saving towards retirement), most clients will find it easier to think about accumulating a certain quantity of capital over a five-year term. That capital then becomes part of their longer-term retirement savings fund, which itself will have five-year targets. This encourages the client to review progress towards long-term goals at regular but not too frequent intervals.

One of the mental short cuts or heuristics people tend to use in dealing with complex issues is mental accounting, the creation of separate 'boxes' for each specific issue. Advisers do well to utilise this characteristic rather than to propose what may appear more rational solutions that fail to engage the client. Clients generally prefer to have separate savings plans for separate objectives, even if from the adviser's point of view these might just as well all be accommodated within a single plan.

A typical client may have requirements for capital from their savings for several purposes over the next 20 years, such as education fees, moving home, a daughter's wedding, a contribution to children's first home purchase. Many clients will prefer to have separate accounts for each of these objectives rather than one plan encompassing them all. A decade ago, setting up such separate plans would have incurred significant additional costs, but today fund supermarkets and wrap accounts permit the creation of multiple accounts with no additional costs, so neither cost nor administration now present obstacles to maintaining multiple plans in this way.

2 Fact-finding for savings and investment

If the fact-finding process has resulted in clear objectives, the requirements for saving and investment are often obvious, at least in general terms. For example, most people in their 20s, 30s and 40s need to save more, but usually face the problem that other priorities may be more important.

Additional themes relevant to saving and investment that may not naturally emerge from a conventional fact-find but that need to be explored by the adviser include the following.

Expectations

The greater the certainty regarding an inheritance, the greater its significance in terms of risk capacity – today's capital of £50,000 may be invested very differently if there is another £250,000 on the horizon. It may be important to try to guesstimate when it will happen; for example, if the elderly relative is in poor health in a nursing home, one can reasonably expect the capital to be inherited sooner than if they are still playing 18 holes of golf.

However, the adviser must also beware of over-optimism. John's belief that he is named as a beneficiary in Aunt Maud's will is not a strong enough foundation on which to base his financial plan. Also, ageing baby boomer parents are not only living longer but are showing no inclination to stint themselves in order to pass on capital to their children. As compared with a generation whose parents died in their seventies, tomorrow's inheritors are likely to receive smaller sums of capital.

> ### Example 18.1
>
> Sue borrowed £100,000 more than she needed to in order to buy a home because she expected about that sum from her one-third share in her father's business. But after his death her brothers Jim and Derek decide they want to continue the business and, because they need to invest capital in the business, do not want to buy out Sue's share at the present time.

Joint inheritances may also pose problems. A family home may have sentimental value which means that it is not sold and converted into investable capital. A sibling who wants to encash their share in a home or a business may come under pressure from those who want to stay invested.

Education

Educating children is the single largest expense most parents incur. Only a minority of parents have absolute clarity on this issue. In this case, little Johnny will go to the same school as his father and uncles did, come what may, and parents will make huge sacrifices, and plan them in advance, to ensure this happens.

Far more common is the situation where little Johnny will go to the local state primary school, and parents will hope for the best as regards what happens next. By then they may – for family or employment reasons – have moved home to a different area where the secondary schools are better or worse. If they are better, Johnny will stay in the public sector, but if the local state schools rate poorly in league tables, they will try to scrape together the cash for a private day-school.

Advisers need to be aware of this pattern and even if parents express no current interest in private education for their children, they need to pursue the issue with 'what if?' questions until they reach the point where the parents definitively say 'never' to private education or admit that, if the public options are really bad, they will reluctantly go private. Then the adviser can ask to what extent they want to provide financially for that possibility.

A further confusing factor is that by the time little Johnny is ready for secondary school, he may be in a different household with a stepfather or stepmother. In this case, the way private education is financed can become a matter of tortuous and difficult negotiations.

Grandparents often contribute to the costs of private education. If this is the case, the adviser needs to know more about their situation. Given their own financial position, they may be unable to enter a firm commitment to pay a set amount. More likely, they will agree to an annual level of contributions they believe they can definitely afford and possibly make additional payments if they feel they are able. If grandparents are to be relied upon for fee payments some years into the future, there is clearly a risk that their situation may change to the extent that they cannot actually afford the intended contributions; for example, one of them may require expensive long-term care. School fee plans for parents should take this risk into account.

> **Example 18.2**
>
> Ian and Lou are in their mid-40s. They plan for their two children, currently aged four and two, to attend a state primary school and to attend a private day school from age 11 to 18. Ian's parents, Fred and Jemma, have agreed to contribute £500 a month to a savings plan towards the fees starting now, to which Ian and Lou will also contribute £500 per month. Fred and Jemma will consider top-up payments when the children start school if they can afford them at the time.

Most parents will want their children to be able to go to university if they have the aptitude and wish to do so. Many parents will be prepared to make some contributions to reduce the amount of debt their child will incur. The extent of their potential contributions will be an important factor in assessing overall savings needs. If a couple have two children whose ages are less than four years apart, there will probably be at least one year in which they have to support both at university. If the adviser provides current figures for parental support, this will enable the clients to decide how much they want to try to save for this purpose.

Business opportunities

Many people have the urge to start their own business either alone or with family or friends. Sometimes the trigger is redundancy, which can provide cash as well as the opportunity, but many other events can give the impetus to a dormant entrepreneurial spirit.

For this reason, advisers should explore this issue. Does the client have friends or family already involved in running a business of their own? If so, what is the client's attitude to the venture? The more positive it is, the more likely the client will be to want to emulate them. If the client is positive about wishing to start their own business, the adviser needs to have at least some idea of the possible timing and of the amount of their own capital the client would want to commit.

When a woman leaves work to have children, the usual assumption today is that she will return to work after an interval. But some women who do not want to return to full-time work find ways of making money on a part-time basis, and these activities can develop into ongoing and growing businesses. This possibility can also be explored by the adviser, since women likely to consider this option may already have friends who are doing so.

Family issues

Increasing longevity creates new issues in family relationships. Society is at an early stage of adaptation to a large shift in life expectancy, so changes in the pattern of family life and relationships can be expected over the next few decades. One that appears likely is that more parents will end up living with their children, partly for support and partly to mitigate the cost of increasingly expensive professional care.

Advisers need to understand clients' attitudes to their parents, the extent to which actual or potential care responsibilities are shared between siblings, and the potential need for care through knowledge of family health history.

Mortgage repayment

The abolition of the ability of employers to set mandatory retirement ages means traditional patterns of mortgage repayment are likely to change. If people are going to work into their 70s there is no reason why they should aim to pay off their mortgages by the age of 65.

For many people, having part of their mortgage on a capital-and-interest and part on an interest-only basis can be a sound strategy.

Debt management is a key aspect of financial planning. Effective management of mortgage liabilities can be rewarding financially. Among the issues the adviser should consider are:

- **Flexibility**. Does the mortgage permit overpayments on a regular or lump sum basis and do they immediately reduce the interest payable?

- **Offset**. Would the client benefit from an offset arrangement where their savings effectively earn interest at a net of tax rate equal to the rate payable on their mortgage?

- **Drawdown**. Does the mortgage permit any overpayments of capital to be re-borrowed without further recourse to the lender?

- **Penalties**. What penalties do the mortgage terms include for early redemption?

3 Debt management

Most people view their mortgage as a debt they would like to pay off as fast as possible, but this is not always the best course of action. In particular, if property owners have loans at rates of 1-2% above inflation, they should consider putting more money into savings plans linked to equities, where the long-term average return is 5% above the rate of inflation, rather than paying off this cheap debt. This strategy requires a ten-year timescale or longer, but securing a 3% margin between the cost of debt and equity returns can result in the accumulation of substantial extra capital.

Example 18.3

John and Julia have a £150,000 mortgage with a remaining term of 20 years. It is a base rate tracker mortgage for life, at a rate of base rate (currently 0.5%) plus 1%. They are currently repaying both interest and capital, with monthly repayments of £724.

If they convert the loan to an interest-only basis (at 1.5%), their repayments will fall to £188 per month. If they start an equity-linked savings plan for (£724 - £188 =) £536 per month, and this earns a real annual return of 5%, its maturity value after 20 years will be £220,000. They will have surplus capital of £70,000 after paying off the loan.

With variable rate mortgages, such a strategy needs to be reviewed regularly. As is explained below, the savings plan contributions should be the difference between the capital-and-interest payments and the interest-only payments.

In the early years of such a strategy, there is little benefit in switching between interest-only and capital-and-interest. Since the prime benefit of regular saving is purchase of cheap investments during market declines, it makes little sense to reduce equity-linked savings and increase capital repayments when interest rates rise — such periods are most likely to coincide with low equity markets.

In later years, when a substantial capital fund has been accumulated, the picture changes.

Example 18.4

Following on from example 18.3, assume the savings plan has accumulated £83,000 (at a steady 5% pa) at the end of the tenth year. At that point base rate rises sharply to 6% so that the mortgage rate is 7%. Monthly interest payments on the £150,000 loan are now £875 per month. The savings plan can be encashed to pay off £80,000 of the debt, leaving a balance of £70,000 on which interest payments are £408 per month. John and Julia may have to reduce their contributions to the savings plan but should be able to keep it going and if contributions are £405 per month or more they should still end up with a capital surplus at redemption.

Advisers will encounter clients who have interest-only mortgages and no savings plans; they are simply hoping to accumulate enough capital to pay the mortgage off in later years. They may say that they will use their tax-free pension commencement lump sum towards this, or sell and downsize. For most people, this is an unrealistic and dangerous strategy.

Issues regarding capital repayment of mortgages from other free capital are covered in chapter 19, 'Capital accumulation for retirement'.

4 Timescales and purposes

Most clients will have saving requirements for different purposes and timescales. These will to a large extent determine the most suitable type of plan and the type of investments it should contain.

Timescale

The period of time alone necessarily plays an important part in determining what types of investment should be used.

Short-term savings

Where the client will need cash within a period of five years, the unpredictable volatility of equities means they are not likely to be a suitable form of investment. Short-term needs for capital will include:

- Tax: payment of known or anticipated tax bills
- Home: repairs, maintenance or improvement costs
- Car replacement
- Education fees

Such short-term needs are usually best provided for by putting capital or accumulating income in short-term deposits or fixed rate accounts from banks, building societies and National savings & Investment (NS&I). Other instruments that can be appropriate include zero coupon dividend shares in investment trusts, guaranteed growth bonds from life insurance companies, structured products and absolute return funds.

Because the ISA is a permanent tax shelter, it is generally most advantageous to use it for long-term investments. If the client can use the annual ISA allowance either for regular savings or capital transfers or a mixture of both, their shorter-term savings and investments will not benefit from ISA tax exemptions. The selection of appropriate investments will then depend to a significant extent on the client's tax position.

Short-term investments suitable for higher rate taxpayers include:

- NS&I tax-exempt products such as index-linked certificates (when they are available).
- Zero coupon dividend shares, where realised gains are subject to capital gains tax, not income tax.

- Structured products, where returns can be obtained in the form of a capital gain rather than income.

- Guaranteed growth bonds, where net returns are not grossed up for the purposes of assessing income tax liabilities.

Longer term savings

With a term of over five years, options widen to include many types of managed fund. Once the timescale exceeds five years, it is the purpose and the client's tolerance for possible variations in returns that will determine the most suitable investments.

Purposes

While the adviser will have investigated the client's attitudes to risk in general terms, advisers need to be aware of the general tendency to use mental accounting (see page 35) in managing multiple plans. In theory, the client could view all their future cash requirements as potential outputs from a single portfolio and consider the optimal division of capital between asset classes on this basis. Few clients do this. Instead they usually allocate specific amounts of capital or income for specific purposes and, given those purposes, set tolerances for variation that in turn determine an appropriate risk profile for the particular investment or set of investments.

An example of this is school fee planning. Because the commitment is emotionally important to the client, and they may not be able to afford to make up any shortfall from income, their tolerance for potential shortfalls is often low. Clients will therefore tend to prefer plans with a high probability of generating the fees required, even if the returns are lower than from more volatile alternatives. On the other hand, if the client is considering the same amount of saving over the same term towards the capital required for a new business venture, they are likely to be prepared to accept a much greater variation in potential returns.

In education fee planning, the amount of income required to fund a fee commitment is often in excess of that generated by the investments, and it is expected that some capital will be used up over the period. The aim in designing such a portfolio is to limit the erosion of capital as far as possible.

One way of doing this is to generate a high income with a portion of the capital, usually through investment in fixed income, possibly including high-yielding equities. The balance (a smaller proportion of the capital) is invested in a range of riskier assets, with the aim of encashing each year those that have generated high returns.

The client's tax position will determine the most efficient ways of holding these investments — see the tax wrapper analysis in chapter 6, 'Investment planning'.

Where parents are intending to save money towards education fees, the preferred method in the past was with-profit endowment policies. Today, however, low bonus rates make such policies relatively unattractive especially given their inflexibility and the penalties for early encashment.

To some extent, the lower-risk aspect of with-profit policies can be created by setting up a regular saving scheme using a fund supermarket and including both lower-risk and higher-risk funds.

To emulate the with-profits policy profile, for example, cautious managed funds, multi-asset funds or absolute return funds could be used. It is also worth noting that equity income funds, because of the reinvestment of their income, normally show significantly lower volatility than growth funds. The proportion of total contributions directed towards lower-risk, lower-return funds like these on the one hand and more aggressive pure equity funds on the other should be based on the client's tolerance for variations in the amounts to be withdrawn for fees and the timescale of the plan. As the time approaches when fees will start to be withdrawn, the risk profile of the funds should be lowered.

Before designing such a plan, advisers need to ensure that the estimates for fee requirements are realistic. This may require the investigation of actual fee levels and their rates of increase. Assuming a ten-year advance funding period, a 4% annual fee escalation will increase the total fees bill over the following five years by 60% compared with today's levels.

Example 18.5

Tony and Jane wish to fund for the private education of their two children (currently aged three and one) from ages 11 through 18. The fees at their preferred school are currently just short of £3,000 per term. Assuming a 3% annual increase in fees (below the recent average), the actual level of fees starting in eight years' time will be £3,800 and by the final year it will be almost £5,000 per term.

Vehicles for saving

If the client is unable to use their annual ISA allowance for longer-term savings or investments, it can be used for education fee savings. But if there is capital or income available to use the allowance for savings to generate retirement income, the lifetime tax savings from this will far outweigh the benefits of using the ISA for a school fee plan.

For basic rate taxpayers, simple unit or investment trust savings plans are tax-efficient. In practice, the client may incur only a small amount more tax (mainly on fixed income investments) by investing in this way than they would through an ISA.

For higher rate taxpayers already using their ISA allowances, use of a ten-year qualifying unit-linked life insurance policy to hold the investments can be worthwhile. Both income and gains from the investments will bear tax at the life insurance company rate of 20% but the proceeds on encashment will not be liable to any further tax.

Capital accumulation through mortgage

Of all the financial issues they have to deal with, clients often find mortgages the most challenging. This is because they often apply the same attitude to the mortgage as to the 'bad' forms of consumer debt discussed in chapter 16, 'Immediate cashflow planning', which it does indeed make sense to pay off as fast as possible.

A mortgage, however, is a means of financing the purchase of a capital asset. Once the mortgage has been obtained and the property has been purchased, the question always needs to be considered as to whether it makes sense to pay off more of the mortgage debt from income or whether to use income to accumulate financial assets instead.

The client benefits from the capital appreciation of the property whether they only make payments of interest or whether they also repay capital. So whether or not to repay capital should depend on the potential return from purchasing other assets as compared with the interest rate payable on the debt.

Over the typical 25-year mortgage term, having an interest-only mortgage throughout the term and investing in equity-linked savings plans would have delivered large capital surpluses in the great majority of periods over the past century. During most such periods, there would have been periods of up to five years during which interest rates were high and equity returns low. But during such periods, more advantage would have been gained from accumulating cheap equity assets than from paying down debt when the interest rate was likely to fall.

The key issue in designing and managing mortgage repayment strategies is a focus on real interest rates rather than nominal interest rates. When both inflation rates and interest rates are erratic, people tend to focus on nominal rates, especially in relation to liabilities such as mortgage interest that account for a large part of their outgoings. This can lead to the behaviour described by Dean Mathey: "People borrow money in good times and pay it back in bad times — just the opposite of what they should do."

Both economic theory and history suggest that extremely high or extremely low real interest rates are unlikely to persist for more than short periods. So a long-term strategy that assumes that real equity returns will on average be significantly higher than mortgage interest rates is soundly based.

The key obstacle to implementing an effective mortgage repayment plan using equity-linked vehicles is the necessity of reviewing it when interest rates change. This makes managing such a plan with a variable rate interest mortgage difficult. It is important to understand that the reason for the shortfalls experienced with endowment mortgages arose primarily because borrowers did not follow the rules necessary to make such an arrangement work (though it is true that neither lenders, insurers or advisers helped people to adopt the correct strategies).

If we compare methods of repayment for a £100,000 mortgage over a 25-year term, the capital-and-interest monthly repayments at a 5% interest rate are £585 per month. Over the term the total cost is £175,400. The interest-only payments are £417 per month with a total cost of £125,100, plus the repayment of the £100,000 capital making a total of £225,100.

The difference between £585 and £417, namely £168 per month, invested in a savings plan delivering a net return of 5% per annum, produces a maturity value after 25 years of £100,000, and this repays the capital.

Why should a borrower use the interest-only method when its total cost is £225,000 or £50,000 more than the capital-and-interest method? Because of the chance of securing higher returns. At 6% pa, the savings plan would deliver £116,000 (surplus over redemption cost 16%), at 7% pa £136,000 (36% surplus) and at 8% pa £160,000 (60% surplus). Surpluses on this scale were earned by many endowment mortgage borrowers whose policies and mortgages matured in the 1970s and 1980s.

The chance of earning such surpluses is considerably higher when the real interest rate payable on the mortgage is well below the historical average return from equities (in the UK, this is inflation plus 5%).

The figures above assume constant rates throughout a 25-year term. But interest rates change. Assume the mortgage is at a variable rate of interest and that at the end of the fifth year the interest rate rises to 7%. Then the capital-plus-interest repayments on the outstanding balance of £88,800 will be £688 per month. The interest-only payments on £100,000 are £583 per month. The difference is £105 per month, and at a constant 7% net return this (plus a 7% return on the £11,200 already accumulated in the savings plan during the previous four years) will deliver a maturity value after 20 years of £100,000.

Instead, assume that at the end of the fifth year the interest rate drops sharply to 3%. The capital-and-interest repayments on the balance of £88,800 are now £497 (instead of £585) per month; the interest-only payments are £250 (instead of £417). The difference is £247 (up from £168), and £247 per month at an annual growth rate of 3% for 20 years (plus a return of 3% on the capital already accumulated in the plan) will return £100,000 at maturity.

The difficulty of managing a mortgage strategy is that clients will resist increasing their savings contributions when interest rates fall – this was the prime cause of the majority of endowment shortfalls.

If the mortgage strategy is based on obtaining a fixed rate for a five-year term whenever rates are attractive, then the adjustments to the savings plan contributions do not need to be so frequent. Nor, in practice, do they need to be as large as shown above. It is unlikely that over a ten-year period the net return from equities will be as low as 3%. So an increase of as much as £80 per month in savings plan contributions would not really be necessary. And if savings plan contributions are maintained rather than reduced when interest rates rise, there will be less need to raise them when interest rates fall.

A further consideration is the capital position at intermediate dates. If a capital-and-interest method is used, then the outstanding capital at any future date can be read off a schedule (provided the interest rate remains the same). If the interest-only plus savings plan method is used, the amount of capital available in a savings plan towards a refinancing or house move at any point – say in the depths of a bear market – can be well below the amount paid off by the capital-and-interest method.

Example 18.6

Mark and Jill take out an interest-only mortgage for £120,000 to buy their home. After seven years Mark gets a much better job offer that requires them to move. This coincides with a low point for the stock market, and the current value of the savings plan is only £15,000, some £2,500 less than their contributions to date. If they had used a repayment mortgage, the current balance would have been £100,000, so they have £5,000 less available towards their next home purchase.

Against this must be set the potential advantage of having ownership of a sum of capital in the savings plan independent of the property, the loan and the lender. Greater capital repayments towards the mortgage reduce the debt, but only in the case of flexible or offset mortgages is the client entitled to increase the debt again if they want to. There are no restrictions on the use of the capital in a savings plan.

These factors mean that despite the potential gains to be derived from operating an interest-only plus savings plan mortgage repayment strategy, there are many clients for whom it will not be suitable. It requires some tolerance of risk, the discipline to make necessary changes, and an ability to focus on the likely long-term benefit even when the short-term results are poor. Nor is it appropriate if the client is likely to move house in the near future, since (given the volatility of equities) this exposes them to more capital risk.

For those who fit the criteria for the interest only mortgage, the strategy remains one of the most reliable methods of accumulating capital.

5 Regular savings benefits

Behavioural finance has confirmed what experienced financial advisers have always known: most people heavily overweight the short-term at the expense of the long-term ('Hyperbolic discounting', see chapter 3, 'The impact of behavioural finance'). This is often cited as the main reason why under-saving is so prevalent. But another important factor that causes people not to commit to regular savings is often overlooked. This is most people's poor level of numeracy and especially of their understanding of the effects of compound interest. This means most people will substantially underestimate the amount that will be accumulated from regular savings and the additional capital that will be gained from an increase in the average annual return that is earned or from lengthening the period of saving.

Advisers can easily test this by asking clients to estimate the capital they will accumulate at different rates of return over various periods. The table shows some examples. Few people will, for example, correctly guess that if £100 per month saved earning an annual return of 7% produces a capital sum of £17,300 after ten years, the encashment value will rise to £31,600 after 15 years. They will (without realising they are doing so) focus on the fact that an extra £6,000 is being invested over this period and overlook the continuing growth of the already accumulated capital of £17,300. Nor would they correctly guess that that if a capital sum of £41,100 is accumulated by regular saving of £100 per month at a 6% rate of return over 20 years, a 9% return will deliver £66,800, which is greater by an amount equal to the entire contributions over the period. The mathematical relationships in compound interest are not linear, which is how most non-mathematicians normally think, but exponential, and most people find this very difficult to understand.

Table 18.1 – Capital accumulation from regular savings of £100 per month

End of year	Annual net rate of return			Total saved
	5%	**7%**	**9%**	
5	£6,800	£7,100	£7,500	£6,000
10	£15,500	£17,300	£19,300	£12,000
15	£26,700	£31,600	£37,800	£18,000
20	£41,100	£52,000	£66,800	£24,000
25	£59,500	£81,000	£112,100	£30,000

A most important part of an adviser's role is encouraging and enabling clients to think long-term. For most clients in their 20s, 30s and 40s the greatest advantage the adviser can secure is through encouraging them to save more in equity-linked savings plans.

Graphic illustrations of historic results are a powerful way to convey this message. The chart shows the results of a £100 per month contribution to a savings plan over a 20-year term. It shows the average returns for funds in three IMA sectors: Emerging Markets, UK Smaller Companies and UK Equity Income. The plan values (as at November 2010) were £75,300 (annual return 10%), £70,600 (9.5%) and £52,000 (7%) respectively. In each case the top quartile funds in the sector would have delivered significantly higher returns.

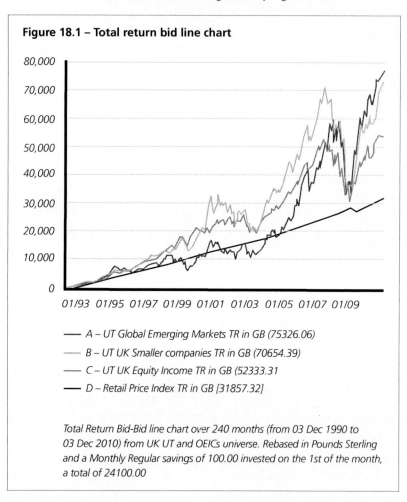

Figure 18.1 – Total return bid line chart

——— A – UT Global Emerging Markets TR in GB (75326.06)
········· B – UT UK Smaller companies TR in GB (70654.39)
——— C – UT UK Equity Income TR in GB (52333.31)
——— D – Retail Price Index TR in GB [31857.32]

Total Return Bid-Bid line chart over 240 months (from 03 Dec 1990 to 03 Dec 2010) from UK UT and OEICs universe. Rebased in Pounds Sterling and a Monthly Regular savings of 100.00 invested on the 1st of the month, a total of 24100.00

To avoid the money illusion, it is important to show the effects of inflation, hence the inclusion of the Retail Prices Index as well as the funds. This shows that the client's £24,000 of contributions would need to have grown to £32,000 to have constant purchasing power.

Designing savings plans

It is worth noting from the chart above that today's favourite sector, Emerging Markets, delivered the worst returns for the first half of the 20-year life of the plan. This highlights the challenge of designing a regular equity-linked savings plan today. Predicting what will be successful even a year or two in the future is hard enough, but with a 20-year timescale it is virtually impossible to pick funds or even sectors that will deliver the best returns.

However, over the long-term (ten years or more) both economic logic and history show that almost all contributions should be directed into equities. The issues concerning the 'de-risking' of an accumulated fund as it approaches the date when capital or income withdrawals are required are dealt with in the following chapter.

There are three possible answers to the problem of fund selection for a long-term savings plan:

- Multimanager fund: entrust the sector and fund selection to a manager, by choosing a multimanager fund with a global remit without constraints in terms of volatility or benchmark.

- Equity Income: over the long-term, value strategies have by far the best record of delivering superior risk-adjusted returns, which points to the selection of equity income funds (UK, regional or global) with long-serving managers.

- Specialist: over any period specialist funds are almost certain to deliver the highest returns. The fact that their volatility will also be high is not a disadvantage for regular savers. In fact it is an advantage, since greater volatility means more benefits are derived from pound cost averaging. Since which specialist funds (gold, technology, resources, financials, etc) will do best is so uncertain, splitting contributions between several such funds is the obvious strategy.

- Regular savings plans through fund supermarkets permit the division of monthly contributions between several funds, so it is possible to establish such a plan on a portfolio basis from the outset. In this case, the fund selection can be reviewed and altered on a regular basis. In practice, therefore, all three solutions described above can be included.

As the time approaches when the client wishes to draw on the accumulated capital, consideration can be given to lowering volatility by switching some of the accumulated capital into funds with lower risk profiles such as cautious managed funds or bond funds.

Example 18.8

Peter has agreed with his adviser that he will contribute £600 per month to a long-term savings plan. Peter has shorter-term plans and capital resources so that he is confident he will not need access to it for at least seven or eight years. The adviser recommends the division of the £600 as follows:

Global equity income fund	£150 per month
Global emerging markets fund	£150 per month
UK smaller companies fund	£100 per month
Global natural resources fund	£100 per month
Global property securities fund	£100 per month

---

6 Key issues in savings

For many clients under the age of 50, accumulation of capital from regular savings is the single most important issue in financial planning. It is this that will create the possibility of financial independence and the ability to achieve their objectives. Since behavioural biases cause most people to save too little, the adviser's principal role is to help clients to understand this and to commit to regular savings at a level greater than the client originally thinks is possible.

In practice, as experienced advisers know, once a commitment has been made to a level of monthly savings, people's spending behaviour adapts and often after a few months the client finds easy what they had originally thought was impossible.

In addition to explaining and illustrating the great power of compounding in accumulating capital, advisers can use behavioural biases to help change clients' views. Among the obvious techniques are:

- Anchoring. Clients often need a definite tangible objective, a pot of gold at the end of the rainbow. If they have a large enough sum in 20 years' time, what dream would they most like to fulfill: the yacht, sports car, motor home, holiday villa, world cruise? Helping clients to articulate this want more clearly can help them commit more strongly to the regular savings required to achieve it.

- Mental accounting. Where the bulk of regular savings is needed for the provision of retirement income, or the payment of school fees, the client may perceive the savings as a necessary but difficult burden. Allocating a small proportion of the savings to a separate fund to meet one of the client's personal wants can help them commit to the whole package.

- Confirmation. Clients who have difficulty in sustaining a savings commitment can be helped by providing regular illustrations of their success to date and projections showing how their objectives will be met.

- Loss aversion. With capital investment, a decline in market prices is usually a negative. When clients are saving regularly in equity-linked plans, however, it is a positive factor, since it means more investments are being purchased for the same outlay. If clients understand this clearly at the outset of a savings scheme, they are more likely to be receptive to the idea of increasing their commitment when markets fall.

Techniques that can help with the implementation of regular savings are:

- Start the month. If contributions to a savings plan are drawn from the current account near the end of the month, they may tip the account into deficit. The client's attitude may then become negative. If the contributions are taken near the start of the month, it will be other items that create this problem and the client is more likely to direct their attention to reducing spending.

- Save more tomorrow. This idea, applied in some retirement saving schemes, requires the client at the outset of a savings scheme to commit to increasing their contributions at regular intervals in the future, or on each occasion when their income increases.

Example 18.9

James commences a £100 per month long-term savings plan with an intended term of 25 years. He agrees to increase his contributions by 20% every five years. Assuming a constant 7% return, his plan will be worth £103,000 at maturity compared with £81,000 for a plan with level £100 per month contributions.

Table 18.2 – Savings solutions pros and cons

Solution	Advantages	Disadvantages
Use of ISA allowance for medium term savings such as school fees	Immediate tax savings	Loss of larger tax savings over the longer term
Use of with profit policies for education fee funding	Certainty of minimum maturity payments	Low rates of return; inflexibility
Use of fixed income to fund for near-term needs	Certainty of returns	Vulnerable to a rise in inflation
Capital repayment mortgage	Certainty over repayment term and cost	Loss of opportunities for capital accumulation
Interest only mortgage and savings plan	Potential for capital accumulation and surplus at redemption; availability of capital	Possible shortfall in capital at intermediate stages compared with repayment mortgage
Savings plan linked to single fund	Potential for large gain if successful	Significant risk of below-average returns
Savings plan linked to multiple funds	Potential for gain and diversification	Greater commitment required to monitoring and management

Chapter 19
Capital accumulation for retirement

1 The biggest financial challenge

Accumulating sufficient capital to provide for a comfortable standard of living in retirement has become the largest financial challenge facing most people today. There are three main reasons for this:

Increasing longevity: the average life expectancy in 1970 was 68.7 for men and 75.0 for women; by 2008 this had risen to 77.8 for men and 81.9 for women.

Reducing pension funds: in the private sector, defined benefit (DB) schemes are mainly closed to new members. Corporate contributions to defined contribution (DC) schemes that have replaced them are typically at significantly lower percentages of earnings.

Lower interest rates: the decline in inflation and interest rates has seen real interest rates on low-risk assets (especially fixed income) fall to very low levels, so that more capital needs to be accumulated to generate the same level of income.

Taken together these factors mean that a person in their 30s needs to accumulate a much larger capital sum to support them in retirement. This often means a monthly savings requirement that is beyond their capacity.

Example 19.1

John is 30 and earns £36,000 a year. He is contributing 3% of earnings to the DC company pension scheme and his employer matches this. Assuming a 3.5% annual earnings increase, and investment returns in line with the long-run historic average, these contributions will produce a fund of £500,000 at age 65. This will generate an inflation-proofed retirement income of about £1,000 per month from age 65, well below his target of two-thirds of earnings or £3,200 per month. To make up this deficit John would need to save £300 per month from now to age 65.

For older people who have made insufficient provision, the challenge is even more demanding since they have a shorter time left to accumulate the necessary funds and will therefore need to save a greater proportion of their income.

Given the scale of the retirement challenge, advisers need to investigate all the options open to the individual and identify all possible means of maximising returns from regular savings and from lump sums.

2 Savings issues

For many clients, the problems of saving for retirement will be aggravated by competing priorities for resources, in particular, housing, family protection and education costs.

It is therefore important to explore all the areas in which clients have commitments or ambitions. The extent of their ambitions may need to be curtailed, and specific objectives may have to be abandoned, if savings targets are to be met.

Housing

It has become an accepted notion that residential property is a good investment which justifies commitment of a large proportion of income to mortgage repayments. Advisers need to make clients aware of the assumptions involved and of the risks of committing too much of their income to mortgages.

Looking at a typical home ownership pattern, the family uses a large portion of its income to own a home. Each property move requires larger amount of finance since on average house prices rise at above the rates of consumer prices or earnings. The result is that at retirement the family has a large proportion of its net wealth invested in the home, whose mortgage is wholly or largely paid off. At this point the family may well be 'asset rich and cash poor', yet by this stage the owners are attached to their property and are reluctant to downsize to release capital. They are also often incurring substantial annual repair, maintenance and fuel costs. In essence, this scenario involves too great a commitment of resources to property and not enough to accumulation of financial assets.

In contrast, a typical pattern in continental Europe is for families to rent during their working lives (when they may move frequently), and to steadily accumulate the capital to purchase a home in retirement.

The UK rental sector has grown considerably in the past decade. Unless current high rates of stamp duty are reduced, these will act as a disincentive to the frequent home moves seen in the 1970s and 1980s. It is therefore likely that the UK rental sector will continue to grow and that many families will remain in rental accommodation rather than purchasing.

When investigating clients' attitudes to housing and plans for the future, advisers need to ensure clients understand all the costs and risks involved in home ownership as well as the benefits. The risks, for example, became apparent to people attempting to sell their homes in 2008-10, when prices declined steadily as many would-be buyers were unable to obtain mortgage finance.

If clients appear likely to need to move frequently in order to pursue their careers, home ownership can become costly. While an owner can let out their own home and rent another, this is usually an inefficient way to run their housing budget, especially if an agent's fees are paid on the letting income.

Financing the ownership of second or holiday homes may be at the expense of contributing to long-term savings plans. Property owners are often unrealistic about how long it can take to sell. Rental income from holiday homes may fall not just due to economic trends but also as a result of changes in general holiday preferences.

Protection

An old US saying about protection is 'Buy term and invest the rest'. If this strategy is used, the requirement for life cover should decline as capital is accumulated in savings plans. Taking this policy to its logical conclusion, if there is a need to devote more cash to regular savings, ways of reducing the cost of protection should be sought.

The adviser should double check the need for cover. In particular, have any occupational life cover benefits been included; have future commitments been accurately estimated; is the replacement income greater than is actually required?

Today, many advisers would normally recommend the purchase of sufficient life cover on a wife with young children to enable the husband to pay for childcare in the event of her death. But this may not be necessary in all cases, as families may cope with lower levels of cover if they can count on the support of parents or siblings.

Critical illness cover is the most expensive form of protection, and though it is often highly valued by clients, it may be possible to substitute income protection cover with a long deferment period at a lower cost. Though the covers are not identical, they deal with the same need in different ways and if there is an urgent need to raise the amount saved each month the option is worth considering, especially if the family history on both sides is of good health into old age.

Education

If parents are set on private education for their children, this will usually take priority over other needs. This can often mean that the amount allocated to long-term savings is lower than the adviser has assessed as desirable. The difference between boarding and day fees is substantial. Clients may consider moving home in order not to pay boarding fees.

Advisers may need to encourage parents to reduce their commitment to additional expenses such as optional school trips or exchange visits in order to release extra cash for long-term savings plans.

Circumstances

The amount of capital that needs to be accumulated to support the client in retirement can readily be estimated based on their present earnings. But for younger clients changes in these circumstances are certain. Advisers need to gain as much information as they can about career and earnings prospects so that they can more realistically project future cashflow.

A couple's decisions about when to have children and whether the mother will return to full-time work will also have a major impact on the level of income and on the savings required.

3 Assessing needs

Advisers will normally attempt to ascertain the level of income that will be required in retirement. As discussed in earlier chapters, this is most easily done by working in real terms, so that the required income level can be expressed as a fraction of today's actual income.

A target of two-thirds of pre-retirement income has normally been regarded as appropriate by financial planners. However, the changing pattern of retirement means it will often be inappropriate to apply a simple rule. Many people will in practice retire later than they originally planned, or will continue to work part-time, so that their actual requirements for retirement income will be increasingly distinct and personal.

The assessment of retirement income needs, and the capital required to fund these needs, can be quite precise for clients nearing retirement, but will be less and less accurate as the term to retirement grows. Changes in personal circumstances, income levels, actual investment returns, pension scheme membership and many other factors can result in very large changes in the amount of capital required to fund the requisite level of income. For this reason, advisers using cashflow projection software will usually show outcomes as probabilistic bands.

With the abolition of mandatory retirement ages, it is increasingly likely that people will work past the age at which they start to receive the state pension (for many people in future this will be the only fixed 'retirement' date). Retirement savings 'gaps' are therefore extremely provisional for people with 20 or more years to go until they start to draw on their capital. Rather than fine tuning assumptions in an attempt to be more accurate, advisers should focus on designing the right strategy for the client, which is certain to require adjustments along the way.

> **Example 19.2**
>
> Tony is 40. He earns £60,000 a year and is a member of an occupational DC scheme. He wants to aim for a retirement income of two-thirds of pre-retirement earnings. The adviser calculates that his preserved pension entitlements and his current pension scheme will (if Tony remains in his current employment until age 67) generate an income of 40% of his pre-retirement earnings. Tony has capital of £30,000 in ISAs that is earmarked for retirement. Assuming a real lifetime return from invested capital of 4% in retirement, Tony needs a capital sum of £400,000 at age 67. Assuming a real annual return of 5%, he will need to save £400 per month, but if returns average 3% the required monthly contribution will be £550.
>
> In this example, assuming a lower rate of return in retirement will dramatically increase the capital requirement and hence the monthly saving required.

4 Savings vehicles

In the past, advisers and providers spent too much time debating the merits and demerits of specific savings vehicles. As should be clear from the sections above, the key issue is assessing the likely need for capital and translating this into a required rate of monthly or annual savings from income. The question of which vehicles to use is secondary and may well change as a result of changes to tax and other legislation as well as variations in personal circumstances.

In this section we consider vehicles for the accumulation of capital through regular saving, while investment of capital is covered later in the chapter.

Tax factors

Tax efficiency is an important factor in the selection of savings plans. The following is a simplified analysis of the tax efficiency of pension plans versus ISAs for retirement provision.

Assuming constant real rates of return and similar charges, the net lifetime return from pensions and ISAs will be very similar where the individual pays the same rate of income tax throughout (capital gains tax can be ignored since both schemes are exempt).

This ignores the effect of the compounding of returns, which favours the pension plan, but a number of analyses, including one by the Financial Services Authority (FSA), have suggested this will be worth no more than 6-8% to a basic rate taxpayer over a 20-year term. It also ignores the effect of withdrawing the maximum pension commencement lump sum and investing it in an ISA, which would marginally improve the figures for the pension relative to the ISA.

Table 19.1 – Lifetime returns from an ISA and a pension for basic and higher rate taxpayer

	Basic rate taxpayer		Higher rate taxpayer	
	ISA	Pension	ISA	Pension
Net contribution	£800	£800	£800	£800
Tax relief	NIL	£200 (20%)	NIL	£533 (40%)
Gross investment	£800	£1,000	£800	£1,000
Gross income yield	5%	5%	5%	5%
Gross income	£40	£50	£40	£66.70
Income tax	NIL	£10 (20%)	NIL	£26.70 (40%)
Net income	£40	£40	£40	£40

However, in broad terms, this analysis makes it clear that clients will only secure large benefits from pension plans compared with ISAs if they pay tax at one of the higher rates during the accumulation period and then pay tax at basic rate during the withdrawal period. The case of someone securing basic rate tax relief during the accumulation period and paying no tax during decumulation can for practical purposes be ignored.

Many financial planning clients are likely to fall into the category of people who pay higher rate tax now but may not pay it during their decumulation period. On the face of it, for them pension plans offer a more tax-efficient method of accumulating capital than ISAs. But when planning for decumulation starting in 20 or 30 years' time, advisers should avoid giving too much emphasis to current tax rules and rates. Where outcomes are projected, the fact that they assume current tax rates and that these are almost certain to be different in 20 or 30 years time are important factors in the decision making process.

Substantial and significant changes have occurred to the tax reliefs and tax treatment of pension benefits in the past decade and it would be unrealistic to assume that no such changes will occur in the coming decades.

Pension plans

The most recent set of changes to pension plan rules include both benefits and restrictions. In effect, they place limits on pension investment for the wealthy while giving slightly enhanced personal control over accumulated capital and lower taxation of residual capital after age 75.

Limits on accumulation

The latest changes (announced December 2010 with effect from April 2011) restrict the maximum amount that may be accumulated in pension plans through two rules:

Lifetime allowance

The lifetime allowance has been cut from £1.8m in 2010–11 to £1.5m from April 2012. Those who exceed this will face a 55% tax charge on the excess.

Individuals with pension funds that may exceed the allowance may apply for fixed protection before April 2012. In this case their fund may rise to £1.8m with no tax charge, but they will not be permitted to make any further contributions to their fund after April 2012.

Annual allowance

This has been cut from £255,000 in 2010-11 to £50,000 in 2011-12. However, individuals may carry forward unused allowances from the previous three years (for each of which an allowance of £50,000 is available).

For DB schemes, the amount counted towards the annual allowance is a multiple of 16 times (formerly ten times) the increase in entitlements over the year.

Any contributions in excess of the allowance are subject to a rate of tax that negates the value of income tax relief. Since withdrawals from pension plans will bear income tax, making contributions without tax relief is disadvantageous.

The reductions in the annual and lifetime allowances mean that high earners will have to use vehicles other than pension plans for a significant part of their retirement funding plans.

Limits on access

Under current rules individuals have no access to the capital in their pension funds except in respect of the pension commencement lump sum, a maximum of 25% of the fund value. This tax-free lump sum can be taken at any time after age 55.

After the lump sum has been taken, any capital remaining at the member's death will be subject to a 55% tax charge if not used to provide a dependants income. If the lump sum has not been taken, death benefits will normally be free of income tax and will not normally be subject to inheritance tax.

The capital in a pension scheme may be withdrawn tax-free if there is medical evidence of terminal illness.

Limits on withdrawals

The standard way in which benefits are taken from a pension plan is through an annuity providing a guaranteed income for life. While many different types of annuity are available (single, joint, inflation-linked, escalating, level, with-profit) the choice of the annuity has to be made at the point at which benefits are taken (at any point from age 55) and cannot be changed thereafter.

Under rules effective from 2011, members may, after taking their pension commencement lump sum, use a capped drawdown scheme, in which case the capital remains invested and a variable annual income can be drawn. The maximum income is 100% of the annuity income available at that age according to tables published by the Government Actuary's Department. Members who have a secure annual income of at least £20,000 (derived from pensions or annuities) may draw variable income from the capital in their fund using the flexible drawdown scheme and may withdraw their entire fund as income if they choose to do so.

Apart from the commencement lump sum, all withdrawals from the fund during the member's life will be subject to income tax.

Occupational schemes

Employers operating occupational schemes usually offer to match employee contributions up to a certain level. From 2012, employers operating their own schemes will need to offer terms at least equal to those of the national employment savings trust (NEST) scheme, which requires 3% employer contributions to match employee contributions of 3%.

Historically, many employees have failed to join schemes even when they offered matching rates better than these. Once auto-enrolment becomes the standard and employees have to make a decision to opt out, an occupational scheme should form the base level of most workers' retirement provision.

Advisers should ensure that employees are maximising their benefits from occupational schemes. In many cases, if additional pension scheme contributions are appropriate, doing this through an occupational scheme can be advantageous given their typically lower costs. Many DC schemes offer access to a wide range of funds, and an intelligent construction of a fund portfolio — often possible with contributions of a few hundred pounds per month — should enable higher rates of return to be secured compared with the default option of a managed fund.

Example 19.3

Steve is 42 and a member of a DC scheme to which his and the employer contributions amount to £500 per month. As part of a retirement planning review, his adviser recommends that he cease using the default managed fund and directs his contributions to funds in the following sectors:

Global equity income	£200
Global emerging markets	£100
UK smaller companies	£100
Natural resources	£100

Lifestyling and target date

Many occupational schemes and some personal pension schemes now offer lifestyling options. Such schemes are effectively fund-of-fund structures where the proportions invested in the main asset classes change over the term to retirement. Usually, such schemes require the member to set an intended retirement date. The further away this date is, the higher the proportion of the fund that is invested in equities. As retirement age approaches, the fund's assets are progressively switched from equities into fixed interest.

Target date funds are similar, in that they assume a particular maturity date. Over the period up to maturity risk assets are steadily reduced as a proportion of the fund's capital. This approach enables people to buy in to one date or to a series of dates if they are not yet sure of their actual retirement date.

Both approaches have advantages and drawbacks.

Advantages

- Risk is actively controlled throughout.

- Because of the risk control, people may accept a higher initial allocation to equities than they would if making the asset choice themselves.

- People do not have to make difficult decisions about asset class choices at any point.

Disadvantages

- For those with very long periods to retirement, a lifestyling allocation to equities may be lower than the optimal – which might be 100% for people in their 30s.

- If an automatic switching system is used, sales and purchases of asset classes may be poorly timed and reduce returns.

- If the individual intends to use drawdown, there is in fact no reason to move wholly into fixed interest as retirement age approaches.

As retirement age becomes less certain and the nature of retirement changes, aiming for a low-risk asset allocation portfolio at a fixed point in time is less and less likely to match individual needs.

Where the adviser is providing an ongoing service, they should be able to provide fund selection advice specifically relevant to the individual.

Other savings vehicles

There are four other methods of regular saving that may be used for capital accumulation for retirement.

1. ISA
2. Qualifying endowment policy

3. Unit trust/open ended investment company (OEIC)/investment trust savings plan
4. Employer-financed retirement benefit schemes (EFRBS) and employee benefit trusts (EBTs)

ISA

The ISA is exempt from tax. The only tax incurred is the 10% tax levied at source on UK dividends, and withholding taxes levied on dividends from other countries. There is no time limit on these exemptions and the ISA can be maintained throughout life.

Each individual has an annual ISA allowance of £10,200 (it rises in line with inflation). Up to £5,100 each year may be invested in a cash ISA.

Individuals may own unit trusts, OEICs and investment trusts within ISAs. They may own LSE-listed shares and shares listed on approved foreign markets but not shares listed on the AIM.

Qualifying endowment policy

The proceeds of a qualifying life assurance policy with a term of ten years or more are exempt from tax. Though the life assurance company bears tax at (approximately) 20% on income and gains, a higher rate taxpayer avoids the higher rates applicable to personal income and capital gains.

Unit-linked policies are available with links to a wide range of funds. Like other life policies, they can be written under trust so that not only the policyholder but also others can receive some or all of the proceeds without personal tax liability.

Unit trust/OEIC/investment trust savings plan

These savings plans are simple low-cost ways of saving regularly. Any income received or receivable (even if reinvested through accumulation units or reinvestment schemes) is part of the individual's declarable income for the year. Any realised gains are potentially subject to capital gains tax.

EFRBS and EBTs

EFRBeS and EBTs were schemes that employers used to provide benefits to higher-paid employees. Rule changes announced in December 2010 eliminated most of the potential tax benefits.

5 Savings strategies

For those with 20 years or more to go before decumulation begins, directing all savings plan contributions to equities is almost certain to deliver the highest returns and is therefore the right strategy. Only if there is a strong likelihood of access being required to capital in vehicles other than pension funds should consideration be given to including other asset classes.

The shorter the period until decumulation begins, the more consideration needs to be given to the asset mix in the savings plans. Relevant factors include:

Resources. If an individual has access to substantial capital from other sources, they can afford to take more risk with their pension fund investments and it will usually be appropriate for them to do so. If an individual will be entirely dependent on their savings for retirement income, then the purchase of an annuity, or the construction of a low-risk drawdown strategy, will be appropriate and progressively lowering the equity exposure as this date approaches will reduce the risk of a retirement income shortfall.

Attitude. People's attitudes to risk are often partly determined by the purpose of the saving or investment. Many people prefer to adopt a lower-risk strategy with savings they expect to use for retirement income provision.

Couples. If one partner adopts a cautious approach and this is expected to provide a baseline level of income, the other partner may feel able to take on more risk than they would otherwise be comfortable with.

Where a client pays higher rate tax now but is likely to pay basic rate tax in retirement, pension plans deliver the best return and should be used for the bulk of the savings programme.

Example 19.4

John is 45 and expects to retire between 67 and 70. He earns £65,000 a year and is contributing £500 per month to a DC pension scheme. The adviser estimates that he needs to save an additional £500 per month to achieve his target retirement income. The adviser recommends that £350 per month is added to pension scheme savings and that John also contributes £150 per month to a Stocks & Shares ISA.

For basic rate taxpayers, the arguments for pension plans are much weaker and if they have no other sources of capital, having capital access through an ISA, and being able to pass on any remaining capital at death, is attractive in its own right.

The ISA is a highly flexible tax shelter and well suited to generating retirement income. In particular, the avoidance of income tax on fixed income investments means high-yielding portfolios can easily be constructed. Where individuals also have capital outside ISAs, this facilitates construction of tax-efficient portfolios where all the income-generating investments are held in ISAs and all the gain-producing ones outside them (see chapter 20, 'Retirement decumulation'). Such a combined portfolio can incur minimal income tax or capital gains tax.

Example 19.5

Susan and Martin are in their late 30s. Both are members of DC schemes with low employer contribution rates. Susan earns £37,000 a year and Martin £43,000. The adviser assesses their combined capital need at age 68 at £650,000. At a 5% annual return this would require monthly savings of £800, but they cannot afford this. They agree to increase their pension contributions at each pay review in future, and to now start contributing £300 each per month into a Stocks & Shares ISA. These ISAs should accumulate a capital sum of £500,000 by age 68.

Self-employed people are rarely certain of their income in future years. Usually, the best strategy for them is to commit to a level of regular savings they are confident they can afford, and to make additional one-off payments annually. Where the contributions are directed may depend partially on the level of income and the consequent income tax bill.

Example 19.6

Paul, 45, is self employed and his earnings vary, usually between £30,000 and £60,000 annually. He is confident of being able to sustain regular savings of £300 per month and his adviser recommends that these go into a personal pension plan. He plans to make additional lump sum contributions each year ranging from £1,000 to £5,000. In years when his earnings are higher and he incurs higher rate tax, the adviser recommends that the bulk of these contributions go into his pension plan, but in lower-earning years all the lump sum contributions are directed into a Stocks & Shares ISA.

High earners may need to make substantial annual savings beyond the limits of pension plans to meet their retirement targets.

Example 19.7

Alexander, 50, is the owner-director of a private business. He earns £230,000 a year and his pension fund is already close to the lifetime allowance, so he cannot make any pension contributions. His adviser estimates he needs a capital fund of an additional £500,000 at age 65 to generate £25,000 a year and meet his £100,000 a year income target. This will require saving about £3,000 per month. The adviser recommends that

---

he contributes the maximum to an ISA at £850 per month and contributes £2,150 per month to a ten-year qualifying unit-linked endowment policy.

6 Investment strategies

People often have sums of capital they can allocate to retirement provision. But they may also wish to consider alternatives, especially reducing mortgage debt.

Business and pension

Advisers will encounter business proprietors who say: "My business is my pension". This is a very high-risk strategy and advisers need to make clients aware of just how exposed they are to the risk of a permanently low standard of living.

Example 19.8

Roger is 53 and runs his own design agency, he is in his seventh year and profits have grown steadily. He has reinvested all his profits in expansion, hiring larger premises and staff, and has not made any pension provision. Then his largest client suddenly becomes bankrupt and cannot pay Roger's bills. Roger cannot meet his liabilities on rent and staff costs and eventually his business fails. He now faces the need to make very large annual savings in order to secure an adequate retirement income.

Where business proprietors use small self-administered schemes (SSAS) or self invested personal pension (SIPP) schemes, to purchase property for the use of their business, they may give too much emphasis to the needs of the business and too little to the investment merits of the property. The question the adviser should ask is what the prospects are of selling or letting the property if the client's business were to move. If the property accounts for a large part of the fund, a similar portion of the client's retirement income could be at risk.

Pension consolidation

Many people have a variety of pension entitlements. These can include DB and DC entitlements from former employer schemes as well as varieties of personal pension. Usually a review of such entitlements will form a major part of the adviser's review of retirement provision and needs. This section provides only a summary of complex issues that are covered in detail in the *Taxbriefs Adviser's Guide to Pensions and Retirement Planning*.

In the case of DB entitlements from schemes sponsored by the state or local authorities, there will almost never be a case for switching out. The benefits are so generous in relation to the transfer values that only by achieving very high rates of return could equivalent benefits be secured in a personal pension scheme. But in these cases, it is not the high critical yield alone (the rate of return in a personal pension plan required to match existing benefits) that makes transfer out disadvantageous: it is the state backing, which makes the benefits completely secure.

In the case of private sector DB schemes, evaluation is more complex, since an apparently good set of benefits may be provided by a pension scheme with a substantial deficit sponsored by a weak employer. In this case the critical yield is not necessarily the most important factor. If the scheme effectively defaults and transfers to the pension protection scheme, then high earners will secure only a fraction of their entitlements — a fact few people are aware of. The risk factor is therefore high. Advisers need to assess the financial strength of both the scheme and the sponsoring employer. Since it is impossible in most cases to predict what will happen, the adviser can only place the facts before the client and ask them to make a final decision. If they feel their pension is at risk, many people will want to switch even if they face a theoretical loss of benefits.

Example 19.9

Jonathan is 60 and has a preserved DB entitlement in a 1/60ths of salary scheme with a company he worked for five years ago. At that time it was a successful business, but it has succumbed to competition and has made losses in two of the last three years. The pension fund (now closed to new entrants) is valued at £150m and had a deficit at its latest valuation of £20m. The benefits include a two-thirds dependant's pension and limited price indexation. The critical yield on transfer to a personal pension is 12.4%. However, Jonathan's entitlement will account for over half his target retirement income, and he does not wish to place this at risk, so he instructs his adviser to effect a transfer.

Some employers have offered financial inducements to members to leave final salary schemes. Such inducements can include a transfer value higher than was formerly offered. While this may seem attractive to the member, the transfer value may still be low in relation to the promised benefits, so that the critical yield remains high. Such offers are a classic case of information asymmetry since the employer making the offer knows far more about the position of the fund than the individual does or than the adviser can find out.

With DC schemes, preserved pensions may be invested in default funds that are unsuitable for the client's needs. While there is no reason in principle why a client should not retain several preserved DC schemes provided they have access to a suitable range of funds and can alter these funds when they need to, clients are almost sure to want to consolidate their pension schemes at the point of retirement, either to go into drawdown or to purchase annuities. So consolidating earlier can make sense provided that the following factors are considered:

Charges. DC scheme charges vary and if the client is in a scheme with low charges and suitable funds, it may be better to remain there until they are close to retirement.

Destination. Consolidation of several preserved DC schemes into a SIPP where a bespoke portfolio can be created can be advantageous, but overall charges in the SIPP are likely to be significantly higher. The adviser needs to justify such a switch with a well-planned investment strategy.

Benefits. It is unlikely that those with preserved DC pensions will be entitled to any other benefits but this can be a feature of older schemes.

Transfer in. Few private sector DB schemes will now accept transfers in on terms that benefit the member. However, if the client is a current member of a good DC scheme with a wide range of funds and low charges, the transfer of other preserved DC pensions into such a scheme rather than into a personal pension/SIPP can be advantageous.

Reducing debt

For many clients, reducing their principal debt, their home mortgage, is a high priority. Since people assume they will want to pay it off before they retire, paying it off even earlier if capital becomes available often seems attractive. The alternative, investing capital for the long-term, appears subject to many uncertainties as compared with cutting the mortgage balance today. The amount of interest saved by doing this is often a large figure, though this simply reflects the long-term remaining to redemption.

In this as in many other issues, behavioural biases including availability, familiarity and hyperbolic discounting are evident. The adviser will need to present a careful analysis of the costs and benefits of debt repayment compared with investing the available capital.

The first issue to address is equity. The client owns the property and benefits from any increase in its value even with a 90% mortgage. They do not own a greater proportion of it if they reduce the mortgage debt, though this is how many clients think. What the client does by paying off debt is reduce gearing. Advisers need to establish this since the framing of the issue in terms of ownership is misleading.

Then the comparison is between interest saved through paying off debt and capital earned from investment returns.

Example 19.10

Henry is 48 and took out a £250,000 mortgage to buy a £400,000 property eight years ago. He pays £1,460 per month at a 5% interest rate on a capital-and-interest basis. He has inherited £100,000 and is considering using it to reduce the debt from the current balance of £200,000 to £100,000. If he keeps his monthly payments the same, he will pay off the loan ten years early and save £79,000 in interest payments.

If instead he reduces the capital balance and maintains the original 25-year term on the reduced balance of £100,000, his monthly payments will reduce to £730 over the remaining 17 years. If he starts a £730 per month savings plan (thus keeping monthly payments the same) and earns a 5% return then at the end of a further seven years (the point at which he would have paid off the loan with the first option) the plan will be worth £73,000. The plan would reach a value of £100,000 in year nine and by redemption would be worth £237,000.

A third option is to switch £100,000 of the loan balance from a capital-and-interest to an interest-only basis, leaving the original term unchanged. In this case his repayments will reduce to £1,160 per month, a £310 per month saving. A £310 per month savings plan at a growth rate of 5% a year will return £99,000 at the redemption date. If the capital is invested to earn 5%, its value after 17 years will be £233,000.

Though the same interest rate has been used for both interest and investment returns in this example, this is unrealistic. Over the long-term it is almost certain that real investment returns will be higher than mortgage interest rates. The capital surplus from investing and not paying off the debt is likely to be substantially greater.

In general, where the term to redemption is 15 years or more, advisers can be confident that investment of capital in equities will earn returns well in excess of interest payments (assuming standard mortgage terms). In this case, establishing a diversified portfolio of investments with capital rather than using it to pay off debt is a superior strategy. Over the full term this is almost certain to generate a substantial surplus. But whether such a strategy is appropriate will depend on the client's likely need to access the capital earlier, which might occur if they moved home and were unable to port their existing loan or were unable to borrow as much as they needed. If such early access is very likely, then the risk of a capital shortfall at the point when access is required will be too high for most people.

The shorter the term to redemption, the stronger the argument for using capital to pay down debt rather than to invest it. Other factors that would point towards debt reduction include:

Ill health This might result in the loss of employment income.

Redundancy If the client's job is insecure, then reducing outgoings should take priority.

High interest If the loan is on unfavourable terms, repayment is beneficial.

There are also circumstances in which not paying off mortgage debt can make sense:

Access Once a conventional loan has been repaid, the client has no further access to it. If the client may need capital in the foreseeable future, the benefit of maintaining the capital sum to which they have unlimited access can outweigh the interest costs.

Low interest rate Clients may have an existing mortgage on terms such as 'base rate plus 1%', and so long as base rate remains at a low level, repayment of such debt would be foolish when capital could be invested to earn more, even on a short-term basis with minimal risk.

Offset Clients with offset or current account mortgages can obtain instant benefits by placing capital in their accounts. This will reduce interest payments and enable a similar amount to be added to monthly savings.

Investment options

The methods most appropriate for the investment of lump sums to fund retirement provision will depend on a number of factors, including:

Timescale The longer the timescale the greater the range of higher-risk investments that can be included in a portfolio.

Resources A client who already has a substantial pension entitlement that meets the bulk of their likely retirement needs can afford to take much more risk than someone who needs a definite level of income from their capital to meet a minimum income target.

Access The greater the likelihood of a requirement to access capital before retirement, the lower the proportion of capital that can be allocated to risk assets.

Health A client in poor health will be eligible for enhanced annuity rates. This may require an investment strategy aiming for a cash sum at a certain age.

A general model for retirement portfolio allocation is shown in the table. This is based on the assumption that the client will be aged 65 or more when decumulation begins and will be aiming to secure a lifetime real return thereafter of 3–4% from their capital. It also assumes no early access requirements.

Table 19.2 – Asset allocation for retirement portfolios

Asset class	Number of years until decumulation begins			
	5	10	15	20+
Fixed income	20%	10%	5%	NIL
Commercial property	10%	10%	5%	NIL
Absolute return/alternative	15%	10%	5%	5%
Equities	55%	70%	85%	95%
	100%	100%	100%	100%

The principles of investment planning covered in chapter 6, 'Investment planning', apply to the construction of portfolios designed for retirement provision.

Higher rate taxpayers investing for retirement may find venture capital trusts (VCTs) appealing. Income tax relief at 30% is granted on the initial investment with a maximum of £200,000 in any tax year. The relief is clawed back if shares are disposed of within five years of purchase. Gains on disposal are not subject to capital gains tax. Dividends are exempt from income tax. This latter characteristic makes them a potentially attractive element in a retirement portfolio, since many VCTs include payment of a steady dividend stream in their objectives.

Chapter 20
Retirement decumulation

1 Introduction

Retirement is the moment when clients stop saving money from their earnings and start to draw on the resources they have built up for themselves and their partners. Some advisers have pithily summarised the situation as the time when the client stops working for their money and their money has to start working for them. The accumulation of investments and assets that may have seemed rather theoretical and remote to many clients suddenly takes on much more importance and urgency. The point of retirement is a time of great change in financial and personal circumstances and also in the approach to financial planning.

There is a very wide range of circumstances facing people at retirement; the divide between rich and poor becomes even more marked at this time. For example, in 2008-09, 53% of single pensioners had a total pension income of less than £10,000 a year. Most of this chapter will focus on the more affluent part of the market that financial planners typically service, where individuals have more income or at least more assets than the average. At the bottom end of the market, the primary need for those who provide financial advice is mostly concerned with developing very considerable expertise in budgeting, debt repayment and social security benefits.

Decisions around pension drawdown are likely to constitute a substantial proportion of the advice that will be given to clients in retirement, especially now that many of the age 75 restrictions are to be removed. The choices, opportunities and potential pitfalls have become much greater and the need for advice for this cohort of clients has suddenly expanded hugely.

2 Timing of retirement

Clients' normal and expected retirement dates tend to be the traditional state retirement ages of 60 for women and 65 for men. But these are already changing as women's state retirement age equalises with men's at 65 and then extends beyond. Retirement itself has become an increasingly fluid concept, as more and more people continue to work full-time or part-time after they start to draw on their state or private pension benefits. The introduction of anti-age discrimination laws may have opened up the possibility of continuing employment for those who want it – at least in theory.

Longevity is still increasing rapidly – seemingly at the rate of about two years in every ten. The prospect of many pensioners living into their early 100s, (and some beyond even that age), increases the financial and lifestyle attractions of continuing to work for the healthy. Even a relatively low income from a part-time job could represent extremely good value, when it takes over £100,000 to generate an income of less than £5,000 a year for a couple in their mid-60s.

There are clients who retire early. Some of them are fortunate city dealers or entrepreneurs who have been lucky or clever enough to make fortunes before they reached their 50s. But most are people who lost their jobs prematurely and were unable to find employment.

Example 20.1

Ellen, Peter and John all worked in the same bank until their late 40s when they were all affected by redundancy.

Ellen went and worked for another bank where she joined their generous defined benefit (DB) scheme, having transferred over her rights from her old employer's scheme. With the transfer value, her ongoing accrual and some AVCs, Ellen qualified for a pension of two thirds of her final salary. She prospered and trebled her final pensionable salary by the time she retired at 60. In 2007 Ellen did a little consultancy work after she retired and invested the entire fee into a personal pension.

Peter started a business when he left the bank, and he hoped that it would have a substantial capital value which he could realise. His business was his pension, in effect. Peter even transferred his accrued bank pension rights into a buy-out bond, which he eventually largely transferred into a SIPP and lent to his company when times got tough. When the company went into liquidation, Peter had virtually only his basic state pension on which to retire.

John built up a consultancy business that prospered on a modest basis. He invested in a personal pension, but could not afford to replace the whole of the final salary pension benefits that he would have built up in his final years with the bank. He continued to work well into his late 60s, partly because he enjoyed it. At 65, John was paid his accrued bank pension and his state pension. But continuing to work allowed him to postpone drawing on his personal pension until annuity rates were more attractive and he had accumulated a much bigger fund.

---

3 The advice process at retirement

The advice process at retirement essentially follows the standard six steps of financial planning generally, but in view of the client's rapidly changing circumstances, it may involve rather more guesswork and estimation about the immediate future than earlier planning exercises. The issues are also often more urgent and important.

Aims, objectives and needs

Just as there is a wide range of circumstances when people reach retirement, there are also many different types of ambition and need.

The basic ambition of most people is to have enough income – and to some extent capital – to enjoy a reasonable standard of living. What this means will vary widely. Some couples may be very content on £20,000 a year, while others would find it hard to survive on a net income of less than £100,000 a year or possibly more. In any event, spending habits may be expected to change as clients grow older and possibly develop more modest spending habits. The 60s and 70s are often the peak periods of expenditure.

The decision where to live in retirement is a key issue. For some clients, staying in their current home is the highest priority, while for others the main goal is to live in a property by the sea or in another country. Some clients are fortunate in being able to afford more than one home. Other clients want to move to a smaller property. As time goes on, many clients may increasingly decide to occupy smaller properties and eventually in advanced old age (or possibly earlier) move to somewhere that provides extra support and possibly even nursing or medical help.

Deciding where to live may be crucial. Moving to a lower cost part of the country or overseas could release some capital and allow clients to live in a congenial location. But such a relocation could also make it harder to move back to a high cost area later on if the differential in prices has widened.

Example 20.2

Bill and Mary moved from London to a seaside town in Dorset where they were very happy during their 60s and early 70s. But then Mary suffered a debilitating fall and Bill found he could no long drive. Unfortunately, the hills and distances of Dorset made driving essential. Bill and Mary wanted to move back to London to be near their children and grandchildren, but even much smaller properties were now no longer affordable.

There is a tension between generating immediate income and making sure that there will be sufficient income in the future. To some extent, this may be offset by declining levels of expenditure in old age. But this pattern is by no means universal and with roughly 1 in 4 or 5 people expected to suffer some kind of dementia in old age, there is a chance that at some point, expenditure levels may increase very sharply indeed.

Clients and their advisers should bear in mind the possible need for long-term care planning, although with the government's plans in limbo, it is hard to make much advance provision except by ensuring that there should be sufficient assets to cover the probable costs. Some clients are keen to ensure that the local authority pays for their long-term care. At least one possible consequence of such planning is that the level of care is limited to the local authority's budget for provision and may not necessarily be as comfortable as more expensive arrangements. There is also a very strong possibility that the rules will change in the future, undermining the effects of these preparations.

The fact-finding process

The fact-finding process can be more complicated and may be more protracted because of the many changes that are being contemplated at retirement.

Personal circumstances

People's family situation can change unexpectedly and markedly at retirement. Family relationships often alter and may become more interdependent (grandparents may become even more important as part of the arrangements for looking after grandchildren); or family members may be more independent of each other, particularly if the clients or their children decide to move overseas.

Sometimes couples decide to split up, because their marriage or partnership cannot survive full time exposure to each other. One of the key issues in retirement is the provision of survivors' pensions and it is important to know the circumstances. It is also very common for people to be in unmarried relationships. The financial planner should be aware of the situation and how this might affect pension planning. If the partner is unmarried and financially dependent on the pension scheme member, the position of death benefits will be important to consider. Pension fund withdrawal may provide a degree of flexibility that clients in these circumstances might prefer. The ownership of income-producing assets could provide opportunities for investment tax planning, as long as the partners are on good enough terms to be prepared to change the ownership to reduce their income tax and capital gains tax.

Clients' state of health is a key factor in retirement planning. It could affect the choice between annuity and pension fund withdrawal. If an annuity is the most suitable approach it could open up the possibility of a higher income from an impaired life annuity.

Example 20.3

Mike and Anna are married. She has a substantial pension income and some earnings; she also has most of their savings and investments in her name. Mike has a basic state pension and a small occupational pension, but very little other income. Anna is a higher rate taxpayer and sometimes even pays capital gains tax on her investment gains. Mike is a basic rate taxpayer.

It would be effective tax planning to move some of Anna's investments over to Mike so that she saved higher rate tax on her income; she cannot move any of her pension income. The question is whether she trusts Mike enough to make such a transfer.

If clients decide to live overseas, the decision will affect their costs, medical care situation, tax position, approach to investment and currency risk. It will be especially important for such clients to understand the potential impact of currency movements on the relationship between their overseas spending needs and the value of their UK pension income and assets.

Example 20.4

Paul and Evelyn retired to Florida when sterling was riding high. A few years later, as Evelyn fell ill, they found that the costs of medical care were becoming unaffordable, even after benefit payments from their medical insurer. They also discovered that the value of their UK pensions had depreciated by about one third in relation to the US dollar. When Paul and Evelyn decided to explore the possibility of moving back to the UK, they discovered that the value of their US home had declined substantially following the American crash in residential property, while UK property prices had been less affected.

Assets and liabilities

By the time clients reach retirement age, they should ideally have built up some wealth represented by property — the main residence and possibly other property — as well as some investments and pension rights.

Property It is important to know the approximate the value of any property, particularly the main residence, especially if it could be used for downsizing and releasing funds at some point in the future. It is also essential to discuss the plans for the property and whether the client intends to stay or move. Issues will include the costs of running the property, its state of repair and the other outgoings including council tax, as well as its size and convenience.

The mortgage Ideally, there should normally be no mortgage on the main residence when the client retires. If there is a mortgage, the aim should normally be to pay it off, because the interest payable on a mortgage is seldom equal to the income from the balancing investment. However this may not be possible in some circumstances.

Example 20.5

Margaret and Bill own several residential properties which they let commercially. One of the properties still has a mortgage which has some five years to run. The interest on the mortgage at 6% is higher than the percentage yield on the property of 4%, although the rent of £12,000 a year easily covers the interest of £7,000 on the relatively small mortgage. They have insufficient liquid resources to pay off the mortgage and they do not want to sell the property at the moment. They decide to keep the mortgage for the time being.

If it is not feasible to pay off the mortgage on the main residence and the clients do not wish to move home, it may be worth considering converting the outstanding mortgage into some kind of equity release, so that the interest rolls up and no longer eats into the client's spendable income. This may not be possible if the loan to value ratio is too high.

Investments

The investments clients have had while they were earning may no longer be suitable for their retirement. The main reason is that they will now require income from their investments, but their risk profile may also have changed. Drawing income may require a lower risk approach to investment.

If the portfolio of investments is to be changed, this will probably involve disposals of previous holdings. It is especially important to know the base values and to be able to explain the tax position on the disposal of investments. The financial planner needs to understand the client's particular circumstances: to know about capital losses carried forward, the times ahead when the client may be able to engineer a tax year of low income, which will affect the rate of tax payable on both capital gains and the encashment of investment bonds. If the client is married, it may be possible to share the ownership of assets that are due for disposal in such a way that both spouses'/partners' tax positions are used to the greatest extent. It is common to find that couples have uneven pension incomes, so one has a much larger pension income than the other. The investments can then be used to balance the income to take maximum advantage of the clients' personal allowances and basic tax bands.

The value of the investments is important. Unlike pensions, it is possible to transfer assets between spouses/partners to minimise the tax on income and capital gains. Investments can generate capital gains, which are more advantageously taxed than income.

Some investments may be in the form of property. Property has the advantage of generating relatively high levels of income. However, property owners may over-estimate the net income they derive from their properties, because they tend to discount such expenses as maintenance, management, and wear and tear of fixtures and fittings. They may also overlook the possible impact of voids. The financial planner should discuss these issues with clients and look at past performance where that is relevant.

Pensions

The main types of pensions from which a client may benefit are state pensions, defined benefit (DB) pensions and defined contribution (DC) pensions.

Clients' expected state pensions can be ascertained from the Department for Work and Pensions. This should be obtained for each partner. Apart from the basic state pension, the client may also benefit from S2P, SERPS and graduated pensions. It may be worth postponing drawing the basic state pension in order to benefit from a higher rate of income.

Many clients have accrued pensions in DB schemes. For couples, it is very important to know about the survivor's rights, in particular whether the member's spouse/partner will in fact benefit on the member's death and if so the level of benefit. The scheme may offer the option to commute some pension benefits for a tax free pension commencement lump sum (PCLS). It is also essential to find out about the security of the DB scheme as far as possible.

DC scheme pension

Many clients have a range of different pension arrangements that need to be valued and assessed. Specialist issues to be considered include: whether there are any rights to guaranteed annuity rates and whether any market value reduction (MVR) applies to with profits policies. In many cases, it may make sense to bring all the arrangements into a single arrangement such as a self-invested personal pension (SIPP) or possibly in some cases a small self-administered scheme (SSAS). The potential costs or penalties of coming out of these schemes as well as the costs of setting up a new one will need to be taken into account.

4 The main choices – defined benefits schemes

The main question for members of DB pension schemes is whether to take the full pension entitlement or the tax free PCLS with a lower pension. Where this choice is available, clients will need advice. In some instances, there is no choice and the member always receives the tax free lump sum, as is the case with the civil service superannuation scheme. In most cases where they have a choice, members tend to take the PCLS:

- The lump sum is certain and does not depend on the client living, unlike the pension which will cease on death or at the end of any guarantee period. Some pensions offer a minimum death pay-out.

- The lump sum is tax free – in contrast to the taxable pension income, which can be subject to tax at up to 50%.

- The size of the survivor's pension is not usually affected by the commutation, although this should be checked.

- Most clients want to have a tax free lump sum to make capital purchases at retirement or pay off any liabilities.

Nevertheless, the basis for the commutation of the lump sum may represent poor value and it is well worth checking, especially if the client will need income and is a basic rate taxpayer for whom the freedom from tax of the lump sum is relatively less valuable than for a higher rate taxpayer. Some clients prefer to have a lifetime index-linked pension rather than a relatively small tax-free lump sum.

The adviser needs to consider the financial security of the scheme; if a scheme is not secure financially, perhaps because of a troubled employer, it might eventually fall into the Pension Protection Scheme or the Financial Assistance Scheme and the member might then be subject to a reduction in pension benefits. If the scheme is not secure, the financial planners should consider obtaining specialist advice about the client transferring out, although it should be recognised that even in these circumstances it might well not be worthwhile.

Example 20.6

Maria is 65 and has reached retirement age and her employer's DB pension scheme is offering her an limited price index (LPI) linked pension of £30,000 a year. The commutation factor is based on a ratio of 11:1 so she could give up £1,000 a year of index-linked income to gain £11,000 of capital as a lump sum. Maria can think of no other investment where she could obtain a comparable and secure lifetime return on £11,000. She does not need the capital, because she has other resources, and so she decides to forgo the tax free PCLS and take all her pension benefits as an income. She is pleased that she is in good health and with any luck, the scheme should carry on paying her well into her 90s – and perhaps even beyond.

Some clients may wish to consider switching their accrued DB scheme pension rights to take advantage of the new DC pension drawdown rules (see below). A pension transfer should be considered very carefully and in most circumstances is unlikely to be advisable.

5 Defined contribution pensions – the main choice

The Government's proposed new rules for pension drawdown and the removal of the effective requirement to buy an annuity at age 75 are already changing some of the basics of planning at retirement and afterwards. The main choices for taking retirement benefits from a DC pension scheme from 6 April 2011 would seem to be as follows:

- Lifetime annuity, which could be single life or joint life, level or escalating, conventional or investment-linked. The terms of an annuity could be affected by the annuitants' health, lifestyle and even their postcode.

- Third way or variable annuities

- Pension drawdown: capped or flexible

- Phased retirement; consisting of tax free cash and annuity payments or tax free cash and drawdown.

- A combination of the above.

6 The new pension maturity rules applying from 6 April 2011

The new rules will have a profound impact on the decision-making of many clients who will no longer have to consider their planning in the context of virtually enforced annuity purchase on reaching age 75. This brief summary was written after the publication of the Government's response to public representations in December 2010 when it was clear that most aspects of the proposals were settled – but by no means all. The Government proposes the following rules that will apply from 6 April 2011.

- DC pension members will no longer effectively have to buy an annuity at age 75, although age 75 will continue to be an important date for a number of the tax features of pension schemes. For example, it will still not be possible to make pension contributions with tax relief after reaching age 75. The new rules will apply to those who are already in pension drawdown. There will continue to be no minimum drawdown of income up to or after age 75.

- If the individual chooses 'capped drawdown', their annual maximum income withdrawal will be 100% of the 'equivalent annuity'. This compares with the previous maximum of 120% of the Government Actuary Department'

(GAD) rate. This is broadly the single life level annuity that could have been bought which is calculated according to the rates set by the GAD. This method has been used as the basis for drawdown since it was first introduced. The maximum capped amount for each client will have to be determined every three years, until the individual reaches the age of 75; after that, the reviews will be carried out annually.

- An individual could choose to take *flexible or uncapped drawdown*, in which case, they would have unlimited access to their drawdown fund. In theory, they could draw the entire amount in a single year. However, to qualify for this flexible drawdown, they would need to have a lifetime pension income of at least £20,000 a year — known as the minimum income requirement (MIR). The aim of the MIR (and the 100% cap on capped drawdown) is to try and ensure that an individual does not fall back on the state after exhausting their savings prematurely. The Government plans to review the MIR level every five years. The income that counts towards the MIR includes:

  - State pensions;
  - Lifetime annuity of dependant's lifetime annuity which can be level or increasing (but not a purchased life annuity);
  - Scheme pension or dependent's scheme pension;
  - Overseas pension payment equivalent to a lifetime annuity or scheme pension.

- Once an individual has decided to access the whole of their drawdown pension fund, they will be liable to the annual allowance charge on all their subsequent pension input amounts. So deciding to take flexible drawdown will mean an end to making further pension contributions with tax relief. The aim is to stop recycling.

- It will be possible to take the PCLS at any time after age 55 in most cases, even past the age of 75.

- The tax rate for all lump sum death benefits will be 55%, except for those who die before age 75 with undrawn pension benefits which will remain tax free. There will typically be no inheritance tax (IHT) on benefits that have born the 55% tax charge (pre-75 death benefits are normally free of IHT). Unused drawdown funds of someone who has died with no living dependants can be left to charity tax free. The Government believe that the 55% tax charge is broadly the equivalent of the tax reliefs on contributions and roll-up of the funds for a higher rate taxpayer.

7 Advice – taking the PCLS

It is always better to take the tax free PCLS than to draw the equivalent amount as an income. The PCLS is certain and tax free; any other form of income is taxable and may be subject to some restriction on access. There are a few people who are enthusiastic about annuities and want to draw all their benefits as an income. For such people, the purchase of a purchased life annuity (PLA) will provide a better return because part of the annual income (the capital element) is tax free.

A more common issue is whether to delay crystallising the pension in order to take a higher level of pension benefits. This is clearly a worthwhile consideration for anyone over 55 who has accumulated pension benefits that are significantly lower than the lifetime allowance (soon to be £1.5m) and who does not immediately need access to the capital. It is of course part of the overall issue of when to draw the pension benefits.

8 Advice on the annuity purchase option

Annuity purchase is currently the most common way to draw the benefits from a DC pension. However, the popularity of annuity purchase may be expected to fall further in the aftermath of further falls in annuity rates and the Government changes to the annuity purchase rules at age 75 set out briefly above. In other countries – e.g. the US – where pension annuity purchase is not compulsory, surprisingly few people buy annuities. Financial advisers should make sure that their clients are aware of the very substantial advantages of annuity purchase, because many clients instinctively recoil from buying them.

- An annuity is paid throughout the member's lifetime, with no danger of its running out. It can also provide a guaranteed income for the partner/spouse, with the same life-long security.

- The pooling of lives by an insurance company provides a cross-subsidy between those who die prematurely and those who live longer than expected. While some annuitants will not receive their money back (or their estates will miss out), some will receive a very high return over the whole of their lifetimes.

- The pension annuity can be protected fully or partially against the impact of inflation, although this will mean that the initial income will be substantially less than a level pension bought with an equivalent fund. Instead of a fixed level annuity, the increasing annuity can be set up to rise at a fixed escalating rate – say 3% a year or 5% a year – or it can be linked to the RPI.

- People with poor life expectancy because of ill-health may expect to benefit from significantly higher annuity rates — possibly 10% better or more.

- Annuity purchase is very simple and low cost to administer once it has been set up. The basis is fixed and cannot be changed.

Conventional annuities are likely to be suitable for clients who want a simple and predictable pension income that is guaranteed for their lifetime and possibly also their partner's/spouse's lifetime. The attractions are not limited to those with relatively small pension funds of, say, up to £100,000, although annuity purchase is almost certain to be more suitable for such clients than pension drawdown and similarly relatively elaborate planning.

Investment-linked pensions

Some clients are attracted by the option of investment-linked pensions that are set up on a with profit or unit-linked basis. They are different from conventional annuities. The return could be higher because the underlying investment of the fund is likely to be wholly or substantially equities, but the return will be much less certain for the same reason.

With profits annuities operate on a broadly similar basis. The initial income is set by the annuitant selecting an assumed bonus rate. The higher the assumed rate, the greater is the initial income, but the less likely it is to grow in the future. HM Revenue & Customs permits a maximum initial growth assumption of 5% a year net of charges; the minimum growth assumption is 0% a year.

Unit-linked annuities operate along roughly the same lines as with profit annuities. The investor chooses an assumed investment return (between 0% and 5% a year). Unlike the with profit version, the returns are volatile because there is no smoothing effect.

The level of risk would probably not suit a cautious investor. However, investment-linked annuities provide a half-way house between conventional annuities and drawdown. The investor has some exposure to the returns from investment markets, but also considerable longevity protection and much greater simplicity than drawdown provides. Investment-linked annuities need to be kept under review, but the advice and administrative issues are much simpler and as a result their cost is likely to be significantly less than drawdown.

The drawbacks of lifetime annuities

The main drawback of lifetime annuities is their inflexibility. Once the annuity has been set up, it cannot be varied and this could have unfortunate consequences in some circumstances:

- If the pension scheme member's spouse or partner died first, the benefit of the joint life provision would then be lost. Then, if the annuitant were to survive and remarry or even co-habit with another person, it would not be possible to add the new spouse or partner as a co-annuitant.

- The member might need to have access to a capital sum – for example, to pay for long-term care – but it would not be possible to draw this from the annuity other than in the form of the prearranged income. It would not even be possible to provide the income as a security for a loan as this is specifically forbidden.

Some of these aspects of pensions might be changed in the future, but this is far from certain and the changes seem unlikely to benefit anyone who buys an annuity before further reforms are introduced.

Another problem arises from the death benefit where there is no surviving spouse or partner and the client dies after the initial guarantee or capital protected period. There are no death benefits in this situation; the resulting surplus is used to cross-subsidise longer-living annuitants. Clients often find this hard to accept. Drawdown can deal with this problem relatively effectively especially under the new rules.

9 Third way annuities

Third way or variable annuities have been introduced in the UK in recent years, although they have been a major type of business in such markets as the US and Japan for some time. They typically offer a guaranteed minimum level of income payments throughout life. The income may then be ratcheted up at regular reviews (e.g. every three years) if the investment performance of the underlying funds has been satisfactory. The guarantees can be for the life of the scheme member or extend to the lifetime of a spouse or civil partner.

There is typically a range of funds to choose from, although it is likely to be restricted to relatively cautious or balanced funds. More adventurous and higher risk funds are generally not available for linking to this type of product.

The initial guaranteed income is normally below the level provided by a conventional level annuity. This could then rise if the plan incorporates ratcheted reviews, but it cannot fall. The guarantees come at a cost expressed in annual charges that vary considerably between providers, but are currently between about 0.65% and 2% a year. The restrictions on fund choice and relatively high costs may be regarded as limiting the scope for future ratcheted increase and reduce the attractiveness of the product. However, these types of contract are becoming increasingly popular.

10 Advice on pension drawdown

Pension drawdown has become the preferred method of taking an income from a DC pension plan for most pension plan members with relatively substantial pension funds and it is set to become even more widely used with the latest proposals to make the rules less restrictive. Personal pension plan holders can indefinitely defer taking their benefits as an annuity. If they wish, they can draw the benefits as a tax free PCLS and they can also take further withdrawals as drawdown directly from the fund. The rules are being changed with effect from 6 April 2011 (see page 319).

Pension drawdown planning strategies

Pension drawdown could involve several different strategies and the range of possibilities has opened up very considerably as a result of the new rules that are being introduced. Most strategies will involve drawing the PCLS and the maximum income that is sustainable over the long-term.

- Most pension schemes are used to generate capital and long-term income in retirement. The drawdown will be used to try and broadly replicate the income that an annuity would provide. The removal of the age 75 rule means that clients can plan their pension portfolios for the much longer term and can therefore afford to hold equities and higher risk investments as a larger proportion of their portfolios than in the past.

- Some clients will wish to withdraw very little or no income — at least initially and possibly never. They might take out the PCLS and perhaps an occasional income withdrawal.

- Some clients who choose flexible drawdown will decide to draw the maximum possible amounts of income with the aim of draining the fund altogether. They would probably aim to do this in years of low taxable income or at least when they are not 50% taxpayers.

There will probably be some clients who intentionally never crystallise their pension funds. The fund should avoid IHT and only be subject to the 55% tax rate after age 75; but the PCLS is tax free and it theoretically could be gifted tax free if the donor survives at least seven years after making the gift; alternatively it could be invested for at least two years in qualifying business assets and pass free of IHT.

Under the Government's proposals, a client who has started taking flexible drawdown would be prevented from obtaining tax relief on further pension contributions. It seems that this restriction would not apply to capped drawdown or annuity purchase, which may be more suitable for clients who wish to be able to make pension contributions while they are taking withdrawals.

Example 20.7

Max, a youthful 63, lived with his long-term girlfriend Jo, 42. They were not keen to get married but Max wanted to make sure Jo would benefit from his pension if he died first. He decided that an annuity would not be suitable for him, because it would have to be single life. He also felt that an annuity would not have been good value for Jo because of her age (even if it could have been set up). So he decided on drawdown for his pension crystallisation planning. That way, Max could have access to the funds when he needed them and if he died, Jo could benefit from the remaining lump sum; 55% tax seemed rather a high penalty, but in view of the fact that he had been a higher rate taxpayer through the period in which he had accumulated the funds, it did not seem outrageous, especially as there would be no IHT to pay on the lump sum on his death. Also, if he and Jo fell out, the situation would be flexible and he could leave any remaining pension fund to his children – or perhaps even another companion in his old age.

Capped or flexible drawdown – the choice

The drawback of capped drawdown is the 100% of GAD limit on drawdown. This will be a limiting factor for those who want flexibility in their income withdrawals or who are used to withdrawing up to 120% under the previous rules. It will be particularly irksome for those who wish to withdraw substantial amounts to pay for long-term care or for some other substantial and lumpy expenditure. It is unlikely to affect couples very adversely because the cap is based on single life annuity rates and the joint life rates are generally much lower, depending on ages.

The complete flexibility of flexible drawdown may be very useful for those clients who wish to run down their pension fund as rapidly as possible or want to have access to large sums from time to time. However, they are likely to be constrained by the impact of 50% tax on any income in a tax year of over £150,000 and even 40% tax on lesser amounts of income. The added flexibility may not be needed in practice and it is worth checking how important it really is.

One of the possible disadvantages of flexible drawdown is the need to meet the MIR. Of course, some clients fulfil the MIR without any inconvenience or cost, if for example they have already secured enough state pension and DB pension benefits. But buying an annuity of £10,000 would typically cost a 65 year old man at least £200,000 and such a sum is likely to represent a significant proportion of a client's total pension fund.

> **Example 20.8**
>
> Flexible drawdown seemed very suitable for Elizabeth. She had a basic state pension plus a pension from a final salary scheme, which gave her secure income of £18,000 a year. So she just needed to invest about £50,000 to buy a level pension annuity with a small portion of her £1.4m pension fund and the rest could be taken exactly as she wished under flexible drawdown. Elizabeth was concerned that her pension fund should be available to pay for long-term care if needed as she felt it would be preferable to selling her home to pay for it. Flexible drawdown would mean she could afford very high quality care at the end of her life.

A further possible problem associated with taking flexible drawdown is the limitation on making any further pension contributions with tax relief. This might well be an issue for clients who aim to have significant levels of earnings after they start drawing their pensions.

Pension drawdown and investment risk

As always, the investment strategy for a pension will depend on the aims for the investments and the client's risk profile. It is also important to consider the investment strategy for the pension in the context of the overall portfolio. The aim for the fund could be to draw substantial amounts of income or it might be to accumulate all or virtually all the fund for the long-term — possibly even to use the fund as a vehicle for IHT planning.

Where the pension fund is being retained for capital growth or the client has a very low dependence on the fund for their income, the client should be able to tolerate a higher risk investment strategy within the fund.

If the main objective is to generate a spendable income for the client, most clients will need to depend on the fund's total return to generate the income, including both the so-called 'natural' income of the investments (i.e. the dividends from the shares, rental income from any property and interest from bonds and cash) as well the capital gains. So, for example, if the long-term capital growth plus income from a portfolio were 7% a year, the aim might be to draw up to that much from the portfolio annually. However, this total return approach means taking on more risk than with a pure growth strategy and there are therefore likely to be considerable variations round this average return. In some years, the client could incur substantial losses and in others there could be big spikes as a result of capital gains. There are broadly three main ways to approach this problem of drawing a constant income from a volatile portfolio:

- Draw a constant amount from across the whole portfolio. The result will be a reverse pound cost averaging effect tending to accentuate the impact of investment volatility. A large number of units and shares will be sold when their values are low and relatively few will be sold when their prices are high.

- Draw from the most successful parts of the portfolio as part of the periodic rebalancing of the asset allocation. This may work well in years when asset classes behave differently. It may be less successful in the years when asset class movements are all in a correlated downward direction.

- Draw from a reserve pool of cash and short-dated bonds into which the rebalancing profits are diverted and which is otherwise generally only topped up in years of overall profitability. The size of the pool could be based on the number of years the client and adviser estimate that markets would take to recover from a very low bear phase; past performance might suggest this could be five years or even longer.

Example 20.9

James has a pension fund of £1m after taking his PCLS. He is 65 and at current interest rates, 100% of the GAD rate is 6.2%. He decides not to draw the maximum under the new rules and settles on a figure of 5%, which should leave a little in reserve for investment fluctuations, although not as much as he would like. James is in good health and his parents are both alive and in their 90s. He therefore concludes that there is a strong chance that he too will be relatively long-lived, possibly surviving to age 100 or even beyond in view of generally increasing longevity. James believes that asset backed investments should provide long-term returns, but he is not comfortable about depending on fluctuating values to produce a stable income. In any case, his chosen portfolio of equities and property for long-term growth will produce a projected yield of just over 2% a year. James is concerned that he should be able to have a safe reserve for a period of at least five years which would be topped up from the natural income of the fund, the proceeds of some of the annual rebalancing of his portfolio and also periodic capital disposals of funds. James' adviser sets up a fund of £250,000 in cash and short-dated bonds.

The important point that financial planners and their clients need to understand is that drawdown should normally make clients more cautious towards investment risk than when they were in the accumulation phase.

Most clients who use pension drawdown should have other sources of income because of the higher risks inherent in this approach. Such clients may have substantial income from property or other investments; they may be beneficiaries of trusts or possibly they may be receiving pension income from a secure DB pension scheme.

Suitability of drawdown

Pension drawdown is likely to be suitable for the following situations:

- The client is not very dependent on their pension for regular income and can therefore afford to invest in relatively high risk assets and see considerable fluctuations in their portfolio. This could be because the client has other assets and other sources of income outside the pension plan. So the pension is a relatively small part of their overall wealth.

- The client should be a reasonably sophisticated investor and be aware of the risk and can tolerate investment volatility.

- The client wants to take the tax free PCLS but possibly little or no income – at least for some time.

- Interest rates appear to the client to be temporarily low but might well increase again, at which point it might be worth buying an annuity. Clients who take this view should be warned that rising longevity and the effects of international regulation of financial services (notably Solvency II) might mean that a major recovery in annuity rates could be a remote possibility.

- The client and/or their partner or spouse is relatively young and an annuity does not appear to be good value. Taking drawdown for a few years before buying an annuity may seem an attractive option.

- The fund from which the drawdown is to be taken is large enough to absorb the additional costs of running the investments, administering the scheme, undertaking the reviews and giving the advice. Some product providers normally insist on a minimum of £100,000 in the fund after taking the PCLS. However it may be worthwhile in some other circumstances, especially if death benefits are the main issue.

- Death benefits are a high priority. For example, if the client were to die prematurely and the surviving spouse or partner is in poor health, the drawdown facility could be used without locking up the whole fund in a survivor's pension annuity. If a surviving partner is not married to the pension scheme member, the death benefits from drawdown could be a valuable financial resource and 'only' subject to 55% tax.

Conversely, drawdown is unlikely to be suitable for clients who do not react well to complexity or investment risk. Drawdown funds need to be large enough to sustain the charging structure. The shorter the timescale, the less likely it is that equities will reliably outperform conventional annuity yields.

11 Short-term annuities

An alternative (wholly or partly) to pension drawdown is to use some of the available fund to buy a short-term annuity; the rest would be invested for capital growth. A five or ten year annuity would buy a reliable income for the term of the annuity, and the balance of the fund would be invested with some of it being used to provide capital growth to buy another temporary annuity at the end of the annuity term when the income ceases. A structured product could be used to buy at least a guaranteed minimum level of performance but with upside exposure to stock market investments.

This approach is similar to setting up a pool of cash and short-term bonds. It might provide a comparable return, with more certainty and simplicity, but with less flexibility.

12 Advice – phased retirement

Phased retirement is the process of gradual crystallisation of a pension arrangement, although it is often achieved by policy segmentation.

One approach is to postpone taking any pension income and simply to drawdown tax free PCLS each year at the rate of say 3% or 4% of the total fund. This could deplete the total PCLS within 15 to 20 years, or possibly longer depending on the assumptions about income and growth from the fund. These tax-free withdrawals could be boosted by additional taxable income if required. The income could be generated by buying a series of annuities each year, but is more likely to be financed by ongoing pension drawdown for the required amounts. An important feature of phased retirement is the position on death of the pension scheme member:

- The uncrystallised pensions would continue to be available free of both income tax and IHT on death before age 75.

- The crystallised pension funds before the client's age 75 and all the funds after that date would be subject to a tax charge of 55%, but no IHT.

Suitability

Phased retirement would be suitable for clients for whom drawdown is appropriate and who:

- Do not need a lump sum when they reach retirement, presumably because they have other assets and have paid off their liabilities;

- Want to provide the maximum death benefits particularly in the years up to age 75; after that the death benefits would be treated the same for tax purposes;

- Are higher rate taxpayers and see the benefit of using the PCLS to provide a wholly or largely tax-free income;

- Can afford relatively higher fees for advice and can cope with complexity and investment risk.

13 Using non-pension investments for retirement income

Pensions are usually not the only sources of income in retirement. As the limitations on pension contributions become more significant, other forms of investment income will become relatively more important for retirement, especially for clients at the top end of the income scale.

The main key issues are the choice of underlying investments to generate income, the selection of tax wrappers and other tax planning.

Income oriented investments

When clients reach retirement and want to start taking income from their investments, they will need to switch their investment strategy from growth to income. There is a broad trade-off between maximising immediate income and providing for future inflation protection, so that the more income a client draws in the short-term, the less they will have available for the longer term. It is at this point that, in assessing their priorities, clients need to understand the difference between nominal and real investment returns.

Several factors erode the value of an income stream from investments. These are the costs of owning the investment, the tax on the gross returns and the impact of inflation. If the client spends more than the net income, the income will not be sustainable in the long-term and the client will effectively have to live on their capital. This may be unavoidable, but the client should be aware of the fact and the implications.

Example 20.10

Paul has a portfolio of funds invested in fixed interest securities. These generate an income of 6% gross. Income tax at 20% will reduce his net yield to 4.8%. If Paul wants to reinvest part of his income to maintain its real value, then he should deduct and reserve an amount equal to inflation (say 2%), so that his effective net inflation-proofed investment return would be 2.8%.

Maintenance and administration costs can be very significant for such investments as property. But costs are also deducted from other investments and in many cases they have to be paid from income, e.g. investments held through a wrap.

Example 20.11

Mary lives partly off the rental income from two properties. They generate at total gross income of £20,000 a year for her. However, the annual costs of running the properties in terms of repairs, renewals and administration are about £3,000. The tax at 20% (of £20,000 − £3,000 = £17,000) is £3,400 and so Mary's net income is £13,600. The hope is that the level of income will keep pace with inflation, because rents tend to increase in the longer term.

Clients should be aware that the income from their investments can go down as well as up and this is normally more important for retired clients than fluctuations in capital values especially in the short-term. Incomes can fluctuate for a range of reasons. Property income can rise and fall because of periods when there is no tenant or one who cannot pay the rent or possibly because supply and demand for property can vary with economic conditions or local circumstances.

Example 20.12

Mary (see example 20.11) might find that her property income has dropped in the last year as a result of a local oversupply of rented accommodation, causing her property to be unexpectedly empty for three months. As a result she could only let the property by reducing the rent by 15%.

Different asset classes provide different income profiles, each with its advantages and drawbacks.

Deposit accounts

Deposit accounts are regarded as 'safe' investments but they tend to provide a very variable income. Even where deposit income is fixed, the fixed periods are generally no more than a year or two. Investors can generally achieve higher levels of income from deposits by tying up their money for several months or even years. The drawback of term deposits is that premature access (e.g. for switching) is usually penalised. Investment returns from deposits are not asset-backed and long-term inflation proofing can therefore only be achieved by reinvesting income.

Fixed interest funds

Fixed interest funds provide a more fixed income stream, although the income will normally vary more than the interest from direct holdings of securities. The main advantage of funds is that they can provide a greater degree of diversification and therefore safety. Capital values are at risk from rises in interest rates and long-term inflation proofing requires some income reinvestment, although capital growth can be generated by the use of convertibles.

Asset backed investments

The most reliable way to generate rising long-term income is through asset based investments that represent an equitable interest in business — property and shares. Of course, both income and capital are subject to fluctuations.

Property

Property can generate relatively high rental yields, although they may not be as high as they initially appear if they are direct holdings. The level of yield is at least partly an indication of the quality of the property investment in question. Lower yields generally indicate a property where the quality of the tenant's covenant is high, although there may be other factors. Historically, about half the total return from commercial property has been derived from the rental yield rather than the capital growth. So deciding to draw the rental income rather than to accumulate it represents a substantial reduction in the potential for growth, although in the long-term, the capital growth from a diversified commercial property portfolio should provide some inflation protection.

The switch from capital growth to income generation for many investors with direct holdings of residential or commercial property may take the form of reducing or eliminating their gearing. Borrowing to buy property has proved to be a successful long-term growth strategy for many investors. Paying off the borrowing will unlock the income from these assets. This may be achieved by disposing of other assets or selling properties. Clients may need reminding that property is generally not a highly liquid asset class and individual properties can prove hard to sell and may even prove to be a drain on income while they are waiting to be sold.

Equities

Equities have traditionally provided steady growth of both capital values and income yields. The UK market has been especially successful at providing a steadily growing level of dividend income, although generally at a lower yield than property. A switch of investment strategy from growth to income may require a higher emphasis on investment in UK shares which have generally offered a higher yield than many other major stock markets. Investing in UK shares helps to reduce the potential impact of currency risk on capital values, but more importantly income. UK dividends were much steadier and more dependable until the end of the 90s. In the last decade or so, UK dividends have risen and fallen more than in earlier periods, although they have been generally less volatile than equity capital values or interest rates.

Capital gains are often needed to top up natural income and the more advantageous tax position of gains makes them an important source of 'income' for many clients. Equity funds and direct holdings are relatively liquid and can be disposed of in relatively small amounts on a regular basis. Direct holdings of property cannot be realised in this way. The volatility of the capital values of equities is the main drawback of depending on them for a regular source of spendable income. Holding a cash reserve for income payments is probably the best way to manage the gradual use of capital gains to top up income. This would allow clients to make disposals when it is convenient to do so, rather than when the client needs the cash. A similar approach is discussed above with respect to pension fund withdrawal.

Tax and investment income

A pension is essentially a tax wrapper with a specific set of rules that govern the client's access to the funds. There are other tax wrappers with different and in some respects less restricting limitations. A financial planner should recommend suitable tax wrappers for income withdrawals on the basis of the client's tax rate (both immediately and in the future) and also the nature of the underlying investment.

ISAs

The ISA is in many ways the most attractive investment for drawing income. Although it does not qualify for tax relief on the initial investment, it is tax-free at the time of withdrawing cash. For a basic rate taxpayer with few other capital gains, an ISA that holds equities has no particular tax advantage because the client's capital gains would normally be free in any case; moreover, the ISA manager cannot reclaim the tax credit and a basic rate taxpaying ISA investor is therefore no better off than the investor who holds the equity investments directly. But the ISA investor would benefit from a tax advantage if the underlying investment were cash, fixed interest or a property fund, because the income from these assets in the ISA is normally paid tax free to the investor. This would save 20% tax for a basic rate taxpayer. The differential is even greater for a higher rate or additional rate taxpayer who would also benefit from holding a high yielding equity in the ISA.

Pension funds

A similar tax logic applies to pension funds. If there is a choice between holding cash, fixed interest securities or high yielding equities inside or outside a pension, it is generally more advantageous to hold them within the largely tax free environment of a pension fund rather than direct. Conversely, growth oriented equities are better held direct or as collectives because they are within the capital gains tax regime.

Life assurance bonds

Life assurance bonds – whether UK or offshore – are almost exclusively only suitable for higher and additional rate taxpayers (and trusts) and the same broad logic applies; growth oriented investments are better held outside bonds. One corollary is that onshore bonds in particular can be useful for higher and additional rate taxpayers who want income, especially if they can take the view that their top rate of tax is very likely to decline in the longer term and their investment bonds will therefore function as tax shelters. Their tax rates might come down because their future income will be generally lower, or tax rates might be reduced, or it might be possible to engineer a year of low income when the investment bonds could be encashed. In the short to medium term, the bond will shelter their taxable income at a lower rate until such time as the clients tax rates are reduced.

Venture capital trusts

Venture capital trusts (VCTs) generate tax free income and can be very attractive to higher and additional rate taxpayers. However, the tax privileges of VCTs are offset by the relatively high risk of the underlying investments and their illiquidity. To some extent, this risk can be reduced by purchasing second-hand VCTs which generally have more reliable track records although they do not benefit from up-front income tax relief.

Independent taxation

An advantage enjoyed by non-pension investments is the owners' ability to switch them from the high taxpaying investor to a lower taxpaying investor. This can be especially advantageous for many couples who need income. Where one spouse or civil partner has a high pension income, an effective tax planning strategy would be to transfer assets to the other spouse or civil partner if they have little or no income and therefore pay lower rates of tax.

14 Equity release

Some people find that they do not have enough retirement income or capital but they live in homes that are very valuable. The obvious answer in most such instances is to move home, downsize to a less expensive property and realise some of the capital. Another possibility that may be feasible in some cases is to let part of the property, although many houses do not easily lend themselves to this solution.

Many clients also consider equity release, which can provide them with a capital lump sum or series of lump sums. This has its advantages, where the client does not wish to move, but the interest rates or costs can be relatively high and the eventual impact on the value of the estate may be considerable. The consequences for the beneficiaries may or may not be important.

Someone in their early 70s could borrow about 20% to 25% of the value of their property as a lifetime mortgage. Older people could borrow more. The interest on the borrowing would be rolled up until final disposal of the property which is assumed to be on death. Some lenders are prepared to release amounts gradually which can be used as income and where the roll-up of the liability and interest on the borrowing is significantly slower and therefore has a lower impact on the estate.

Example 20.13

Paul and Judith owned a home in the South East of England that was worth £1.8m. The property was becoming too large for their needs and required some considerable amounts of expenditure to keep it in good repair. They had some income from pensions but it was not enough to meet their needs and they could no longer afford to keep up the house.

They were in their early 70s and decided to look at the alternatives. It was not possible to carve out any part of the garden and sell it off for development; the land was not large enough for this. Likewise the house was not really suitable for dividing up and sub-letting part; Paul and Judith would have had to live cheek by jowl with their lodgers.

They considered equity release carefully and decided that if they lived a long time and the house did not increase in value very substantially in the future, the net loss to the estate would be very considerable and they did not want to deprive their children and grandchildren of so much of their inheritance. They were also concerned that the equity release arrangements would prescribe to some extent their freedom to move and go into long-term care if necessary. Their financial planner looked at the potential impact on their entitlements to various state means-tested benefits but concluded that whatever they did, these entitlements were likely to be affected.

They therefore decided to sell the property and move to a property costing about £850,000. The net £900,000 they released was invested to generate a very helpful income.

From the point of view of the estate, the issue will be the relationship between the rate of interest that rolls up on the borrowing and the increase in the value of the property. If the interest rate is less than the growth in the property value, there should always be some equity left in the property. But if the interest rate is higher than the average annual growth, the equity will disappear more rapidly. For example, on a loan to value of 20% with interest at 5% a year more than property growth (e.g. property growth of 2% a year and interest at 7% a year), the equity will be eaten up within about 32 years. Of course, virtually all lifetime mortgage arrangements have a provision that guarantees that the borrower will not suffer from negative equity.

15 Pension decumulation plans compared

Type of pension decumulation	Advantages	Disadvantages
Conventional level annuity	Lifetime income guaranteed Predictable income Secure Simple Single or joint life provision High initial income	Inflexible if change of spouse/partner Inflexible if capital or change of income is needed Cannot provide for non-spouse partner or non-dependants No inflation protection
Conventional escalating annuity	Same as level annuity but also provides some inflation protection in return for lower initial income	Same as level annuity but also provides low initial income which will take many years to break even
Investment linked annuity	Some longevity protection A choice of high initial income or some inflation protection Exposure to equity and other investment markets	Unpredictable returns Opaque funds in the case of with profits Inflexibility of all lifetime annuities
Third way annuity	Some longevity protection A choice of high initial income or some inflation protection Exposure to equity and other investment markets	Limited fund choice High costs in some cases Complexity of contract
Capped drawdown	Considerable flexibility of income withdrawal up to 100% of GAD A choice of high initial income or some inflation protection Exposure to equity and other investment markets	Costs Complexity and need for ongoing advice and fund management Limited annual drawdown Possibility of running out of funds
Flexible drawdown	Maximum flexibility of drawdown A choice of high initial income or some inflation protection Exposure to equity and other investment markets	Costs Complexity and need for ongoing advice and fund management Possibility of running out of funds Limitation of the MIR Cannot make further pension contributions

Chapter 21
Estate planning

1 Introduction – the scope of estate planning

Estate planning consists of much more than the mitigation of inheritance tax (IHT). IHT issues are important but they are part of a wider picture of financial planning for a family. This should include making sure that assets are passed down to younger generations fairly, appropriately, at the right time and in the most tax efficient ways. Estate planning means balancing many different and often competing interests and priorities, both between generations and also between people of the same generation. It is very concerned with the consequences of death but it also involves lifetime planning and disposals. For most clients, estate planning becomes a higher priority as they grow older, but there are also many estate planning issues to consider for clients who are still relatively young, especially if they are parents of minor children.

The scope of estate planning extends to wills, trusts, lasting powers of attorney and even includes philanthropy in the view of an increasing number of advisers. Marital issues such as marriage, divorce and separation can come under the heading of estate planning. Making provision for the care of minors and incapacitated dependants is also crucial for many families.

Sizes of estates

As with all financial planning, estate planning varies considerably according to the size of the estates in question, the nature of the assets comprised in the estates and the circumstances of the family. Much of the basic strategy for IHT planning involves making lifetime gifts that should escape IHT if the donors survive at least seven years. Where a client is contemplating making gifts of assets, the financial planner cannot ignore the impact of capital gains tax and stamp duties on transactions.

A large estate involves potentially a higher proportion of it being subject to IHT; but paradoxically it is generally easier to plan for larger estates than relatively small ones (under about £750,000). Essentially, this is because it is more straightforward for people with larger estates to make lifetime gifts without endangering their future standard of living. For example, in most circumstances, a client with an estate of £5m (in addition to their home) could comfortably dispose of £3m or even more and live on the remaining £2m. But people vary; some clients would regard this as impossible and would still feel insecure with £5m; much would depend on the nature of the individual and the types of assets in question. Some assets are valuable but are illiquid and incapable of generating an income for their owners.

Type of assets

The type of assets that a client owns can be crucial to the planning that has to be undertaken for them. Liquidity is very helpful because easily disposable assets like cash and shares are relatively simple to transfer – although a gift of shares might trigger a capital gains tax (CGT) charge. However, certain illiquid assets qualify for very generous IHT reliefs, in particular business assets, historic houses and agricultural land and are therefore privileged. But they can cause their own particular complications, especially if one member of the family is set to inherit most of the estate in this form and the remainder are likely to receive relatively small inheritances. Valuable main residences and other properties can cause planning difficulties and the rules about reservation of benefit and pre-owned assets tax (POAT) can inhibit planning.

Availability of income

The availability of enough income can have a substantial impact on estate planning. An individual or couple with a reasonably secure income – often from a pension – can consider making substantial lifetime gifts, while those with a small or uncertain income generally have much less scope for IHT mitigation.

Family circumstances

Family circumstances make a big difference to estate planning. Increasingly, and especially with wealthy families, estate planning can involve providing assistance to several generations of a family at the same time. A financial planner can consider a family group in the round, extending the advice strategy to cover parents, children and grandchildren and beyond, where the clear and agreed purpose is to cascade wealth down through the generations. However, advisers should realise that taking on this coordinating and planning role could open up conflicts of interest that will need to be managed.

There is a possible danger that some older family members will use their wealth to try and impose their values and wishes on other family members. But at its best, this kind of inter-generational collaboration can lead to better understanding of each others' wishes and needs. At a relatively simple level, it could mean that parents and grandparents ask the younger members of the family to undertake some financial planning. Intermediate generations can ask the more elderly family members to pass down assets to grandchildren and skip a generation or two in order to avoid creating unnecessary potential IHT liabilities. Where there is a family business with ownership spread over several generations, consultation and discussion of the issues and the future of the business is essential.

2 Lifetime gifts

Making lifetime gifts is likely to save IHT but there could be other equally important reasons for making substantial lifetime gifts. They could include providing funds for house purchase, helping with children's education and maintenance costs, helping to set up a new enterprise, passing over business assets to secure the succession of its ownership and management.

Very often, it is better to make lifetime transfers than to hold onto assets until death. The need for financial help might have passed or diminished by the time the donor has died and in any case there is often much pleasure to be derived from making lifetime transfers. Intergenerational discussions and planning may identify areas where lifetime gifts – sometimes quite modest ones – could make a major difference to the recipients.

Potential donors of lifetime gifts should consider various key issues, which are discussed further below:

- A trust might provide a suitable vehicle for helping members of the family by providing flexibility and some continuing control to the donor. Some recipients are not always capable of behaving entirely responsibly if they receive large outright gifts or they might become entangled in marital or other relationship difficulties.

- Selling property or other investments to finance a transfer or making a gift of an asset could trigger a CGT charge and may involve stamp duty and other costs that will need to be taken into account.

- Transferring wealth to younger people might facilitate the use of their lower rates of tax on income and possibly capital gains.

Providing funds for house purchase

Giving a young relative enough funds to buy a property could make the difference between their buying and renting or between a suitable property and one that is too small or badly placed. It may be sufficient to finance the deposit or to increase its size to help arrange the mortgage or make it cheaper. Such timely finance could be especially welcome for self-employed people who increasingly find it hard to raise finance particular with a business.

Other ways in which members of the older generation can help the younger members of a family are with loans or loan guarantees. These arrangements are usually best set up formally and preferably with legal assistance.

Helping with children's education and maintenance costs

School fees can be expensive and university fees and associated costs are increasing rapidly. Older members of the family may be able to help with regular gifts to parents and older students.

Business

The owner or part-owner of a family business may wish to pass down shares in the business to a son or daughter who is intended to take over running it. A lifetime transfer could be timely, giving the recipient a direct stake in the company as well as allowing profits to be distributed to the new shareholder as dividends.

There should normally be no IHT on such a transfer, but it might trigger a CGT charge. The rate of tax might only be 10% because of entrepreneur's relief, but that would still represent a leakage of wealth that would have to be balanced against the tax, financial and other advantages of a lifetime transfer. Business assets generally qualify for held over gains relief, under which the recipient of the transfer would take over the assets at the donor's base value for CGT. The tax liability would then be postponed indefinitely until the next disposal. There would be no CGT on death.

A young family member may have ambitions to set up or expand their own business. An older and wealthier family member may wish to help with the finance by way of a gift, loan or loan guarantee, or possibly some mix of all these.

3 Wills

Wills are important for IHT planning (see page 343) but they are just as essential to ensure that the right people benefit and to set up the appropriate arrangements after a death. This is particularly crucial for clients who are parents or responsible for bringing up children. Some of the key issues are as follows:

- The intestacy rules are unlikely to be appropriate for many clients and they are certainly unsuitable for most unmarried couples. Where a couple have children, the surviving partner — whether married to the deceased or not — will almost certainly be inadequately provided for. The intestacy rules are likely to exclude various members of the family who should benefit and some others might receive too much or too little in relation to the deceased person's wishes and assessment of needs.

- If a couple die without leaving a will or have a very simple will, the guardianship arrangements for their minor children might not turn out to be what they would have wanted.

- Sometime wills are the best way to even up the distribution of assets between beneficiaries who have been given unequal lifetime gifts.

- Specific possessions will probably not go to the intended beneficiaries unless there is a will and perhaps an accompanying letter of wishes.

- Many people wish to leave money or assets to chosen charities; this is unlikely to happen unless they have made provision for it in their will.

- If a person has just become married or divorced, the chances are that their old will is void. In any event, this is a moment when it is appropriate to make a new will.

- Some people think that any tax inefficiency or inappropriate distribution of their estate under the will can be put right by a deed of variation after they have died. However, it is not safe to rely on such deeds: they need the agreement of the beneficiaries — which might not be forthcoming, or at least could cause family dissension at a difficult time; they are not normally effective where minor children are beneficiaries, and the tax efficiency of the arrangements might be reviewed by a future government.

Example 21.1

Tim and Maria want to rewrite their wills. They are keen to leave all their assets to each other and for the time being none to their two young children. Their top priority is the financial security of the survivor and family if one of them were to die. They do not want to set up a trust for the children if one of the parents were to die, although they recognise that it might be tax efficient; they think it would probably be an excessive hassle. However, if Tim's parents die and leave a significant estate, which seems likely, then they would want some of the estate to pass to the grandchildren and that would require setting up a trust. At that point, they would want to review the arrangements in their own wills.

Tim and Maria are keen that if they both died, their old friends and near neighbours, Ros and Peter, should act as the guardians of the children. They think Tim's parents would probably be too old to do the job and they do not share the same values about child-rearing. Ros and Peter have similar values to theirs, and the children know and like them well. They have children of their own and so the two couples have set up reciprocal arrangements and have talked through all the arrangements. Tim and Maria know that is important for there to be enough money to provide for the survivor and the children if just one parent died and then for the other couple to be able to look after the children if they both died. They achieve this goal with the substantial help of life assurance. They have checked that Ros and Peter have set up comparable arrangements.

---

4 Trusts

Trusts are widely used for IHT planning but they have other uses as well. A trust is essentially a way of giving property to other people without giving them control over it. During their lifetime, the settlor can be a trustee and even after death, they can influence how the trust is used through the choice and the terms of the trust. It is essential to take care to choose the right trustees.

Trusts can be useful in a number of circumstances that are more or less independent of tax issues. Outside the sphere of private trusts for families, trusts are also used for such purposes as charities, employee benefits and pensions.

Advantages of trusts

Trusts have several non-tax uses and advantages for holding property.

- The intended beneficiaries may be too young, too irresponsible or simply not capable of looking after the trust property themselves.

- Where there are several beneficiaries, the trust can provide a convenient way to hold and look after their collective interests.

- A trust can help ensure that the assets are used according to the settlor's wishes. A spouse might want to make sure that their surviving spouse has enough income during their lifetime. But when the survivor eventually dies, the settlor would want the assets in the trust to go to their children rather than some other person (such as a new spouse or partner and possibly even the children of this new union). This aim can be achieved with a life interest trust or a discretionary trust.

- A discretionary trust provides a very useful way to have flexibility about who will benefit. Capital and income can be diverted to those who need it most from time to time.

Drawbacks of trusts

Financial planners should also be aware of the various drawbacks and limitations of trusts. Some of the main ones are as follows.

- Trusts can be expensive to set up and administer and offshore trusts can be especially costly. The benefits may not match the costs. Accountants', lawyers' and other professional trustees' charges can eat into the trust income and investment values.

- Trusts can mean complexity and lead to legal disputes. Clients and advisers should remember that the long-running although fictional case *Jarndyce v Jarndyce* in Charles Dickens' novel 'Bleak House' concerned a complicated family trust. Nowadays these disputes are generally avoided but trusts can lead to difficulties. One answer to some of these problems is to break the trust and distribute the assets. The authority is the old case of *Saunders v Vautier*, but all the beneficiaries must have come of age.

- Trustees can cause difficulties if they behave in a way that is uncooperative or unsympathetic to the needs of beneficiaries or most likely of all, if they are just inefficient. Problems commonly arise from trustees' employing poor investment strategies. Trustees have a duty to look after a trust's investments and poor performance may open opportunities for financial planners.

- The income tax and capital gains tax position of discretionary trusts is not generally advantageous and reflects the suspicion of both HM Revenue & Customs and the government that many trusts are vehicles for tax avoidance. Trusts are certainly the object of much anti-avoidance legislation, which increases the cost and complexity of dealing with them.

Financial advisers who work with clients with trusts will need to cooperate with specialist legal and tax advisers. Trusts are, of course, extensively used in IHT planning.

5 Outline of IHT issues for planning

The value of a person's estate for IHT on death is the total market value of their assets net of their liabilities. An individual is treated as owning the underlying assets in which they have an interest in possession – broadly speaking a right to the income from those assets.

IHT is chargeable on the cumulative value of the lifetime transfers an individual has made in the seven years before their death, as well as their estate at death. UK domiciled people are subject to IHT on their world-wide assets, although non-UK assets might qualify for some double taxation relief, depending on its location. A non-UK domiciled person is generally not subject to tax on their overseas assets. Someone who has been resident in the UK in 17 out of the previous 20 years is treated as UK domiciled for IHT, even if they are not UK domiciled for other purposes.

If an individual makes an outright gift to another person, there will be no IHT as long as the donor survives for at least seven years after making the gift. Such a gift is called a 'potentially exempt transfer' (PET), because it will be exempt if the donor does not die in the seven year period.

Each person has a nil rate band of £325,000 in 2010-11 and it is due to remain at this level until 2014-15. The rate of IHT above that is a flat 40%. Where tax is charged on a lifetime gift, it is normally at the rate of 20%.

Transfers between UK domiciled spouses are free of IHT. But a transfer from a UK domiciled individual to a non-UK domiciled spouse or civil partner only qualifies for an exemption of £55,000. An individual can inherit the unused nil rate band of a deceased spouse, so that in most cases, the total available nil rate band is £650,000 after the death of both spouses or civil partners. If a deceased spouse used part of their nil rate band (e.g. by leaving some assets to their children), only the proportion of the unused band would pass to the surviving spouse or civil partner.

Example 21.2

George died in November 1997, when the IHT nil rate band was £200,000. He left £50,000 to his son Anthony and the rest of his estate of £1m went to his wife Mildred. When Mildred died in May 2010, her nil rate band was the full £325,000 and in addition she passed on three-quarters of George's nil rate band. Uprated to 2010 levels, this was £243,750, making a total of £568,750 that will be passed onto her heirs.

The maximum inherited nil rate band is 100% of the current level; so it is not possible to pass down more in addition to one's own nil rate band.

Example 21.3

Peta inherited a third of the nil rate band of her first husband Nick. She remarried Fred after Nick's death and their financial planner explained how to structure his will. Peta's estate could eventually benefit from up to two thirds of Fred's nil rate band. So they agreed that Fred should just leave a third of his nil rate band to his son Edward. That way, they could both make the maximum use of their nil rate bands.

There are various exemptions, apart from transfers between spouses. Regular gifts from income are exempt as long as they do not reduce the donor's usual standard of living. There is also an annual exemption of up to £3,000 per donor, as well as other minor exemptions for small gifts and certain gifts on marriage up to limited amounts. Lifetime gifts for the maintenance of a spouse, child or other dependent relative are generally free of IHT. Transfers do not count as gifts if there is no intention to confer a bounty (broadly speaking, something for nothing) so commercial transactions in which one party makes a loss are not normally counted as gifts.

Trusts

There are special rules for trusts, and they vary according to the type of trust.

- **A discretionary trust** is flexible; income can be distributed or accumulated and the trustees can decide how income and capital may be distributed, subject to the terms of the trust. A transfer into a discretionary trust is taxable, unlike outright gifts. There is a 10 yearly periodic IHT charge which is based on the value of the assets in the trust and the settlor's cumulative gifts made in the seven years before they set up the trust. Finally, there may be an exit charge.

- A flexible trust that is set up for a **disabled or vulnerable person** will not be subject to the discretionary trust regime.

- Transfers into **bare trusts** are treated as outright gifts to the individual recipient. This is because the beneficiary is absolutely entitled to the capital and income of the trust assets, unless they are a minor, in which case they will become fully entitled at age 18.

- Transfers into **accumulation and maintenance settlements** are special kinds of discretionary trusts with tax privileges. Transfers into these settlements are also treated as outright gifts to the beneficiaries, as long as the trust meets certain conditions: the beneficiaries must be grandchildren of the same grandparents; the beneficiaries must become entitled to the capital by the time they are 25 and any income that is not used for the beneficiaries' education, maintenance or benefit has to be accumulated. There is no tax charge if the beneficiaries become fully entitled at age 18, but there is a small potential exit charge which progressively rises to a maximum of 4.2% if their entitlement is postponed to age 25.

Payment of IHT

The most common time for paying IHT is at a person's death. The IHT charge is due six months after the death. It is often necessary to pay the tax on account before an estate is fully wound up in order to avoid interest charges. This should not present a problem, if there is enough cash available from liquid assets or the proceeds of a policy in trust. Otherwise, it might be necessary to borrow. Tax can be paid by instalments on land and some other assets.

Business assets

There are special reliefs for business assets; 100% relief is available for the business of a sole trader or an interest in a trading partnership, as well as for shareholdings in unlisted trading companies. 'Unlisted' for this purpose includes shares listed on the Alternative Investment Market (AIM) and the Plus Market (previously OFEX). Certain other assets may qualify for 50% relief, including land and buildings owned by the individual and used by a company that they controlled or by a partnership of which they were a member. There are several conditions that must be fulfilled, which include the following:

- The individual must normally have owned the business assets for at least two years before the transfer.

- The relief does not apply to investment holding or dealing companies.

- The business assets must have been used mainly for business purposes.
- There must be no binding agreement to sell the business.

Agricultural relief and woodlands relief

Agricultural property relief is given on the agricultural value of farmland and farm buildings. The rate of relief is 100% for both the land that is owned and farmed by the transferor and land that is tenanted. Otherwise there may be 50% relief. Farm houses may not be given full relief and some farm houses may not qualify at all.

Gifts with reservation

A special rule stops people from obtaining an IHT advantage as a result of giving away assets and then continuing to benefit from them. The classic example is the person who gives away a property but then continues to use it. The donor must be excluded, or virtually excluded, from enjoying the property.

There is also a special income tax charge on people who have found various artificial ways to get round the gifts with reservation rule. It is called the POAT.

Capital gains tax and IHT

The lifetime gift of an asset is treated as a disposal for CGT and may be subject to tax on any gain that is deemed to be realised. Financial planners should take this into account when recommending gifts of assets or their disposal to fund a gift. In contrast, life assurance policies such as investment bonds can be gifted outright without a tax charge and then disposed of by the recipient at their rate of income tax.

Some assets can be transferred with the benefit of held-over gains relief. There is no CGT at the time of the gift, but the recipient takes over the donor's base value.

Example 21.4

Max bought an asset for £100,000 and transferred it to his daughter Petronella when it had grown to a value of £160,000. He had a choice. The default position is that he would make a taxable gain of £60,000 which would have been subject to CGT. On a future disposal Petronella would have a base acquisition value of £160,000. But in this case, Max is able to claim held-over gains relief and so Petronella can take over the asset without Max paying any CGT. Max decides to hold over the gains and as a result, the base value she uses on her eventual final disposal will be Max's original acquisition value of £100,000.

The main transfers for which it is possible to claim held-over gains relief are:

- Between spouses or civil partners;
- Into a discretionary trust;
- Qualifying business assets.

6 IHT planning

In general terms, the earlier an individual starts to plan for IHT, the easier it is to reduce the incidence of the tax. This is not always the case, but early consideration of IHT can avoid unnecessary IHT charges, for example on a premature and unexpected death.

The first and perhaps most important priority is to ensure that clients have enough income and capital to live on for the rest of their lives so that they can afford to make gifts. This planning can start very early in clients' lives. Initially, the basic planning strategy should be to ensure that pension and other sources of retirement income are adequate. When the client has reached retirement, the priority could be to ensure that they have enough income. Income is essential for clients to be able to use the gifts from income exemption.

Marriage

Unmarried couples should consider whether they should marry. Leaving aside any other considerations, IHT has proved to be one of the most persuasive reasons for older couples to marry. If a person leaves their unmarried partner a house, a share in a house or some other asset, after the impact of the nil rate band, there will be a 40% tax charge on the estate. Marriage eliminates IHT, as long as the potential recipient of the estate is UK domiciled or deemed to be such for IHT purposes.

Spouses and registered civil partners should normally consider sharing some of their assets, so that each can make use of their exemptions and possibly also their nil rate bands. There is usually no IHT or CGT on such transfers, so they can be made without tax penalties. There could also be income and CGT advantages to such transfers. Of course, it makes sense to ensure that the marriage is likely to be sustained in the longer term before making this type of recommendation to clients.

Wills for tax planning

A key decision is whether to leave the nil rate band to the surviving spouse or registered partner, or to pass down assets up to the value of the nil rate band when the first partner dies. In the past, wills were often designed to leave wealth to children or grandchildren in order to make sure that a couple's nil rate bands are both used. With the advent of the scope for surviving spouses/civil partners to inherit a deceased spouse's or civil partner's unused nil rate band, this is generally no longer so essential. It may now be worth reviewing wills that pass down assets on the first death to see if they are still appropriate.

There can still be a tax advantage in using the nil rate band at the first death, especially if the assets to be passed down are likely to grow at a faster rate than the nil rate band. From a purely IHT planning viewpoint, it generally makes sense to pass down assets that are growing rapidly as early as possible. However, the future of the nil rate band is more problematic. It is due to be frozen at £325,000 until 2014/15, but the Conservative Party has a declared intention to increase the nil rate band to £1m and at some point in the future, that possibility might become a reality. So in the short-term, any growth will be ahead of the increase in the nil rate band. In the long-term, however, it is less easy to be certain, especially if there is a major uplift in the nil rate band.

Example 21.5

Paul has some land worth about £300,000 which he thinks will grow in value reasonably well. He could leave it to his children in his will — probably in trust — or he could leave it to his wife. If he uses his nil rate band now and the asset barely increases in value, the long-term value of the nil rate band would still be about £300,000. However, if the nil rate band were to rise to £1m and Paul had left it all to his wife, she could have left an extra £1m tax free. In the event, he decides not to use his nil rate band if he dies first and in his will he leaves the property to his wife.

It is almost certainly not worth a couple passing down taxable assets worth more than the nil rate band at the first death, because it would involve paying IHT earlier than necessary. If there is an excess and the plan is to pass down assets at around the time of the first death, the chances are that it would be more tax efficient to make a tax free transfer to the surviving spouse. They could then immediately make a transfer to the next generation as a PET, which will be tax free if the donor lives for at least seven years.

Another approach for a couple to consider is to set up a discretionary trust at the first death for the amount of the nil rate band. The assets of the trust can be distributed as required, but they could be lent to the survivor and the loan could rank as a debt against their estate. The loan should reduce the potential IHT on their estate, as long as it has been correctly set up.

Example 21.6

John died leaving his nil rate band in a discretionary trust. There was no periodic IHT charge on the trust because, it was below the nil rate band and John had not made any lifetime transfers in the seven years before his death. The trustees, who included his widow and three children, then lent most of the funds to his widow Joan. Her estate on death has not been boosted by the amount of the nil rate band and has also been reduced by the amount of the loan.

Potentially exempt transfers (PETs) — outright gifts

Outright gifts have many non-tax advantages and count as PETs. But of course, there is very little scope for gifting in a trust and retaining some control over the assets without falling under the discretionary trust IHT regime.

The possibility of IHT arising on premature death during the seven year period after the transfer could be covered by an appropriate life assurance seven year term policy. This should be level term to the extent that the transfer is covered by the donor's nil rate band, because premature death would lead to an effective increase in IHT at the flat rate of 40%. For the excess that exceeds the donor's nil rate band, a special decreasing term policy would be suitable to match the declining tax liability under the IHT tapering relief.

Use of the annual exemptions

The main annual exemptions are gifts from income and the separate £3,000 a year per donor exemption that can be made from capital. So a client could make, say, £4,000 annual gifts from income plus the £3,000 annual exemption, making total regular gifts of £7,000 a year. The real value of the £3,000 has reduced greatly over the years as it has not been increased. As a result, the gifts from income exemption has become the more important of the two. In general, the main uses of the annual exemptions are to help with topping up a younger relative's income possibly to help with school fees and also to cover life assurance premiums.

7 The uses of life assurance in inheritance tax planning

Life assurance has been used extensively for mitigating estate taxes in the UK and in many other parts of the world. It is versatile and can assist in several ways. The proceeds can be used to pay IHT on large lifetime transfers if the donor dies in the seven year period. Another role of life assurance is as the main tax wrapper for trust investments. Finally, life assurance can be the means of using the annual exemptions to fund the eventual IHT liability at death.

Annual premium policies

Life assurance can be a very effective way to achieve the maximum financial return from the annual exemptions. If the annual exemptions are simply used to fund cash gifts, they could have relatively little impact on the inheritance tax liability, although the cashflow could be greatly appreciated by the recipients. If the aim is to help fund the eventual IHT liability on the death of the donor or perhaps after a couple have both died, then a whole life assurance policy gifted in trust could be the answer. Such life assurance policies could also be regarded as a very effective way of building tax free capital for future generations. Each partner has their own exemptions which could be combined for the purpose of funding joint life policies.

Paying annual amounts into a life policy is also a way of gradually reducing the value of the donor's estate. In the long-term, there will be a large tax free lump sum with which to pay the IHT. If the donor or donors die prematurely, after making only a very few gifts, there will still be a very large lump sum paid out by the policy.

The normal approach is to use a whole life policy. This could be a unit linked or with profit policy, where the sum assured increases with the growth in the underlying fund. More usually it is a policy that provides a constant amount of cover assuming that the underlying funds provide a certain level of investment performance. If they fail to achieve the target growth rate over a set period (typically ten years initially), the client will have to pay higher premiums to keep the same amount of cover; alternatively the cover will have to be reduced. Some life companies also offer guaranteed policies with fixed cover and premiums; a few policies have no surrender value. Many policies can be set up as increasable, so that the client can increase the amount of cover regardless of their state of health.

A discretionary life assurance trust usually provides the maximum flexibility to cope with changes in family circumstances such as births and deaths or new tax rules. In practice there is unlikely to be an IHT periodic charge or exit charge in most circumstances, although a tax charge of up to 6% of the value of the policy is conceivable. If the premium exceeds the available exemption, the excess should normally be regarded as a PET.

Example 21.7

As an indication of the premiums and life cover, a man aged 70 and a woman aged 77 (next birthday) could effect a whole life guaranteed policy (i.e. non-profit) for a sum assured of £100,000 on a joint life second death basis for a premium of just under £250 a month (Legal and General). That would almost exactly use up one of their £3,000 annual exemptions.

It is worth financial planners probing to find out if clients are really concerned to fund the potential eventual IHT liability in this way. The beneficiaries may prefer to receive money now perhaps to help with the pressing costs of paying the mortgage or bringing up the children. The gifts from income may get easier for a donor to make over the years, but they may turn out to be a burden. A whole life policy that is stopped early often turns out to be poor value. The possible hardship (or perceived hardship) of paying life assurance premiums may not seem to be worth the benefit of making what are effectively advance payments of the tax.

Lump sum IHT plans

There are a number of lump sum IHT plans that can be used for mitigating the tax. They have several factors in common and financial planners should know when they are appropriate and their various advantages and drawbacks. There is only room for brief details here; more information is contained in the Taxbriefs adviser's guide to Life and health insurance.

One common element is the use of life assurance investment bonds as the basic investment vehicle for trustees. It is not essential for life assurance policies to be the tax wrappers for these plans; collectives or other investments could be used. The main advantage of single premium life assurance policies is that they offer a wide variety of underlying funds and produce no taxable income. This tends to keep administration and tax compliance costs to nil in most years. The drawbacks are mainly to do with the treatment of capital gains, which are arguably less advantageous than with collectives. But discretionary trusts are taxed as 50% taxpayers with respect to income and the CGT situation is less advantageous than that of most individuals. The tax position of life assurance bonds is therefore generally attractive as trustee investments.

Discretionary trusts may be used for these plans to achieve maximum flexibility but there is the possibility of ongoing tax charges. The alternative is a fixed trust into which the transfer counts as a PET. The lump sum plans can be used by single donors or by couples setting them up on a joint basis. If the gifts into a discretionary trust are substantial and in danger of exceeding the nil rate band, they can be split into several smaller gifts that are made over several days, thereby reducing the chance of a periodic charge arising. This type of planning relies on the decision in the tax case *Rysaffe Trustee Co (CI) Ltd v IRC (2003)*.

There are several different types of packaged life assurance based lump sum IHT plans. The following two are among the most common.

Gift and loan schemes

The client makes a gift into a trust and then a loan, which is generally (but not always) much larger than the gift. The loan is then gradually repaid to the client by making 5% annual tax deferred withdrawals from the bond, which the client can use as an income. After the loan has been repaid, the 'income' will run out.

The gift and loan scheme is attractive because it provides an 'income' to the donor and they can largely unravel the scheme prematurely by asking for the loan to be repaid. Equally, these plans transfer wealth from the donor's estate relatively slowly. The amount transferred will be the initial gift plus any growth in the value of the trust fund, so assuming that the initial gift is just £1,000 and the loan is many times that amount, the value building up will be the excess growth in the fund over the annual withdrawals of 5% of the initial investment. In the early years, the excess will be probably be small and could take 20 years or more to make a significant impact on the estate planning objective of building up value outside the donor's estate. If the donor then died soon after setting up the plan, the IHT saving would be very small.

Discounted gift trust

One of the most widely used plans is the discounted gift trust. In essence, the settlor places a sum of money in trust which carves out two separate elements. The settlor retains the right to a fixed sum for the rest of their life and all the other proceeds of the policy will accumulate and eventually be paid out to the trust's chosen beneficiaries. The trustees then invest in a single premium life assurance bond and take withdrawals — typically 5% of the original investment — to fund the payments to the settlor. The gift at outset would be a chargeable transfer unless an absolute trust were used. The purpose of the withdrawals is to provide the clients with an income to spend; if they decide to save the income and accumulate it in their estate, they would defeat the purpose of the plan. Alternatively, if the income turned out to be more than they needed, they could give it away — although advisers should remember that bond withdrawals do not count as income for the purposes of the gifts from income exemption.

If the settlor dies in the early years of the plan, the value for the trust fund would pass to the beneficiaries, but the value for IHT purposes would be discounted to less than 100% of the value of the fund. This is because the amount put into the trust would be subject to a deduction for the present value of the settlor's right to a lifetime income from the trust. This is based on the logic that a gift of £100,000 is worth significantly more than £100,000 less deductions of £5,000 a year. How much this discount is worth will depend on the settlor's age, sex and state of health at the time of the transfer.

The discounted gift trust provides the potential for larger and more immediate IHT savings than the gift and loan plan, but it is also less flexible and requires more commitment to estate planning; it is very hard to unwind and the income is fixed.

Example 21.8

A husband and wife both aged 80 together make a transfer of £100,000 into a discounted gift trust. They are both in good health for their age. The value transferred by the husband is £50,000, less the discount of £20,900, i.e. £29,100. The value transferred by his wife would be deemed to be less because of her longer life expectancy, meaning that the income would be paid out longer to her.

Using business assets relief

Business assets may qualify for 100% business assets relief, and will therefore pass down free of IHT, as long as the client transfers them at least two years after acquiring them, either as a lifetime or death transfer. In many cases, the client may have been involved in the management of the business in question, but there are also many ready-made business assets investments that are mainly designed to provide the investors with IHT business assets relief. They often have other tax advantages as well e.g. enterprise investment schemes and Alternative Investment Market shares.

One advantage of using qualifying business assets for IHT planning is that the client retains control of the asset and any income from it until they die. So there is no need to make a lifetime gift. It also requires action that is no further away from death than two years; in contrast making a lifetime gift requires a minimum period of seven years survival to escape IHT.

The main drawback — apart from the need to survive the two year period — is that most qualifying business assets are relatively high risk investments and may be hard to dispose of. The tax relief of 40% might not be enough to outweigh the potential investment loss. However, there are some specially designed business asset investments that have been very substantially de-risked. As a consequence, they provide relatively low investment returns and are therefore not particularly attractive long-term investments.

Some clients may be tempted to leave IHT planning to last the possible moment and use business assets relief schemes. This is a relatively high risk approach to planning. The rules may well be subject to change at short notice;

the investments would not be highly diversified and in any event the clients might not survive the two year ownership period.

8 Pension death benefits

Spousal by-pass trust

The death benefits from registered pension schemes payable before benefit crystallisation or age 75 are generally free of both income tax and IHT. However, in many cases, they will be paid to the deceased individual's spouse and end up as part of the survivor's taxable estate. The spousal by-pass trust is one way of providing the survivor with access to the funds while achieving worthwhile potential IHT savings on their estate.

The pension death benefits, including life assurance and the return of the uncrystallised pension fund should be made subject to a discretionary trust. The surviving spouse can be among the class of beneficiaries and there should be powers for the trust to make loans to them. The assets would be outside the survivor's estate and available to be passed onto the next generations, but loans could be provided to the survivors and they should count as liabilities to be set against the survivor's net taxable estate. This strategy could achieve a double IHT saving: avoiding adding to the survivor's estate and then also reducing the eventual taxable estate by the value of the loan. The approach could be used for any life policy, although the periodic and exit charges would be a factor to consider.

Post-crystallisation or post age 75 death benefits

If a client dies with pension death benefits after the age of 75 or after crystallising their benefits at an earlier age, there will be a tax charge of 55% of the value of the fund but normally no IHT. This represents an attractive IHT saving scheme considered as a whole, taking the tax relief on the pension input into account of 20%, 40% or even 50%.

But clients mostly do not consider their pension benefits as a whole. Clients are faced with a choice between:

- Either withdrawing income from the pension fund and spending it while gifting other assets,
- Or running down other assets to finance expenditure and leaving the pension fund to pass at death subject to the possible 55% tax charge.

This tax cost can be compared with alternatives.

Passing down other assets in the form of lifetime transfers at least seven years before the donor's death would involve a lower tax charge. If a client made a gift of an asset that avoided IHT, the tax charge as a result of the transfer would be less than the 55% charge. Even income tax on an offshore bond would be less where the profit (rather than the entire proceeds) might be taxed at up to 50%.

Passing down assets where the transfer would trigger IHT at 40% would also involve a lower total outlay than the 55% charge on the pension fund. Capital gains are not subject to tax on death and the recipient of assets that are subject to CGT normally benefits from an uplift in their base value.

There are some circumstances in which an investment that is transferred could be subject to both IHT and a tax charge on the profit. An investment bond might be subject to income tax on the gain on the insured person's death, as well as IHT on its net value after the income tax liability. In some cases, this might come to more than 55%, but generally it should be possible to avoid this with planning. Moreover, the lifetime gift of an asset that suffers both CGT on realisation and IHT because the donor dies within seven years, might suffer more than an aggregate tax charge of 55%. But these circumstances should be relatively rare and often avoidable.

In general, it would probably be preferable to draw on the pension fund for expenditure, so that relatively little of the fund is subject to the 55% tax rate and either make gifts of other assets or leave them to pass down on death.

9 Equity release

In theory, it might seem that equity release is an attractive basis for an IHT mitigation plan. A client could borrow funds and make a gift of cash. The loan would be a charge against the taxable estate and the gift would take assets out of the estate. Equity release appears to offer a tax planning opportunity to those who own a substantial residential property and relatively little other wealth.

In reality, the costs of the rolled up interest tend to outweigh the tax saving, especially if the gift is not very profitably invested and the increase in the IHT nil rate band reduces the potential IHT charge.

10 Long-term care and lasting powers of attorney

Long-term care has several main estate planning implications.

The costs of long-term care will have a major impact on the value of an individual's estate. Nursing home bills can easily exceed £1,000 a week (double that amount is not uncommon). So an estate could be depleted at the rate of £50,000 to £100,000 a year. In most cases, this will be paid for from the proceeds of the sale of a home – unless a surviving spouse or partner is continuing to live there, in which case, other resources may well be needed. This could be a moment when flexible drawdown comes into its own, with the costs of meeting the minimum income requirement greatly reduced by the ability to purchase an impaired life pension annuity.

The need to provide for the possibility of long-term care reduces the scope for clients to make very substantial gifts, in case they need large amounts to pay for their long-term care.

Virtually everyone should consider setting up a lasting power of attorney (LPA). The purpose is of an LPA is to have someone the client trusts to make decisions for them if they are incapable because of old age, illness or perhaps an accident. The LPA can cover their property and finances and also separately their health and wellbeing. Financial advisers should recommend that clients have these legal arrangements. However, they should normally avoid becoming individual attorneys or trustees for clients.

Some clients are very keen to avoid paying personally for the long-term care of their spouse/civil partners or themselves and undertake elaborate planning to make sure that their home is not available to finance this. In some cases, they aim to deprive themselves of assets to bring down the value of their estates in order to stay within the very low limits above which they do not qualify for public financial assistance. This latter approach runs the risk that the consequences of such intentional self-deprivation will be disregarded by the local authority and the individuals will not qualify for the assistance sought. However, a common strategy to protect a main residence owned by a couple is to sever the joint tenancy and create a tenancy in common, and this can often be helpful in IHT mitigation as well.

11 Marriage, prenuptial agreements and divorce

Marriage has an important role in estate planning. For example, it provides both parties certain financial rights under the intestacy rules, which unmarried partners do not have. If an individual leaves a will and does not provide adequately for their spouse, the courts may be more prepared to overturn or amend the provisions. Marriage also allows assets to pass between spouses free of IHT and this fact alone has led to many marriages, especially among prosperous couples who might otherwise prefer simply to live together. Marriage and divorce essentially have the effect of nullifying the couple's previous wills and are therefore events that should prompt making new wills.

Marriage is sadly often a precursor to separation and divorce, which can have a very substantial detrimental impact on family wealth. With most families, there is little that can be done in the form of legal or financial planning to affect the divorce court's decisions about the distribution of a couple's assets between them. However, with very wealthy couples, the courts are increasingly prepared to take account of prenuptial agreements. This is another area where family-wide inter-generational estate planning may be relevant.

Some advisers suggest to wealthy families that prenuptial agreements should be made before a marriage. Not surprisingly, most couples consider this to be a sensitive matter. The difficulty of raising the issue might be overcome by an older member of the family having already set up a trust for members of the younger generation. An important condition of their benefiting from the trust would be that in the event of their marrying, they should do so subject to a prenuptial agreement. In these circumstances it should be easier for the prospective family member to raise the issue with the intended spouse or civil partner and present it as an unfortunate but unavoidable fact. If they do not sign the agreement, the couple will not benefit from the trust. Some advisers find this tactic ingenious but possibly a little distasteful.

12 Philanthropic advice

Advising clients on their philanthropic gifts and activities is an intrinsic aspect of estate planning in the view of an increasing number of advisers. They are taking their cue from US and other overseas financial planners, for whom philanthropy planning has been a mainstream activity for many years, particularly for their wealthiest clients.

Giving money and other resources to good causes can become a major life goal for some clients, especially if they have accumulated or inherited substantial wealth. As part of the goal setting exercise, it is often important to understand clients' philanthropic aims. For many clients, this is may be linked to their attitude to ethical or socially responsible investment and there may be areas where investment and philanthropy might overlap, for example with respect to backing social entrepreneurship ventures of a non-commercial or partly commercial nature. Clients may welcome a discussion of the areas where they wish to focus their giving and how their donation policy could make a difference. Part of the discussion might revolve round their motivations in giving, which might vary considerably according to the nature of the cause. Giving to an educational institution like the client's old school or university may be based on rather different needs and wishes than making gifts to a church, cultural body or charities for the relief of suffering or poverty. Some clients may wish to be closely involved in the activities of their chosen charities and causes; others may wish to stay more distant.

Clients may want guidance on how much they can afford to give to charity, both as lifetime donations and at their death. This is part of the budgeting process and also part of the discussion that should take place about the will.

The tax issues around giving to charity can make a considerable difference about how clients give as well as how much they reserve for charitable donations. Lifetime gifts should be made through gift aid as far as possible. In some circumstances, it might additionally be possible to qualify for CGT relief on the gift of an asset.

Clients who give to a number of charities over the course of a year might find it convenient to use a centralised charitable account like the Charities Aid Foundation to make the process of giving much more convenient and simpler in terms of completing their tax return. Pension funds in drawdown could provide a very tax efficient way of giving; the death benefits avoid the 55% tax charge if they are given to a registered charity.

Clients with substantial wealth and the intention to make charitable gifts could consider setting up their own charitable trust. A charitable trust can receive gifts with tax relief in the normal way but it can have some advantages over direct giving. The aim would be to accumulate a capital sum and then make distributions of income and capital to the chosen good causes. The income and capital gains of a charity are free of UK tax in the same way as a pension fund. The trust may be able to make gifts to non-charities, as long as the purpose is charitable; it can become a focus for the family whose adult members could become trustees. The possible drawbacks are the costs of running the charity and the administration required, and it is only worthwhile where the funds to be given to the charity are sufficiently substantial. Organisations like the Charities Aid Foundation can help with establishing charities or lawyers can be consulted.

Chapter 22
Reviewing and revising

1 An ongoing process

A few clients may simply require a one-off review of their position or of a specific aspect of their finances, such as pension provision. In general, though, clients who have decided to use a financial planner will generally want to benefit from an ongoing service.

The adviser can make ongoing reviews and recommendations a key part of their advice proposition. But even if clients respond to this, they may lose sight of the importance of reviewing and updating their plan. So advisers usually have to work at keeping clients engaged with their plan and encouraging them to take the actions that they recommend.

The adviser's client agreement needs to specify:

- The scope of the service
- The frequency of reviews and reports
- The costs

Scope of the service

The ongoing service should normally include the following:

- Updating the information on which the plan is based
- Reviewing client needs and priorities
- Reviewing plans, policies and investments
- Recommendations

Updating information

Advisers need to establish a process for updating client information. Among the methods in use by advisers are:

Review form. The adviser sends the client a form several weeks before the review date, requesting details of any changes in circumstances

Telephone. The adviser or an assistant telephones the client to gather relevant information.

Fact-find. The adviser prints off the data currently held and sends this to the client with a request for them to notify any changes.

Meeting. The adviser updates information at a meeting with the client.

Reviewing client needs

Changes in circumstances may alter the client's needs or their priorities. When a circumstance was part of the grounds for a recommendation and that circumstance has changed, the recommendation should be reviewed. This is only likely to require changes to recommendations with major changes such as:

Income: a large rise or fall in income, resulting in a change in the client's income tax rate. Among the items that will need to be reviewed are pension contributions and savings contributions.

Family: arrival of a new child probably requires a review of protection requirements, which are likely to be higher.

Inheritance: consideration may be given to paying off all or part of a mortgage and to long-term investment choices.

Employment: a new employment may have a very different package of associated benefits that could increase or reduce the client's need for protection or retirement provision.

Reviewing plans, policies and investments

If there are no changes in circumstances, long-term plans and policies may only need to be reviewed at intervals of several years. Advisers operating a time-based fee charging system may structure their service so that comprehensive reviews are undertaken at three- or five-yearly intervals, with more limited reviews on an annual basis.

However, there are some aspects of planning that require an annual review, for example:

- **ISA allowance**: if this is not being used from income, then transfer of other investments into an ISA on an annual basis will usually be advantageous.

- **Inheritance tax exemptions**: where an adviser recommended their use in the initial plan, they need to ensure the client continues with the necessary payments.

- **Drawdown**: for those aged over 75 an annual review of income withdrawals will be required.

Changes in legislation may require a review of every client holding a particular type of plan. For example, in the wake of the December 2010 announcement of new rules affecting pension decumulation, advisers would have had to review all clients either in drawdown or on the verge of entering drawdown or of purchasing pension annuities.

Investments managed on an advisory basis will need to be reviewed more often, usually half-yearly. Discretionary fund managers also normally report to clients half-yearly.

Advisers using model portfolios need to set a policy for rebalancing portfolios. The asset allocation agreed at the outset was the adviser's recommendation best matched to the client's needs and risk profile. If these are unchanged, then any significant change in the asset allocation of the portfolio as a result of market movements will result in a greater or lesser degree of risk being incurred.

Example 22.1

Keith and Jane's portfolio was constructed using a Balanced risk profile, which allocated 60% to equities. The stock market has risen strongly over the past year while other asset prices have not changed, so that equities now account for 67% of the portfolio.

Modern portfolio theory and the notion of the efficient frontier are based on regular portfolio rebalancing. So if tools using probabilistic portfolio theory methods are used to construct portfolios, it would be inconsistent if they were not rebalanced. Even if the adviser uses less mechanical ways of creating model portfolios, they need to take account of the changing level of risk arising from alterations to the asset allocation. Looked at more simply, rebalancing applies the discipline of selling assets that have risen strongly and buying those that have performed less well, and since 'reversion to the mean' is a well established fact in financial markets, it is likely that over the long-term rebalancing will enhance returns.

With wraps it may be possible for advisers to automatically rebalance portfolios to the original allocation. In this case all holdings are adjusted down or up through simultaneous sales and purchases. For large portfolios, the transaction costs are not likely to be material, but for smaller portfolios such rebalancing may be a costly drag on performance. The alternative is to make sales and purchases of only one or two funds to adjust the allocation without returning it precisely to its original level.

Automatic rebalancing has advantages for the adviser but can only be implemented straightforwardly for pension, bond and ISA portfolios. For direct portfolios, there may be capital gains tax consequences, which mean that a rebalancing policy cannot be applied across all client portfolios without regard to their personal circumstances.

Recent research suggests that no advantage is gained from rebalancing portfolios more frequently than six-monthly, and that setting a threshold of a 10% change from the original allocation for rebalancing is sufficient to avoid incurring too much risk.

Recommendations

Advisers will consider any fresh information together with their initial needs analysis and recommendations. Where the needs have altered, recommendations may need to be revised or completely changed.

The frequency of reviews and reports

Financial plans do not generally require review more often than annually. But investment portfolios managed on an advisory basis may need more frequent reviews and most advisers in practice review portfolios at least every six months.

Advisers may provide an annual review of a financial plan. This will cover all the major goals, any changes to them as a result of changes in circumstances, the progress made towards achieving them, together with any fresh recommendations. It will update all the sections of the financial plan, where appropriate revising cashflow projections, retirement income forecasts and savings plan values. Deviations from expectations or projections built into the original report are of most significance. They may require some action now, or the adviser may take the view that the deviations are temporary and will soon be reversed.

Inbetween these reviews, advisers should monitor the investment portfolio. With an advisory mandate, recommendations for change can be made at any time and best practice is to recommend changes as soon as the adviser considers it appropriate. The client may be provided with valuations half-yearly or quarterly, but if assets are held on a wrap the client can normally access current valuations at any time. Normal practice is to report on the portfolio at half-yearly intervals as discussed in chapter 6, 'Investment planning'.

The frequency of review is a key factor in setting the cost of the service. Advisers need to estimate the number of hours taken to review a plan and produce a client report. This, and client meetings, will account for the bulk of the adviser's time. For most clients, the time spent in portfolio monitoring should be very similar if model portfolios are being used.

With discretionary mandates, the manager will usually report at half-yearly intervals.

Advisers may operate a tiered service in which the frequency of review is one element that varies. Many elderly people, for example, with portfolios designed to generate a steady long-term level of income, do not need half-yearly reviews. The adviser may be able to offer them a service at somewhat lower cost if only annual reviews are provided.

However, for some clients regular contact with the adviser is a key aspect of the service, and they may wish to consult the adviser about minor matters such as switching deposit accounts. Some clients with relatively modest assets may be happy to pay a somewhat higher fee if they are assured of receiving the adviser's attention when they think they need it.

Business people, on the other hand, are often short of time. They may prefer to have an annual meeting with the adviser as part of a comprehensive review of their plan and receive only essential 'must-do' communications inbetween.

The costs

The client agreement will specify the costs of the service. Fees may be payable monthly, quarterly or half-yearly. Where client assets are held on wraps, fees are often deducted from clients' wrap cash accounts. Where fees are charged as a percentage of assets, a statement should show the calculation and the amount.

2 Responding to change

People who engage a financial planner value having control over their finances. Sometimes, though, clients' enthusiasm for their plan can diminish. They may be less disciplined in their implementation of the plan than they had hoped to be. Or they may have undertaken the planning exercise because they know they will not pay it enough attention and they want to rely on the planner to tell them what they need to do.

Identifying relevant clients

To respond effectively to external changes that affect clients, such as legislative changes and market movements, advisers need to be able to identify relevant clients. Usually back office systems permit advisers to identify those holding particular products or plans, and this is often adequate for finding out which clients will be affected by a change in pensions legislation, for example. Likewise, knowing which clients own a particular fund or set of funds is often all that is needed to make a necessary recommendation.

However, if advisers can search their client databases using circumstantial data they will be much better placed to identify those whose needs have changed. For example, the adviser might wish to identify all clients between the ages of 40 and 65 with incomes in excess of £50,000 who are making contributions to personal pension plans. If this is done manually by reviewing client files, the adviser may not find every such client. If it can be done by searching the back office system the adviser can be confident that every relevant case has been identified.

Responding in a timely way to changes that affect clients has high perceived value, and a failure to do so can cause clients to be dissatisfied or leave. This is therefore an important concern for advisers, who need to set aside sufficient time to ensure that they do in fact identify and review those clients who are affected by events. Even if no action is required, the adviser can enhance the perceived value of the service by telling the client that their situation has been reviewed but that no action is required in their case.

Legislative changes

An example of a legislative change affecting many clients was the October 2007 change in inheritance tax (IHT). From that date an individual whose spouse had died without using their nil rate band was able to claim this second nil rate band on their own death. This effectively doubled the amount that the surviving spouse could pass on at their own death without incurring inheritance tax.

Before this, many planners had recommended that married clients should make use of the nil rate band on the first spouse's death. This avoided or reduced the payment of inheritance tax on the second death. But the use of the nil rate band on the first death was not always easy or ideal from the client's point of view. It often required giving up access to funds they might need later in their own lives.

The change therefore enabled advisers to simplify estate planning for many couples, whose combined estates was below the level of the two nil rate bands (at current rates this is £650,000).

Example 22.2

John and Julia were in their 70s in 2005 when their adviser undertook an inheritance planning review for them. Their estate (totalling £500,000) would incur substantial inheritance tax if their wills remained as they were, with all assets passing to the survivor on the first death. As a result of the review, the assets were equalised so that their two children would each receive £25,000 on the first death, with a further £100,000 going into a trust with the surviving spouse as a beneficiary.

Following the October 2007 change, the adviser recommended that the provisions of the wills were altered so that all of John's and Julia's assets passed to the surviving spouse. The survivor could then make their own decision about when to make gifts to the children.

Some changes require a more fundamental review to produce the most suitable advice for the client, such as the changes to pension drawdown announced in December 2010.

Example 22.3

Arthur has a self invested personal pension (SIPP) containing £450,000 of assets. He will be 75 in January 2012. In 2006, his adviser had recommended that a progressively lower-risk strategy be applied to his portfolio with the aim of purchasing annuities at aged 75. The portfolio in December 2010 therefore contained 50% bonds, 20% cash and 15% each in equities and absolute return funds.

Arthur has been drawing an income of £12,000 a year, well below the maximum available. He has been drawing on other capital for income but expected to have a substantially greater income from annuities at age 75 when he would be able to stop these capital withdrawals.

His adviser told Arthur that with capped drawdown under the new rules he would be able to draw over £25,000 in annual income. Arthur had never been keen on annuity purchase, since he was fearful of a rise in inflation and much preferred to keep his capital invested. However, he and his adviser now had to agree a strategy for the portfolio to support annual withdrawals of £25,000 without incurring too much risk.

Personal circumstances

Updating client information prior to plan reviews is essential to ensure the adviser is aware of changes in circumstances.

Significant new data, from the adviser's point of view, includes:

- Income/employment: change of job or earnings.
- Family: birth of child, commencement of education.
- Home: change of residence.
- Inheritance: receipt of any capital sum.
- Health: any deterioration in health.
- Intentions: retirement date, residence, business.
- Transactions: any giving rise to potential capital gains tax liabilities.

Where a circumstance was a factor in a previous recommendation, then a change in that circumstance should prompt a review of the recommendation.

Priorities and attitudes

People's attitudes and priorities can change without any change in their external circumstances.

Example 22.4

On holiday in India, Jean witnessed a poor mother grieving over a dead child. This affected her so strongly that on her return to the UK, she got involved with a development charity and planned to leave her current job and get another, probably at lower pay, at this or another such charity. Her previous projection had been of a steady rise in salary and her lifetime earnings were now likely to be significantly lower.

Example 22.5

Judy separated from her husband Mark four years ago. She has prime responsibility for their two children, aged six and four. Mark and Judy had planned to educate them privately. Judy developed a relationship with Tim, a teacher in a local school who believed strongly in the state educational system. As a result, she decided not to proceed with private education for her children.

Example 22.6

At a party Jim met Owen, who was involved in the Fairtrade movement. Jim became more and more interested in this and after several months told his adviser he wanted to have all his investments and savings invested only in ethical funds.

Often such a change in priorities will require a complete revision of a financial plan.

Investment conditions

For clients with substantial investments, major changes in financial markets can require plan reviews. Usually, such changes affect long-term expectations.

Example 22.7

Hilary and Trevor are in their late sixties and have been drawing an income of some 6% from their portfolio. The rate of inflation has been under 2%, but has now averaged over 3% for six months and there are no signs of it falling back again. Their adviser suggests they should review their strategy and portfolio, a large part of which is invested in fixed income investments. These have performed well during the low-inflation era but will be hard hit if higher inflation continues.

Example 22.8

Graham's adviser had completed his financial plan in autumn 2008. Graham had £150,000 on deposit and the plan included a long-term investment portfolio. The failure of Lehman Brothers prompted considerable anxiety and turbulence in financial markets. Graham's adviser proposed that instead of proceeding with the planned portfolio, Graham should invest £10,000 each month in assets and funds that appeared best value at the time.

Milestone events

For many people, a specific date or event in the future provides an anchor for their expectations and desires. Though clients have many objectives, one is usually more important to them and in this case, reports and reviews should focus on the progress towards this goal. Typical of such goals are:

'I would like to pay off the mortgage by the time I am 60.'

'I would like to have £400,000 in my pension fund before I am 65.'

'I would like to have a fund of £40,000 built up before my son starts at university.'

These objectives, and methods of achieving them, are built into the original plan. The adviser should respond to events that affect these goals.

Example 22.9

Maria, 45, had made paying off her mortgage before her 60 birthday a major objective of her plan. The plan provided for this in two ways: she would continue with her capital-and-interest mortgage but would also pay into a monthly equity-linked savings plan.

When the base rate-linked interest rate on her mortgage fell sharply in 2008, Maria's adviser recommended that she used half of the monthly saving to increase her mortgage repayments, and the other half to top up her savings plan contributions. He calculated this would bring forward the mortgage redemption date by at least two years.

---

3 Communications

The personalised reports clients receive contain the specific advice the client needs. But people vary greatly in their ability to assimilate long reports. Advisers usually benefit from using other less formal means of communicating with clients. Often, a more informal approach makes it easier for clients to grasp complex issues.

Informal client communications

Reports and reviews are the formal part of the adviser's service. Many clients value the provision of information and advice in other ways. For this reason many advisers issue regular client newsletters. Today, advisers also use their websites to provide updated news and views through news sections, blogs or email alerts.

Client newsletters

Regular newsletters to clients maintain the client's awareness of the adviser and the newsletter can contain prompts for actions that were agreed in the plan but the client may not have implemented, for example the use of the annual inheritance tax exemptions.

Financial legislation is often complex and hard to understand, so presenting it in simpler terms that clients do understand is beneficial.

Email

The merit of a printed publication sent through the post is that it is certain to be seen and may be read. With email this is not the case. People receive so many emails that they usually scan subject lines and senders and only open ones they want to read at the time. Yet the probability of their returning to an unopened message to read it later declines rapidly from that moment on.

Advisers usually offer clients the option of having communications by email, but usually this will be action-oriented and linked to plans, reports and recommendations. Rather than sending clients more general information, updates etc by email, it is usually better to post these items to a website and send a short email with a link so that clients can read them there if they wish.

Websites

Advisers increasingly use their websites as a means of communicating with clients. The advantage of using a website in this way is that the adviser can add a comment, report or article to their website and send a brief email to clients alerting them to it, so that they can communicate news or views within hours of the event. This can be especially useful where clients have an ongoing interest in an issue — for example Equitable Life, where many members of the Society had a strong ongoing interest in the long-running compensation issue and were keen to hear about the latest developments as soon as they happened.

Some advisers make clips of interviews available on their websites and many now have Facebook pages where an informal communication can be maintained with clients. Others add extensive content to their websites including calculators and news feeds.

The key to a successful communications strategy is knowing what types of information and communication the clients like. Often, advisers will have groups of clients with different preferences. Many older clients still prefer to receive printed communications and newsletters, while younger ones are often happy to have almost all communications in electronic form.

Feedback

Obtaining client feedback on the service provided by the adviser was covered in chapter 12, 'Client management'. Adviser firms may consider it worthwhile to undertake a separate survey on client communications, asking clients to rate the value to them of the communications they currently receive and indicating which alternatives they would prefer.

Chapter 23
Ten golden rules of financial planning

1. **Base your financial planning for clients around their life, their goals and their ambitions.** Their money is not an end in itself; it is the means for them to live the life they want. Most clients are not used to thinking seriously about their longer term future and need help to work through these issues. Don't be worried that this seems to be beyond the normal remit of a financial adviser. It is essential that financial planning is properly grounded in what the clients really want; if it isn't, the plan will be built on shaky foundations.

   A potential difficulty with trying to induce clients to think long-term is the universal tendency to hyperbolic discounting. People find it hard to put much value on the relatively distant future or make immediate sacrifices for future benefits. Remind clients that this is how everyone feels and suggest that they look back ten or 20 years and consider how recent that seems. The same period in the future should then feel less remote and unimportant. And help them to visualise their desired future more clearly, which will increase their commitment to the actions needed to bring it about.

   Don't be in too much of a hurry to leave the exploration of goals in order to move onto the purely financial planning. Goal setting with clients can take time. Increasing numbers of advisers use the life planning approach developed by George Kinder and charge for the process separately from the rest of the planning process and report much success with it. Others do not take the process so far, but expect to develop a close and lasting relationship, giving them a secure position as the trusted adviser to their clients.

2. **Be very selective about the clients you take on as a financial planner.** You can only afford to work with a limited number of clients. So make sure that the relationship is one that is likely to last and be profitable for you both — as financial planner and as client. It is essential to have both positive and negative filters.

   On the positive side, your clients should come within the financial criteria that you have set. That probably means that the clients have a minimum level of financial assets (investments and pensions) and/or income. It is quite likely that you will also have set a maximum level of wealth and income. For example, if you normally deal with people who have between £500,000 and £1m investable wealth, don't go too far outside your comfort zone. The chances are that a client with £10m or more will present you with problems that may place you outside your depth. This is fine, if you make a conscious decision to move into a new market; but then you should recognise that you will need to change your processes, skills, knowledge and service proposition to focus on this market seriously.

On the negative side, steer clear of people who seem desperately indecisive, have quarrelled with a succession of previous advisers, seem like crooks (they might want you to do something illegal) or are people you simply dislike. The adviser relationship almost certainly won't last and will end in tears. And don't be frightened to sack a client who turns out to have any of these tendencies.

3. **Give clients really good value for money and make sure that the value of your services really shows.** Adviser charging will mean that clients are going to see even more clearly just how much they are paying for their advisers' services. What's more, it will seem much easier for clients to manage without an adviser and so advisers will need to work harder and smarter to retain their income streams. The period until 1 January 2013 provides an unrepeatable opportunity for all financial planners to practise for the new world of adviser charging. Many advisers are already succeeding with a variety of different approaches to charging. One thing they all agree on; it takes time to adjust and you have to use trial and error to find the tactics that do and do not work in this new context.

Remember that clients will value the benefits that they receive from your services, not necessarily the time and effort that you put into providing the service. Clients are much more interested in the value of the outputs for them than in the cost of the inputs by you. Just because you put five hours into carrying out a task and your hourly charge-out rate is £150, it does not mean client will think that your work is actually worth £750 plus VAT. The client might value the work at more than this amount or possibly less. Always consider what the job is worth to the client.

This approach to charging might also help advisers decide what jobs they should be doing to add value for clients or whether other members of the team could do the work more cheaply or more efficiently. Clients may understand hourly charging for some types of work but not for every kind of service; value-based charging may be much more appreciated in many situations.

Clients need to relate their adviser charges to the totality of their funds and this should help them see your fees in perspective. Your advice may be about the whole of their financial assets, and often much more as well. Remember about framing; context is crucial. Clients will find fees much less acceptable if they just relate them to their investment income rather than their overall wealth.

4. **Keep advice as simple as possible; clients need to understand and remember the benefits of what their adviser is doing for them.** Money isn't simple, and it is important not to mislead, but the key benefits can be presented simply, clearly and memorably. Being a good adviser is much more than knowing a lot about financial planning; it is being able to understand what the client wants, find the solutions and communicate them in such a way that the client wants to take action. Knowledge is a vital foundation but it is not enough by itself. You need to keep improving your skills as well as your knowledge. If you cannot explain a concept, then in a very real sense you probably do not understand it.

   The best advisers think of themselves as teachers and communicators, always looking for ways to explain such concepts as risk, tax relief, diversification, investment growth, insurance and compound interest. The simple diagram and the memorable image or simile can communicate an idea rapidly and effectively.

   Try to keep explanations as brief as possible and always relate them to what the client wants. See if you can sum up your advice in three sentences. If clients cannot remember why they are taking a particular action, there is a fair chance they will not persist with it, especially if the recommendation does not provide them with an immediate benefit. Take the same approach to the services that your firm provides for clients. Prepare a salient, vivid and memorable phrase to explain how you help clients and make sure that you always use it with clients, prospective clients and professional associates. People can be very hazy about the benefits of using a financial planner. Make sure they know and remember.

5. **Combine your tax planning and investment planning knowledge to provide a service that clients will really value highly.** Clients often keep tax and investment planning in separate mental compartments, when in fact we know that sound tax planning with investments is one of the best ways to generate alpha. Tax is not just for those accountants whose main responsibility is to complete the client's tax return. Choosing the appropriate mix of tax wrappers for a client's circumstances now and in the future can make a major contribution to meeting their goals.

   From time to time, quite a few clients think they are capable of running their own investments; but many will also admit to not being able to master the ever changing pattern of investment tax planning.

   Tax rules change every year and there are two reasons to remind clients of this. One is that they depend on their financial adviser to make sure that their tax and investment planning is up-to-date in the light of the ever-changing tax reliefs, allowances and rules. So you have a duty to keep on top of those changes yourself. The other is that clients should understand that the advice given to them about tax planning is not set in concrete. Tax rules change, for better and for worse and sometimes with retro-active effect, as we saw with both pensions and capital gains in the course of 2010. Clients need reminding of this constant changeability. The FSA require it as one of the stock warnings, but it is much more than that. Clients really need reminding of this fact of financial life.

6. **Always look for the potential downside risk of any investment; it is the financial planner's role to be sceptical.** Be imaginative about all the things that could possibly go wrong with an investment. It is all too easy to fall prey to the extrapolation effect, where one believes that current trends will always continue: for example, interest rates will always remain low; inflation is a temporary blip; house prices cannot fall; stock market prices will follow the pattern of the last ten years. The history of the last 100 years contains examples of the demolition (often abrupt and painful) of every trend popular opinion had taken as gospel.

Due diligence on products and solutions is set to become even more important in the post-Retail Distribution Review whole-of-market world. It will be even more important to develop stress-testing skills to consider what can go wrong with strategies under different circumstances. If you don't understand a proposition or a track record, don't recommend it.

Clients generally prefer their advisers to preserve their capital rather than to take large risks to increase it. Remember when making a recommendation that most clients dislike making losses roughly twice as much as they like making the equivalent profits. Be sceptical about providers: where do they make their returns? Where are the underlying risks, the counterparty risks, the unknown unknowns?

At the same time, recognise the potential upside of investments and understand how the downside risk is an integral part of the proposition. The tax advantages of the pension are counter-balanced by the restrictions and drawbacks. The guarantees of the structured product are only possible because of their costs, illiquidity and other risks. But make sure that clients understand the snags and drawbacks without paralysing them into indecision; your recommendations need to be clear.

7. **Help clients to understand risk.** Because of our hard-wired behavioural biases, most of us both over-estimate and under-estimate risk in different contexts. Avoiding unnecessary risk is part of your job as an adviser, but just as important is enabling the client to understand the unavoidable risks that exist and that good planning can mitigate but never abolish. The salience and availability effects mean clients can be very aware of stock market risks (though only after a crash), but do not often see the risks of changes in tax legislation, economic trends and governments. Many things clients perceive as a risk (interpreted as giving rise to the possibility of personal loss) are simply features of uncertainty and an indeterminable future.

Most people are not mathematically minded and few have higher mathematics qualifications. So avoid mathematical expressions of risk wherever possible — you will simply add the fear of not understanding the maths to the fear of the risk.

In your own allocation of risk profiles, always give objective factors (the capacity for risk) more weight than subjective factors, which are sure to change.

8. **Aim for continuous improvement.** Clients rarely reach the ideal solution at the first pass. It may take years for them to get to grips with some of their biases and preconceptions, so that their attitudes — to risk especially — are almost certain to change significantly over time. Their prioritisation of needs will probably also change as they engage in the planning process and start to see its results. So you must be ready to re-engage with clients on many issues, and need to be creative in thinking of ways to help clients move forward.

You will inevitably develop your own style and methods of presenting issues, and there is a risk of becoming too tied to one way of doing things. So you can benefit from attending seminars and workshops where you can learn about other methods and approaches.

From time to time it is worthwhile looking at how your planning process for clients has worked over a period of time. This is likely to give you insights into how to accelerate progress and improve your presentation of key issues.

9. **Put everything important on the record.** The regulators take the view that if you did not record it, it did not happen. So failure to record swiftly and accurately places you and your business at risk. Financial issues are often complex and the understanding the client takes away from a conversation may be quite different from what you expected or wanted. So help them by sending them brief summaries of all important conversations.

In your internal processes as an adviser you will inevitably use a lot of jargon, but try to keep as much of this as possible out of your reports and other communications with clients, and instruct your administration staff too to adopt a no-jargon approach.

Writing clearly is a rare skill and most people need to draft and then redraft what they write — allow for this in your report-writing process. With client reports, try to put yourself in the client's shoes when reading it. Make sure the important points are well signposted and all action points clearly summarised.

10. **Look for the silver lining.** If you are involved with savings and investments, some of your clients will lose money. In adverse conditions like 2008-09 they can lose a lot of money. The fact that they are 'paper' losses does not

stop people feeling unhappy about this. But clients will feel less unhappy if you maintain contact and communication with them in difficult times – and they may lose their trust in you if you don't. If you have confidence in your investment planning methods, remind clients of the irrational tendencies of markets and of the danger of selling during a panic. Seek the views of the most respected and experienced professional investors and relay them to your clients – these views are sure to diverge widely from the news headlines, giving your clients a different perspective.

Aim to benefit from your errors. Mistakes happen, and the normal approach is to say: "We must make sure that this never happens again". This focus on improving processes is necessary, but you should also make a bigger effort to apologise for your mistakes. A substantial gesture along with an apology sends two signals to the client: that you really do care about having made a mistake, and that mistakes must be rare if you can afford this kind of gesture. You could, for example, offer to donate a stated sum to the client's favoured charity.

Index